TIME®
LIFE
BOOKS

The Complete Book of

Kitchen & Bathroom Renovation

Other Publications

DO IT YOURSELF
The Time-Life Complete Gardener
Home Repair and Improvement
The Art of Woodworking
Fix It Yourself

COOKING
Weight Watchers® Smart Choice Recipe Collection
Great Taste~Low Fat
Williams-Sonoma Kitchen Library

HISTORY
The American Story
Voices of the Civil War
The American Indians
Lost Civilizations
Mysteries of the Unknown
Time Frame
The Civil War
Cultural Atlas

SCIENCE/NATURE
Voyage Through the Universe

TIME-LIFE KIDS
Family Time Bible Stories
Library of First Questions and Answers
A Child's First Library of Learning
I Love Math
Nature Company Discoveries
Understanding Science & Nature

*For information on and a full description of any
of the Time-Life Books series listed above, please
call 1-800-621-7026 or write:*

Reader Information
Time-Life Customer Service
P.O. Box C-32068
Richmond, Virginia 23261-2068

The Consultants

Kenneth A. Long, a licensed master plumber, is co-owner and chief executive officer of Long's Corporation in northern Virginia and a past president of the Virginia Association of Plumbing, Heating, and Cooling Contractors. "Plumbing," says Long, " is the art of running pipe."

Jeff Palumbo is a registered journeyman carpenter who has a home-building and remodeling business in northern Virginia. His interest in carpentry was sparked by his grandfather, a master carpenter with more than 50 years' experience. Palumbo teaches in the Fairfax County Adult Education Program.

Mark M. Steele is a professional home inspector in the Washington, D.C., area. He has developed and conducted training programs in home-ownership skills for first-time homeowners. He appears frequently on television and radio as an expert in home repair and consumer topics.

The Complete Book of
Kitchen &
Bathroom
Renovation

BY THE EDITORS OF TIME-LIFE BOOKS, ALEXANDRIA, VIRGINIA

CONTENTS

Kitchen Repairs Made Easy

A kitchen's daily ration of heavy traffic and hard use frequently leads to drooping cabinets, scratched countertops, and marred floors. Instead of replacing worn items with new ones, you can often restore them to near-original condition with the simple repairs shown on the following pages.

Laying new adhesive for a loose tile →

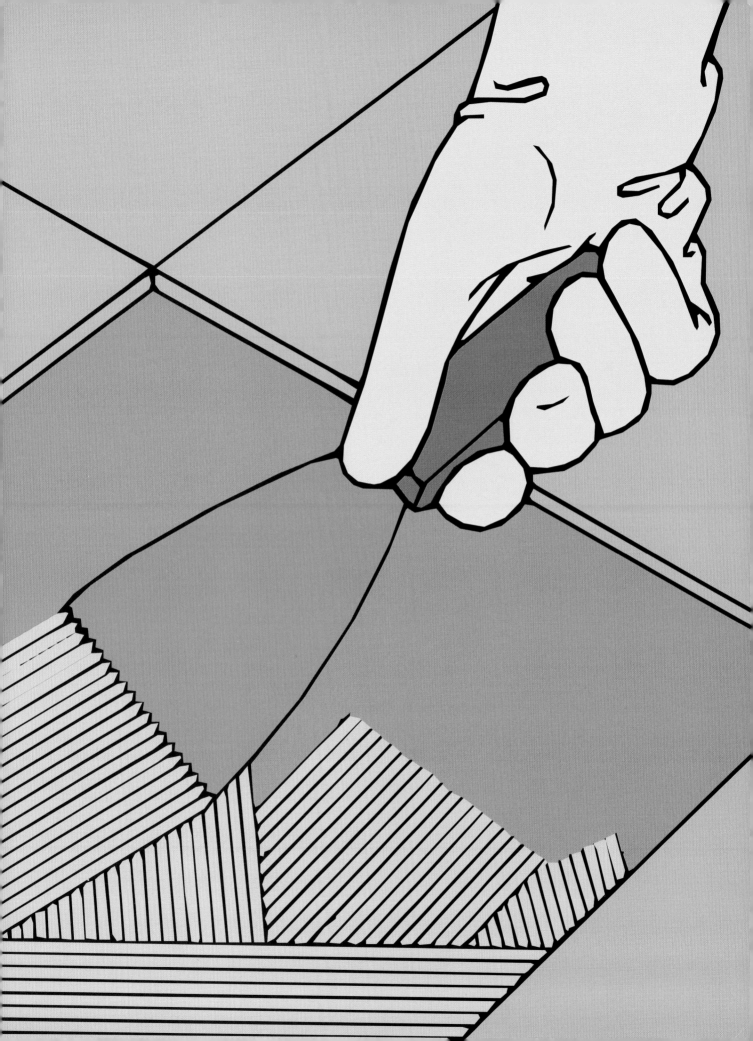

Mending Kitchen Cabinets

Cabinets are an indispensable component of any kitchen; they keep pots and pans, dinnerware, utensils, and foodstuffs close at hand but out of the way until needed. Because of their constant use, however, they are prone to a variety of ailments.

Over time, the cabinet frame can twist—or rack—under its heavy load. Inserting shims—thin pieces of wood—between the cabinet and the wall may be enough to push a racked cabinet back into square, but usually it must be taken down and repaired *(right)*. While the cabinet is off the wall, the joints should be reinforced to strengthen the frame.

Removing Cabinets: Newer cabinets are screwed to the wall through hanging bars—pieces of wood attached to the upper, and often the lower, cabinet back. Screws will be visible inside, but the hanging bar is usually hidden behind it.

Older cabinets without hanging bars are most often nailed to the wall through the inside of the cabinet. To take them down, gently pry the outside edges of the cabinet with a pry bar until it is $\frac{1}{2}$ inch away from the wall, then push the cabinet back against the wall to expose nailheads.

Reinforcing Shelves: Shelves can become bowed under the weight of stacks of dishes or canned goods. In many cabinets, the shelves are removable and need only be turned over. For fixed shelves *(page 10)*, a wooden partition will provide permanent support, but remember that all shelves beneath it must be similarly braced or the sag will be transferred downward. In cabinets with a center stile, wooden strips attached to the back of the stile and the back of the cabinet can support the sagging shelf without taking up valuable space inside the cabinet.

Drawers and Hinges: The moving parts of the cabinet are particularly susceptible to wear. Drawers are most likely to break down at points of special strain—bottoms, backstops, and guides. In many drawers, you can remove the back, slide a damaged bottom out, and replace it. If intricate joints prevent this, measure the bottom, cut a piece of $\frac{1}{4}$-inch luan plywood to size, and glue it on top of the damaged bottom.

Door hinges can work loose, and the doors themselves sometimes warp out of shape. If not too severely bowed, the door can be straightened with an oak brace.

 **TOOLS**

Pry bar
Bar clamps
$\frac{1}{4}$- or $\frac{3}{8}$-inch power drill
Hacksaw
Chisel
Rabbet plane
Block plane
Utility knife

 **MATERIALS**

Wood shims
Carpenter's glue
Masking tape
Hardwood dowels
Wire brads
Angle braces
Metal center drawer glides
$1\frac{1}{4}$-inch dry-wall screws

SQUARING A RACKED FRAME

1. Straightening the cabinet.

◆ First, remove the doors; then, with a helper supporting the cabinet, detach it from the wall, saving the screws and any shims that fall. If working alone, read the box on page 14 before removing the cabinet.

◆ Glue any joints that have popped open. If they are not open enough to apply glue, tap them apart with a hammer and wood block.

◆ Close the joints with two bar clamps set near the ends of the top and bottom rail as shown in the picture below. Protect the finish by placing pieces of scrap wood between the cabinet and the bar clamps.

◆ Before the glue dries, make sure that the cabinet is square. Hook a tape measure on one corner of the cabinet and measure diagonally to the opposite corner, then measure the other diagonal (below). If the measurements differ, loosen the clamps, and with a helper, gently push the two corners that are farther apart toward each other. Remeasure the diagonals and repeat the adjustment until the measurements are equal. Retighten the clamps and let the glue dry.

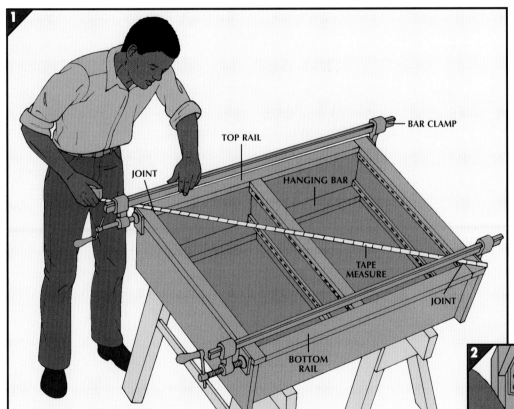

2. Strengthening the joints.

If your cabinet has protruding shelf supports on the inside frame that extend the full height of the cabinet, install metal angle braces (top of diagram) near the front and back of the cabinet. If the shelf supports are recessed or stop short of the corner (bottom of diagram), position a 1- by 1-inch wood block at each joint.

◆ Cut the block as long as the depth of the shelf.

◆ With the block flush against the joint, drill three pilot holes (right) through one side of the block and into the cabinet.

◆ Then, without intersecting those three holes, drill three more pilot holes through the other side of the block.

◆ Apply glue to the remaining two sides of the block, those that rest against the cabinet. Press the block into place with the pilot holes properly aligned, then drive a $1\frac{1}{4}$-inch dry-wall screw into each pilot hole.

9

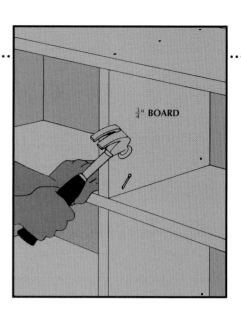

A shelf partition.

Always work from the bottom up. When each partition is inserted, the wood grain should be vertical to match the sides of the cabinet.

◆ First, measure the depth of the cabinet's shelves and cut a $\frac{3}{4}$-inch board along the grain to this measurement.

◆ At the side of the cabinet where the shelves meet the frame, measure the distance between the two lowest shelves, and cut the $\frac{3}{4}$-inch board across the grain to that length.

◆ At the centerline of the cabinet, insert a partition between the bottom two shelves, and drive three nails straight through the shelf into the top of the partition.

◆ Near the bottom of the partition, drive two nails at a 45° angle through each side of the partition into the shelf below (right).

◆ Working upward toward the shelf that is sagging, repeat for the remaining shelves.

Center stile cabinets.

As with the partition method described above, all the shelves beneath the sagging shelf must be supported.

◆ At one end of the cabinet, measure the distance between the bottom two shelves and cut two 1-by-2 pieces of wood to that length.

◆ Wedge one piece behind the center stile and the other against the center of the back of the cabinet directly opposite the stile.

◆ Drill two pilot holes through both pieces of wood and into the cabinet frame about 1 inch from each end. Drive a $1\frac{1}{4}$-inch wood screw into each hole.

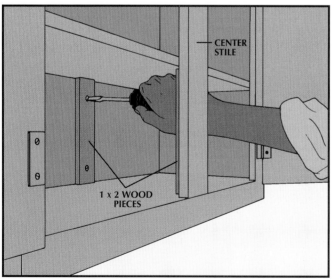

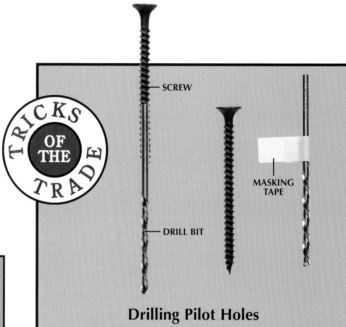

Drilling Pilot Holes

Small pieces of wood tend to split when screws are driven into them. Drilling pilot holes first makes it much easier to seat screws properly.

A pilot hole must be slightly narrower than the screw. Hold a drill bit at eye level directly in front of the screw. The screw's shank should be hidden by the bit but the threads should be visible (above, left). To measure the proper depth for the pilot hole, mark the bit with a piece of masking tape about $\frac{2}{3}$ the length of the screw.

In many cases you will want to countersink the screws—that is, drive them flush with, or even below, the surface of the wood. Combination bits, available in a variety of sizes, will drill the pilot hole and the countersink hole at the same time.

Redrilling screw holes for hinges.

◆ If the hinges are loose, try tightening the screws. If a screw won't tighten, the hole is stripped and must be plugged, then redrilled.

◆ Unscrew the door from its hinges, and remove any hinge where holes in the cabinet frame need to be plugged. Save the screws.

◆ With a hacksaw, cut pieces of a hardwood dowel to the length of the screws, then splinter them with a chisel. Squirt glue into the stripped screw holes, and plug them tight with the hardwood splinters (*inset*), tapping them with a hammer to ensure a tight fit. Wipe off any excess glue.

◆ Let the glue dry, then drill pilot holes into the plugs (*right*) and re-mount the door to the cabinet with the old screws. Close it and see if it is properly aligned with the cabinet. If necessary, loosen the screws slightly, shift the door, and then retighten the screws.

HARDWOOD DOWEL

⅛" GUIDELINE   RABBET PLANE

INSIDE DOOR EDGE

Planing an edge that sticks.

◆ On the inner side of the door, mark a line $\frac{1}{8}$ inch from the edge that rubs. Secure the door in a vise.

◆ On a lipped door *(left)*, use a rabbet plane or a block plane to shave the inside edge down to the marked line.

◆ On a flush door, use a block plane. Take special care not to shave the outside edge to avoid creating a gap between the closed door and the frame of the cabinet.

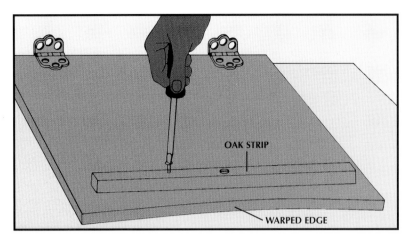

Bracing a warped door.

◆ Cut a 1-by-1 piece of oak 2 inches shorter than the length of the warped edge of the door. Set the door facedown, and center the strip 1 inch in from the warped edge.

◆ With a combination bit, drill a pilot hole through the center of the oak strip and into the door. Countersink a 1½-inch No. 6 screw through the strip, but do not tighten it.

◆ Working toward the edges, drill pilot holes, and countersink screws one at a time at 6-inch intervals along the strip. To avoid cracking the door, attach the 1-by-1 strip fairly loose at first, then gradually tighten the screws, starting in the center.

◆ When the warp is removed, unfasten the strip, glue it in place, and rescrew it to the door.

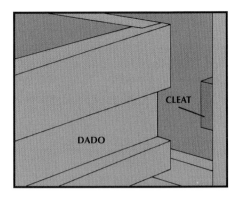

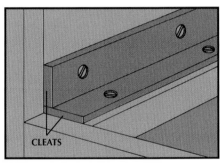

Replacing wooden drawer guides.

Some drawers have grooves—or dadoes—along the sides (above, top) that fit a cleat attached to the cabinet, while others slide on two cleats (above) that form a guide for the drawer's lower edges.

◆ To replace a damaged guide of either type, first trace its outline onto the cabinet with a pen or pencil. At the edge of the outline, mark the positions of the screw holes, then remove the screws. Dislodge a glued guide by gently tapping it with a hammer.

◆ Using the old guide as a template, cut a duplicate piece, then glue it to the cabinet at the traced position. Drill pilot holes for new screws, taking care to offset them about ½ inch from the old screw holes, and secure the block with screws.

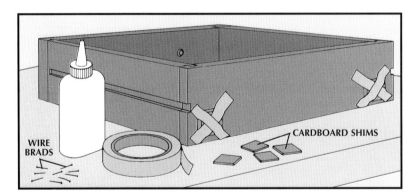

New stops on flush drawers.

◆ First, remove the worn or damaged stop blocks, then push the drawer in as far as it will go, and measure the gap between the cabinet face and the drawer front.

◆ Cut two blocks 1 inch square and slightly thinner than the measured distance, and tape them to the drawer back in place of the old stop blocks (above).

◆ Replace the drawer and test the fit. If necessary, insert cardboard shims between the drawer back and the wood blocks until the drawer front is flush with the cabinet face.

◆ Glue the stops and shims to the drawer, then gently hammer in wire brads.

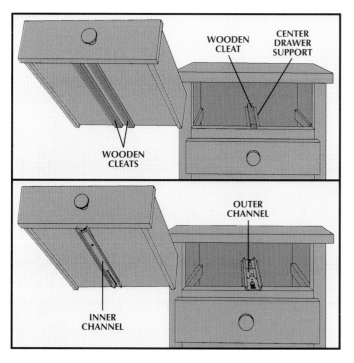

A substitute for wooden bottom guides.

If a wooden center cleat breaks, replace it with metal center guides, which come in sizes to fit most drawers and are more durable.

◆ Gently pry off the wooden cleats from the bottom of the drawer and from the center support *(left, top)*.

◆ Measure the drawer depth, and buy a metal center guide to match it.

◆ Draw a line down the center of the drawer bottom and the center drawer support.

◆ Attach the inner channel to the drawer bottom, and the outer channel to the center drawer support *(left, bottom)*.

ANCHORING A CABINET TO STUDS

1. Shimming the top of the cabinet.

◆ Check the old screw holes in the studs to make sure they are not stripped. If necessary, plug the holes and redrill them *(page 11)*.

◆ While a helper holds the back of the cabinet against the wall, using old paint lines or other markings as a guideline, check the cabinet's vertical and horizontal alignment with a level. If there is no one available to help hold the cabi-

net, see the box on page 14.

◆ If the top of the cabinet must move out from the wall, insert a shim (use the old ones if you have them) at each stud, and tap it down until the cabinet is plumb.

◆ If the cabinet is already plumb, use shims only to fill any gap at the studs between the cabinet and the wall, gently tapping them into place without moving the cabinet.

A Substitute for Another Pair of Hands

If there is no helper available to steady the cabinet against the wall while you remove or re-hang it, a prop constructed of four pieces of $\frac{3}{4}$-inch plywood will serve nicely. One horizontal piece supports the cabinet bottom while the other provides a broad, sturdy base on the countertop. The two vertical pieces that bear the cabinet's weight are screwed together at right angles for added stability. Slide the prop under the cabinet, and insert shims, if needed, until it fits snugly between the cabinet bottom and the countertop.

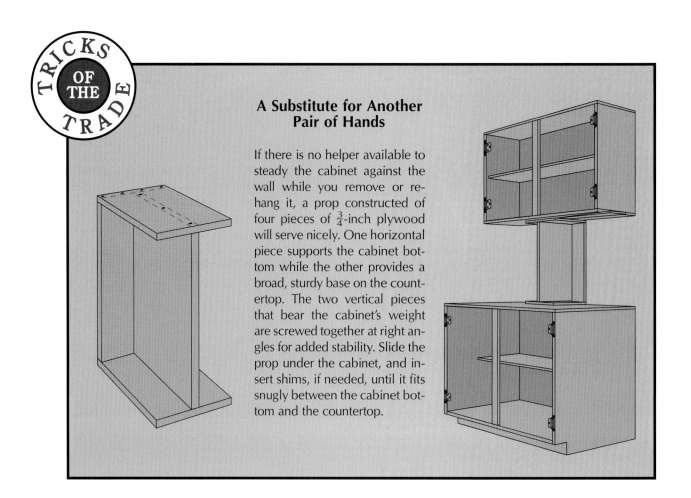

2. Plumbing the cabinet bottom.

◆ Drive screws into the studs through the top hanging bar, cabinet back, and shims *(left)*.

◆ If the cabinet must move out at the bottom, install shims at each stud as you did for the top.

◆ If your cabinet has a lower hanging bar *(not shown)*, shim any gap at the studs between the cabinet back and the wall, then attach it as you did the top hanging bar.

◆ Trim all the protruding shims with a handsaw or utility knife; cut almost to the wall, then snap off the waste.

Fixing Damaged Countertops

Although countertop surfaces—plastic laminate, ceramic tile, or hardwood butcher block—are strong and durable, daily use and accidents eventually take their toll. But much damage to most surfaces can be repaired.

Quick Repairs for Minor Damage: Scratches and gouges in laminate can be hidden with a matching plastic seam filler, available from countertop fabricators. Broken or lifted edges can be reglued. Stains on butcher block can usually be scraped or sanded away.

With care, a cracked ceramic tile can be removed and replaced without marring the surrounding tiles. Scrape away old grout around the edges of the tile with a grout saw. A damaged tile at the edge of the sink presents special problems; you must remove the sink

(page 102) and cut the new tile to fit (pages 108-109).

Replacing a Section of Countertop: Extensive damage to a laminate countertop can be cut out and replaced with an inset of heat-proof glass—available as a kit from home-supply centers—or ceramic tiles. Since the metal-rimmed glass inset requires that the countertop be cut through, check for braces or crosspieces under the countertop before proceeding.

To install a tile inset, remove the damaged area with a router and a $\frac{3}{8}$-inch double-fluted bit. To determine the depth of the cut, add $\frac{1}{4}$ inch for a plywood underlayment to the thickness of your tiles, then subtract $\frac{1}{32}$ inch so that the tiles will sit slightly higher than the surface of the countertop.

 **TOOLS**

 **MATERIALS**

 **SAFETY TIPS**

Putty knife	Electric drill with $\frac{1}{4}$-inch bit	Plastic seam filler	Ceramic tiles
Steel scraper		$\frac{1}{4}$-inch plywood	Carpenter's glue
Orbital sander	$\frac{1}{4}$-inch masonry bit	Silicone caulk	Epoxy-based or
Saber saw with laminate blade	Utility knife with laminate blade	Grout	acrylic tile adhesive
Router	Grout saw	Silicone sealer	
$\frac{3}{8}$-inch double-fluted bit	Pry bar		
C clamp	Cold chisel		
	Notched trowel		

Protect your eyes with goggles when using a hammer and chisel, power saw, sander, or router. Never start the router with the bit touching the surface to be routed. Wear rubber gloves when handling tile adhesive.

A quick fix for countertop scratches.
◆ Squeeze a small quantity of plastic seam filler onto a plastic plate, and work it with a clean putty knife until it begins to thicken.
◆ Wipe the scratch with a cloth dipped in the solvent that comes with the filler, then press the paste into the scratch with the putty knife. Immediately wipe away excess filler with the cloth. If the filler shrinks as it hardens, wait an hour and repeat the process.

Restoring a blemished butcher block.
◆ Set the edge of a steel scraper against the butcher block at a 60° angle, beveled edge up *(left),* and pull it across the blemished area.
◆ If scraping fails, run an orbital electric sander with medium-grit sandpaper over an area slightly larger than the stain. Keep the sander moving to avoid grinding a depression into the surface.
◆ Smooth the surface with fine-grit sandpaper, and apply vegetable oil or a nontoxic finish.

REGLUING PLASTIC LAMINATE

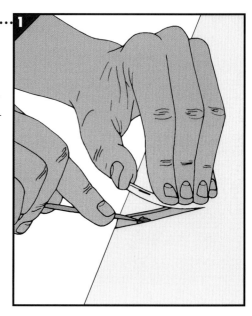

1. Applying the adhesive.
◆ First try reviving the old adhesive by placing a cloth over the area and heating it with a cool iron, then press the loose piece down with a roller.
◆ Alternatively, lift the loose edge gently and scrape out dried glue with a utility knife. Blow out any loose debris with a straw.
◆ Using a toothpick, spread carpenter's glue sparingly on the exposed countertop core *(right).*
◆ Press the laminate back into place and wipe off excess glue.

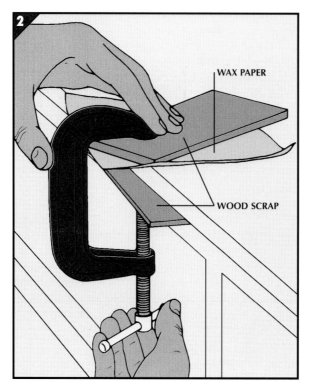

WAX PAPER

WOOD SCRAP

2. Clamping down the repair.
◆ Lay a piece of wax paper over the repair, then cover it with a scrap of wood. With another scrap protecting the underside of the countertop, clamp the repair tightly *(left).*
◆ Wait 24 hours for the glue to set, then release the clamp.

REPLACING A CRACKED CERAMIC TILE

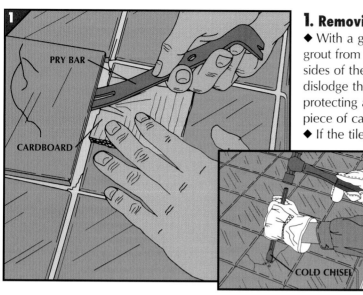

1. Removing the tile.

◆ With a grout saw, scratch the grout from the joints on all four sides of the tile, then attempt to dislodge the tile with a pry bar, protecting adjacent tiles with a piece of cardboard *(left)*.

◆ If the tile resists prying, drill four holes near the center with a masonry bit, then chip out the tile with a cold chisel and hammer *(inset)*.

◆ Scrape any old adhesive or grout from the opening in the countertop with a putty knife or a cold chisel, making the surface as even as possible. Wipe away dust with a damp cloth.

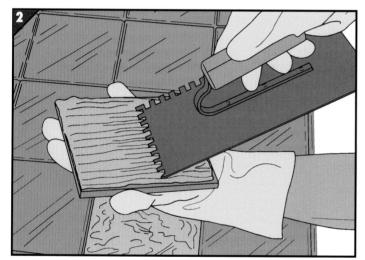

2. Applying the adhesive.

Use the flat edge of a notched trowel to coat the back of the replacement tile with adhesive, then comb the adhesive with the notched edge, leaving visible ridges *(above)*.

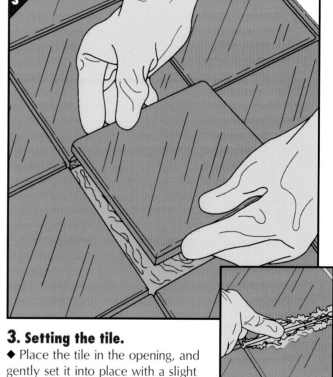

3. Setting the tile.

◆ Place the tile in the opening, and gently set it into place with a slight back-and-forth twisting motion.

◆ Remove any adhesive from the tile surface with a damp cloth.

◆ Lay an 18-inch length of 2-by-4 on the replacement tile. Tap the board with a hammer to bring the surface of the replacement tile even with the surfaces of the other tiles.

◆ Allow the adhesive to cure, then grout the surrounding joints with your fingertip *(inset)*.

A GLASS INSET FOR A SCARRED COUNTERTOP

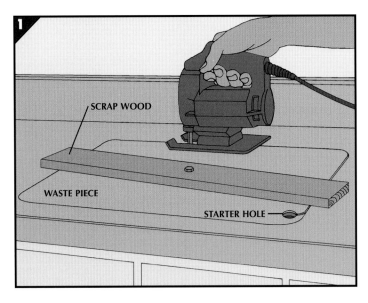

1. Cutting the hole.
◆ Set the rim of the inset or the template provided by its manufacturer over the damaged area, and mark a cut line on the countertop.
◆ Loosely bolt a piece of scrap lumber to the countertop to support the cutout as you saw (left).
◆ Just inside a corner of the marked area, drill a starter hole for a saber saw. Cut out the opening, rotating the board ahead of the saw as you go.
◆ Lift out the waste piece with the board, and test-fit the metal rim in the opening. If necessary, enlarge the opening slightly with a coarse file.

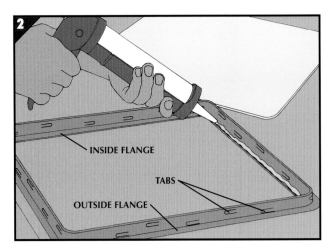

2. Preparing the inset.
◆ Set the rim of the inset upside down and squeeze a thin bead of silicone caulk around the inside flange (left).
◆ Turn the glass piece upside down and press it into the rim of the inset. With a screwdriver, bend the metal tabs along the rim outward to hold the glass in place.
◆ Apply a heavier bead of caulk to the outside flange of the rim, then set the assembly into the countertop.

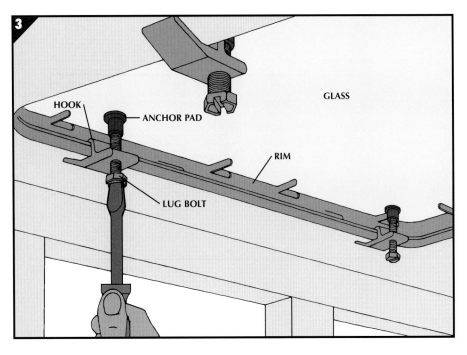

3. Fastening the inset.
◆ Underneath the countertop, hook one of the lugs provided by the manufacturer over the edge of the metal rim, insert the lug bolt and thread it into an anchor pad, then screw the pad against the underside of the inset piece (left).
◆ Repeat this procedure on the lug and bolt diagonally opposite, then on the remaining bolts.
◆ On the countertop, use a putty knife to scrape off excess caulk around the edge of the rim.

AN INLAY OF CERAMIC TILES

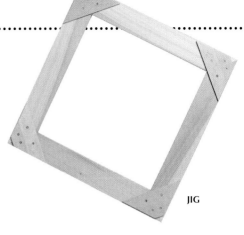

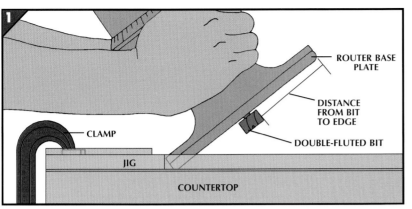

JIG

1. Measuring the area.

◆ Draw a rectangle on the countertop $\frac{1}{4}$ inch larger in each dimension than the area that is to be tiled.

◆ In each corner of the rectangle—and touching its edges—drill a $\frac{1}{4}$-inch hole to the depth of the router cut you plan.

◆ Measure between the router bit and the base plate edge. Double the measurement, and add the result to the dimensions of the rectangle. Make a jig for the router *(photograph)*, using these figures as inside dimensions.

◆ Clamp the jig in place. After adjusting the router to cut half the planned depth, place the router base against the jig *(above, left)*.

2. Routing the inset area.

◆ Turn on the router, lower it into the countertop, and move it to the center.

◆ To ensure support for the router, cut a clockwise spiral *(right)* to the edge of the jig, then rout along the perimeter. Set the bit to the full depth and retrace the spiral.

◆ Beginning in the center, finish routing the remaining countertop inside the jig.

◆ To remove small countertop remnants in corners around the drill holes, score the laminate with a laminate blade in a utility knife, then chisel away the under-lying wood.

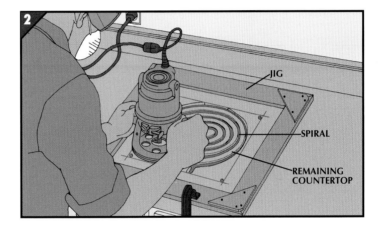

3. Laying the tiles.

◆ Cut a piece of plywood to fit the routed area, and glue it in place.

◆ With a notched trowel, spread adhesive over the plywood. Then set the tiles in the inset *(right),* and let the adhesive cure according to the manufacturer's recommendations.

◆ Grout and seal the joints between tiles as de-scribed on page 111.

◆ After the grout has cured, caulk the $\frac{1}{4}$-inch space between the tiles and the countertop with silicone caulk.

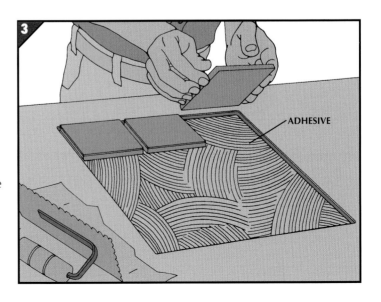

Kitchen floors are high-traffic areas that take a beating in normal everyday use. For this reason, most are made either of durable, resilient vinyl—laid in sheets or square tiles—or of tough, rigid ceramic tile.

Rugged as they are, these materials can still be damaged by common household accidents. Dropped utensils can gouge resilient flooring or crack ceramic tile, and hot liquids can blister a vinyl surface.

Fortunately, such flaws can usually be patched, and it is not necessary to tear out the entire floor. Replacing a broken ceramic tile is described on page 17. Before under-

taking any repairs on resilient flooring, read the information on asbestos on page 22.

Sometimes vinyl tiles or sections of sheet flooring work loose from the plywood underlayment to which they are bonded. This problem should be corrected immediately, before the flooring becomes damaged or kitchen spills seep through to the underlayment and subfloor.

Damaged Wall Base: Also prone to nicks and splits from accidental blows is the wall base—either quarter-round wooden lengths called shoe molding or flexible vinyl

strips—which conceals the joint between the kitchen floor and the walls. Sometimes a section of undamaged wall base must be removed in order to repair the adjacent flooring. If shoe molding is removed carefully, the same piece can be remounted afterward.

Vinyl molding usually needs to be replaced, because it is not practical to try to remove the adhesive from the old piece. New molding in various widths and colors is available at any building-supply center. If you buy it in one long roll, cut it into workable lengths—4 to 6 feet—before installing it.

 TOOLS

 **MATERIALS**

 SAFETY TIPS

Utility knife
Linoleum knife
Putty knife
Pry bar
Nail set
Heat gun
Hand roller
Notched spreader
Glue injector

Wood filler
Vinyl-tile adhesive
Seam sealer

◆ *Heat guns heat a stream of air to between about 250° and 1,100° F. The lowest temperature setting on the gun will usually suffice to soften the adhesive under kitchen flooring. Always wear thick work gloves to protect against burns.*
◆ *Wear rubber gloves when mixing, removing, or applying flooring adhesive. Open all doors and windows in the room, and avoid inhaling the fumes.*

REPLACING SHOE MOLDING

1. Loosening the molding.
◆ First, run a utility knife between the molding and the baseboard to break the paint seal.
◆ Starting at a door or an outside corner, work the blade of a wide putty knife into the seam. Gently lever the piece of molding far enough from the baseboard to allow the insertion of a pry bar into the gap.

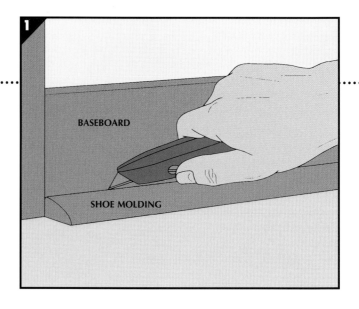

BASEBOARD

SHOE MOLDING

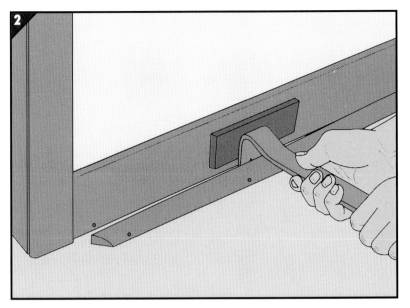

2. Removing the molding.

◆ Using a piece of wood or cardboard to protect the baseboard, work the pry bar along the molding, levering it out slightly at each nail. When the entire piece is thus loosened, return to the first nail and repeat the process. Work slowly; do not try to force the piece out all at once.

◆ If you are replacing damaged molding, save the old pieces as a guide for cutting strips of new molding.

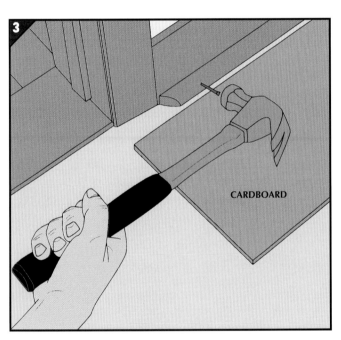

CARDBOARD

3. Installing new molding.

◆ Lay the old pieces of molding against a strip of new molding, and mark the proper lengths. Cut the new pieces with a backsaw. Use a miter box to achieve accurate 45° angles where two pieces meet at a corner.

◆ Install the new pieces in the reverse order from which you removed the old molding, ending at a door or an outside corner.

◆ Lay a piece of cardboard on the floor to protect the finish, then drive a $1\frac{1}{2}$-inch finishing nail through the center of the molding 1 inch from its end. Drive a nail every 12 inches along the length of the piece.

◆ Place a nail set against the head of each finishing nail in turn and, with a hammer, tap the nail set until the heads are below the surface of the molding.

4. Filling the holes and gaps.

◆ Use a putty knife to work wood filler into nail holes and any gaps between molding pieces.

◆ When the filler is dry, sand the wood and the filler, then finish the shoe molding with paint or stain.

BASEBOARDS OF VINYL

1. Removing the wall base.

◆ Hold the nozzle of a heat gun a few inches from the end of a section of wall base, and sweep it back and forth for about 15 seconds to soften the adhesive.

◆ Work the tip of a putty knife behind the heated wall base, and separate it from the wall. Continue moving down the length of the section with the heat gun and putty knife until the entire strip comes off.

◆ Soften any adhesive left on the wall, and scrape it off with the putty knife.

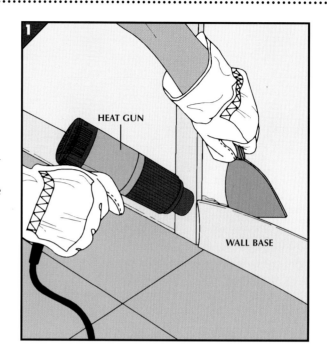

HEAT GUN

WALL BASE

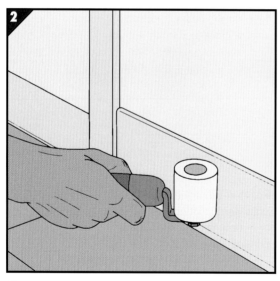

2. Installing new wall base.

◆ Use a notched spreader to coat the back of the wall base evenly with adhesive to within $\frac{1}{2}$ inch of its edges.

◆ Press the section into place on the wall, making sure the bottom edge touches the floor. Where a strip must fit around a corner, warm the strip with the heat gun so that it bends easily.

◆ When the entire section is in place, run a hand roller back and forth over it several times to bond it to the wall (*above*).

⚠ CAUTION

Asbestos

If your resilient kitchen floor was installed before 1986, the flooring or the adhesive underneath may contain asbestos. When damaged, these materials can release microscopic asbestos fibers into the air, creating severe long-term health risks. Unless you know for certain that your floor does not contain asbestos, assume that it does, and follow these precautions when making any repairs:

❗ *Always wear a dual-cartridge respirator. Asbestos fibers will pass right through an ordinary dust mask.*

❗ *Never sand resilient flooring or the underlying adhesive.*

❗ *Try to remove the damaged flooring in one piece. If it looks likely to break or crumble, wet it before removal to reduce the chance of raising dust.*

❗ *When scraping off old adhesive, always use a heat gun to keep it tacky or a spray bottle to keep it wet.*

❗ *If vacuuming is necessary, rent or buy a wet/dry shop vac with a HEPA (High Efficiency Particulate Air) filtration system.*

❗ *Place the damaged flooring, adhesive, and HEPA filter in a polyethylene trash bag at least 6 mils (.006 inch) thick, and seal it immediately.*

❗ *Contact your local environmental protection office for guidance as to proper disposal.*

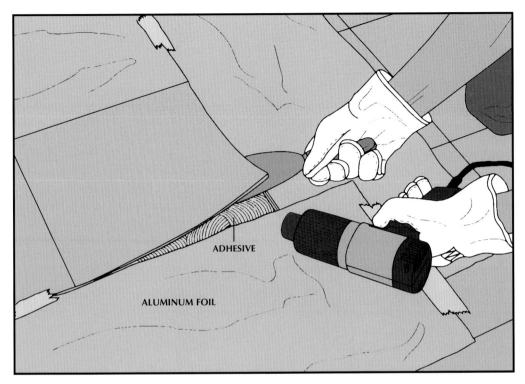

Resealing tiles.

◆ Tape sheets of aluminum foil over the adjacent tiles to protect them from being damaged by the heat gun.

◆ Lift the loose corner of the tile with a putty knife, and move the heat gun back and forth until the adhesive on the underlayment and the bottom of the tile is tacky.

◆ Press the tile down firmly, cover it with a cloth, and place several thick books or some equivalent weight on the cloth. After 30 minutes, remove the cloth and check the tile. If it lifts again, the tile must be removed and reglued.

Regluing tiles.

◆ Soften the adhesive with the heat gun while gently lifting the tile with the putty knife until it can be pulled off.

◆ Using the heat gun and putty knife, remove the old adhesive from the back of the tile and the exposed underlayment.

◆ With a notched spreader, coat the underlayment evenly with vinyl-tile adhesive, leaving visible ridges in it (left).

◆ Let the adhesive set according to the manufacturer's instructions, then fit the tile into the opening and press it down firmly with a hand roller.

REPLACING DAMAGED TILES

1. Removing tiles.

To remove a damaged tile that is still securely bonded to the underlayment, lay a straightedge across the tile about 1 inch from its edge to protect the adjacent tile from the heat gun. Cut through the tile along the straightedge with a linoleum knife.

◆ Sweep the nozzle of the heat gun back and forth along the slit until the adhesive is soft enough to allow the insertion of a putty knife under the edge of the tile, then work the tile loose and remove it. Remove adjacent damaged tiles the same way.

◆ If any damaged tiles were cut when installed to fit against a wall or around an obstruction, use them as templates to make matching replacement tiles.

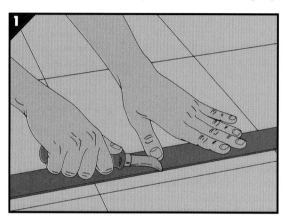

2. Spreading the adhesive.

◆ Remove the old adhesive from the underlayment with a heat gun and putty knife.

◆ With a notched spreader, coat the underlayment with vinyl-tile adhesive, leaving ridges, and let it set according to the manufacturer's instructions.

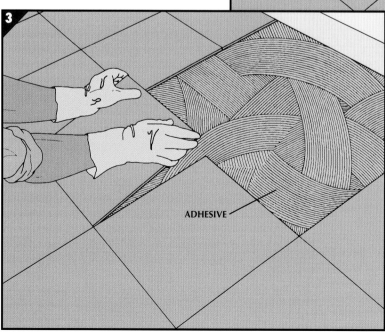

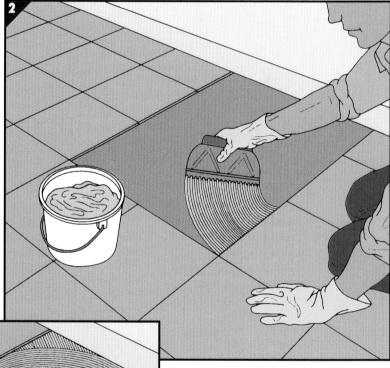

ADHESIVE

3. Installing the new tiles.

◆ Fit a replacement tile in a corner of the opening where it abuts two existing tiles.

◆ Lay whole tiles first, and finish with those that have been cut to fit.

◆ With a hand roller, firmly press down all the new tiles flush with each other and the surrounding tiles.

◆ With a damp cloth, immediately wipe up any excess adhesive. Don't walk on the replacement tiles until the adhesive has dried completely. This usually takes 24 hours.

REGLUING A LIFTED EDGE

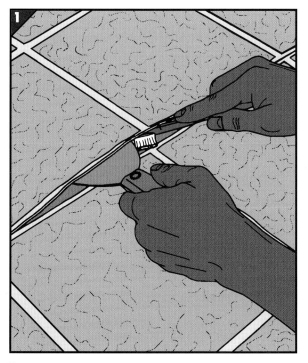

1. Removing the old adhesive.
◆ Raise the loose edge with a putty knife, then use an old toothbrush moistened with undiluted liquid floor cleaner to scrub under it.
◆ While the old adhesive is still wet, use a sharp knife to scrape it from the area along the seam.
◆ Wipe the area clean with a cloth, and let it dry.

2. Applying the adhesive.
◆ Raise the lifted edge again, and use a small putty knife to spread a thin layer of adhesive on the underlayment. Let it set for the specified time.
◆ Pressing firmly, run a hand roller along the edge to bind it to the adhesive.
◆ Immediately wipe up any excess adhesive with a damp cloth, then cover the seam with a dry cloth and place several thick books on it.

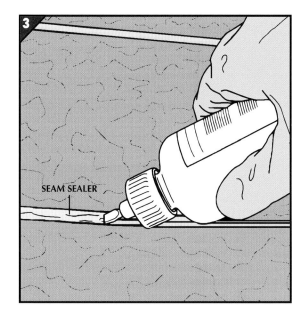

SEAM SEALER

3. Sealing the seam.
◆ Let the adhesive dry according to the manufacturer's instructions, then seal the edge using a commercial seam sealer recommended for your type of flooring.
◆ Working from one end of the edge to the other, hold the applicator at an angle and gently squeeze out a continuous bead.
◆ Keep traffic off the edge until the sealer is dry.

⚠ **CAUTION** *Seam sealer is toxic and flammable. Follow all safety precautions on the label.*

FLATTENING A BLISTER

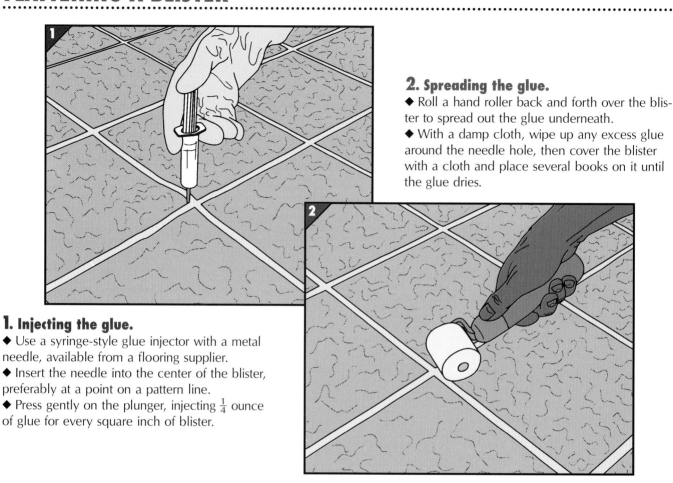

2. Spreading the glue.
◆ Roll a hand roller back and forth over the blister to spread out the glue underneath.
◆ With a damp cloth, wipe up any excess glue around the needle hole, then cover the blister with a cloth and place several books on it until the glue dries.

1. Injecting the glue.
◆ Use a syringe-style glue injector with a metal needle, available from a flooring supplier.
◆ Insert the needle into the center of the blister, preferably at a point on a pattern line.
◆ Press gently on the plunger, injecting $\frac{1}{4}$ ounce of glue for every square inch of blister.

A PATCH FOR SHEET FLOORING

1. Making a patch.
◆ Place a matching, slightly larger piece of flooring over the damaged section, and carefully align the pattern.
◆ Secure the replacement piece to the floor with masking tape.

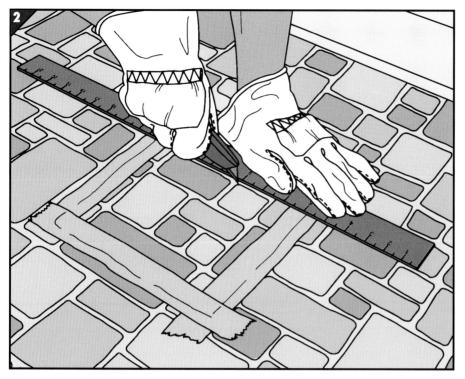

2. Cutting out the damaged section.

◆ Use a utility knife and a straightedge to cut the replacement piece and the damaged section simultaneously, following pattern lines wherever possible.

◆ Lift off the replacement piece, and dispose of the tape and cut edges.

◆ If the damaged section remains adhered to the underlayment, work the tip of the knife between the upper wear layer and the backing, and peel off the upper layer.

◆ Wet the backing with a solution of dishwashing liquid and water, and scrape it off the underlayment with a putty knife.

3. Installing the replacement section.

◆ With a notched spreader, coat the underlayment with an even layer of adhesive.

◆ Let the adhesive set according to the manufacturer's instructions, then fit the replacement piece into the hole.

◆ Press it firmly into place with a hand roller, and immediately wipe up any excess adhesive with a damp cloth.

◆ When the adhesive is dry, seal the edges of the patch with seam sealer *(page 25, Step 3)*.

Simple Fixes for Appliances

Major kitchen appliances are built to give many years of reliable service, but when a problem arises, it can often appear more serious than it really is. In many instances, you can make repairs easily—and safely—without specialized knowledge of the machines. Doing the work yourself not only spares you the cost of a service call, but may well save money on parts, too.

Inspecting a burner receptacle on an electric range ➞

The most common complaints about dishwashers—they leak, don't drain, or don't clean well—often arise from clogs or mechanical breakdowns that are easily fixed, and in some cases the dishwasher may not be at fault.

Hot Water Helps to Clean: Dirty or spotted dishes, for example, may simply be the result of insufficiently hot water. To check your water supply, place a candy thermometer or meat thermometer in a coffee mug,

then turn the kitchen tap to its hottest setting and run water into the mug for 2 minutes. If the temperature is below 120°, raise the setting on your water heater to 120°.

Fixing Those Leaks: Inspect the gaskets around the door, and check hose connections at the water inlet valve, pump, and drain valve. Reseat a slipped gasket in its track, and tighten or replace any loose hose clamps. Replace hoses that look as

if they are cracked or brittle.

More serious are problems involving the pump, motor, or timer, as these three parts are the hardest to fix. Only disassembling and cleaning the pump is shown (*page 34*)—in all other cases you should call for service.

⚠ **CAUTION** *Before attempting any repair of a dishwasher, turn off the power to the machine at the house service panel.*

TOOLS

Multitester	Candy thermometer or
Slip-joint pliers	meat thermometer
Screwdriver	Tweezers
Adjustable wrench	

Anatomy of a dishwasher.

To begin a cycle, the timer signals the water inlet valve to open, allowing water into the tub. The water mixes with detergent, is heated to about 140° by the heating element, and is pumped through the small apertures of the spray arm against the dishes to clean them. Then the dishes are rinsed and the tub drained, and the heating element turns on again to dry the dishes.

To drain the tub at the end of the wash cycle, a dishwasher will have either a drain valve or a reversible motor to pump out the water. Most models have a spray tower—a pipe that carries water to the upper spray arm, as shown here.

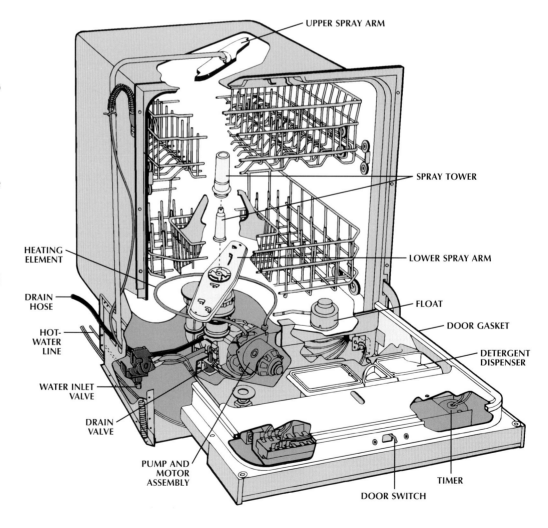

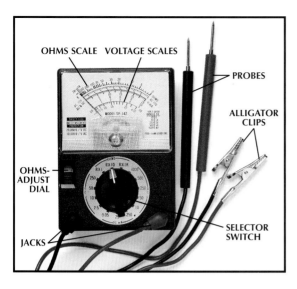

OHMS SCALE   VOLTAGE SCALES

PROBES

ALLIGATOR CLIPS

OHMS-ADJUST DIAL

JACKS

SELECTOR SWITCH

The versatile multitester.

A multitester can measure the voltage and current (amperes) reaching an electrical component, as well as its resistance in ohms.

◆ Turn the selector switch to the correct value of amperes, AC volts, DC volts, or ohms you want to measure, and read the scale on the meter. Always use a setting higher than the value expected. The ohms scale is particularly useful in appliance repairs for identifying which part of the machine has failed.

◆ To calibrate the multitester for resistance measurements, select the RX1 (resistance times 1) scale and touch the probes together. Turn the ohms-adjust dial until the meter reads 0 ohms. For other tests, follow the directions in the owner's manual.

Troubleshooting Guide

PROBLEM	REMEDY
Dishes dirty or spotted.	Test water temperature. Check for binding or broken parts in detergent dispenser. Look for obstructions, such as utensils, that fall and block spray arm. Check and clean spray arm *(page 32)*. Check and clean pump *(page 34)*; replace impellers if corroded or chipped. Check and clean filter screen, if there is one *(page 32)*.
Dishwasher doesn't fill with water.	Test water inlet valve solenoid and inspect filter screen *(page 33)*. Check for obstruction propping up float; test float switch *(page 33)*. Check door latch; test door switch *(page 32)*. Check and clean filter screen, if there is one *(page 32)*.
Dishwasher drains during fill.	Inspect drain valve; test valve solenoid and replace it if necessary *(page 34)*.
Water doesn't shut off.	Remove any debris on underside of float; test float switch *(page 33)*. Test water inlet valve *(page 33)*.
Motor doesn't run.	Check for blown fuse or tripped circuit breaker. Adjust door latch if necessary; test door switch *(page 32)*.
Motor hums but doesn't run.	Check and clean pump *(page 34)*; if it still doesn't work, call for service.
Poor water drainage.	Check for clogged air gap *(page 32)*. Check the drain hose for kinks and clogs; remove any that you find. Check and clean filter screen, if there is one *(page 32)*. Check for clogged drain valve and test drain valve solenoid *(page 34)*. Check and clean pump *(page 34)*; replace impellers if corroded or chipped.
Dishwasher leaks around door.	Adjust door latch so door closes tightly *(page 32)*. Replace door gasket if the rubber is hardened or damaged.
Dishwasher leaks from bottom or below door.	Seal any cracks in tub with silicone rubber sealant or epoxy glue. Tighten water inlet valve connection. Look for loose pump seals or heating element nuts. Check spray arm, especially bottom of arm, for holes.
Door is difficult to close.	Adjust or oil door catch *(page 32)*. Replace catch if broken.

Opening a clogged air gap.
◆ Find the air gap on the back rim of the sink between the dishwasher and the sink faucet. Pull off the chrome cover, and unscrew the plastic cap.
◆ With tweezers, remove any debris from the small tube in the center of the air gap *(right)*.
◆ Clean the cover and cap if necessary; screw on the cap and snap the cover in place.

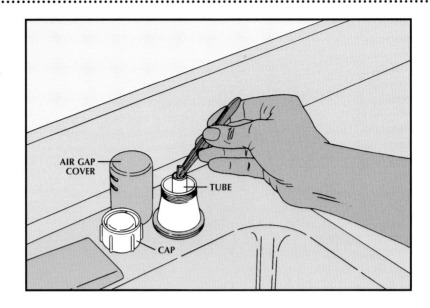

Cleaning the spray arm and filter screen.
◆ After sliding out the lower dish rack, twist off the plastic hubcap, if there is one, that holds the lower spray arm in place, and lift off the arm.
◆ If your machine has a removable coarse strainer and filter screen, unsnap and remove them; otherwise, clean them in place.
◆ Clean out the slotted holes in the spray arm with a wire. Scrub the strainer and filter screen with a stiff brush, and then rinse all three before reinstalling them.
◆ Unclog the holes in the upper spray arm without removing the arm from its holder.

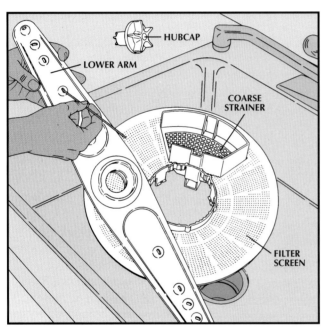

Checking the door latch and switch.
◆ If the latch is difficult to close, lubricate the mechanism with light machine oil. On many models, the latch can be adjusted for a better fit by loosening the mounting screws, sliding the latch in or out, then retightening the screws.
◆ To test the door switch *(above)*, remove the screws on the inside of the door that secure the control panel. Close and lock the door. Gently pull off the panel and disconnect the wires from the door switch terminals, behind the latch. Attach multitester clips to the terminals, and check switch resistance *(page 31)*; any reading other than 0 ohms indicates a faulty switch.
◆ Replace the switch by removing its retaining screws, installing a new switch, and reconnecting the wires.

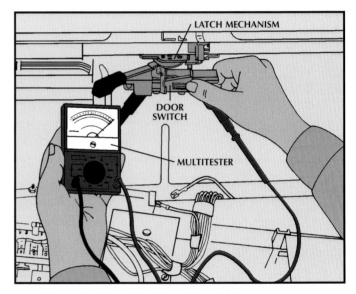

CHECKING THE WATER CONTROLS

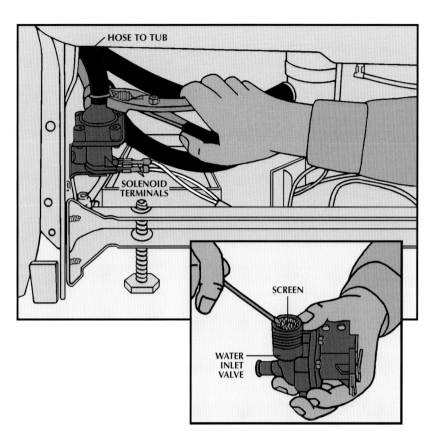

Servicing the water inlet valve.

◆ Turn off the power and water supply to the dishwasher.

◆ With a shallow pan handy, use slip-joint pliers to remove the hose that connects the inlet valve to the tub *(right)*. Then disconnect the flexible copper hot-water line with an adjustable wrench.

◆ Unscrew the valve from its mounting bracket. Without removing the filter screen, scrape it clean *(inset)* and rinse. If the valve appears cracked or otherwise damaged, replace it.

◆ With the multitester, check the solenoid. You should get a reading of between 60 and 500 ohms. Replace the valve assembly if the solenoid is faulty.

◆ Reinstall the valve, then reattach the hot-water line and hose, and tighten all connections.

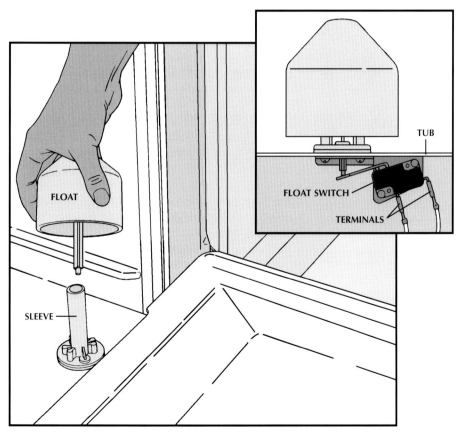

Cleaning and testing the float and its switch.

◆ Lift the float out of its sleeve, and remove any debris from the bottom of the float. Clean out the sleeve as well.

◆ Slide the float into the sleeve and run the dishwasher. If no water enters the machine or if it overflows, turn off the power to the dishwasher at the main service panel, bail out any water in the tub, and remove the access panel below the door.

◆ Test the float switch *(inset)* located under the tub by touching the multitester probes to the terminals. You should get 0 ohms with the switch on *(float down)* and infinity with the switch off *(float up)*.

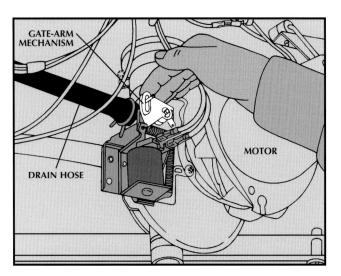

Inspecting the drain valve assembly.

Remove the panel below the door and count the number of wires attached to the motor. Two or three wires indicates a nonreversible motor; four or more is reversible. Only nonreversible motors have drain valves. Locate the valve and its gate-arm mechanism. Move the arm by hand *(above)*; if it doesn't move freely up and down on its two springs, replace them.

Testing the drain valve solenoid.

Disconnect the wires from the drain valve solenoid terminals and check resistance. If you do not get a reading between 60 and 500 ohms, replace the solenoid.

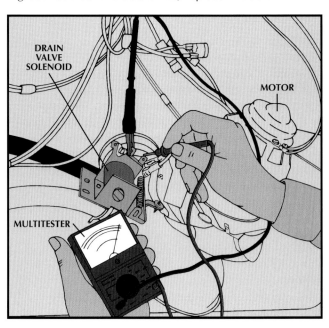

CLEANING THE PUMP

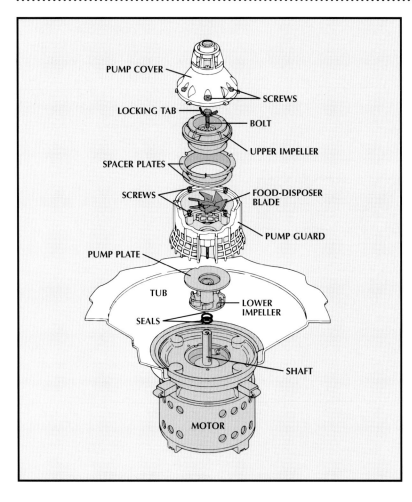

Getting to the impellers.

◆ Take off the lower spray arm *(page 32)*, then remove all screws from the pump cover, exposing the upper impeller.

◆ If there is a bolt-locking tab, bend it up to clear the bolt, then unscrew the bolt, freeing the upper impeller. Check the impeller for debris and for worn or broken blades; clean or replace it as necessary.

◆ Lift out the spacer plates and the food-disposer blade under the impeller; clean the blade.

◆ To reach the lower impeller, unfasten the screws holding the pump guard and remove it. Pull off the pump plate and clean the impeller.

◆ If the lower impeller is damaged, pry it off the motor shaft with a screwdriver or remove it with a pair of locking pliers. When installing a new impeller, replace the underlying seals before pushing the impeller onto the shaft. If the impeller will not slide on easily, sand any rust off the shaft to make it smoother.

◆ To reassemble the pump, first replace the pump plate and screw on the pump guard. Attach the food-disposer blade and spacer plates, then the upper impeller. Secure with the bolt, and put the locking tab, if there is one, on top of the bolt. Screw on the pump cover, and replace the spray arm.

Dealing with a Stuck Garbage Disposer

When a disposer stops working, it is usually because the grinding mechanism has jammed. Bits of food, glass, metal, plastic, or rubber can get caught between the spinning flywheel and the stationary grind ring, causing the motor to overheat and cut off. This may also happen if you pack the unit too tightly. Before starting to work on the disposer, check for a blown fuse or for a tripped circuit breaker at the main electrical panel.

If the suggestions below don't fix the problem, the disposer should be replaced because repairs will probably cost as much as a new unit. Check your warranty; most run from 3 to 7 years and cover repairs or replacement.

⚠️ **CAUTION** *Always turn off the power at the main panel or unplug the disposer—if it is an outlet unit—before reaching into it.*

Resetting the motor.
If the motor doesn't hum at all, reach into the disposer and feel around for any objects that may be jamming it. Let the motor cool down for 15 minutes, then switch on the power at the main panel and gently push the reset button on the bottom of the unit until you hear it click *(below)*.

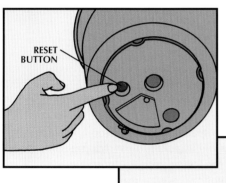

RESET BUTTON

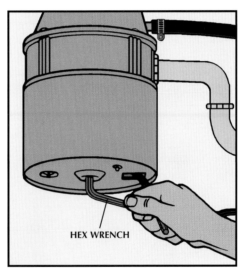

HEX WRENCH

Freeing the grind ring.
If the motor hums but the disposer doesn't grind, take a $\frac{1}{4}$-inch hex wrench (or the wrench that came with the disposer) and insert one end into the hole on the bottom of the disposer *(left)*. Turn the wrench back and forth to rotate the motor shaft until it moves freely.

IMPELLER BLADE

FLYWHEEL

Unjamming the works with a broom handle.
If you are unable to clear the jam by using a hex wrench, stick a broom handle into the disposer and wedge it against one of the impeller blades on the flywheel *(left)*. Apply force until the wheel begins to turn freely, then work the wheel back and forth until it moves easily in both directions.

When a microwave oven begins to cook erratically, the fault may lie with one of several easy-to-service components within the machine. If it stops working altogether, first check that the cord has not become unplugged and that the circuit breaker has not tripped.

Defective Door Switches: The parts that fail most often are door-interlock switches. A faulty one can keep the oven from turning on and

cause it to turn off unexpectedly.

As many as five switches may be present, one behind each door latch and others positioned around the door perimeter. Test each one in turn as shown on page 38.

Other Culprits: If a door switch is not to blame—and the oven light stays off when the door is open—check for a blown fuse inside the appliance. Next test the diode; diagnosis of electronic control panels is

best left to a professional. However, if your oven has a dial timer and a mechanical start button, you can test two additional switches where problems originate *(page 39)*.

⚠ CAUTION *An interior component called a capacitor stores an electric charge that can deliver a strong shock. Discharge the capacitor before any test or repair. The procedure* (right) *can produce a large spark.*

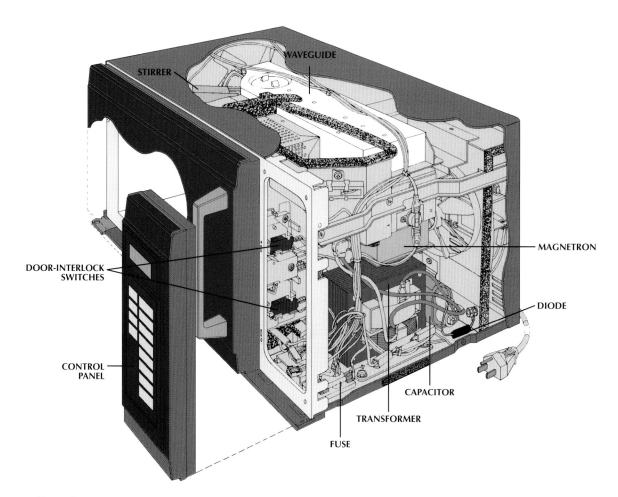

Anatomy of a microwave oven.
The heart of a microwave oven is a magnetron, which produces microwaves that travel through a waveguide into the oven. A stirrer bounces the waves around the cooking chamber, where they heat the food. Supplying

the magnetron with power are a transformer, a capacitor, and a diode. These components boost 120-volt alternating-current household service to direct current (the kind provided by a battery) at 4,000 volts. A control panel on the front of the oven provides for the se-

lection of cooking times and cycles. Safety devices include door-interlock switches, which prevent the unit from starting with the door ajar, thus prohibiting harmful microwaves from escaping, and a fuse that protects the unit from power surges.

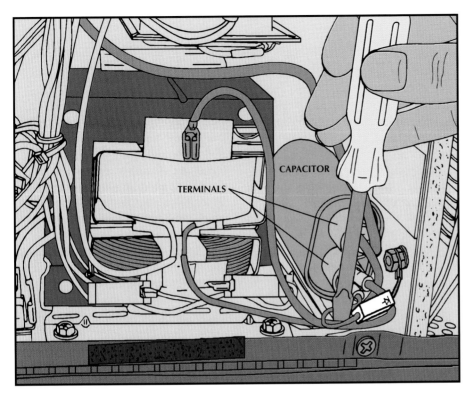

Removing the cover and discharging the capacitor.

◆ Unplug the oven, then remove the screws that secure the cover. Set the cover aside.

◆ Hold an insulated screwdriver by the handle, and lay the shaft across the metal sleeves on the capacitor's two terminals *(left)*.

◆ If this produces a spark, touch the screwdriver to the terminals again to completely discharge the capacitor. If this procedure produces no spark, the capacitor has already discharged.

UNIVERSAL MICROWAVE REPAIRS

Checking the fuse.

◆ With the oven unplugged and the cover off, locate the fuse, usually a cartridge fuse.

◆ Pull the fuse from its holder with your fingers or with a fuse puller if your fingers can't dislodge it *(right)*.

◆ To test the fuse for resistance *(page 31)*, touch a probe of a multitester to each end of the fuse.

◆ If the tester reads infinite ohms, the fuse is blown; replace it with a fuse of equal amperage.

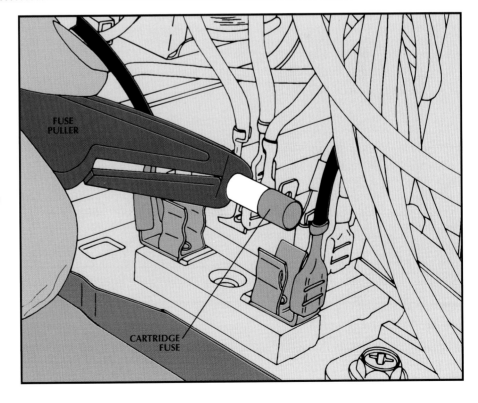

Replacing a diode.

◆ Locate the diode, which is connected to the capacitor and to the frame of the cabinet.

◆ Disconnect the diode from the capacitor and the cabinet *(right)* and examine it. Replace a diode that is cracked or burned.

◆ If there is no visible damage, set a multitester to RX1K and calibrate it *(page 31).* Touch a probe to the end of each wire *(inset),* and note the multitester reading. Then reverse the probes and check the reading again. One reading should indicate a resistance of several thousand ohms, the other infinite ohms. If the diode fails the test, replace it.

◆ Connect the new diode as the old one was connected. If the wires end in identical fittings, attach the one nearer the diode symbol to the cabinet.

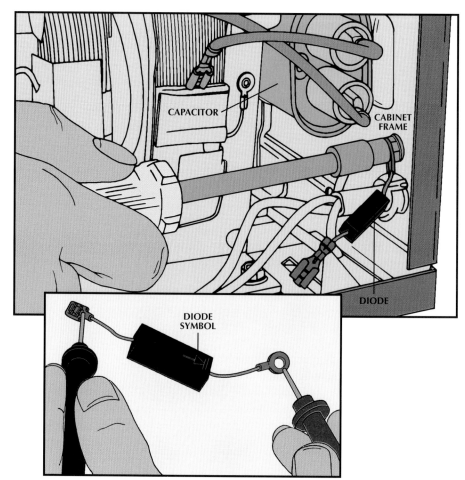

Testing a door switch.

◆ With a two-terminal switch, remove the wire from one of the terminals and check the switch for resistance *(left),* first with the door open (infinite ohms), then with it closed (0 ohms). Replace the switch if it fails either test.

◆ If a door switch has three terminals *(inset),* detach all three wires, then touch one probe to the COMMON terminal and one to the OPEN or NO terminal. A working switch will register 0 ohms with the door closed, infinite ohms with it open.

◆ Next, check for resistance between the COMMON terminal and the CLOSED or NO terminal with the door both open (0 ohms) and closed (infinite ohms). If the switch fails either test, replace it.

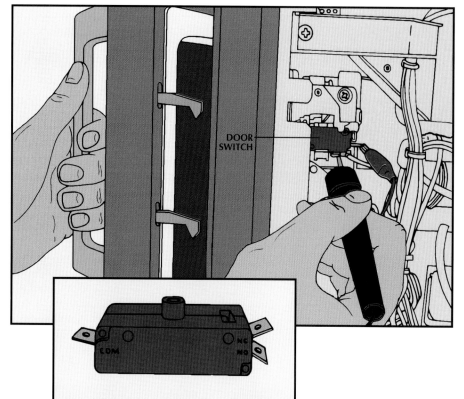

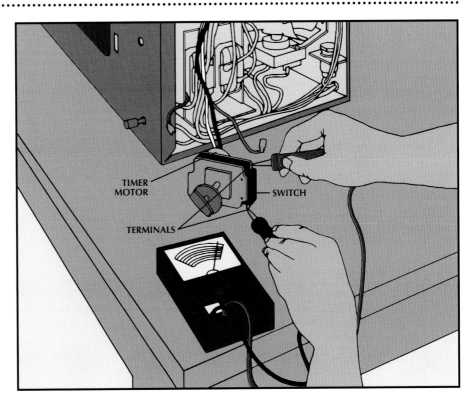

Identifying a faulty timer switch.

◆ Unscrew the timer assembly from the inside front panel and detach the wires from the two switch terminals, located on the back of the timer next to its motor.

◆ Set a multitester to RX1, set the timer for at least 1 minute, then touch the tester probes to the switch terminals *(right)*. Replace the switch if the meter registers more than 0 ohms.

On some ovens the timer switch is integrated with the timer and cannot be bought separately. Replace the entire timer assembly.

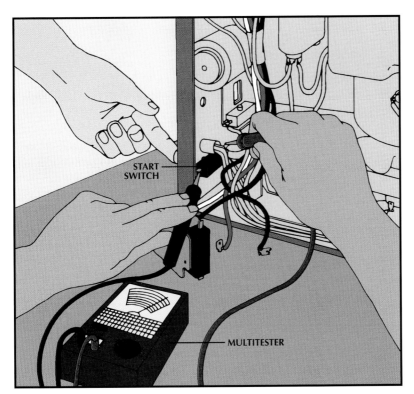

Testing the start switch.

◆ Disconnect the wires from the terminals on the switch behind the start button.

◆ Touch multitester probes to the switch terminals. There should be resistance of infinite ohms.

◆ Have a helper push the button; the meter should read 0 ohms while the button is depressed *(left)*.

◆ If the switch fails either test, replace it by unscrewing or unclipping it from the timer assembly. Install a new one, and connect the wires to its terminals.

You can often locate the source of trouble on an electric range just by looking. Visible burns, pits, or cracks make it easy to identify faulty parts. If no damage is noticeable, continue your diagnosis with a multitester as shown on the following pages.

Checking the Voltage: The heating elements on an electric range run on a 240-volt circuit. High-rise buildings, however, often have three-phase 208-volt current, in which case normal readings on the multitester will be in the range of 197 to 210 volts.

Holding the Right Temperature: One common complaint about electric ranges is that the oven temperature does not match the reading on the control. A frayed or torn door gasket could be the cause, and the thermostat is also a likely culprit. To test the thermostat, place an oven thermometer in the center of the oven and set the thermostat to 350°. Let the oven heat up, then check the thermometer every 10 to 15 minutes for the next half-hour. If the temperature is within 50° of 350°, calibrate the thermostat *(page 44)*; for digital ranges, adjust the temperature at the control panel. If the temperature is more than 50° off, replace the thermostat *(page 45)*.

⚠️ **CAUTION** *Before starting repairs, unplug the range or cut the power at the main service panel, then test the terminal block for incoming voltage (page 41).*

Anatomy of an electric range.

When you turn on a surface unit or the oven, current flows through a calibrated control to a heating element. The element provides resistance to the current, and the energy created radiates outward as heat.

In the oven, a rodlike capillary tube attached to the wall senses the temperature and relays the information to the thermostat, which cycles the current on or off to keep the temperature even. Digital ranges have an electronic temperature sensor.

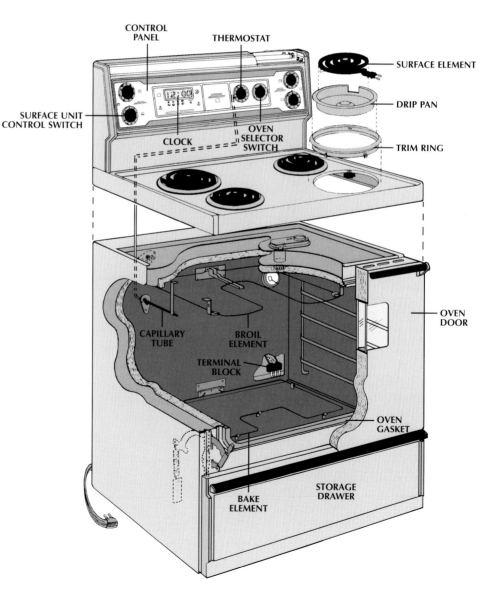

CONTROL PANEL — THERMOSTAT — SURFACE ELEMENT — DRIP PAN — TRIM RING — SURFACE UNIT CONTROL SWITCH — CLOCK — OVEN SELECTOR SWITCH — OVEN DOOR — CAPILLARY TUBE — BROIL ELEMENT — TERMINAL BLOCK — OVEN GASKET — BAKE ELEMENT — STORAGE DRAWER

Troubleshooting Guide

PROBLEM	REMEDY
Nothing works; the elements do not heat, or heat only partially.	Check fuses and circuit breakers at the main service panel. Test terminal block and replace if necessary *(page 41)*.
Surface element doesn't heat.	Test element for resistance and for short; replace if necessary *(page 42)*. Check connection at receptacle, and visually inspect the receptacle *(page 42)*. Test the voltage at the receptacle and, if necessary, at the control switch *(page 43)*. Replace the receptacle if it is faulty.
Oven doesn't heat.	Check the oven element and power to the element *(page 44)*. Test thermostat for resistance; replace if necessary *(page 45)*.
Oven temperature is not the same as temperature setting on control.	Test oven temperature and calibrate thermostat *(page 44)*. On digital ranges, calibrate at control pad, then test the temperature sensor *(page 44)*. Inspect the door gasket and replace if it is frayed or torn. Adjust oven door by loosening screws that secure inner door panel to outer door. Twist door to fit snugly, and tighten screws.
Self-cleaning oven doesn't clean.	Test the bake and broil elements *(page 44)*. Test thermostat for resistance; replace if necessary *(page 45)*.
Oven door doesn't close properly.	Adjust oven door *(see above)*. Adjust or replace door springs.

RESTORING THE INCOMING POWER

Testing the terminal block.
◆ With the power off, pull the range out and remove the back panel.
◆ Set a multitester *(page 31)* for 250 volts and clip the leads to the block's line terminals—marked L_1 and L_2 *(right)*. Restore power. If the meter doesn't show 230 to 240 volts, check for a blown fuse or tripped circuit breaker at the main service panel.
◆ Shut off the power and move a probe to the ground-wire terminal on the lower center screw. Restore power; the meter should now read 120 volts. If it does not, there may be something wrong with the house wiring; call an electrician.
◆ If the block appears burned, replace it by removing the wires and unscrewing it from the range.

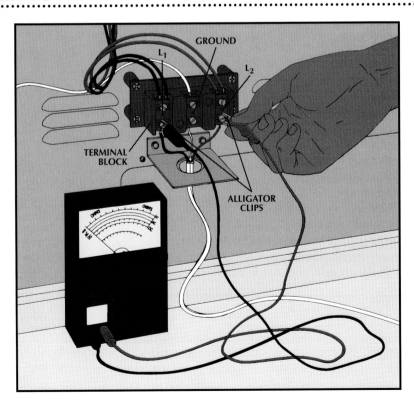

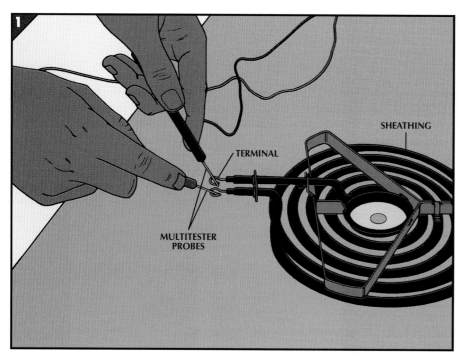

1. Testing the element.

◆ Detach the faulty element from its receptacle and inspect the coil terminals. If they are burned or pitted, replace the element and the receptacle.

◆ To test the element for resistance *(page 31)*, set a multitester to RX1 and touch the probes to the terminals *(left)*. The meter should read below 60 ohms. If it doesn't, the element should be replaced.

◆ If the element shows the correct resistance, check for a short circuit by leaving one probe on a terminal and placing the other probe on the sheathing. A reading of 0 ohms indicates a short; replace the element.

2. Inspecting the receptacle.

◆ Unscrew the receptacle and pull it out. Check for visible damage to the terminal blades inside the slots and for loose or damaged wires leading into the receptacle. If you find any of these, replace the receptacle.

◆ Cut the wire leading into the old receptacle as close as possible to the back of the receptacle. Strip $\frac{1}{2}$ inch of bare lead with wire strippers and splice it to the short length of wire attached to the new receptacle. Twist a wire cap over the bare ends.

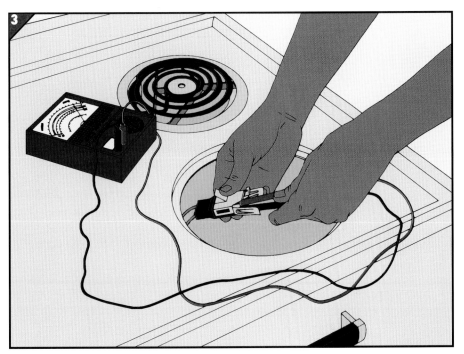

3. Checking the voltage at the receptacle.

◆ With the power off, insert a multitester probe into each receptacle slot so that the probe touches the terminal blade *(left)*.

◆ Set the multitester for 250 volts, restore power to the range, and turn the control knob to HIGH. If the meter does not read 230 to 240 volts, check the control switch *(Step 4)*. If the control switch is fine, replace the receptacle *(Step 2)*.

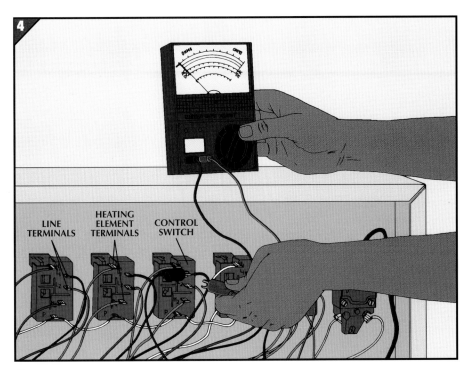

LINE TERMINALS

HEATING ELEMENT TERMINALS

CONTROL SWITCH

4. Testing the control switch.

◆ Locate the switch behind the rear top panel. Cut the power and put multitester clips on the switch's line terminals, marked L_1 and L_2 *(above)*. Set the multitester for 250 volts and restore power; you should get 230 to 240 volts. Turn off the power and move the clips to the heating element terminals, marked H_1 and H_2. Restore power and turn the knob to HIGH. The meter

should again read 230 to 240 volts.

◆ If you only get power at L_1 and L_2, or any terminals appear burned, replace the switch. No power at L_1 and L_2 indicates loose or burned terminal block connections; tighten the wires, or replace the block *(page 41)*. If H_1 and H_2 have power but the receptacle does not, splice new range wire— available at appliance-repair shops or electronics stores—between them.

ADJUSTING AN OVEN TEMPERATURE CONTROL

Calibrating the thermostat.
◆ Pull off the thermostat knob and loosen the setscrews on the back *(near right).* Turn the disk slightly to recalibrate the thermostat—here, moving the disk pointer one notch for each 25°. Retighten the setscrews.

◆ Some ranges have a calibration screw instead. Pull off the thermostat knob and locate the screw inside or beside the shaft *(far right).* Adjustments vary; consult your owner's manual for which way and how far to turn the screw.

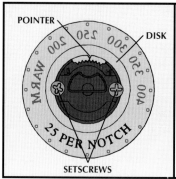

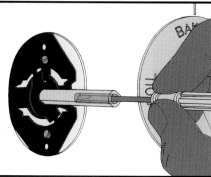

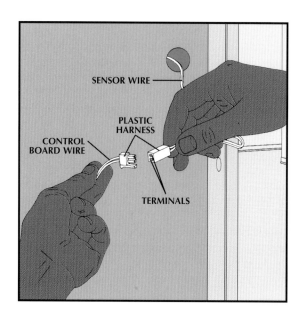

Testing digital oven controls.
◆ To test the temperature sensor—a rod inside the over on the rear wall—for resistance, pull out the range and remove the back panel. Unclip the plastic harness *(left),* and touch multitester probes to the terminals inside the harness. Check the owner's manual for the proper resistance reading.

◆ To replace a faulty sensor, unscrew the retaining plate, and pull out the sensor; then insert the new one and re-attach the plate. Connect the harness and replace the back panel.

◆ If you get the proper reading, the electronic control board is defective; call for service.

GETTING HEAT FROM A BALKY OVEN

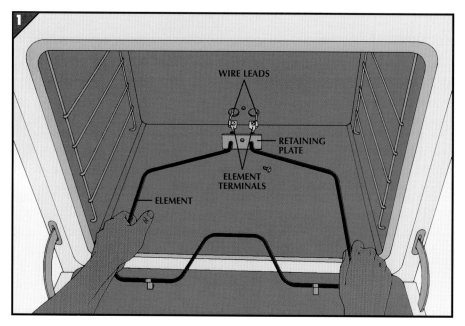

1. Examining the bake or broil element.
◆ Unscrew the element's retaining plate from the rear wall. Pull the element out and unplug the leads from their terminals or loosen the screws and disconnect the wires.

◆ Replace the element if it has burns and cracks. Cut off a burned or pitted terminal, strip about $\frac{1}{2}$ inch of its wire lead, and attach a new one.

◆ Touch multitester probes to the element terminals to check resistance. You should get 10 to 60 ohms; if you do not, replace the element.

◆ Leave one probe on a terminal and touch one to the element. A 0-ohms reading means the element is shorted; replace it.

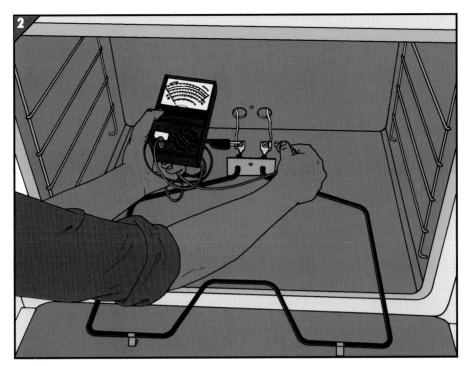

2. Testing for power to the element.

◆ Reconnect the leads and attach the multitester clips to the terminals or, if your range has them, to the screws in the element terminals *(above)*.

◆ Set the multitester for 250 volts, then restore power to the range and turn the oven to 300°. If the meter registers 230 to 240 volts after about a minute, power is reaching the element, so the element must be faulty. Turn off the power and replace the element.

◆ If the multitester does not show the proper voltage, turn off the power and check for loose wires at the oven selector switch and thermostat behind the back panel of the range.

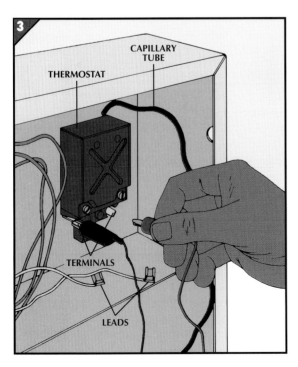

3. Checking the thermostat.

◆ Turn off the power, remove the leads from the back of the thermostat, and attach multitester clips to the terminals *(left)* to test for resistance. With the knob turned to 300° and the power off, the meter should read 0 ohms; if it does not, replace the thermostat.

◆ Examine the capillary tube; if it is damaged, replace the whole thermostat.

◆ To replace a thermostat, shut off the power, remove the leads, and unscrew the thermostat from the back panel. Unclip the capillary tube from the oven wall and pull it out from the back. Push a new tube into the oven, clip it on, and screw on the new thermostat. Reattach the leads.

A gas range is, in essence, a network of pipes that carry gas to burners on the cooktop and in the oven, where it is mixed with air and ignited to produce a controlled flame.

Lighting the Gas: Some ranges have a high-voltage ignition module on the back panel of the range that sends current to an electric igniter when the burner is turned on. Other types use pilots that pro-

duce small, constantly burning flames that ignite the gas. Most problems with either system are caused by accumulated dirt and grease, which can foul the electrodes of electric igniters or clog the small apertures of the pilots.

Routine Maintenance: Keeping the cooking surfaces clean is the best way to avoid problems, and modern ranges are designed with

this in mind. Burner grates and drip pans lift off, and the hinged cooktop can be propped open. Oven doors slide off, and both the oven bottom and the oven burner baffle are removable for easy cleaning and access to the oven burner.

⚠️ **CAUTION** *If the pilot has been out for some time or if you detect an odor of gas, ventilate the room before relighting.*

Anatomy of a gas range.

Natural gas enters the range through the supply pipe in the back. Inside, the pipe branches to carry gas to the oven burner and the manifold, which runs across the front of the range beneath the cooktop and distributes gas to the four surface burner units. An air shutter on each burner's pipe mixes air with the natural gas.

Turning the burner-control knob on the front of the range opens a valve that lets the air/gas mixture flow into the burner tube and the flash tube—where it is ignited—and then through the small holes in the burner head. The oven burner is governed by a thermostat, which senses the temperature inside the oven by means of a capillary tube.

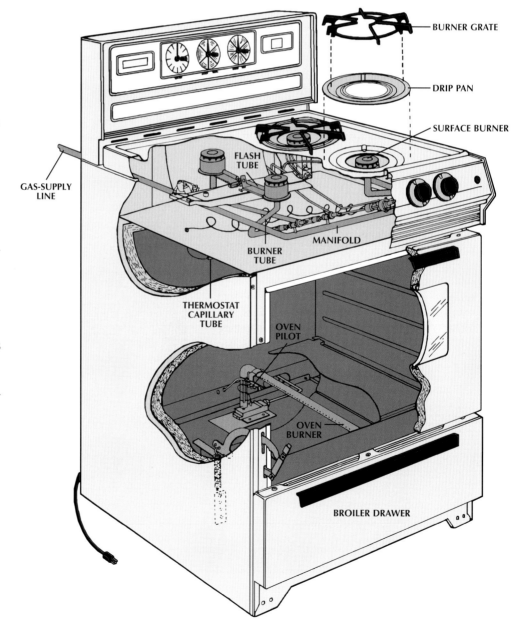

- BURNER GRATE
- DRIP PAN
- SURFACE BURNER
- FLASH TUBE
- GAS-SUPPLY LINE
- MANIFOLD
- BURNER TUBE
- THERMOSTAT CAPILLARY TUBE
- OVEN PILOT
- OVEN BURNER
- BROILER DRAWER

Troubleshooting Guide

PROBLEM	REMEDY
Gas odor.	Ventilate the room. Turn burner controls to OFF. Check burner and oven pilots. Relight them with a match if necessary. If the gas odor persists, turn off gas to the range and call the gas company.
Burner won't light.	Relight extinguished pilot flames *(page 48)* or clean igniter electrodes. Clear the burner portholes with a thin needle *(page 48)*. Close the air shutter slightly *(page 48)*. Reposition a surface burner to align its flash tube with the pilot flame or igniter *(page 48)*. For ovens, check the flame switch *(page 49)*.
Pilot flame won't stay lit.	Clear the pilot opening with a thin needle *(page 48)*. Adjust the pilot flame *(page 48)*.
Electric igniter won't spark.	Check incoming power to the range. Clean igniter electrodes with a cotton swab or cloth. If the igniter still doesn't spark, the igniter, the wiring, or the ignition module is faulty; call for service.

The ideal flame.

In the upper photograph at right, a properly adjusted burner shows a steady, quiet flame with sharply defined blue cones about $\frac{1}{2}$ to $\frac{3}{4}$ inch high. Insufficient air reaching the burner produces a weak red or yellow flame *(below)* that may leave soot deposits on pots and pans. In the lower photograph at right, the burner is getting too much air, resulting in an uneven, noisy flame.

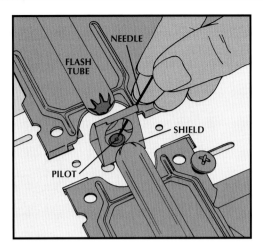

Cleaning the pilot opening.
◆ Insert a needle into the hole in the center of the pilot and move it up and down, taking care not to enlarge or deform the opening. If the metal shield over the pilot presents an obstacle, gently lift it out of the way.
◆ With all burner controls turned to the off position, relight the pilot frame with a match held at the opening.

Clearing the portholes.
◆ With the range top propped open, lift out the burner assembly. It is usually unanchored, held in place by its own weight.
◆ Push a needle through each porthole (some burners have a vertical slot instead of portholes), then wash the burner head in warm, soapy water.
◆ To reinstall the burner, slip the burner tube onto the gas manifold and align the flash tube with the pilot.

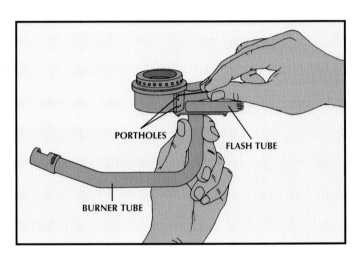

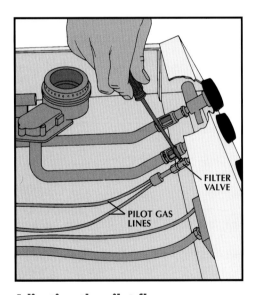

Adjusting the pilot flame.
◆ Follow the thin pilot gas lines to the filter valve at the front of the stove.
◆ Find the screw on the side of the valve, and turn it with a screwdriver until the pilot flame is a compact blue cone with little or no yellow at the tip.

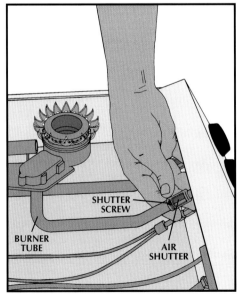

Regulating the burner flame.
◆ To adjust the airflow to a burner, first turn off all the burner controls. Locate the air shutter on the burner tube near the front of the stove.
◆ Loosen the shutter screw until the shutter either twists or slides freely, then turn the burner on high.
◆ Adjust the shutter by hand until the burner has the correct airflow (page 47) and retighten the shutter screw.

Exposing the pilot and burner.

Loosen any tabs or screws holding the oven floor in place, and lift it from the oven. Below the floor is the burner baffle *(inset),* often held in place by wing nuts. Remove them and the baffle, then pull the broiler drawer out of its opening and set it aside.

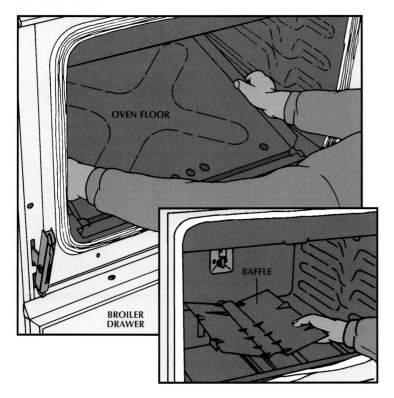

OVEN FLOOR

BROILER DRAWER

BAFFLE

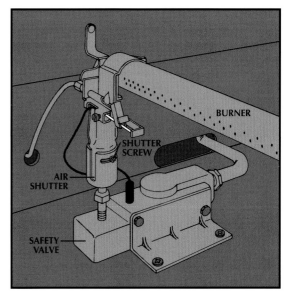

BURNER

SHUTTER SCREW

AIR SHUTTER

SAFETY VALVE

Adjusting pilot and burner flames.

◆ Relight the pilot if it has gone out. If not, increase its height. Pull the oven thermostat knob from its shaft to reveal an adjustment screw labeled "constant pilot," and turn it clockwise.

◆ Replace the knob and turn on the oven. If the burner still does not light, the thermostat or safety valve must be replaced. Call a repair service.

◆ To adjust the burner flame, turn off the oven and loosen the air-shutter screw. Change the shutter opening, then remove your hand from the oven and turn on the oven to observe the flame *(page 47).*

◆ Make additional adjustments as needed, each time turning off the burner before reaching into the oven.

◆ When the flame is satisfactory, turn off the oven, tighten the shutter screw, and replace the baffle and oven floor.

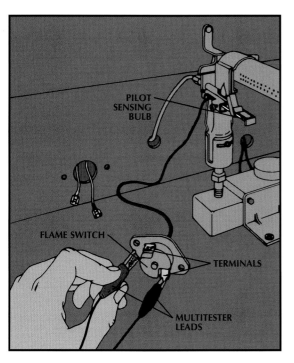

PILOT SENSING BULB

FLAME SWITCH

TERMINALS

MULTITESTER LEADS

Testing the oven flame switch.

◆ Turn off electrical power to the range, check that the pilot flame is burning, then unscrew the switch from the rear oven wall.

◆ Detach the wires from the two terminals on the back of the flame switch. Check for resistance between the flame switch terminals with a multitester set at RX1 *(page 31).* A reading of 0 ohms indicates a properly working switch; call a repair service, and expect to have the oven thermostat replaced.

◆ If the multitester shows high resistance, replace the flame switch. Remove it by gently working the pilot sensing bulb from its bracket. To install a new switch, attach the wires to its terminals, screw it to the oven wall, and slip the sensing bulb into the bracket.

Two Kinds of Range Hood Ventilators

Many ranges, electric and gas, are topped by a venting range hood. The hood will contain either a fan or "squirrel-cage" blower impellers that draw smoke and grease through an aluminum mesh filter and out an exhaust duct.

To keep grease from building up around the motor and on the fan blades or on the blower impellers, wash the filter regularly in hot, soapy water or in the dishwasher, and replace it annually.

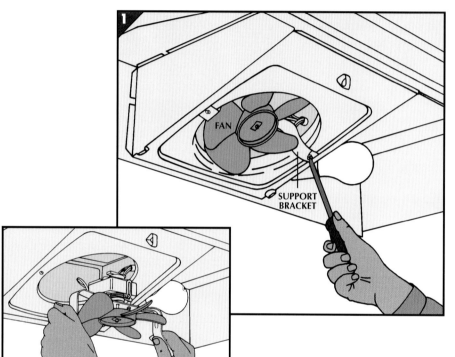

1. Removing the fan.
◆ First, turn off power to the range hood. Then remove the aluminum grease filter, which is secured by clips.
◆ To release the fan, remove the screws that hold the support bracket to the housing *(left)*.
◆ Holding the fan assembly by its support bracket, lower it from the housing *(inset)*.

2. Oiling and cleaning the fan.
◆ Hold the fan by its support bracket, and put a few drops of oil on the motor shaft at the rear of the fan *(right)*. Even permanently lubricated motors benefit from a few drops of machine oil.
◆ Wipe the fan motor and blades with a cloth moistened with a kitchen cleaner that contains ammonia.
◆ Before reinstalling the fan, clean the range hood surfaces and as much of the ductwork as you can reach.
◆ To reassemble the range hood, screw the support bracket to the fan housing, and reattach the grease filter.

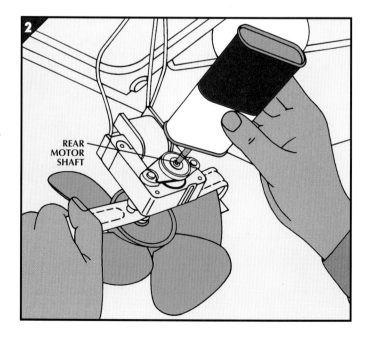

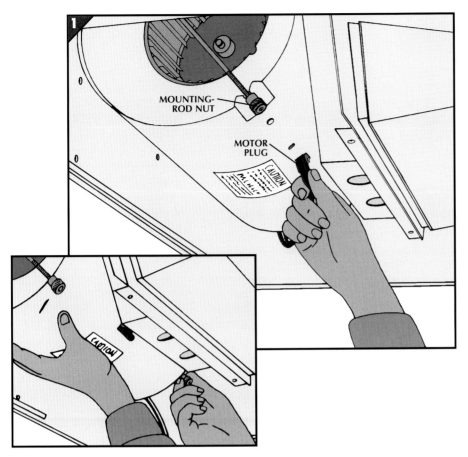

1. Removing the filters and blower assembly.

◆ With power to the range hood turned off, pull out the aluminum grease filters at both ends of the blower cover, and wash them in hot, soapy water.

◆ Remove the screws holding the cover in place, and take it off to expose the blower assembly.

◆ Unplug the motor as shown at left.

◆ Supporting the blower assembly with one hand, loosen the mounting-rod nuts on both sides *(inset)*.

◆ Move the rods out of the brackets, and lower the blower assembly.

2. Cleaning the impellers.

◆ With a hex wrench, loosen the setscrews holding the squirrel-cage blower impellers to the motor shaft.

◆ Grip the hub of each impeller in turn and slide it off the shaft. Use locking pliers, if necessary, to free balky impellers.

◆ Wash the squirrel cages in hot, soapy water, then replace them on the motor shaft and tighten the setscrews.

◆ Clean the interior of the range hood and as much of the ductwork as you can reach.

◆ To reinstall the blower assembly, lift it into position under the hood, keeping the discharge vent aligned with the duct opening.

◆ Slip the mounting rods into the brackets and tighten the nuts by hand.

◆ Plug in the motor, then screw the cover in place and reinsert the two grease filters.

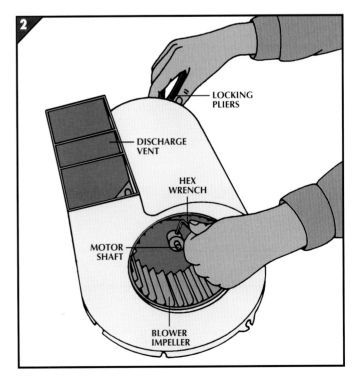

Refrigerators usually provide years of trouble-free service. When a problem does arise, you can often make the diagnosis and repairs without any special tools.

Common Problems: A refrigerator usually signals a malfunction by not cooling or by making too much noise. There are many possible causes for a cooling failure, some of them quite simple (*see Troubleshooting Guide, right*). Before taking things apart, make sure that the door closes all the way and that the interior light (which produces heat) switches off properly. You should see the light go off just as the door of the refrigerator closes.

A refrigerator that makes a screeching or rattling sound probably has a faulty evaporator or condenser fan motor. Replace a motor rather than trying to lubricate or repair it. Repairs to the compressor, evaporator, or condenser, which require special skills and tools, should be left to professionals.

Side-by-Sides and Icemakers: The parts of a side-by-side refrigerator may be located in places other than those shown on these pages, but the methods for testing and repairing them remain the same.

Many refrigerators include an icemaker or fittings for installing one. Problems that commonly occur with these devices are leaks and loose shutoff arms; for repair instructions, see page 60.

⚠️ **CAUTION** *Before starting any repair, always unplug the refrigerator or shut off the power at the house service panel. After the repair, wait 15 minutes before plugging in the refrigerator. This delay allows pressures in the cooling system to equalize, lessening the start-up strain on the compressor.*

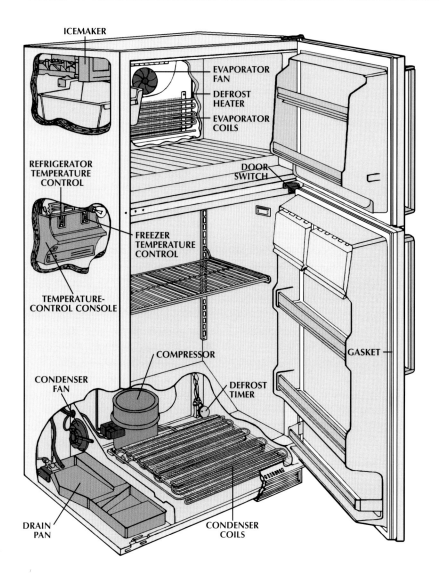

ICEMAKER — EVAPORATOR FAN — DEFROST HEATER — EVAPORATOR COILS — REFRIGERATOR TEMPERATURE CONTROL — DOOR SWITCH — FREEZER TEMPERATURE CONTROL — TEMPERATURE-CONTROL CONSOLE — COMPRESSOR — GASKET — DEFROST TIMER — CONDENSER FAN — DRAIN PAN — CONDENSER COILS

Anatomy of a refrigerator-freezer.

The cooling process begins when liquid refrigerant passes through the evaporator coils in the freezer, where it absorbs heat and becomes a gas. The refrigerant then flows to the compressor, which pumps it into the condenser coils. Cooled by air from the condenser fan, it releases its heat, returns to a liquid state, and begins the cycle again.

An evaporator fan circulates cold air within the freezer and, through vents, to the refrigerator area. A temperature control in the freezer regulates the airflow. Another in the refrigerator sets a thermostat that switches the compressor on and off to maintain the proper temperature in both compartments. Gaskets on the doors seal cold air inside. A door switch controls the light in the refrigerator compartment that comes on when the door is opened.

To prevent ice buildup, a defrost heater activated by a timer melts frost from the evaporator coils. A defrost-limit switch turns off the heater before the freezer gets too warm. Meltwater flows down a tube in the back wall and into a drain pan underneath.

Troubleshooting Guide

PROBLEM	REMEDY
Refrigerator not cold enough.	Test thermostat *(page 57)*. Clean condenser coils *(page 54)*. Replace the gasket *(page 55)* if door seal is not tight. Remove and test the door switch *(page 56)*. Replace evaporator fan *(page 57)*. Test defroster components; replace faulty ones *(page 59)*.
Refrigerator too cold.	Test thermostat *(page 57)*
Refrigerator doesn't run, but light works.	Test thermostat *(page 57)*. Clean condenser coils *(page 54)*. Check condenser fan and motor *(page 58)*. Test defrost timer *(page 59)*.
Refrigerator starts and stops frequently.	Clean condenser coils *(page 54)*. Check condenser fan and motor *(page 58)*.
Refrigerator runs constantly. **See "Freezer doesn't defrost automatically"** **(below).**	Replace the gasket *(page 55)* if door seal is not tight. Clean condenser coils *(page 54)*. Remove and test the door switch *(page 56)*. Check condenser fan and motor *(page 58)*.
Moisture around refrigerator door or frame.	Reset energy-saver switch. Replace the gasket *(page 55)* if door seal is not tight.
Ice in drain pan or water in bottom of refrigerator.	Clean drain hole *(page 54)*.
Water on floor around refrigerator.	Reposition drain pan. Clean drain hole *(page 54)*.
Interior light doesn't work.	Replace bulb, or test the door switch *(page 56)*.
Refrigerator noisy.	Reposition drain pan. Check condenser fan and motor *(page 58)*. Replace evaporator fan *(page 57)*.
Freezer doesn't defrost automatically.	Test defroster components; replace faulty ones *(page 59)*.
Icemaker doesn't make ice.	Open cold-water-supply valve fully or check water inlet valve *(page 60)*. Set freezer to colder temperature. Test icemaker's thermostat *(page 61)*. Test water inlet valve solenoid *(page 60)*.
Icemaker doesn't stop making ice.	Reseat a loose shutoff arm; test on/off switch *(page 61)*.
Water on the floor behind the refrigerator.	Tighten water inlet valve connections behind refrigerator.
Water overflows from icemaker.	Test water inlet valve and switch *(page 60)*; replace if necessary.
Icemaker doesn't eject ice cubes.	Test holding switch *(page 61)* and icemaker's thermostat *(page 61)*.

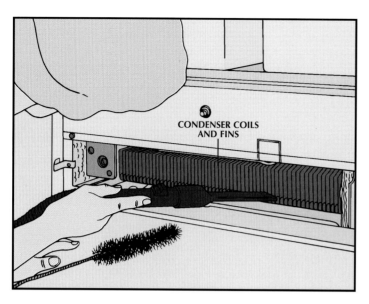

CONDENSER COILS
AND FINS

Dusting cooling-system components.

Condenser coils and metal cooling fins, which are best cleaned twice a year, are located either at the bottom front *(left)* or on the back of the appliance. To dust bottom-mounted coils, remove the floor-level grille. Use a long-handled brush to dust the coils and fins, taking care not to bend them. Vacuum up debris.

To expose the coils and fins on the back of a refrigerator, roll or walk the appliance away from the wall. Brush dust from the coils and fins, or use a vacuum cleaner with an upholstery-brush attachment.

BASIC REPAIRS FOR DOORS AND DRAINS

HINGE

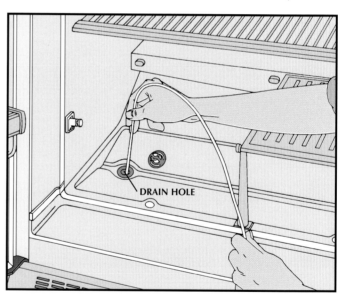

DRAIN HOLE

Adjusting a sagging freezer door.

◆ Using a nut driver or a socket wrench, loosen the two hex-headed bolts in the hinge at the top of the freezer door *(above)*.

◆ Reposition the door squarely over the opening of the freezer compartment by pulling upward on the door handle. Hold the door firmly in place and tighten the hinge bolts.

◆ Check the new position by opening and closing the door several times. It should clear the refrigerator door and align with the top of the unit.

Unclogging the drain hole.

◆ Remove the storage bins at the bottom of the refrigerator compartment to expose the drain hole, if there is one. Pry out the stopper plug with a screwdriver.

◆ Clear the drain by inserting a length of flexible $\frac{1}{4}$-inch plastic tubing or a pipe cleaner into the hole and pushing it through the drain canal into the drain pan *(above)*.

◆ Flush the drain with a solution of soapy water and ammonia, forcing it through the canal with a baster.

◆ Empty and wash the drain pan.

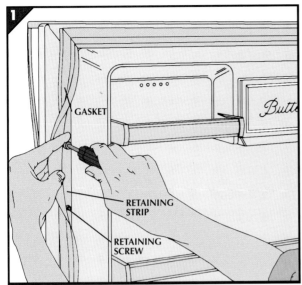

1. Loosening the retaining screws.

◆ Starting at the top outer corner of the door, roll back the rubber gasket with one hand, exposing the metal retaining strip beneath *(left)*.

◆ Use a nut driver to loosen the retaining screws two turns. Working across the top of the door and one-third of the way down each side of it, loosen each of the screws an equal amount.

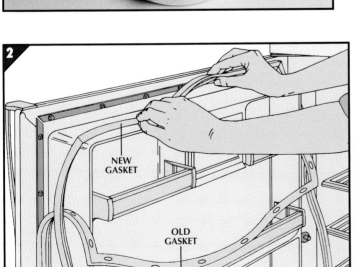

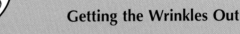

Getting the Wrinkles Out

New gaskets come folded in boxes and are usually kinked and wrinkled. Before installing one, you must straighten it. There are two effective ways to do so: Spread the gasket out in the sun on the hood of a car on a warm day, or soak it a little at a time in a skillet or pan of boiling water *(left)*. Allow a few hours for the first approach. Boiling water should unkink the gasket immediately.

2. Installing a new gasket.

◆ Pull the old gasket straight up to free it from behind the retaining strip at the top of the door.

◆ Let the old gasket hang out of the way, and slide the new gasket behind the retaining strip *(left)*, beginning along the top of the door and working down the sides. Partially tighten the screws.

◆ Working down each side, loosen the screws and strip off the old gasket; then insert the new gasket and partially tighten the screws.

◆ At the bottom of the door, slip out the old gasket at one corner, and replace it with the new gasket before loosening the retaining screws at the other corner. Then complete the last few inches of the installation.

3. Squaring the door.

◆ Close the door and look for gaps between the gasket and the body of the refrigerator. Usually found on the handle side of the door, a gap indicates a slight twist in the door, introduced during gasket installation.

◆ If the door is twisted, open it and have a partner push on the top or bottom of the doorframe to counter the twist. If you don't have any help, support the door with your foot *(left)* while pushing on the frame. Tighten the screws once the door looks straight.

◆ If a gap still shows when you close the door, open it again, loosen the screws a half-turn, and repeat the squaring process.

A NEW DOOR SWITCH

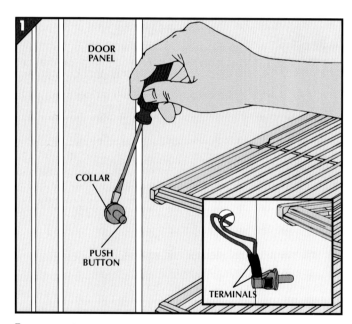

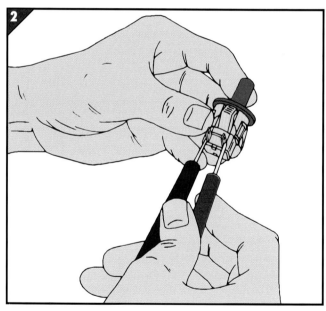

1. Removing the push-button switch.

◆ Unplug the refrigerator, cover a screwdriver tip with masking tape, then gently pry the collar encircling the push button from the door panel.

◆ Tilt the push button so you can get the right-angle terminals through the hole *(inset)*, then pull the switch out of the door panel along with its wires.

2. Checking switch operation.

◆ Pull the wires off the terminals and, using a multi-tester, test the switch for resistance *(page 31)*. The switch should show 0 ohms when the push button is up *(above)* and infinite ohms when it is depressed.

◆ Replace a faulty switch by attaching the wires to the new switch and inserting it into the hole in the door panel.

REGAINING CONTROL OF THE TEMPERATURE

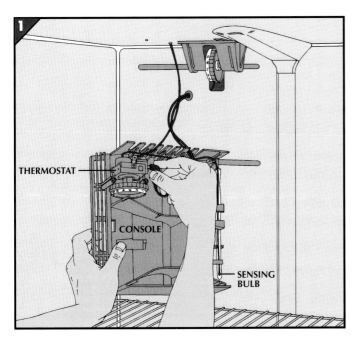

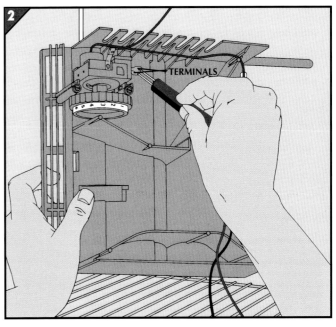

1. Getting at the thermostat.

◆ Unplug the refrigerator and unscrew the temperature-control console. For a control recessed into the top of the compartment, unscrew the breaker strips securing the console and remove it.

◆ Disconnect the wires that are attached to the thermostat terminals (above).

◆ Rest the console on a shelf, taking care not to bend the tube of the sensing bulb.

2. Putting the thermostat through its paces.

◆ Test the thermostat for resistance (page 31) by turning the control dial to OFF and touching a multitester's probes to the two terminals (above); the meter should show infinite resistance.

◆ With the probes still touching the terminals, turn the dial to ON and gradually rotate it toward the coldest setting. The meter should show 0 ohms at some point. If it does not, replace the thermostat.

A MOTOR FOR THE EVAPORATOR FAN

1. Gaining access to the fan.

◆ Unplug the refrigerator and remove the icemaker and any shelves from the freezer.

◆ On some models, you must unscrew and remove a fan grille to get at the rear panel. If the grille is also secured by plastic tabs at the freezer floor, bend the grille gently inward to free it from one tab at a time.

◆ Unscrew the freezer's rear panel to reveal the evaporator coils and fan. Lift out the panel (left) with its insulation, if any. Cover the exposed evaporator fins with a towel before beginning work on the fan.

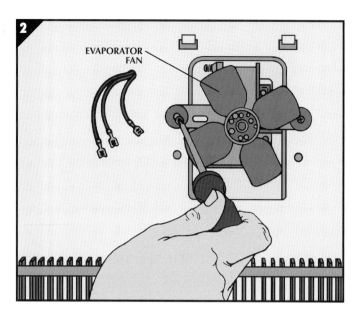

EVAPORATOR FAN

2. A new fan.

◆ If the fan's plastic grille is located behind the rear panel, unscrew it and remove it.

◆ Disconnect the wires from the fan motor, remove the screws that secure the fan to the cabinet *(left)*, and pull out the fan assembly.

◆ Before discarding the old fan, unscrew the blades from the motor shaft. Examine them for cracks and replace them if they are damaged; otherwise reuse them.

◆ Secure the fan blades on the shaft of the new motor, then insert the fan in the opening located at the back of the freezer, positioned so that the terminals face the loose wires.

◆ Screw the fan to the cabinet, reattach the wires, and replace the fan grille. Reinstall the rear panel, as well as any equipment removed earlier.

RENEWED AIRFLOW TO THE CONDENSER

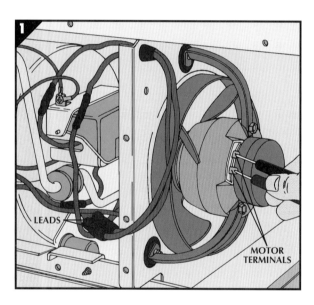

LEADS

MOTOR TERMINALS

1. Testing the motor.

◆ Unplug the refrigerator, move it away from the wall, and remove the rear access panel.

◆ Spin the condenser fan to see if it turns freely. If it does not, the motor bearings are worn; replace the motor *(Step 2)*.

◆ If the fan turns without binding, disconnect the wire leads from the motor and test it for resistance at the terminals *(left)*. With a multitester set at RX1, the meter should read between 200 and 500 ohms; a reading other than that means that the motor should be replaced.

2. Replacing a faulty motor.

◆ With the refrigerator unplugged, unscrew the condenser fan's mounting brackets from the divider panel *(right)* and lift out the fan assembly.

◆ Unfasten the mounting bracket from the motor and remove the hub nut that holds the fan blades in place.

◆ Wash the blades if they are dirty.

◆ Attach both the blades and the bracket to a new motor, then align the fan assembly in the refrigerator and screw the bracket to the divider panel.

◆ Reconnect the leads to the terminals.

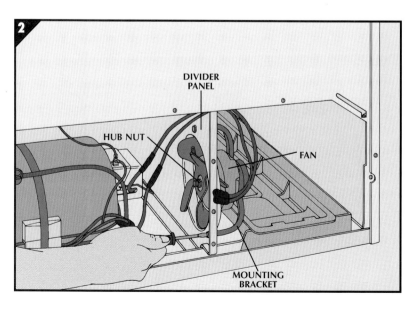

DIVIDER PANEL

HUB NUT

FAN

MOUNTING BRACKET

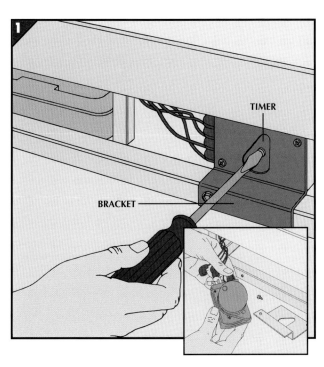

1. Trying the defrost timer.

◆ Locate the defrost timer, which may be behind the bottom front grille or rear access panel, or in the temperature-control console.
◆ With the compressor running, insert a screwdriver blade in the timer slot *(left)* and turn it clockwise until it clicks. If the compressor stops and the freezer begins defrosting, you have a faulty timer.
◆ To replace a timer, unplug the refrigerator and unscrew the timer's mounting bracket. Unscrew the timer from the bracket. If a ground wire is attached to the cabinet, disconnect it. Pull the wires from the timer terminals one by one *(inset)*, transferring each to the corresponding terminal on the new timer.
◆ Screw the new timer to the mounting bracket and reconnect the ground wire. Reinstall the timer on the refrigerator frame.

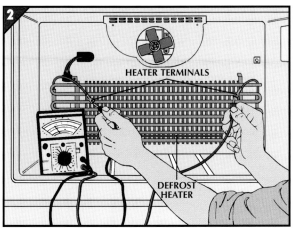

2. Checking the defrost heater.

◆ With the power off, remove the rear panel to reveal the defrost heater—a glass or steel tube that runs behind the evaporator coils and often along the sides. (If the heater is embedded in the coils, leave servicing to a trained technician.) Tighten loose wires to the heater and replace burned ones.

◆ Test resistance *(page 32)* by removing the wires and touching multitester probes to the terminals *(left)*. A reading between 5 and 100 ohms indicates a functional heater.
◆ To replace a defective heater, put on gloves for protection against sharp evaporator fins. Twist the tabs holding the heater in its brackets, remove it, and clip in the new one.

3. Replacing the defrost-limit switch.

◆ If the other defrost components are working, replace the defrost-limit switch; it is usually above or attached to the coils.
◆ Unscrew or unclip the switch and pull off the wire connectors if they are detachable; otherwise cut the wires to the switch and connect a new switch with wire caps *(right)*.
◆ Squeeze silicone caulking into the wire caps' base to protect the connections from moisture.
◆ Clip or screw the switch in place, then replace the insulation and the rear panel.

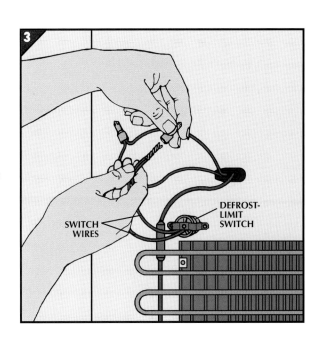

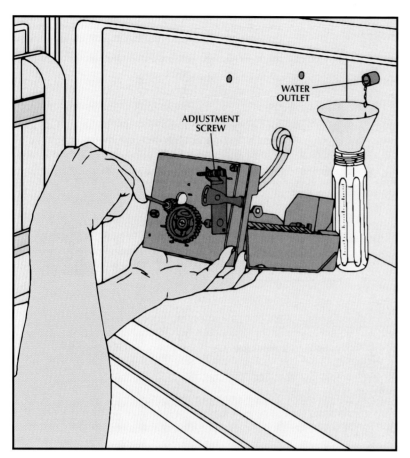

Adjusting the water fill.

◆ Remove the icemaker cover, and if your ice-maker has no label warning against rotating the drive gear on the front of the device, unscrew the unit from the freezer. Do not unplug it. If there is a warning label, try turning the water-adjustment screw as needed.

◆ Put a small funnel in the mouth of a baby bottle or other container marked in ounces and place it under the water outlet.

◆ Insert a screwdriver in the gear slot *(left)* and gently turn the gear counterclockwise about a half-turn, until you hear the motor start.

◆ Allow the unit to complete a cycle, then check the level of the water in the bottle; it should be about 5 ounces.

◆ Increase or reduce the water flow by turning the water-adjustment screw a small amount toward the + or - sign. Run another test cycle to check your adjustment.

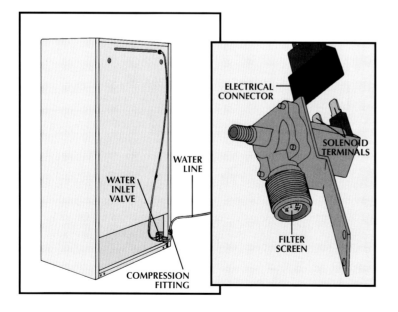

Correcting the water flow.

◆ Close the valve in the water line to the refrigerator and remove the rear access panel to expose the water inlet valve. Place a shallow pan under the line to catch drips, and unscrew the compression fitting at the valve. Discard the used brass ring from the fitting, and obtain a new one for the reinstallation.

◆ Unplug the refrigerator, pull the electrical connector from the water inlet valve *(inset)*, and test the resistance between the solenoid terminals *(page 32)*. If the reading is less than 60 ohms or more than 500 ohms, replace the valve.

◆ If the resistance falls within these limits, try cleaning the filter screen. Remove any screws on the valve and take it apart; scrape the screen, rinse it well, and reassemble the valve.

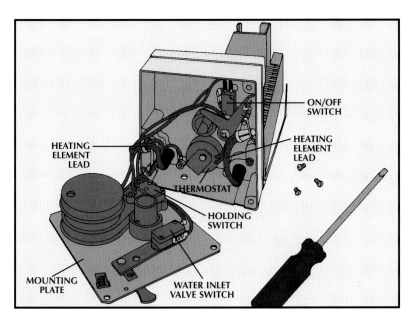

Testing the electrical components.

◆ Unplug the icemaker and remove its cover and mounting plate. To check the thermostat for resistance *(page 31)*, leave the icemaker in the freezer. Remove the heating element leads and touch a probe to each terminal; at temperatures below 15° F., you should get 0 ohms. Retest the icemaker at room temperature. It should read more than 0; if not, replace the thermostat.

◆ Unscrew a clamp to remove the thermostat. Put metallic putty on the back of the new thermostat and stick it down. Screw in the clamp.

◆ To test a switch, disconnect its leads and unscrew the switch. Test each terminal against its common contact (marked "C"); when the switch button is down, one terminal should show 0 ohms, the other more than 0. Readings should be opposite when the button is up.

REPLACING AN ICEMAKER SHUTOFF ARM

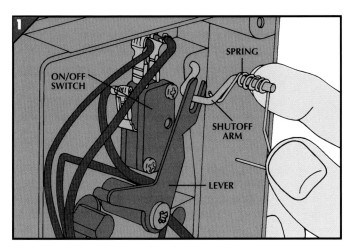

1. Reseating the spring and arm.

◆ Unplug the refrigerator, take out the icemaker, and remove the mounting plate.

◆ Check that the spring is engaged on the shutoff arm *(left)* and that the arm is in the slot in the end of the lever that links it to the on/off switch. If necessary, seat the spring as shown and put the arm back in the slot.

◆ If the shutoff mechanism still does not work, replace the shutoff arm *(below)*.

2. Replacing the shutoff arm.

◆ Carefully disengage the spring and separate the old arm from the lever. Push the arm forward, turning it as required to work it out through the hole in the housing *(right)*.

◆ Slide the new shutoff arm through the front of the housing. Engage the arm in the lever slot and replace the spring *(above)*.

◆ Replace the mounting plate and cover, and reinstall the icemaker.

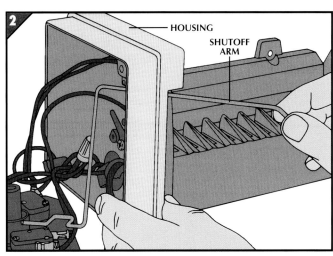

Custom Solutions for Storage Problems

3

No matter how large your kitchen, it never seems to have enough space for everything you need to store. Often, the solution is to organize the available space for greater efficiency. Options range from adding simple screw-on attachments to restructuring cabinet interiors. Or, from a pair of cabinets, you can build a handy movable island that increases both storage capacity and counter space.

Installing a frame for a stow-away recycling bin →

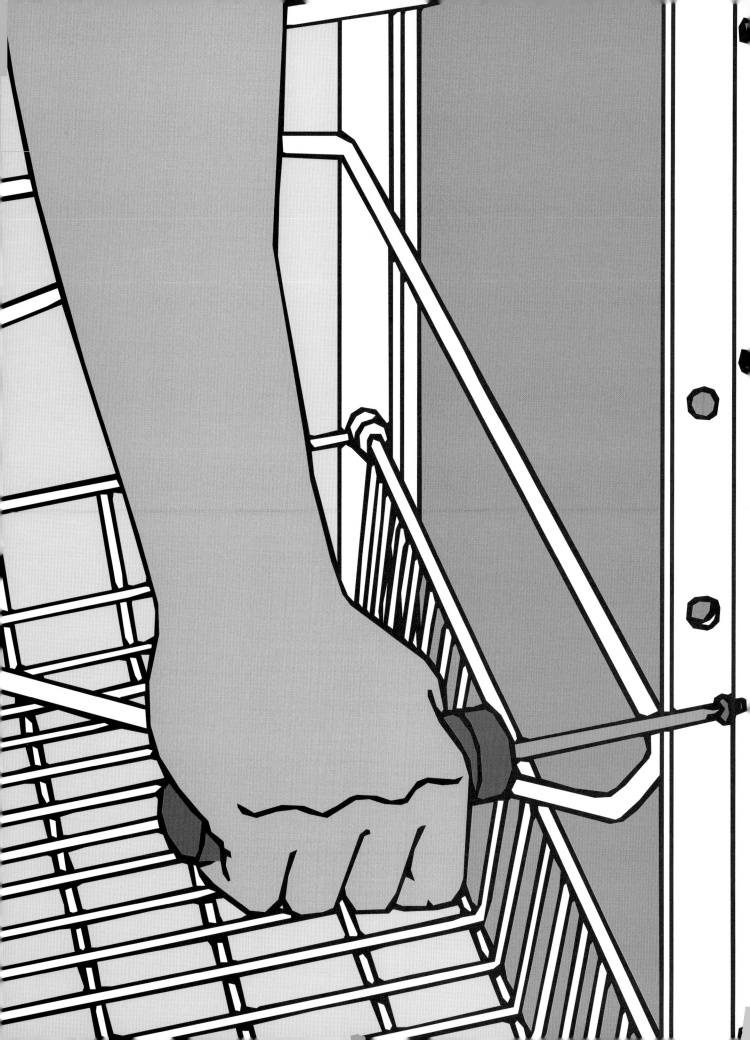

Whether your kitchen cabinets are old or new, you can make them more efficient and increase their capacity with attachments and ready-made space organizers.

External Attachments: If you know the manufacturer of your cabinets, the local dealer can supply a catalog showing current kits and accessories. The kits come with hardware, instructions, and templates to make installation easy.

The underside of a wall cabinet lends itself to space-saving accessories such as a swing-out cookbook holder or a hanging glass rack that keeps fine stemware protected yet easy to reach.

Internal Modifications: You can also transform drawers and storage spaces in base cabinets. A tilt-out tray at the sink front keeps items like sponges, brushes, and rubber gloves right where you need them. A conventional drawer box with a removable front can be replaced with a combination cutlery tray and pull-out cutting board.

The ample storage space in blind corner cabinets is often wasted because it is so hard to reach. Half-moon shelves that pivot as a lazy Susan does and then slide out on glides give easy access to the deepest recesses of the cabinet.

Most modern cabinets have removable shelves, which simplifies converting the interior space to another purpose. Permanent shelves need to be cut out *(page 68)*. With the cabinet space cleared, you can choose whichever of the units profiled on the following pages suit your particular needs.

Ensuring Correct Fit: Knowing the exact dimensions of drawers and cabinet openings will help you pick accessories that fit perfectly. To make sure racks, shelves, and glide-out trays will be absolutely level, always check screw hole locations with a carpenter's level before you drill pilot holes.

TOOLS

Screwdriver	Awl
Power drill	Saber saw
Tape measure	Combination square
Carpenter's level	

SIMPLE ATTACHMENTS TO A CABINET FRAME

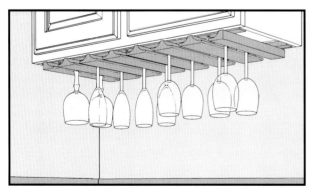

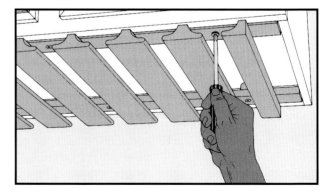

A hanging stemware rack.

◆ Hold the preassembled wooden rack in place under the cabinet and mark with a pencil through the predrilled screw holes in the mounting rail. Drill a pilot hole at each mark with a $\frac{3}{32}$-inch twist bit, making sure not to drill through the cabinet bottom.

◆ Insert a $1\frac{1}{2}$-inch No. 8 wood screw through each hole in the rail, and slip plastic spacers over each screw. Then drive the screws into the pilot holes *(above)*.

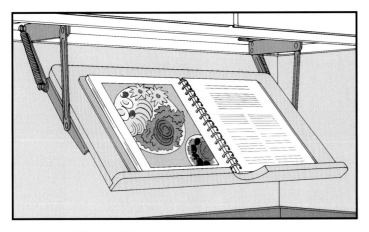

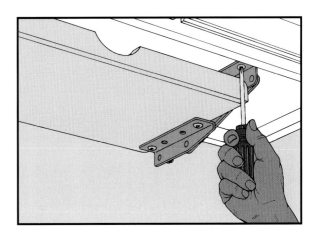

A retractable cookbook rack.

◆ Place the rack against the cabinet bottom with the spring-loaded hinges in a closed position and the front edge of the hinge plates $\frac{1}{2}$ inch behind the overhanging lip of the cabinet face. Outline the location of the hinge plates on the cabinet bottom with a pencil.

◆ Open the rack and reposition the hinge at the penciled outline. Mark the location of the hinge screws and drill $\frac{3}{32}$-inch pilot holes. Fasten the holder to the cabinet with the screws provided *(above, right)*.

A TILT-OUT TRAY IN THE SINK APRON

1. Attaching hinges to the cabinet frame.

◆ Reach up through the cabinet door below the sink to find the opening in the cabinet face directly in front of the sink. With a pencil, trace the opening on the back of the decorative face panel, then unscrew the panel from the cabinet.

◆ Position the left-hand hinge flush with the cabinet face and $\frac{3}{32}$ inch above the bottom of the opening. Mark the location for the hinge screws at the center of the oblong holes in the hinge plate and drill $\frac{3}{32}$-inch pilot holes at the marks.

◆ Fasten the hinge to the frame without tightening the screws all the way *(left)*. Repeat for the right-hand hinge.

65

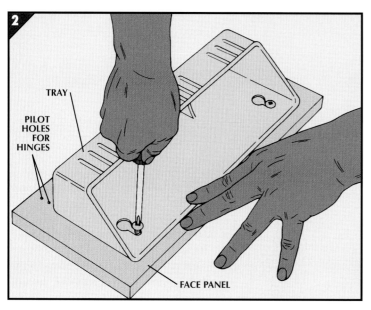

TRAY

PILOT HOLES FOR HINGES

FACE PANEL

2. Attaching the tray.

◆ With the hinges extended from the cabinet, align the hinge plates with the bottom of the penciled outline on the face panel. Mark the screw holes and drill pilot holes. If a handle is provided, center it on the front of the panel, then mark and drill those holes, too.

◆ Lay the front panel facedown on a worktable and center the tray $\frac{1}{8}$ inch below the penciled line that indicates the top of the cabinet opening. On the panel, make a mark at the narrow end of each of the tray's two keyhole-shaped slots.

◆ Drill pilot holes at the marks, then screw two $\frac{1}{2}$-inch panhead screws into the holes just deep enough to allow the tray to slide over them *(left)*. Set the tray aside for now.

3. Remounting the face panel.

◆ Attach the handle, if there is one, to the front of the panel.

◆ Screw the panel to the hinges without tightening the screws completely. If the countertop is in the way, use a stubby screwdriver as shown at right.

◆ Adjust the position of the hinges so the panel fits flush against the cabinet face and is parallel to the countertop, then tighten all the hinge screws. Finally, slip the tray onto the mounting screws on the inside of the panel.

A COMBINATION CUTLERY DRAWER AND CUTTING BOARD

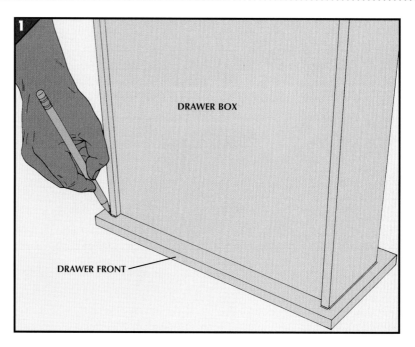

DRAWER BOX

DRAWER FRONT

1. Marking the drawer face.

◆ Remove the drawer by pulling it open and lifting it slightly to disengage the metal glides from their channels inside the cabinet.

◆ Trace the outline of the sides and bottom of the drawer box on the back of the drawer front *(right)*. Remove the screws that hold the box to the front, but do not remove the drawer handle if there is one.

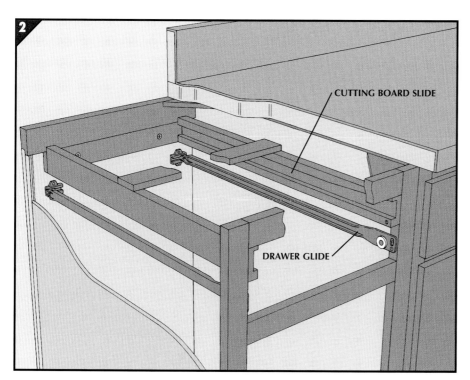

2. Installing the cutting board.

◆ Insert the cutting board slide into the drawer opening. Hold its upper surface against the opening's top and its front flush with the cabinet face.

◆ Mark the inside of the cabinet for pilot holes by pushing an awl through the predrilled screw holes on the sides and the back rail of the assembly. Remove the assembly and drill $\frac{3}{32}$-inch pilot holes.

◆ Screw the cutting board slide to the cabinet, then insert the cutting board.

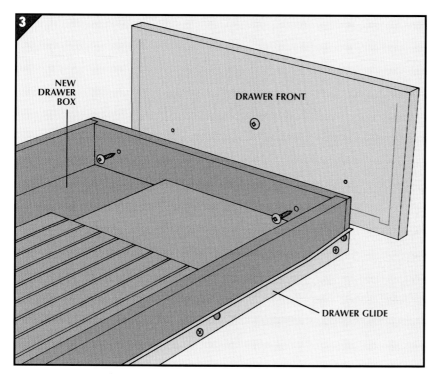

3. Attaching the cutlery tray.

◆ Set the front of the new drawer box with the cutlery tray against the back of the drawer front, aligning the bottom and sides of the box on the corresponding outline of the old drawer. Mark the drawer front through the predrilled screw holes at the front of the tray. Drill pilot holes and attach the box to the drawer front.

◆ The drawer box comes with metal glides that match those of the original drawer box. Tilt the box into the cabinet opening and slip the rollers at the rear of the glides into the channels in the cabinet.

REMOVING CABINET SHELVES

1. Cutting a fixed shelf.
◆ Using a saber saw fitted with a flush-cutting blade, cut a wedge from the shelf as shown at left. Tape a scrap of metal to the back of the cabinet to protect it from the saw blade.
◆ Tap the top and bottom of the shelf around the edges with a hammer several times to break the glue bond that holds the shelf in the dado joint.

2. Taking out the pieces.
◆ Gently work each half of the shelf up and down until it comes loose, then remove it. If necessary, cut each piece in half, parallel to the cabinet front, to facilitate removal.
◆ Fill the dado joint with wood putty and let dry. Then sand it with fine-grit sandpaper until it is flush with the cabinet wall.

VERTICAL DIVIDERS FOR HARD-TO-STORE ITEMS

Installing vertical dividers.
◆ Cut lengths of metal, plastic, or wood tracks as long as the cabinet is deep. Screw tracks to the cabinet bottom, perpendicular to the cabinet face, at about 4-inch intervals. Also cut $\frac{3}{8}$-inch plywood panels equal in width to the cabinet depth and $\frac{1}{4}$ inch shorter than the door opening.
◆ If the cabinet door opening has no frame (far left), slide a panel fitted with a top track into each bottom track. Holding the panel vertical, draw position lines for the upper track, then screw it to the cabinet top.
◆ For a framed door opening (left), hang the top tracks between the bottom edge of the frame and a crosswise board screwed to the rear wall.

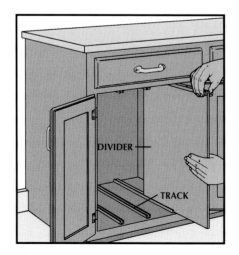

DIVIDER

TRACK

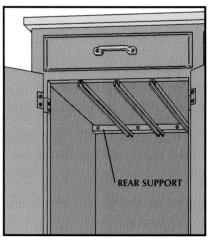

REAR SUPPORT

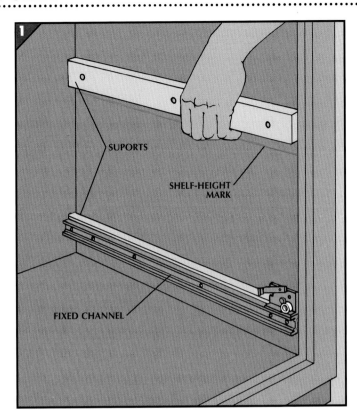

SUPORTS

SHELF-HEIGHT MARK

FIXED CHANNEL

1. Mounting the glides.
◆ Mark both cabinet side walls at the height you have chosen for shelves.
◆ Cut glide supports to match the depth of the cabinet. Use stock no thinner than the distance from the door opening to the adjacent cabinet wall. Plane the pieces to this thickness as needed.
◆ Bore screw holes 6 inches apart in each support. Align the bottom edge of a support with a shelf-height mark and drill pilot holes into the cabinet. Glue and screw the supports in place.
◆ Mount the fixed channels of the drawer glides flush with the bottom of the supports.

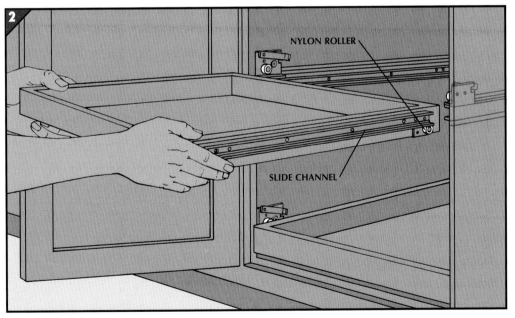

NYLON ROLLER

SLIDE CHANNEL

2. Installing the shelf.
◆ Align the slide channel of the drawer glide so that the nylon roller is flush with the bottom edge of the drawer (above). Drill pilot holes, then screw the slide channel to the drawer.
◆ Repeat for the other side of the drawer, then position the nylon rollers in the fixed channel and push the drawer into the cabinet.

A HIDDEN RECYCLING BIN

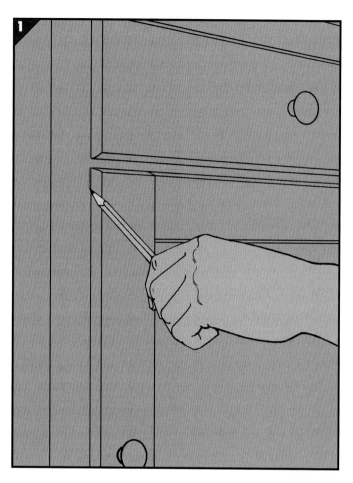

1. Marking the door position.

◆ First, lightly outline the door on the cabinet face with a pencil *(left)*, then unscrew the door from the hinges and set it aside.

◆ Remove the hinges from the cabinet frame and fill the holes with wood filler of a color similar to the cabinet finish. To avoid damaging the finish, do not sand the filler.

2. Centering the wire frame in the cabinet.

◆ Attach the wire frame of the recycling bin to the slide channels of the glides with a hex wrench *(right)*.

◆ Place the assembly in the cabinet, centering it in the opening and making certain that the front edge of the wire frame is parallel to the face of the cabinet.

◆ With a pencil, mark the screw holes for the glides on the cabinet floor.

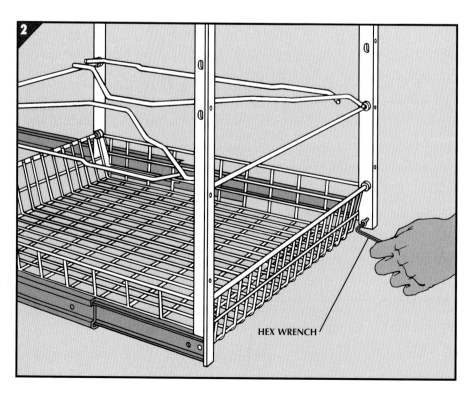

HEX WRENCH

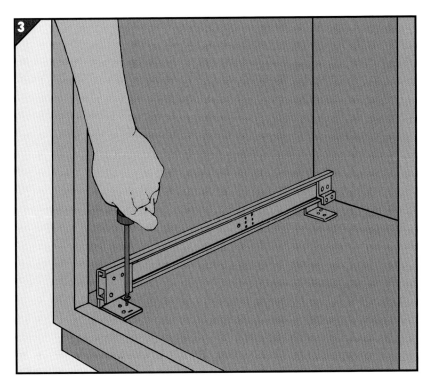

3. Attaching the glides.

◆ Remove the assembly and unscrew the wire frame from the glides.

◆ Drill pilot holes at the pencil marks and screw the glides to the cabinet floor *(left)*.

◆ Extend the inner channels of the glides from the cabinet, then set the wire frame between them.

◆ Starting at the back, reattach the frame to the glides.

4. Measuring the door position.

◆ Push the wire frame in until it is flush with the cabinet face. Hold a combination square against the cabinet and measure the distance between the penciled door outline and the center of a mounting hole in the recycling bin frame *(right)*. Then slide the square body to that point on the ruler.

◆ Using the square to guide a pencil down the inside of the door *(inset)*, draw a line along both vertical edges.

◆ On the cabinet, measure down from the top pencil outline to the first hole on the wire frame, and mark this distance on both of the lines drawn with the square on the door. Drill a pilot hole at each mark.

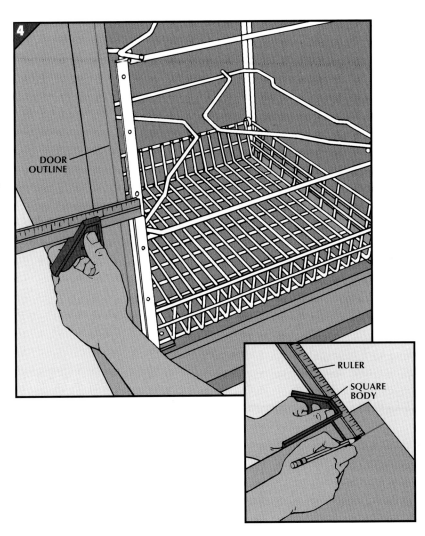

DOOR OUTLINE

RULER

SQUARE BODY

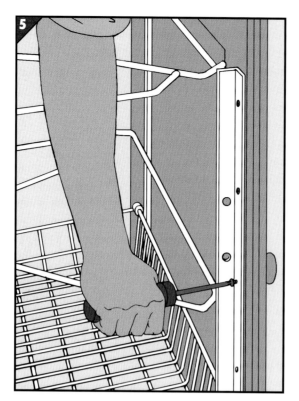

5. Attaching the door.

◆ Pull out the wire frame and have a helper hold the door against it. Drive a screw in each of the two pilot holes, then close the door and make sure it is square on the cabinet face.

◆ Open the door and mark it for the remaining screws, using holes in the wire frame as a guide. Drill pilot holes and drive the screws.

◆ Finally, place the plastic recycling bins in the wire frame.

HALF-MOON SHELVES FOR A CORNER

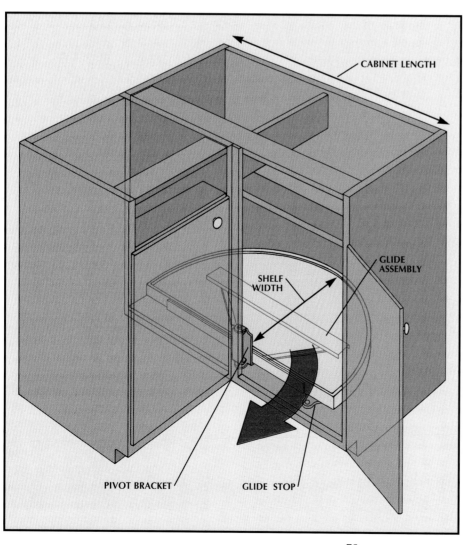

CABINET LENGTH

SHELF WIDTH

GLIDE ASSEMBLY

PIVOT BRACKET   GLIDE STOP

Getting the right size.

The glide assembly that supports a half-moon shelf pivots on a bracket attached to the cabinet frame. A glide stop prevents the shelf from being pushed into the cabinet too far and bumping the wall. A wheel on the glide stop blocks the hardware from marring the cabinet door when the shelf is pulled out.

Three cabinet dimensions govern shelf size: depth, length, and the width of the door opening. The standard cabinet depth is 24 inches, but door openings and lengths vary. A good rule of thumb is to buy a shelf 3 inches shorter than the length of the cabinet and about 1 inch narrower than the width of the door opening.

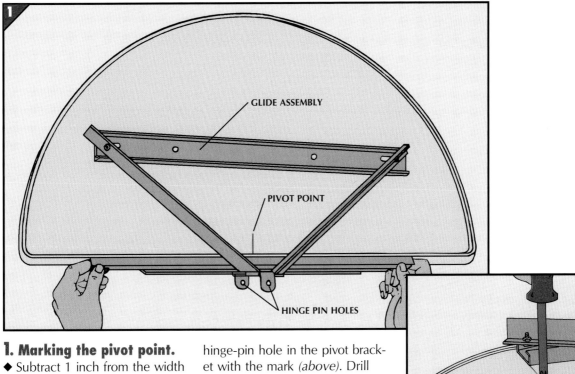

GLIDE ASSEMBLY

PIVOT POINT

HINGE PIN HOLES

GLIDE STOP

1. Marking the pivot point.

◆ Subtract 1 inch from the width of the cabinet door opening. Mark this distance on the bottom of the shelf, measuring from the end that will be farthest from the door opening after the unit is installed.

◆ Hold the glide assembly against the shelf and align the hinge-pin hole in the pivot bracket with the mark *(above)*. Drill pilot holes into the bottom and the edge of the shelf and attach the glide.

◆ Next, mount the glide stop on the bottom of the shelf at the end of the glide nearest the cabinet opening *(inset)*.

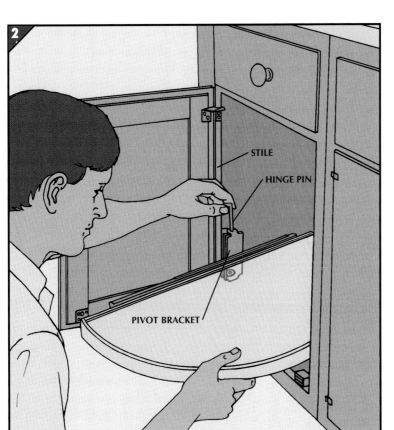

STILE

HINGE PIN

PIVOT BRACKET

2. Installing the shelf.

◆ Hold the pivot bracket against the inside of the stile at the shelf height you have chosen, but no closer than $\frac{3}{4}$ inch from the cabinet bottom. Mark the screw positions, drill pilot holes, and mount the bracket on the cabinet.

◆ Hold the shelf in position to align the hinge-pin holes on both halves of the bracket, and drop the pin into place *(left)*.

No kitchen is complete without a selection of herbs and spices. Yet the small jars that hold these seasonings are a nuisance, wasting space on regular cabinet shelves or getting lost behind larger containers. The two simple projects shown here allow you to organize spice jars in their own separate space.

The door-mounted spice rack can be hung on any solid raised-panel or European-style cabinet door at least $\frac{3}{4}$ inch thick. Only 3 inches deep, the rack uses very lit-tle of the interior when the door is closed. Consider hanging two or three racks on the door, fitting them between the cabinet shelves.

A kitchen drawer that is at least $3\frac{1}{2}$ inches deep can accommodate an easy-to-build rack that provides convenient storage for standard 2-inch-diameter, $4\frac{1}{4}$-inch-tall spice jars. Any leftover space in the back of the drawer can house seldom-used utensils. Either of these spice racks can be painted or stained be-fore it is installed.

TOOLS

Backsaw	Nail set
Miter box	Hammer
$\frac{1}{4}$-inch drill	Ruler

MATERIALS

1- by 3-inch clear pine	$\frac{3}{4}$-inch quarter-round molding
$\frac{1}{4}$- by $1\frac{3}{8}$-inch wood lath	Carpenter's glue
$\frac{1}{4}$-inch hardwood dowel	$\frac{5}{8}$-inch oval-head wood screws
$\frac{1}{4}$-inch plywood	$\frac{3}{4}$-inch brads

A DOOR-MOUNTED SPICE RACK

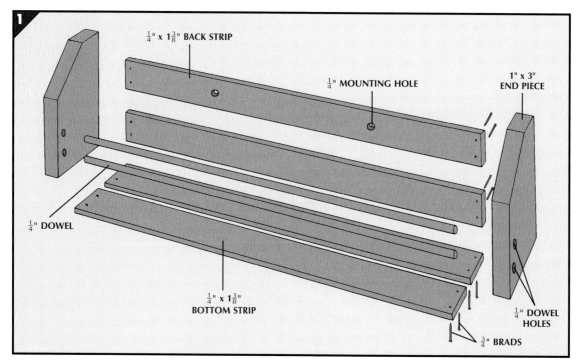

1

$\frac{1}{4}$" x $1\frac{3}{8}$" BACK STRIP

$\frac{1}{4}$" MOUNTING HOLE

1" x 3" END PIECE

$\frac{1}{4}$" DOWEL

$\frac{1}{4}$" x $1\frac{3}{8}$"
BOTTOM STRIP

$\frac{1}{4}$" DOWEL HOLES

$\frac{3}{4}$" BRADS

1. Measuring the pieces.

The diagram above shows the individual pieces that are required to assemble the spice rack. The two end pieces are made from one 10-inch length of pine, sawed in half. The back and bottom strips are thin pieces of wood called lath, and the front rails are made of hardwood dowel. The length of these pieces depends on the size of your cabinet.

◆ Measure the inside width of the cabinet door and subtract at least 2 inches to allow for clearance at each end of the rack. Note any hinges or hardware on the door or cabinet frame that might interfere, and adjust the width of the rack accordingly.

◆ Use this measurement to mark four lengths of the wood lath and two lengths of dowel.

2. Cutting the wood lath and dowels.

◆ Place a backsaw in the miter box's right-angle slots. Hold the wood tightly against the side of the miter box with one hand, and saw through it with light, smooth strokes.

◆ Saw all four pieces of lath and the two dowels, then lay them side by side. Sand if necessary until all are the same length.

3. Making the end pieces.

◆ On a 10-inch length of 1-by-3 pine, measure and mark $1\frac{3}{4}$ inches from a corner in both directions. Using a straightedge, draw a line between the two marks *(below)*.

◆ Set the backsaw in the miter box's 45° slots, and saw along the line.

◆ Repeat this step at the other end, then cut the board squarely in half midway between the beveled ends.

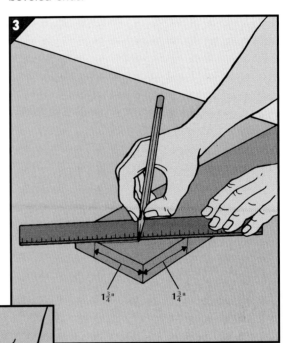

4. Drilling the dowel holes.

◆ On the face of each end piece, draw a straight line $\frac{3}{8}$ inch from, and parallel to, the shorter edge. Mark the line 1 and 2 inches from the bottom edge of the end piece.

◆ Hold the end piece down firmly on a piece of scrap wood, and drill a $\frac{1}{4}$-inch hole straight through the board's face at each mark.

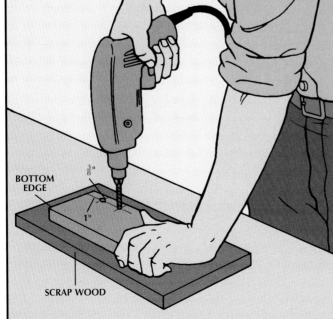

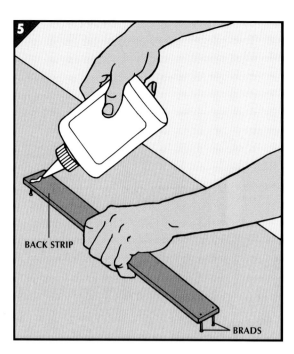

5. Assembling the back.

◆ To attach the back strips, place a piece of lath on the scrap wood, and, $\frac{3}{8}$ inch from one end, tap down two $\frac{3}{4}$-inch brads until their tips emerge on the other side.
◆ Repeat at the other end, then squeeze a thin bead of glue across all the tips.
◆ Nail the lath to the back edge of each end piece, flush with the bottom.
◆ Prepare a second piece of lath the same way. Then measure $1\frac{3}{8}$ inches above the first strip, and nail the second strip to the back of the end piece.

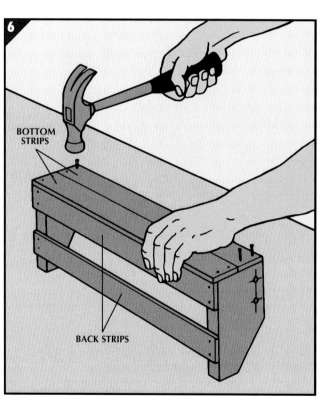

6. Adding the bottom strips.

◆ Tap brads through the remaining two pieces of lath, and add glue as in Step 5.
◆ Then turn the rack upside down and nail one piece of lath to the bottom of the end piece, flush with the back strip.
◆ Nail the last piece to the bottom, flush with the front of the end piece (above).

7. Gluing the dowels.

◆ Test-fit the dowels by sliding them through the holes in the end pieces; if a dowel binds, lightly sand it down.
◆ Pull the dowels out slightly and smear glue on their ends (above), then push them in so that the ends are flush with the outer faces of the end pieces. Wipe off any excess glue and let dry.
◆ To mount the rack, drill two $\frac{1}{4}$-inch holes in the center of the upper back strip, 3 inches from each end.
◆ Hold the rack against the cabinet door, making sure it fits between the cabinet shelves, and mark the mounting holes on the door. Drill pilot holes at the marks, then attach the rack with $\frac{5}{8}$-inch oval-head wood screws.

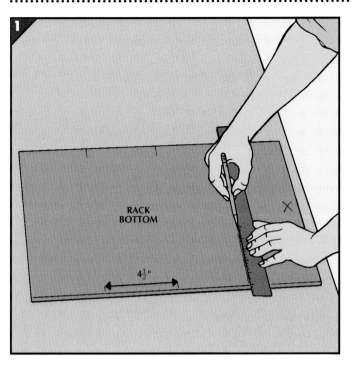

1. Laying out the rack.

◆ Measure the interior of the drawer bottom and subtract $\frac{1}{8}$ inch from the length and width. Then cut a piece of plywood—birch veneer plywood has a nice, smooth finish—to those dimensions for the rack bottom.

◆ Mark an X at what will be the bottom of the rack—that is, the edge nearest the drawer front. Starting at that edge, place marks along the sides of the plywood at $4\frac{1}{2}$-inch intervals.

◆ With a ruler or carpenter's square, draw parallel lines connecting the marks. You will need to make one divider for each line.

2. Cutting the dividers.

◆ Measure and mark pieces of $\frac{3}{4}$-inch quarter-round molding to match the width of the piece of plywood.

◆ Use a backsaw and the right-angle slots on a miter box to cut the pieces squarely.

◆ On each piece, tap $\frac{3}{4}$-inch brads into the center of the molding's round face at 5-inch intervals until the tips just protrude through the flat side.

3. Final assembly.

◆ Take one of the dividers and squeeze a thin line of glue between the protruding tips.

◆ Place the divider on the first line above the X marking the rack bottom. The divider's 90° angle should be flush on the line, with the rounded face toward the bottom.

◆ Hammer the brads until their heads barely show, then use a nail set (left) to drive them just below the surface. Repeat this procedure with the remaining dividers.

◆ Fill the nail holes with wood putty, sand smooth, then finish as desired.

Making Deep Cabinets Accessible

The back part of a deep cabinet is often hard to reach and difficult to see, making it less than ideal for storage. To open up this space, you can build movable storage units that pivot on hinges or roll out on drawer glides. Tailored to fit your cabinet, these units can provide more accessible space for anything from canned goods to kitchen utensils.

A Swing-Out Shelf Unit: Pivoting on a hinge at one side to allow access to the back of the cabinet, this unit has shelves on front and back sized for standard jars and cans. The weight of its contents demands solid support, which you can provide by attaching its mounting cleat with screws long enough to penetrate into the side of an adjoining cabinet. To avoid excessive stress on the mounting hardware, do not load a swing-out unit with heavy items such as large juice cans.

Dual Bins: Side-by-side glide-out bins, with partitions and shelves that fit your needs, are more complicated to build but accommodate awkward items. In the examples on pages 82-87, one bin has a rear compartment for long-handled skillets and a front one for saucepans with space below for lids. The other bin combines shelves with a compartment for tall items and a top tray for large cutlery and other utensils.

Planning: The dimensions of the swing-out and glide-out units shown depend on the size of the original cabinets and your storage needs. The arrangement you choose may include shelves for cans and jars, trays for flatware, or compartments for tall items that are hard to store in conventional cabinets and drawers. In determining the number and spacing of shelves, allow at least 1 extra inch between shelves, to facilitate storing and removing objects.

If your existing cabinets have permanent shelves, you may need to cut them back *(page 80)* or remove them entirely *(page 68)* before installing a new storage unit.

Materials: Most of the parts of the units shown here are made of clear birch plywood, which has smooth surfaces that are easily prepared for painting or staining. The vertical pieces, which carry most of the structural loads, are made from $\frac{3}{4}$-inch plywood, as are the shelves for the swing-out unit. Shelves and rails for the dual bins are cut from $\frac{1}{2}$-inch sheets, and the broad panel that closes one side of a glide-out bin is made from lighter $\frac{1}{4}$-inch plywood. Cleats that support hinges or drawer glides are 1-by-2 clear pine.

Building Tips: When cutting plywood, use a circular saw with a plywood blade or a combination blade that makes both crosscuts and rip cuts. To insure the proper alignment of joints in the dual bins, cut the pieces with dadoes, rabbets, and cutouts first. Make the remaining pieces as you go along. For both units, hold pieces together with bar clamps while you drill pilot holes *(page 10)* for inconspicuous trimhead screws. Protect the unit's finish with scrap wood under the clamp. Test assemblies for fit and alignment before gluing.

 **TOOLS**

Bar clamps
Tape measure
$\frac{1}{4}$-inch or $\frac{3}{8}$-inch power drill
Circular saw
Saber saw
Hacksaw
Metal file
Router
Level
Framing square

 **MATERIALS**

$\frac{3}{4}$-, $\frac{1}{2}$-, and $\frac{1}{4}$-inch clear birch plywood
$\frac{1}{4}$-inch wood lattice
1-by-2s for cleats
Carpenter's glue
Sandpaper (medium grit)
Shims
Drawer-glide assemblies
$1\frac{5}{8}$-inch trimhead screws
No. 6 finishing nails
No. 8 flathead screws
1-inch wire brads
$1\frac{1}{2}$-inch piano hinge
Magnetic catch

CONSTRUCTING SWING-OUT SHELVES

1. Determining the dimensions.

A swing-out shelf unit *(disassembled at right)* is made of $\frac{3}{4}$-inch birch plywood, with shelf rims of $\frac{1}{4}$-inch lattice. The pieces are held together by glue and $1\frac{5}{8}$-inch trimhead screws.

◆ The height of the unit is 1 to $1\frac{1}{2}$ inches less than the height of the cabinet opening. To ensure swinging clearance, make the width of the unit narrower than the cabinet opening by a third of the unit's depth.

◆ The unit's total depth is the sum of the shelf depths plus the thickness of the partition and shelf rims. In the example shown here, with $3\frac{3}{4}$-inch shelves for standard-size cans, the depth is $8\frac{3}{4}$ inches.

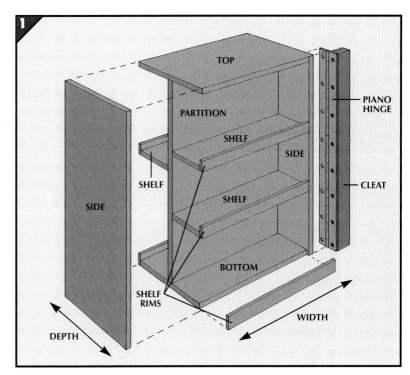

2. Assembling the sides and partition.

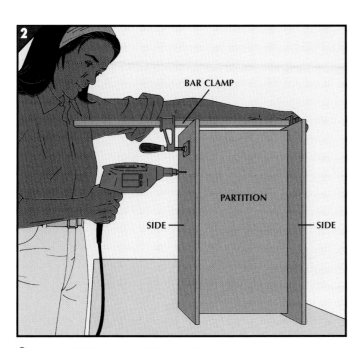

◆ Cut two sides from $\frac{3}{4}$-inch plywood to the planned height and depth of the unit. Cut the partition $1\frac{1}{2}$ inches shorter and narrower than the height and width.

◆ Clamp the partition between the sides so that it is centered top to bottom as well as front to back.

◆ Mark the thickness of the partition on the top edge of each side. Use the marks as guides for pilot holes for $1\frac{5}{8}$-inch trimhead screws at 6- to 8- inch intervals through each side *(above)*.

3. Adding the top and bottom.

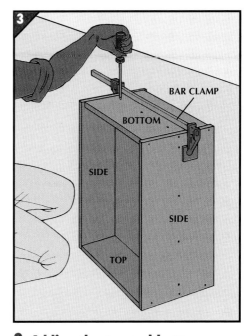

◆ Cut top and bottom pieces $1\frac{1}{2}$ inches shorter than the width of the unit. Match the top piece to the unit's total depth, and make the bottom piece $\frac{1}{2}$ inch narrower to accommodate shelf rims.

◆ Slide the top into position atop the partition; clamp the sides against it. Drill pilot holes for $1\frac{5}{8}$-inch trimhead screws to attach the top piece to the partition and side pieces. Screw the top in place.

◆ Turn the unit upside down and attach the bottom piece in the same way *(above)*, centering it between the sides to leave room for rims.

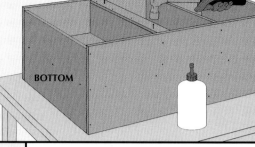

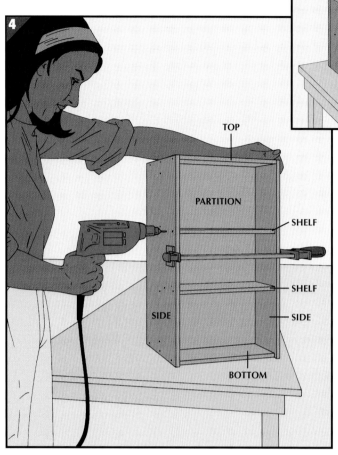

4. Installing the shelves.

◆ Cut shelves as long as the width of the partition and $\frac{1}{4}$ inch narrower than the distance from the partition to the front edge of the side, to leave space for shelf rims.

◆ Position a shelf between the sides, making sure it is level, and clamp the sides to hold it.

◆ Drill two pilot holes through each side into the shelf, placing one about an inch from the front edge of the shelf and the other an inch from the partition *(left)*, and secure the shelf with $1\frac{5}{8}$-inch trimhead screws.

◆ Install the remaining shelves on both sides of the unit in the same way.

◆ Cut a rim for each shelf from $\frac{1}{4}$-inch lattice, as long as the shelf. Apply glue to the front edge of the shelves, and nail the rims flush with the shelf bottoms with 1-inch wire brads *(inset)*.

FINISHING AND INSTALLING THE UNIT

1. Cutting the cabinet shelf.

◆ On each permanent shelf in the cabinet, mark a cutting line parallel to the front edge and as far from the inside of the cabinet frame as the depth of the swing-out unit plus 1 inch. Start the line 1 inch from the same side of the cabinet as the unit's hinge, and make the line several inches longer than the width of the unit, in order to allow swinging clearance. Check these measurements by holding the unit inside the cabinet against the shelf.

◆ Use a saber saw *(left)* or a handsaw to cut the shelf along the line. Smooth the cut edges with medium-grit sandpaper.

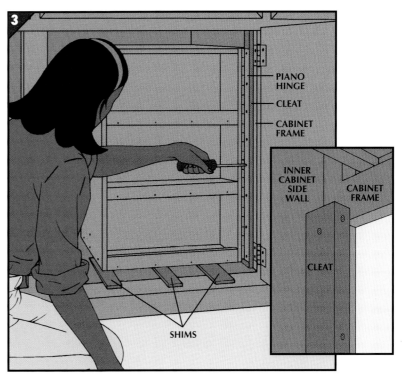

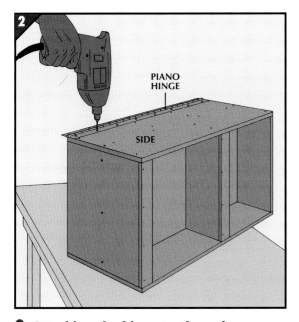

2. Attaching the hinge to the unit.
◆ Position the hinge at the front edge of the pivot side. Center it vertically between the top and bottom and align the hinge barrel with the edge. Drill pilot holes through the screw holes *(above)* and use the screws provided by the manufacturer to attach the hinge.
◆ If the hinge is too long, use a hacksaw to cut it at a joint, but not more than 2 inches shorter than the height of the unit. Smooth the cut edges with a fine metal file.

3. Mounting the unit in the cabinet.
◆ Cut a 1-by-2 cleat to the height of the cabinet wall on the pivot side. Attach the cleat to the back of the cabinet frame *(inset)* with $1\frac{5}{8}$-inch trimhead screws driven every 6 to 8 inches through the cleat into the frame.
◆ Drive 3-inch trimhead screws through the side of the cleat and into the cabinet's side wall, at intervals that avoid the screws that are already in place.
◆ Set the unit on shims inside the cabinet and check for swinging clearance at the top.
◆ Position the free hinge leaf on the cleat with the barrel against the cleat's back edge. Mark the hinge holes on the cleat.
◆ Drill pilot holes and use 2-inch No. 4 or No. 5 screws (the largest that will seat flush against the hinge) to secure the hinge to the cleat *(above)*.

4. Installing the magnetic catch.
◆ Screw the steel strike plate of the catch to the inner bottom corner of the unit on the side away from the hinge. Be sure the edges of the plate are flush with the edges of the corner.
◆ Swing the unit inside the cabinet and position the magnetic catch on the cabinet floor against the strike plate.
◆ Mark the position of screw holes on the cabinet floor, swing the unit out, and use the screws provided with the catch to secure it *(left)*.

DUAL BINS FOR CONVENIENT STORAGE

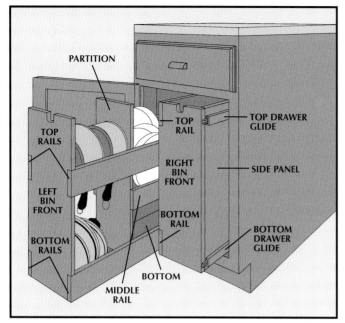

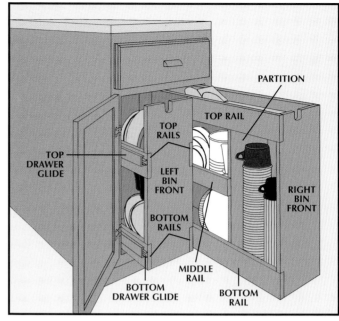

Determining the dimensions.

The overall dimensions of glide-out bins *(above)* allow clearance for sliding and closing the door. The bins are at least 1 inch shorter than the height of the opening and $2\frac{3}{4}$ inches narrower than the width. The depth is $\frac{1}{4}$ inch less than the distance from the back of the cabinet to the inside edge of the front frame. Individual parts, including the width of each bin, are sized according to use.

The bins are made of clear birch plywood: $\frac{3}{4}$ inch for the fronts, backs, and partitions; $\frac{1}{4}$ inch for the side panel, and $\frac{1}{2}$ inch for other parts.

CUTTING THE MAJOR PIECES

Grooved right bin components.

Start by making the front, back, and partition, as well as the rails.

◆ The front and back are as high and wide as the bin; the partition is $3\frac{1}{4}$ inches shorter and $\frac{3}{4}$ inch narrower. The 3-inch-wide top and bottom rails are as long as the unit's depth; the length of the 2-inch-wide middle rail is determined by the position of the partition *(Step 2, page 84)*.

◆ A routed notch 1 inch wide and $\frac{3}{4}$ inch deep at the top front serves as a pull. Corner cutouts sawed in the front and back are 3 inches by $\frac{1}{2}$ inch; a middle cutout in the back is 2 inches wide.

◆ Dadoes $\frac{1}{2}$ inch wide and $\frac{1}{4}$ inch deep across the top of the front and back and in the top rail form a continuous groove after assembly; so do dadoes at the bottom of the front and back and in the bottom rail. A dado $\frac{1}{4}$ inch from the bottom of the middle cutout aligns with dadoes across the partition and in the middle rail. A rabbet $\frac{1}{4}$ inch wide and $\frac{1}{4}$ inch deep on the right edge of the front and back fits the side panel.

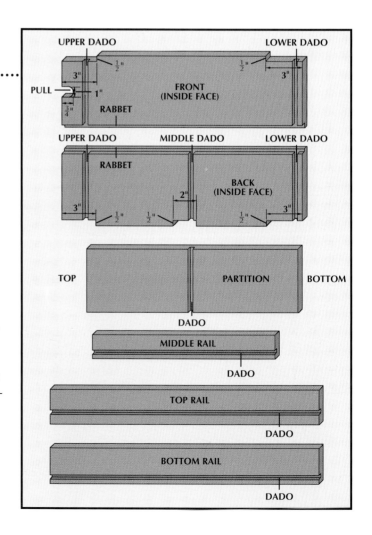

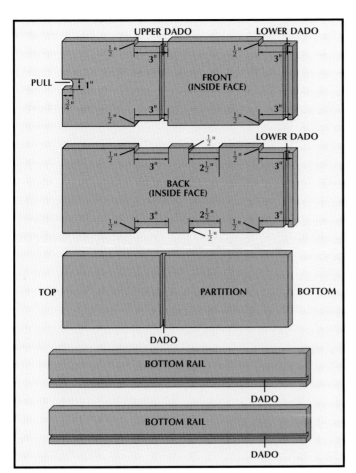

Grooved left bin components.

As with the right bin, make the front, back, and partition. Cut the bottom rails, but make the top and middle rails once the partition is in place *(page 87)*.

◆ The front and back are the planned height and width of the bin, and the partition is $\frac{1}{2}$ inch shorter and 1 inch narrower. Two 3-inch-wide bottom rails are as long as the unit's depth.

◆ The upper cutouts on the front and back are positioned to allow room for planned storage, as are the middle cutouts on the back. The upper and bottom corner cutouts are 3 inches by $\frac{1}{2}$ inch, and the middle cutout is 2 inches by $\frac{1}{2}$ inch.

◆ A notch routed at the top front serves as a pull. A $\frac{1}{2}$-inch-wide dado cut $\frac{1}{4}$ inch deep across the front is $\frac{1}{4}$ inch from the bottom of the upper cutout; the partition's dado aligns with it. The lower dadoes on the front and back are $\frac{1}{4}$ inch above the bottom, as are the dadoes running the length of the bottom rails.

STRAIGHT CUTS WITH A ROUTER

A router makes fast work of the precise cuts crucial to cabinet joints. The variety of available bits and the router's adjustable cutting depth allow cuts of almost any size or shape. A rabbeting bit *(photograph, far right)*, which cuts a notch on the edge of a board, usually has a ball-bearing guide on its tip that rides along the edge, keeping the cut at a uniform width. A straight bit *(photograph, bottom right)*, which makes a square-bottom groove or dado, has no such guide. To ensure straight cuts, clamp a perfectly straight board to the workpiece, parallel to the cutting line and at a distance that allows the bit to just cut the line. Hold the router firmly against the guide when cutting *(right)*. For either type of cut, grip the router with both hands and move it against the resistance of the cutting.

⚠️ **CAUTION** *Always wear goggles when routing, and never start the router with the bit in contact with the workpiece.*

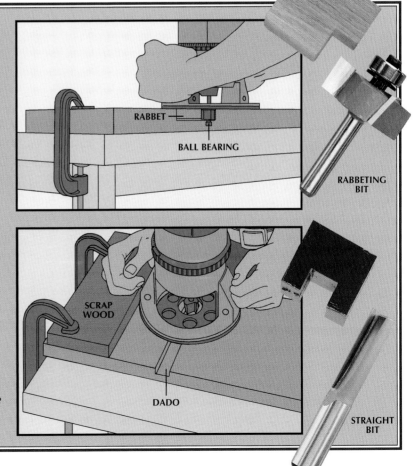

ASSEMBLING THE RIGHT BIN

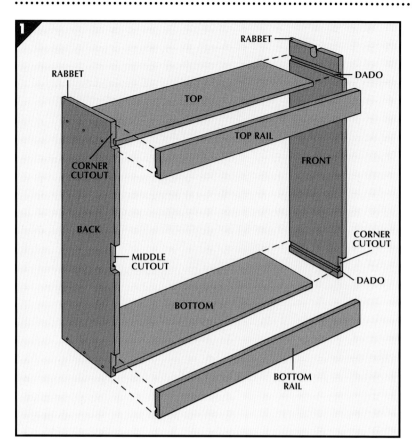

1. Building the frame.

◆ Cut top and bottom pieces from $\frac{1}{2}$-inch plywood, 1 inch shorter than the depth of the cabinet and $\frac{1}{2}$ inch narrower than the front and back.

◆ Apply glue to both ends of the top and bottom and slip them into the dadoes on the front and back, positioned so that one edge extends $\frac{1}{4}$ inch into the cutouts while the other edge is flush with the inner face of the rabbets.

◆ Clamp the pieces together, and drill three pilot holes through the front and back into the top and bottom. Secure these joints with trimhead screws.

◆ When the glue has set, remove the clamps. Apply glue to the long edges of the top and bottom and slip the dadoes of the top and bottom rails over the edges. Drill pilot holes through the rail ends into the edges of the front and back panels and through the rails into the edges of the top and bottom. Secure the rails with trimhead screws.

2. Constructing the middle shelf.

◆ Cut a shelf from $\frac{1}{2}$-inch plywood, $\frac{1}{4}$ inch wider than the partition and $\frac{1}{2}$ inch longer than the distance from the back to the planned partition location.

◆ Apply glue to one end of the shelf and slip it into the dado on the partition so that the shelf edge on the open side extends $\frac{1}{4}$ inch beyond the partition. Drill pilot holes and secure the joint with trimhead screws through the partition into the shelf.

◆ When the glue is dry, apply glue to the other end of the shelf and to the top and bottom of the partition, and position the assembly in the bin with one side of the shelf extending $\frac{1}{4}$ inch into the middle cutout, and the other side flush with the inner face of the rabbets. Complete the joints with screws through the back, top, bottom, and rails.

◆ Glue and screw the middle rail to the protruding edge of the shelf.

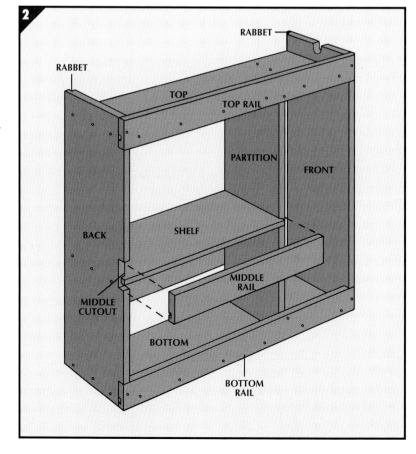

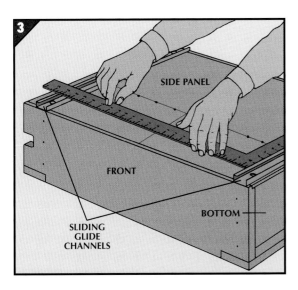

3. Attaching the side panel and sliding channels.

◆ Cut the side panel from $\frac{1}{4}$-inch plywood, to fit snugly within the rabbets.

◆ Position the panel in the rabbets and use a pencil to outline the edges of the top, bottom, shelf, and partition on the panel. Transfer the outlines to the other side of the panel, and reposition it with these marks facing up.

◆ Place the glide channels on the panel, with their front ends flush with the front of the bin and their mounting screw holes centered over the outlines of the top and bottom. Mark the screw holes.

◆ Glue the side panel to the bin and secure it with No. 6 finishing nails countersunk along all the outlines, taking care to avoid the marked screw positions.

◆ Align the top sliding channel with the screw hole markings, and attach it with the screws provided, driven through the panel into the top.

◆ Position the bottom sliding channel over its markings and use a framing square to make sure the distance between the top and bottom channels is equal at both ends (left), then secure the channel with screws through the side panel into the bottom.

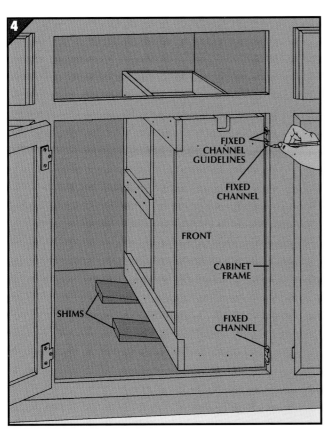

4. Positioning the bin.

◆ Slip the fixed glide channels over the sliding channels on the bin. Position the bin in the cabinet on shims so it is level and clears the top and side of the opening.

◆ Mark the locations of the upper and lower fixed channels on the edge of the cabinet frame (above).

◆ Measure the distance between the fixed channels and the cabinet wall. Use 1-by-2 clear pine to make two mounting cleats of that thickness and as long as the cabinet depth.

5. Installing the bin.

◆ Extend lines from the marks on the cabinet edge along the sides and 1 inch onto the back of the cabinet.

◆ Position a fixed channel against a cleat, flush with the front edge, and drill mounting holes in the cleat.

◆ Center a cleat on the upper guidelines, and avoiding the mounting holes, drill four pilot holes through the cleat into the side wall. Attach the cleat with No. 8 screws (above).

◆ Mount the lower cleat the same way.

◆ Screw the fixed channels to the cleats using longer screws than those provided, for added strength.

◆ Install the bin by inserting the sliding channels into the cabinet-mounted fixed channels.

ASSEMBLING THE LEFT BIN

1. Making the bottom.

◆ Cut a bottom piece 1 inch shorter than the depth of the cabinet, and $\frac{1}{2}$ inch narrower than the front and back.

◆ Apply glue to the ends of the bottom piece and slip it into the lower dadoes on the front and back, with its edges extending $\frac{1}{4}$ inch into the cutouts on both sides. Clamp the bottom in place, drill pilot holes into its edge through the front and back, and secure it with trimhead screws.

◆ Apply glue to the edges of the bottom, then attach the two bottom rails with screws into the bottom on the front and back.

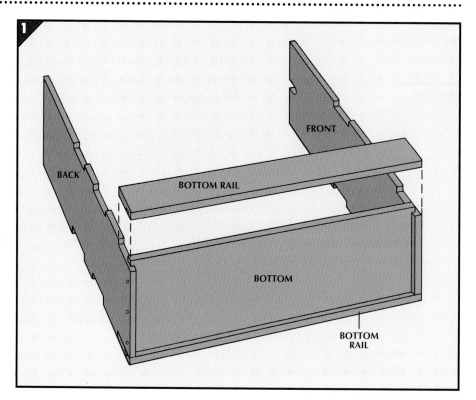

2. Building the long supports.

◆ Cut long supports *(left)* from $\frac{1}{2}$-inch plywood to the length corresponding to the planned position of the partition, adding $\frac{1}{2}$ inch to allow for the dadoes. Make each support wide enough to leave a gap between them for pot handles when their outer edges are flush with the edge of the partition.

◆ Apply glue to one end of each support and slip them into the partition dado, outer edges flush with the edges of the partition. Clamp the pieces together, drill pilot holes through the partition, and secure the pieces with trimhead screws.

◆ Apply glue to the free ends of the supports and the bottom of the partition, then set the assembly in the bin with the supports fitted firmly into the front dado.

◆ Secure the assembly with screws through the front, bottom, and rails.

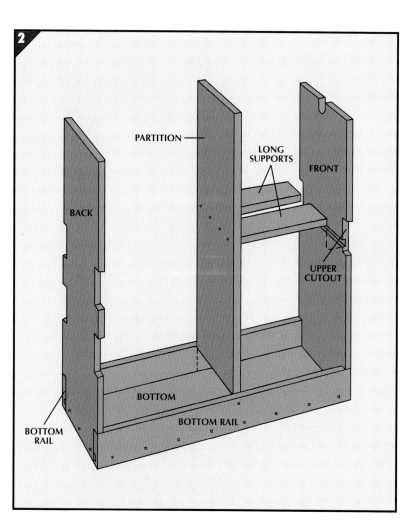

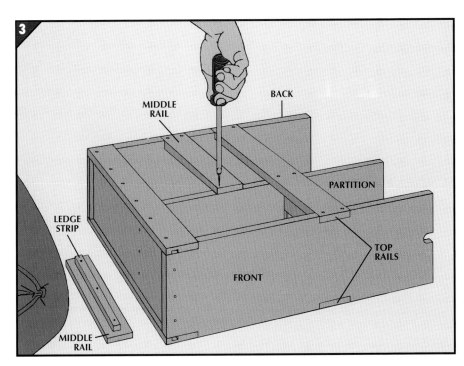

3. Constructing the top and middle rails.

◆ Make two top rails with the same dimensions as the bottom rails. Glue and screw them into the upper cutouts on the front and back.

◆ Make two middle rails $2\frac{1}{2}$ inches wide and as long as the distance from the outside of the back piece to the front side of the partition.

◆ Cut two ledge strips, $1\frac{1}{2}$ inches shorter than the middle rails and $\frac{3}{4}$ inch wide, and center one on each middle rail. Secure them with glue and trimhead screws.

◆ With the ledge strips facing inward, glue and screw the middle rails to the partition and the middle cutouts on the back (left).

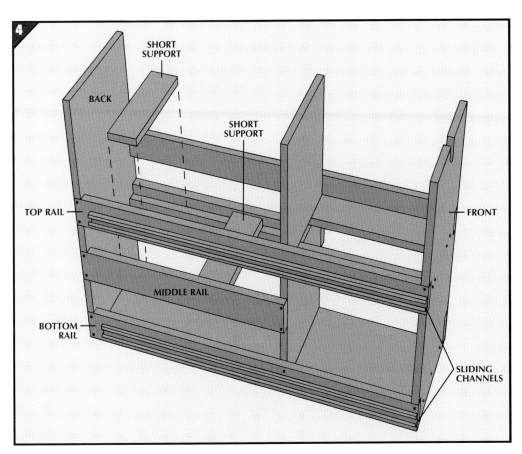

4. Completing the left bin.

◆ Make two short supports as long as the distance between the inside edges of the middle rails. Their width can vary, but they must be wide enough to support the smallest item you plan to store.

◆ Lower the short supports onto the ledge strips and leave them loose or glue them.

◆ Attach the sliding channels to the top and bottom rails of the bin, centered and flush with the front, and mount the bin in the cabinet (page 85).

87

An Island That Rolls

Four swivel casters and a butcher-block top can transform a pair of kitchen cabinets into a movable island. With the cabinets fastened back to back, this unit offers additional storage space with adjustable shelves and doors on opposite sides, plus an extra work surface that goes where you need it.

Buy two preassembled wall cabinets, 12 inches deep and anywhere from 18 to 60 inches wide, depending on your needs and the size of your kitchen. To make the island the same height as your countertop—typically 36 inches—choose cabinets 30 inches high; the swivel casters and butcher-block top will add the rest. The top should overhang the cabinets on all four sides by 3 inches, providing handholds for rolling the island. Select cabinets with tops and bottoms of plywood or particle board at least $\frac{1}{2}$ inch thick and add solid wood reinforcing boards to support the casters and butcher block.

If the joint where the two cabinets fit together is noticeable, fill it with wood putty or conceal it under $1\frac{1}{4}$- by $\frac{1}{4}$-inch wood lath, fastened with carpenter's glue and countersunk brads.

 TOOLS

$\frac{3}{8}$-inch power drill
Circular saw
Awl
Medium-size flat-blade
  screwdriver
Adjustable wrench

 **MATERIALS**

Two matching kitchen wall
  cabinets
Laminated maple butcher
  block, at least $1\frac{3}{4}$ inches
  thick
Four 1-by-8 pine or fir boards
Four flat-plate locking swivel
  casters, with $2\frac{1}{2}$-inch wheels
  and 75-lb. load capacity
  rating

Six $\frac{1}{4}$- by 3-inch stove bolts,
  each with 1 nut, 2 flat washers, and 1 split lock washer
Eight No. 8 $1\frac{1}{4}$-inch round-
  head wood screws
Sixteen No. 8 $\frac{3}{4}$-inch round-
  head wood screws
Six No. 10 3-inch round-head
  wood screws, each with 1
  flat washer

JOINING TWO CABINETS

2"
$\frac{1}{2}$"

1. Drilling holes for bolts.
◆ Remove the doors and shelves from the cabinets and lay them facedown, tops facing each other and sides flush.
◆ With a pencil, mark $\frac{1}{2}$ inch down from the top edge and 2 inches in from each side of the cabinets. Make a third mark halfway between.
◆ Make sure the marks on both cabinets align with each other, then turn the cabinets around and repeat along the bottoms.
◆ Drill $\frac{1}{4}$-inch holes through the lip of the recessed area at each mark (*left*).

2. Bolting cabinets together.

◆ Set the cabinets upright, back to back, and push an awl through each pair of holes to align them. Slide flat washers onto three stove bolts, and push each bolt through the holes in both cabinets. Put a flat washer and a split washer on each bolt, followed by a nut; then turn each nut finger tight.

◆ Turn the cabinets over by tipping them on their sides, not on a front panel. Bolt the bottom edges together the same way as the top. After all six bolts are in place, hold each bolthead with a screwdriver and tighten the nut with a wrench until the split lock washer is compressed.

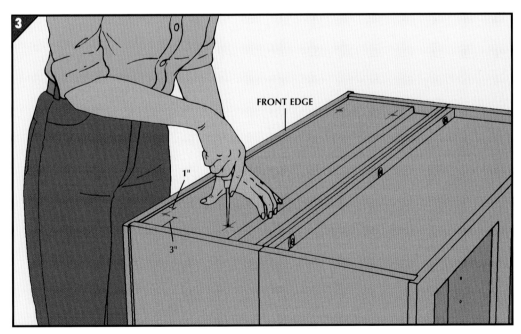

FRONT EDGE

1"

3"

3. Fitting the reinforcement boards.

◆ Measure the length of the recessed area on the cabinet tops and bottoms and cut four pieces of 1-by-8 to that length.

◆ Make four marks on each board, 3 inches from the ends and 1 inch from the edges, and drill $\frac{3}{32}$-inch holes at each mark.

◆ Set a board in one of the cabinet recess-es, snug against the front edge of the cabinet. Insert an awl into each hole in the board and push the point firmly into the cabinet (*above*). Remove the board, and drill a $\frac{3}{16}$-inch hole through the cabinet at each awl mark. Repeat the process for each reinforcement board in each of the remaining three recesses.

4. Fastening the boards to the cabinets.

◆ Set one of the reinforcement boards into its cabinet recess and push the awl through the holes to align them.

◆ Then, reach inside the cabinet and drive a $1\frac{1}{4}$-inch No. 8 wood screw through each hole in the cabinet and up into the board (*below*). Install the remaining reinforcement boards the same way.

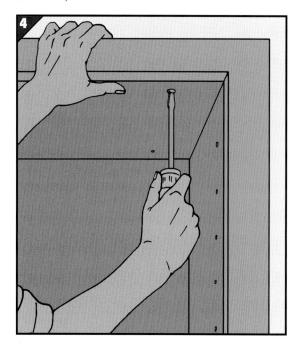

5. Attaching the casters.

◆ Turn the cabinets bottom side up. Set a caster in each corner with the holes in the mounting plate at least $\frac{1}{2}$ inch from the edges of the reinforcement board. Mark the board through the holes in the plate.

◆ With a $\frac{3}{32}$-inch bit, drill $\frac{3}{4}$-inch-deep pilot holes (*page 10*) at each mark. Fasten the casters to the board with $\frac{3}{4}$-inch No. 8 wood screws.

◆ Unfinished cabinets—including the doors and shelves—should be painted or stained before proceeding to the next step.

MOUNTING A BUTCHER-BLOCK TOP

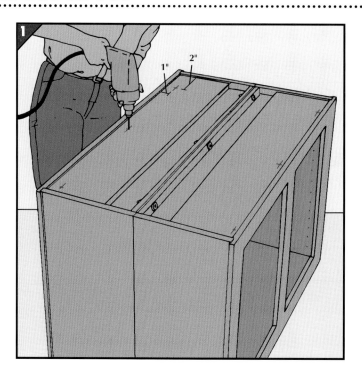

1. Drilling through cabinet roof.

◆ Turn the cabinets upright again, then measure and mark 2 inches in from each side and 1 inch back from the front edge of the reinforcement boards. Center a third mark between these two.

◆ Drill $\frac{1}{4}$-inch holes through the reinforcement boards and the cabinet tops at each mark.

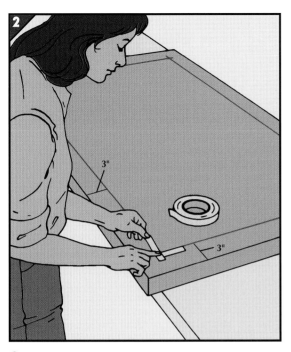

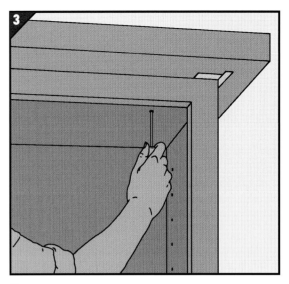

2. Marking the butcher block.

Set the butcher block upside down and, with a straightedge, draw a line 3 inches in from and parallel to each edge. Affix two pieces of masking tape at each corner as shown above, aligning the inner edges of the tape with the lines.

3. Positioning the butcher block.

◆ Set the butcher block on the cabinets, aligning the tape strips with the cabinet corners. Push an awl through each hole in the cabinet roof to mark the underside of the butcher block.

◆ Remove the butcher block and turn it over. Then, with a $\frac{1}{8}$-inch bit, drill $\frac{1}{2}$-inch-deep pilot holes at each mark.

4. Attaching the butcher block.

◆ Reposition the butcher block on the cabinet. With the awl, align the holes in the cabinet roof with those in the block.

◆ Slip flat washers onto six 3-inch No. 10 wood screws, and drive the screws partway into the block. When all the screws are in place, go back and tighten each one completely.

◆ Remove the masking tape. Replace the shelves and rehang the doors.

Face-Lifts for Timeworn Kitchens

You can bring an old-fashioned kitchen up to date by building on what you already have. Modern amenities such as soap dispensers and water filters are easy to add, as is a new countertop in a fresh color. Instead of replacing old cabinets, consider sprucing them up with new doors, drawer fronts, and matching veneer for the frames. Very often, a new floor can be installed right over the old one.

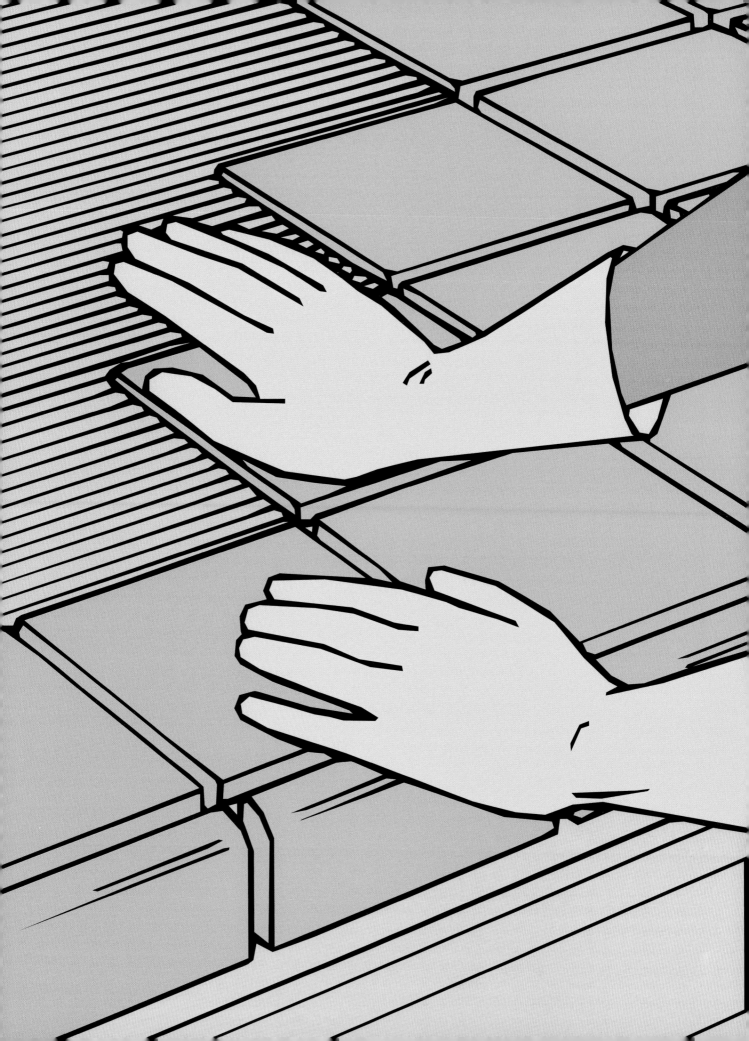

A Safer Electrical Receptacle

Since the mid-1970s, the National Electrical Code has required that any electrical receptacle that is installed within 6 feet of a sink must be protected by a ground-fault circuit interrupter, or GFCI. This device detects the smallest leakage of electrical current—called a ground fault—and turns off power in the receptacle within $\frac{1}{40}$ second.

Replacing an old receptacle with a new GFCI is economical insurance. Because one GFCI protects all receptacles that are downstream from it on the same circuit, you can install the device anywhere on the kitchen circuit between the service panel and the receptacles that require this protection.

For a GFCI to function, the wires must be properly connected to the terminals labeled "line" and "load." Reversing these connections will still allow electricity to flow through the receptacle, but it will render the GFCI protection inoperative.

Before Proceeding: Some jurisdictions require a permit for any work on a house's electrical wiring and an inspection once it's completed. Also check your house for aluminum wiring; it is dull gray in color, sometimes coated with copper. The code allows only specially licensed electricians to work on it. If you have any doubts, consult an electrician.

⚠️ **CAUTION** *First, trip the circuit breaker or unscrew the fuse in the service panel that protects the receptacle's circuit. Then remove the cover plate and set a multitester for 250 volts AC. Touch one probe to the green grounding screw and the other in turn to each silver- and brass-colored screw. Repeat the test at the 10-volt AC setting. Any reading other than 0 volts indicates that there is a problem in the circuit; call an electrician.*

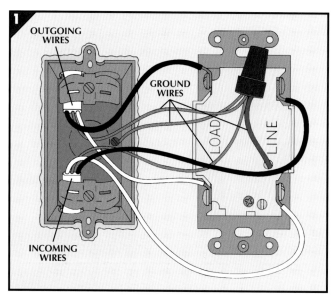

1. Wiring the GFCI.

◆ With the power off, remove the receptacle and disconnect the bottom set of black and white wires. Plug a radio into the receptacle and turn the power back on; if the radio is silent, you have disconnected the incoming wires.

◆ Turn off power at the service panel. Attach incoming wires to the "line" side of the GFCI, black to the brass-colored screw post and white to the silver-colored post. Connect outgoing wires to the "load" side of the GFCI, black to brass and white to silver. Attach a short length of bare copper wire to the box's green screw post. Use a wire cap to join this wire with all other green or bare copper wires in the box and the GFCI *(above)*.

◆ Some GFCIs have wire leads instead of screws. Proceed as instructed above, but match wires by color and connect them with wire caps.

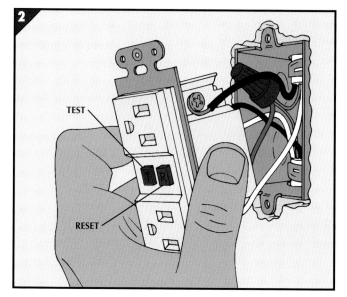

2. Mounting the GFCI.

◆ Tuck the wires back into the electrical box, then secure the GFCI receptacle to the box with the mounting screws and replace the cover plate.

◆ Turn on power at the service panel and test the GFCI and any protected receptacles between it and the end of the circuit. To do so, plug a radio into each receptacle in turn and push the test button on the GFCI. If in each case the reset button pops out and the radio goes silent, all is well. If the radio does not go off, or if you cannot push the reset button to restore power, turn off power at the service panel and check the wiring of the GFCI.

◆ If the wiring is correct and the problem persists, either the GFCI is faulty or there is a problem elsewhere. If replacing the GFCI doesn't work, call an electrician.

Soap and hot water at your fingertips, pure water for drinking and cooking, a seemingly endless supply of ice, and bright, glare-free light on a kitchen countertop—any of these add to the efficiency and convenience of a kitchen.

Soap and Hot Water: A soap dispenser and a tap that delivers near-boiling water are usually mounted to a stainless steel sink through a hole cut in the back rim of the sink with a knockout punch *(page 96)*. Piercing the rim of a cast-iron or porcelain sink is impracticable, but either device may be installed in the countertop, provided the soap dispenser or waterspout is long enough to reach the basin.

Installing a hot-water tap requires not only the existence of a new, GFCI-protected receptacle *(page 94)* for an uninterrupted flow of electricity, but also the proximity of a cold-water line that can be tapped. For this purpose, use a saddle valve *(page 98)*, an ingenious, virtually foolproof device for drawing water from copper or plastic pipe. Buy a valve that fits your supply pipes and the flexible tubing for the tap.

Clean Water: Under-the-counter water filters fit into the cold-water line supplying the kitchen sink. The replaceable cartridges in some filters trap sediment, particulate matter, and unpleasant tastes found in water, while others remove lead, chemicals, and bacteria.

Ice on Tap: Almost all models of refrigerators made since the early 1970s allow for the installation of an icemaker, usually obtained from the manufacturer as a kit.

The icemaker must be connected to a cold-water-supply pipe by $\frac{1}{4}$-inch copper tubing. Use a saddle valve to tap into a water pipe convenient for routing the tubing to the back of the refrigerator.

Under-Cabinet Lighting: A fluorescent light mounted under a cabinet provides bright, glare-free illumination for a countertop or sink.

Home-improvement stores sell ready-to-install lighting that can be plugged into any handy receptacle.

TOOLS

Center punch or nail set	Adjustable wrench
Knockout punch	Open-end wrench
Basin wrench	Wire stripper
Hacksaw or tube cutter	Wirecutters
Pipe reamer	Drill
Emery board	Utility knife
Torpedo level	Screwdriver or nut driver

MATERIALS

Plumber's putty	Compression fittings
Plumbing tape	Insulated wire
Saddle valve	staples
$\frac{1}{4}$-inch flexible copper tubing	$\frac{3}{8}$-inch wood screws

MOUNTING A SOAP DISPENSER AT THE SINK

1. Drilling a starter hole.
◆ Pick a location on the back rim of the sink where there is sufficient space underneath for the soap reservoir.
◆ Mark a point on the rim so that the pump flange *(far right)* rests fully on metal and does not overhang the sink or extend over the countertop. Dimple the rim at that point with a center punch or nail set *(right)*.
◆ Drill a starter hole at the dimple with a $\frac{1}{8}$-inch bit. Then widen the hole to $\frac{7}{16}$ inch with increasingly larger bits.

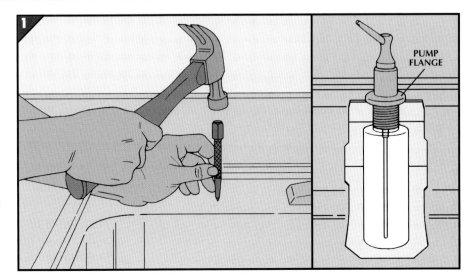

PUMP FLANGE

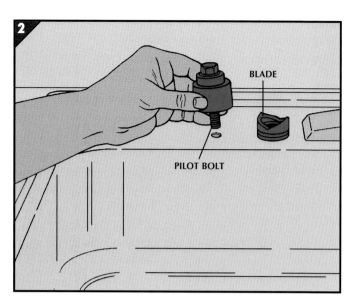

2. Finishing the hole.

◆ Insert the pilot bolt of a knockout punch into the starter hole from the top *(left)*. From beneath the sink, screw the bladed part of the tool onto the bolt hand tight.

◆ Turn the bolt with a wrench until the blade cuts through the stainless steel. To avoid bruised knuckles as the punch breaks through, never push the wrench handle away from you; instead, always pull it toward you.

THE KNOCKOUT PUNCH

This ingenious tool cuts precise holes in stainless steel quickly and easily. A bolt, passed through a pilot hole drilled in the metal, connects the top and bottom halves of the punch. Turning the bolt head at the top pulls the bottom—with its finely honed cutting edge—upward through the steel. Most tool-rental stores carry a selection of knockout punches in diameters from $\frac{1}{2}$ inch to as large as $4\frac{1}{2}$ inches, usually in $\frac{1}{8}$-inch increments.

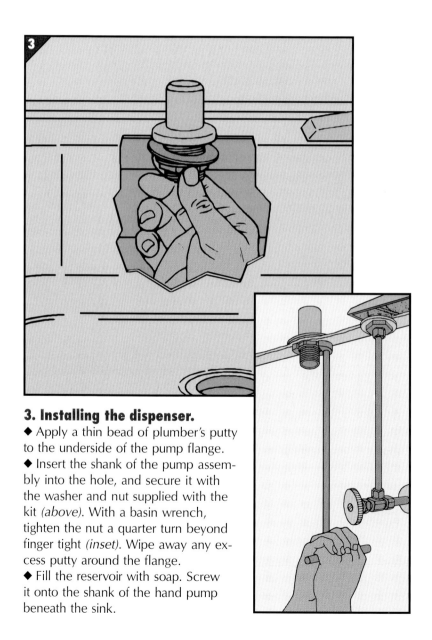

3. Installing the dispenser.

◆ Apply a thin bead of plumber's putty to the underside of the pump flange.

◆ Insert the shank of the pump assembly into the hole, and secure it with the washer and nut supplied with the kit *(above)*. With a basin wrench, tighten the nut a quarter turn beyond finger tight *(inset)*. Wipe away any excess putty around the flange.

◆ Fill the reservoir with soap. Screw it onto the shank of the hand pump beneath the sink.

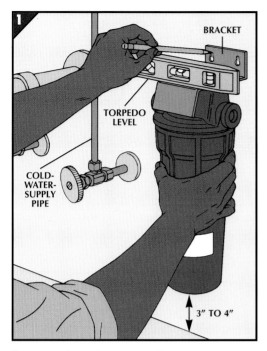

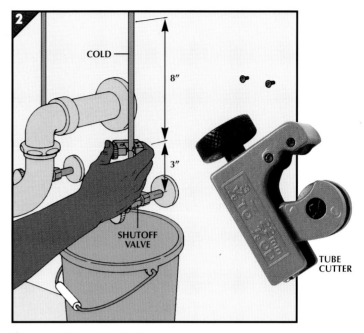

1. Attaching the mounting bracket.

◆ Place the filter housing on the mounting bracket. Choose a location for the bracket to the right of the cold-water-supply pipe leading to the faucet. Also allow 3 to 4 inches above the floor for clearance when changing filter cartridges.
◆ Hold the bracket level against the wall, and mark the holes for mounting screws *(above)*.
◆ Set the bracket aside, and drive the screws into the back of the cabinet, leaving about $\frac{1}{4}$ inch of each screw exposed.

2. Attaching the fittings.

◆ Close the cold-water shutoff valve, then mark the cold-water pipe 3 inches above the valve and 8 inches above that mark.
◆ Place a bucket below the pipe to catch drips, then cut out the piece of pipe between the marks with a tube cutter *(above)* or hacksaw.
◆ Smooth the pipe edges on both sides of the gap with an emery board, and clean out the cut ends with a pipe reamer. Then slip one of the dual compression fittings that come with the filter kit over each end of the cut pipe. To avoid damaging the compression rings, tighten each fitting only one turn past hand tight with an adjustable wrench.
◆ Working in a clockwise direction, wrap two layers of plumbing tape around the threads of the fittings that screw into the in and out ports of the filter housing. Screw the fittings into the ports, and tighten one turn past hand tight.

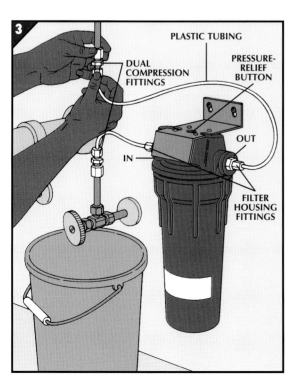

3. Hooking up the filter.

◆ Shorten the flexible plastic tubes so that they reach from the dual compression fittings on the pipe to the in and out ports of the filter without being either too long or so short that they curve sharply.
◆ Insert a length of plastic tubing in the dual fitting coming from the shutoff valve, and connect it to the threaded fitting occupying the in port of the filter housing. Fasten another tube to the fitting in the out port, and connect it to the upper dual fitting on the pipe.
◆ Hang the bracket on the mounting screws and tighten them. Open the cold-water shutoff valve and press the pressure-relief button on the filter to release air displaced as water enters. Tighten any leaky fittings by a quarter turn until the seepage stops.
◆ Run cold water from the tap for 2 or 3 minutes, both to saturate the filter cartridge and to flush out loose material.

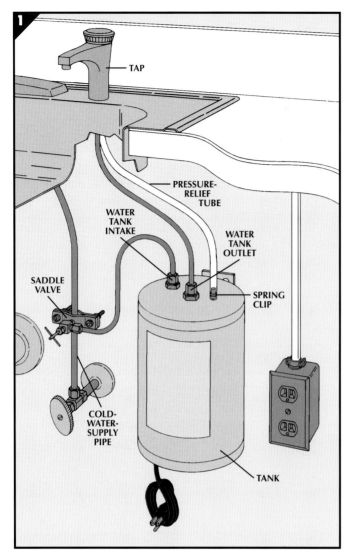

1

TAP

PRESSURE-
RELIEF
TUBE

WATER
TANK
INTAKE

WATER
TANK
OUTLET

SADDLE
VALVE

SPRING
CLIP

COLD-
WATER-
SUPPLY
PIPE

TANK

1. Mounting the tap and tank.

◆ Choose a location for the tap on the sink rim where the spout will overhang the sink. Then cut a hole in the rim with a knockout punch as shown on page 96.

◆ Lay a thin bead of plumber's putty around the tap's flange, or use the gasket supplied with some kits. Insert the shank of the tap in the hole. Secure it with the washer and lock nut supplied with the unit, and tighten gently with a basin wrench *(page 96)*. Some models use bolts and a metal brace to hold the tap from the underside of the sink rim.

◆ Below the sink, level the mounting bracket for the water heater tank, and screw it to the inside cabinet wall as close as possible to the cold-water-supply pipe. Mount the tank onto the bracket.

⚠️ **CAUTION** *The water tank gets hot; rags or flammable substances should not be stored in the same cabinet.*

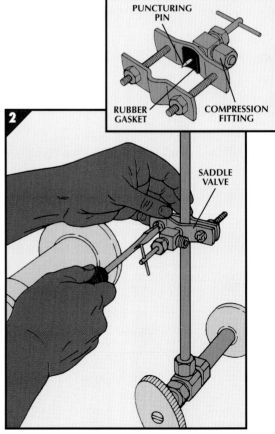

PUNCTURING
PIN

RUBBER
GASKET

COMPRESSION
FITTING

2

SADDLE
VALVE

2. Tapping a water line.

◆ Close the shutoff valve to the cold-water-supply pipe.

◆ Turn the handle of the saddle valve counterclockwise until the puncturing pin is fully recessed beneath the rubber gasket *(inset)*.

◆ Join the two pieces of the valve around the pipe, and draw them together snugly with the nuts and bolts provided *(right)*.

◆ Insert a length of flexible copper tubing into the compression fitting of the saddle valve. To avoid damaging the compression ring inside it, turn the nut one turn past hand tight.

◆ Use a compression fitting to

fasten the tubing to the water-tank intake *(above)*. Use copper tubing and compression fittings to connect the tank's outlet port to the underside of the tap.

◆ Attach the pressure-relief tube, which is connected to the tap at the factory, to the small brass nipple at the top of the tank, and secure it with the spring clip supplied with the kit.

◆ Open the cold-water shutoff. Turn the handle of the saddle valve clockwise until the pin punctures the pipe, then open the valve to adjust water flow. Check for leaks, and tighten fittings as needed.

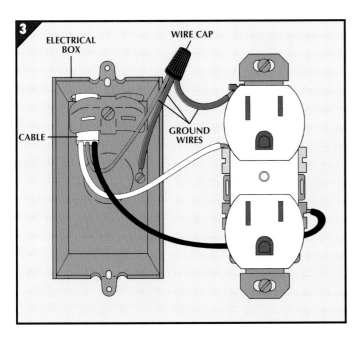

3
ELECTRICAL BOX
WIRE CAP
CABLE
GROUND WIRES

3. Wiring a new receptacle.

◆ Extend a 20-amp circuit to a convenient spot below the sink, and install a surface-mounted electrical box there for the new receptacle. If the circuit is not protected by a GFCI, install one *(page 94)*.

◆ Connect the black wire in the cable to one of the brass-colored screws on the receptacle and the white wire to a silver-colored screw. Cut short ground wires for the receptacle and the box, and join them with a wire cap to the bare wire in the cable as shown *(left)*.

◆ Push the receptacle into the box, and secure it with the screws provided. Then install the cover plate.

◆ Plug in the water heater.

AN ICEMAKER FOR THE FREEZER

1. Mounting the icemaker.

◆ Unplug the refrigerator and pull it away from the wall.

◆ Inside the freezer, lift out the removable back panel to expose the end of the internal water-supply line.

◆ Remove the covers from the mounting holes and the power outlet in the freezer wall. Plug in the icemaker, then screw it into the mounting holes so that the supply line overhangs the water basin on the icemaker.

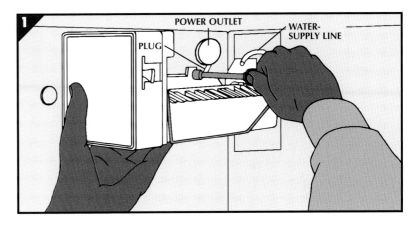

1
POWER OUTLET
WATER-SUPPLY LINE
PLUG

2. Hooking up a water line.

◆ Locate the most convenient cold-water-supply line and close its shutoff valve.

◆ Tap into the line with a saddle valve *(page 98)*. Attach flexible copper tubing to the valve's compression fitting, and run it to the back of the refrigerator. Cut the tubing about 12 inches longer than necessary to reach the water inlet valve.

◆ Slip a compression ring and nut onto the tubing, and insert it in the inlet valve for the icemaker's internal water-supply line *(right)*. The valve can be found at the back of the refrigerator, usually near the floor.

◆ Plug in the refrigerator, turn on the water at the shutoff valve, and open the saddle valve. Check all connections for leaks, and tighten them if necessary.

◆ Adjust the water fill lever and icemaker shutoff arm as described on pages 60 and 61.

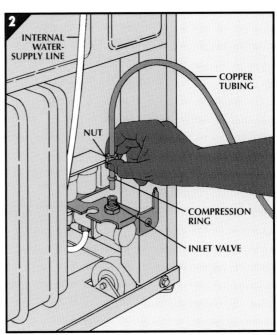

2
INTERNAL WATER-SUPPLY LINE
COPPER TUBING
NUT
COMPRESSION RING
INLET VALVE

1. Mounting the housing.

◆ Where you choose to install the under-cabinet lighting is a matter of personal taste. The closer it is to the front edge of the cabinet, the more direct light you get on the countertop work area. If it is mounted farther back, the unit itself is hidden from view, but you also get less direct light on the work area.

◆ Hold the housing against the underside of a cabinet and mark the bracket holes, then drill pilot holes $\frac{1}{4}$ inch deep for the mounting screws *(page 10)*.

◆ Attach the fixture housing to the cabinet with wood screws no longer than $\frac{3}{8}$ inch.

2. Attaching the light.

◆ Take the fluorescent bulb out of the light fixture to avoid breaking it as you work.

◆ Secure the fixture to the housing. Some models screw to the housing, others slip into support brackets.

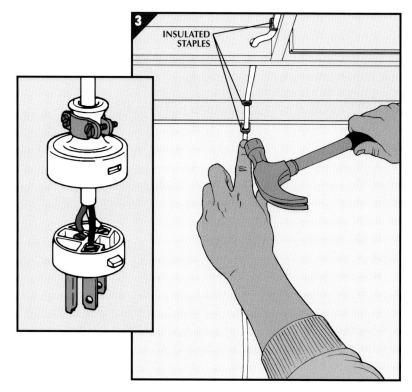

3. Hiding the cord.

◆ Run the fixture's cord under the cabinet frame to the nearest grounded wall outlet. Anchor the cord with insulated wire staples every 4 to 6 inches *(left)*.

◆ To overcome an obstacle such as an adjacent cabinet frame, drill a hole through the frame large enough for the cord to pass but not the plug.

◆ If the cord is attached to a plug with screw terminals *(inset)*, take the plug apart, thread the cord through the hole, then reattach the plug. Snip off a molded plug with wirecutters and attach a new grounded plug to the end of the cord.

◆ Install the fluorescent bulb and plug the unit in.

Replacing an old laminated countertop with a new one can make a quick and dramatic change in the appearance of your kitchen. Aside from the cutting of an opening for the sink, the job consists mostly of simple steps—drilling holes, driving screws, hooking up the sink—and can usually be completed in a single day.

Critical Measurements: The most important element in a smooth installation is the precise measurement of the existing countertop *(below)*. Check your results carefully, and take them, along with a sketch of the counter layout, to the supplier, who will provide the replacement.

Choosing a Style: Available in a wide variety of laminate colors and patterns, countertops also come in two styles: custom self-edge and postform. The difference lies in the treatment of the front edge and of the joint between the work surface and the backsplash, the short vertical surface that catches overflows and spills at the counter's rear.

In a custom self-edge countertop, the work surface and the backsplash meet in a sharp 90° angle. The front edge is also perpendicular to the work surface. Custom self-edge is the style to choose if you wish to finish the edge with wood trim called bullnose.

A postform counter has a gently rounded front edge and backsplash joint, with the laminate curving smoothly over them. For the neatest job whichever style you choose, specify that the countertop ends, even those that abut a wall or appliance, be covered with laminate.

TOOLS

Tape measure	Utility knife
Basin wrench	Flashlight
Open-end	Drill
wrenches	Saber saw
Screwdriver	Caulk gun

MATERIALS

Prelaminated count-	Masking tape
ertop segments	(2-inch)
Corner fasteners	Utility handle
2-by-2s	Silicone caulk
Roll of paper	Denatured alcohol
(25-inch-wide)	

Taking the measurements.
◆ First, measure the length of the countertop. For an L-shaped counter *(left)*, hook the end of a tape measure over the backsplash and measure the length of each leg of the old countertop.
◆ Check the distance from the back of the backsplash to the front edge. If the distance differs from the standard 25 inches, specify the actual measurement when ordering the replacement.

1. Removing the sink.

◆ Turn off the water supply to the faucet. Open the faucet to drain the supply lines, then disconnect them from the faucet with a basin wrench. Use the same tool to remove the dishwasher air gap *(page 32)*.

◆ Cut power to the dishwasher and garbage disposer at the service panel. Disconnect drain and dishwasher plumbing from the disposer, then detach it from the sink *(left)*, either by turning it to unlock it or by loosening mounting screws under the sink. Set the disposer on the cabinet floor.

◆ Unscrew the anchors under the countertop that hold the sink. Separate the countertop and the sink edge with a utility knife, then lift out the sink and set it aside.

2. Making a sink template.

◆ Cut a sheet of paper long enough to extend from one end of the countertop past the sink cutout. Tape the paper even with the end of the countertop and with one edge against the backsplash. Mark these edges of the paper *(Xs)*.

◆ Using the corners of the sink cutout as guides, cut through the paper with a utility knife to make an opening at each corner *(right)*.

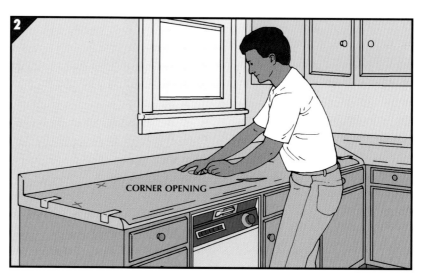

3. Removing the old countertop.

◆ Using a flashlight to illuminate the dark corners, examine cabinet corner braces for screws in the underside of the countertop. Remove any screws you find and save them for securing the new countertop.

◆ Remove the screws that secure the dishwasher to the underside of the countertop.

◆ If the space between the backsplash and the wall is filled with caulk, cut the caulk away with a utility knife.

◆ With a helper, lift the old countertop from the cabinets.

INSTALLING THE NEW COUNTERTOP

1. Marking a sink cutout.
◆ Cut 2-by-2s to support the new countertop when marking and cutting the sink opening. With a helper, set the countertop on the supports.
◆ Tape the template to the countertop using the marks that were made earlier to position it.
◆ With a marker, transfer the corners cut into the template to the countertop *(left)*. Remove the template and join the corners with the marker and a straightedge.
◆ Cover the resulting outline of the sink cutout with strips of 2-inch-wide masking tape to protect the laminate when you saw it. If the cutting line is not visible through the tape, remove the tape and darken the line, then replace the tape.

2. Cutting the sink opening.
◆ Screw a handle to the countertop in the center of the cutout, then drill a 1-inch-diameter hole inside the cutout area, near a corner.
◆ Fit a blade suitable for cutting laminate into a saber saw. Start the saw with the blade in the hole and cut toward the line, then along it *(left)*.
◆ As you approach the end of the cut, grasp the handle to prevent the waste piece from sagging, which might split the laminate.

3. Positioning the countertop.

◆ While you lift the countertop slightly at the sink cutout, have a helper slide out the front 2-by-2 support, followed by the rear support *(above)*.

◆ For an L-shaped cabinet, lift the other countertop section onto the cabinet to help align both pieces while you finish installing the first one.

◆ Set the sink in the cutout, adjusting sink and countertop so that the sink drain aligns with the drainpipe in the wall and the backsplash fits against the wall.

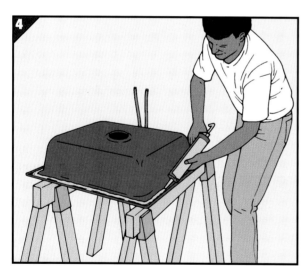

4. Caulking the sink.

◆ Pencil a line perpendicular to the front edge of the sink and continue it onto the countertop to mark the sink position. Draw a similar line at one edge of the sink, then remove the sink and support it upside down above the floor.

◆ Clean any old caulk from the underside of the sink, then apply a thin bead of caulk around the outer edge of the sink lip *(above)*.

◆ Apply a $\frac{1}{4}$-inch-thick bead of caulk to the countertop around the edge of the sink cutout.

5. Reinstalling the sink.

◆ To avoid disturbing the fresh caulk, lift the sink by the base of the faucet and the drain hole.

◆ Set the sink into the cutout, aligning the pencil marks on the sink edges with those on the countertop.

◆ Reconnect all plumbing detached during removal of the sink.

◆ Screw in the anchors that hold the sink in place, drilling pilot holes for the screws if necessary.

◆ Wipe excess caulk from around the sink edge with a rag dampened with denatured alcohol.

6. Securing the countertop.

◆ To bore pilot holes for the anchoring screws from the old countertop, use a drill bit slightly narrower than the screws. Prevent the bit from going all the way through the countertop by wrapping the bit with tape. Place the tape at a distance from the drill tip equal to the screw length less $\frac{1}{8}$ inch.

◆ Drill pilot holes through the existing holes in the cabinet corner braces as shown at left. (Pilot holes need not be vertical.) Screw the countertop in place.

◆ Screw the dishwasher to the underside of the countertop.

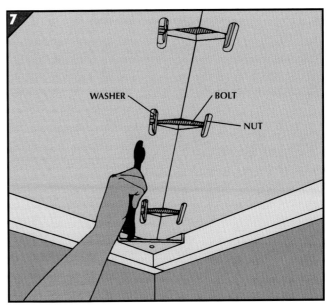

7. Completing an L-shaped countertop.

◆ Slide the unfastened section along the cabinet and apply a thin bead of caulk to the mitered edge. Then slip the sections together again.

◆ Insert a corner fastener—a bolt with a rectangular nut and washer—in each of the channels precut at the joint. With a helper to hold the countertop sections flush with each other, tighten the fasteners with a wrench, back to front *(right)*. Wipe excess caulk from the joint.

◆ Screw the countertop to the cabinet.

8. Caulking the backsplash.

To prevent water seepage between the countertop and the wall, fill the gap between the top of the backsplash and the wall with a bead of caulk. It is not necessary to seal the ends of the backsplash.

Durable glazed tile is virtually impossible to scratch, stain, or scorch, and the shiny, nonporous finish provides a sanitary work surface. Standard $4\frac{1}{4}$-inch-square tiles and latex-based grout both come in a wide variety of colors.

Buying Tile: First, calculate the square footage of your countertop, then add 10 percent to allow for wastage when cutting tiles and in case you ever need a replacement. Measure the countertop edge to determine how many trim tiles you'll need, and note your requirements for special tiles—mitered pieces for inside corners and caps for outside corners. The top row of the backsplash requires bullnose tiles, including a pair of double-bullnose units for the ends.

The Layout: The most appealing design will satisfy three goals: uniform grout joints, a symmetrical arrangement around the sink, and no tiles less than 1 inch wide—they are hard to cut and unsightly.

Make a dry run using plastic spacers or the molded-in tabs on some tiles to provide $\frac{1}{8}$-inch grout joints. If that approach fails, try the suggestions at the bottom of the opposite page. You can make all the necessary cuts yourself to fit tiles around the sink and against the wall. The trim tiles, however, must be cut by a tile supplier.

Preparing the Countertop: Remove the sink, as shown on page 102, and the old backsplash. If removing the backsplash is impracticable, you can tile over it *(page 111)*. Fill any nicks or cracks in the countertop with wood putty, then sand it with coarse (60-grit) sandpaper.

If the counter overhangs the base cabinets, either glue and nail strips of wood to the underside to make the edge as deep as the trim tile, or cut off the overhang with a circular saw; set the blade to the thickness of the countertop and adjust the saw guide to cut it flush with the edge of the cabinets.

 **TOOLS**

Framing square
Notched spreader
Tile nippers
Tile cutter
Tile sander
Rubber-faced grout float
Caulk gun

 **MATERIALS**

Epoxy adhesive and solvent
Latex-based grout
Silicone caulk
Silicone-based grout sealant

SAFETY TIPS

Rubber gloves protect your hands when you are mixing and applying tile adhesive, grout, and sealant. Wear safety goggles when cutting tile to shield your eyes from flying chips.

LAYING OUT A DRY RUN

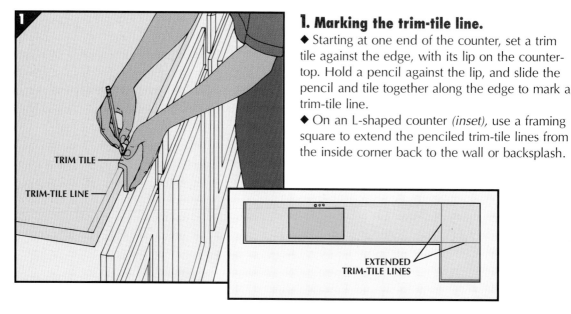

TRIM TILE
TRIM-TILE LINE
EXTENDED TRIM-TILE LINES

1. Marking the trim-tile line.
◆ Starting at one end of the counter, set a trim tile against the edge, with its lip on the countertop. Hold a pencil against the lip, and slide the pencil and tile together along the edge to mark a trim-tile line.
◆ On an L-shaped counter *(inset)*, use a framing square to extend the penciled trim-tile lines from the inside corner back to the wall or backsplash.

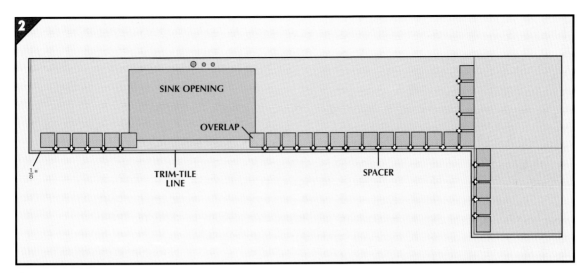

2. Laying a dry run.

◆ Place two rows of tiles on the countertop, one of them $\frac{1}{8}$ inch—the width of a spacer tab—behind the trim-tile line, the other at right angles to the first and continuing to the wall. On a straight countertop, position the first tile $\frac{1}{8}$ inch inside the trim-tile line at the end of the countertop. For an L-shaped counter *(above),* begin at the extended trim-tile line in the corner.

◆ Where a tile protrudes over the sink opening, measure the overlap and match it when positioning the first tile at the opposite side of the opening. Continue the dry run to within a tile width of the end of the countertop. Repeat the procedure for the other arm of an L-shaped unit.

◆ Place tiles along the front of the sink opening, working from the corners toward the center.

◆ Examine the dry run. If it requires tiles less than 1 inch wide to fit around the sink opening or to fill any gaps, widen the tile spacing *(below).*

Adjusting the Layout

One way to fix a dry run that calls for tiles less than 1 inch wide is to spread the tiles farther apart—the joints can be up to $\frac{1}{4}$ inch wide. If this approach fails, try marking the centerline of the sink opening on the countertop. Then center either a tile or a grout joint on the mark and work outward to the corners. Should neither of these tactics solve the problem, you may have to settle for an asymmetrical arrangement of tiles around the sink.

Spacers are of no help in achieving uniform grout joints if they are wider than $\frac{1}{8}$ inch. Instead, make a joint gauge from a 3-foot piece of $\frac{1}{4}$-inch wood lath. Without disturbing the dry run, lay the lath flush with a tile edge and mark its edge at the corners of several tiles *(left).* Use this gauge to position tiles on the countertop, left to right and front to rear.

3. Working around the sink.

◆ Remove the tile next to the one overlapping each corner of the sink opening, and lay a framing square against the cabinet face as shown at right. Pencil a line on both sides of the opening from the front of the counter to the wall.

◆ Set a row of tiles along these lines, using spacers or the joint gauge to keep the joints uniform, then lay a row of tiles behind the opening flush against the wall.

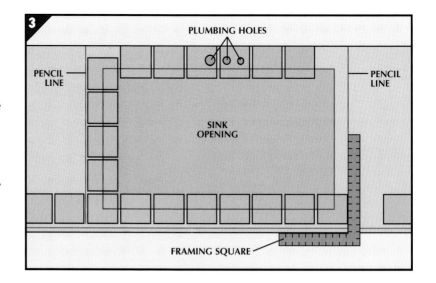

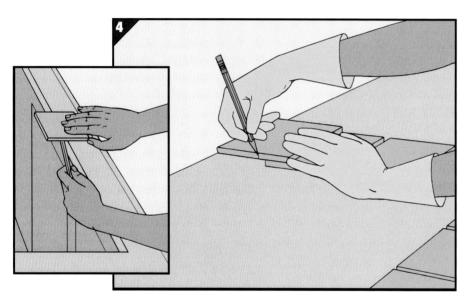

4. Marking the tiles for cutting.

◆ Wherever tiles extend over the sink opening, mark a cutting line on the underside by drawing the pencil along the edge of the opening *(far left)*. At the back of the opening, mark tiles to fit between the wall and plumbing holes in the countertop.

◆ For a row of partial tiles against the wall *(left)*, place a tile facedown on top of a full tile in the preceding row, edge against the wall. Mark both sides of the overlapping tile one joint width from the edge of the underlying tile, then join these marks across the face of the tile.

TWO TECHNIQUES FOR CUTTING TILE

A tabletop tile cutter.

◆ Set a marked tile on the padded base, lift the handle, and push it forward until the scoring wheel touches the tile's far edge.

◆ Then place the wheel on the cutting line, set the adjustable fence against the side of the tile, and tighten the thumbscrew. The fence helps hold the tile and simplifies cutting several tiles to the same width.

◆ Pulling up on the handle, slide it toward you to score the tile *(right)*.

◆ To break the tile, rest the heel on the tile and press firmly on the handle.

⚠ CAUTION *Cut tiles are sharp. Dull the edges with a tile sander, available from any tile supplier.*

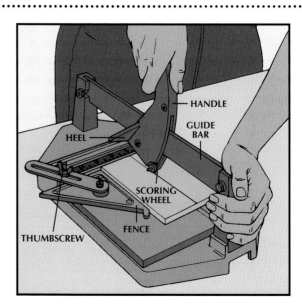

Irregular cuts with tile nippers.

◆ Position the jaws of the nippers to take a $\frac{1}{8}$-inch bite from the edge of the tile, then squeeze the handles to nip off a small piece of tile.
◆ Continue taking $\frac{1}{8}$-inch bites until you reach the cutting line.

SETTING TILES IN ADHESIVE

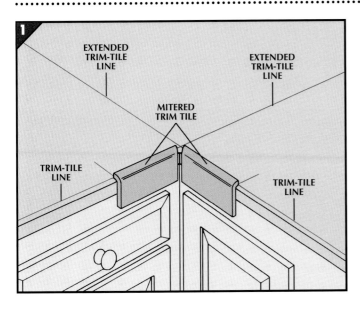

1. Setting the trim tiles.

◆ For an L-shaped counter *(left)*, make two marks at the countertop edge, each a tile width from one of the extended trim-tile lines.
◆ Using a notched trowel, spread epoxy-based adhesive on both inside surfaces of a mitered-corner trim tile. Align the tile with the marks and the trim-tile line at the L's inside corner, and press the tile firmly in place without sliding it along the surface. Repeat for the other corner trim tile, then, using spacers or a joint gauge, proceed to both ends of the counter. Stick caps to outside corners, then continue to the walls with trim tiles.
◆ On a straight counter, start the row of trim with an outside corner cap—or with the tile at one end of a countertop that is set between walls or cabinets.

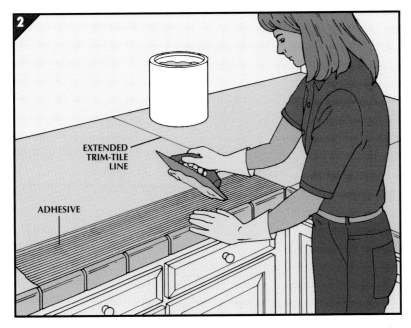

2. Spreading the adhesive.

◆ Starting at one end of a straight counter or the inside corner of an L-shaped counter, spread a band of adhesive one tile wide about 24 inches along the countertop.
◆ On a straight counter, start in one corner and align the edges of a square tile with a trim tile. Press it down firmly without sliding it across the adhesive. On an L-shaped counter, align a square tile with the mitered trim tile and the extended trim-tile line.
◆ Then set a row of tiles along the entire band of adhesive.

3. Laying surface tiles.

◆ Spread adhesive between the first row of tiles and the wall. Working from the edge of the countertop toward the wall, set a row of tiles along the edge of a straight counter or the extended trim-tile line of an L-shaped counter *(left)*.

◆ Continue to set tiles in diagonal rows until all the adhesive is covered.

4. Tamping the tiles.

◆ Level the tiles you have laid so far with a straight 2-by-4 about 18 inches long. Place the board facedown on the tiles and move it around, gently tapping it with a hammer to force protruding tiles into the adhesive. Wipe away excess adhesive with a solvent recommended by the manufacturer.

◆ Finish tiling the countertop, a section at a time.

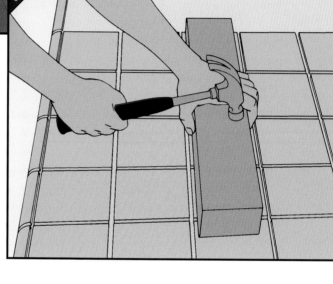

5. Making a backsplash.

◆ Mark the height of a bullnose tile on the wall at several points. Add the width of a grout joint to this mark, and draw a pencil line across the wall at this level.

◆ Spread a band of adhesive 24 inches along the wall between the countertop tiles and the pencil line. Set bullnose tiles into the adhesive, each with the curved edge at the line and the sides aligned with the corresponding tile on the countertop. Continue setting tiles along the length of the backsplash. At each end of the backsplash, set a double-bullnose tile—one with two rounded edges.

◆ Let the adhesive cure for 24 hours.

BULLNOSE TILE

PENCILED LINE

ADHESIVE

Most laminate countertops have built-in backsplashes, typically $\frac{3}{4}$ inch thick and 4 inches high. If the backsplash cannot be detached easily, you can tile it to match the countertop.

The front face is covered with regular square tiles; measure and cut them two joint widths shorter than the backsplash height. In addition, cut two tiles to leave one joint width uncovered at the ends of the backsplash.

Cover the top of the backsplash with bullnose tiles, cut so that the rounded front edges are even with the faces of the vertical tiles. On the rectangular end of the backsplash, use a double-bullnose tile—rounded on two adjacent sides—with the rounded edges even with the top and front of the backsplash.

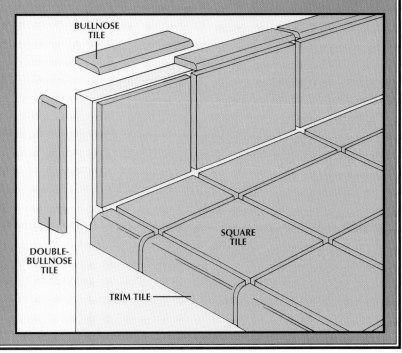

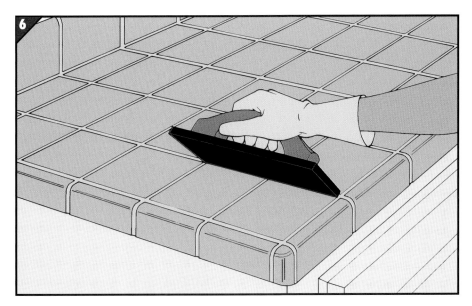

6. Grouting the counter and backsplash.

◆ Press twisted strips of newspaper into the joint between countertop and backsplash tiles to prevent grout from entering.

◆ Scoop grout onto the tiles, 1 cup at a time. Sweep the edge of a rubber-faced float diagonally across the surface several times to force the grout into the joints.

◆ Compact the grout in each joint with the edge of the float (above) so that the grout is slightly below the surface of the tiles.

◆ When all joints are filled, clean the float and sweep it across the tiles like a squeegee to remove excess grout. Wipe the surface with a damp sponge, and let it dry. Polish off any grout haze with a soft cloth. Caulk the joint between the countertop and the backsplash.

◆ Let the grout cure for three days, then spray the joints with a silicone-based sealer to prevent stains and leaks.

New Faces for Old Cabinets

One economical alternative to installing new kitchen cabinets is to reface the old ones. The job consists of replacing old doors and drawer fronts with new ones and veneering the cabinet frames to match.

Acquiring Materials: Supplies for the job are available through millworks, cabinetmakers, or firms that specialize in cabinet refacing. After choosing a style and finish for the new doors and drawer fronts, order veneer in a matching finish to cover the ends and faces of the cabinets.

Two kinds of veneer are required. Thin peel-and-stick veneer for the cabinet faces comes in sections that are 2 by 8 feet and are precoated with a pressure-sensitive adhesive. Veneer for cabinet ends is mounted on $\frac{1}{8}$-inch plywood and is available only in 4- by 8-foot sheets. Ask your supplier to cut the veneer for you slightly larger than the ends of your cabinets.

Things Not to Overlook: Besides the veneer, you'll want prefinished molding to trim the tops of eye-level cabinets and the ends where they meet the kitchen ceiling and walls. To fill joints and nail holes, ask for a touch-up kit containing a wood crayon—a stick of filler that matches the finish on the veneer.

The face of many a cabinet extends $\frac{1}{4}$ inch beyond the ends, creating a void that must be filled before the ends can be veneered. For this purpose, purchase $\frac{1}{4}$-inch luan plywood, which is named for the tree whose wood gives the material a smooth surface ideally suited to adhering veneer.

 **TOOLS**

Utility knife	Level
Hand roller	Circular saw with
Fine-toothed hand-	plywood blade
saw	Backsaw
Combination square	Miter box
Nail set	$\frac{1}{4}$-inch drill

 **MATERIALS**

Doors	Drawer pulls
Plywood-backed veneer	Drawer fronts
Peel-and-stick veneer	Contact cement
Trim molding	$\frac{1}{4}$-inch luan plywood
Hinges	Medium sandpaper
Door handles	Clear lacquer spray
	$1\frac{1}{4}$-inch finishing nails
	Wood filler
	Wood crayon
	Felt or plastic bumpers

VENEERING CABINET ENDS

1. Preparing the cabinet frames.

◆ Remove drawers, doors, and hinges from the cabinet frames. Pry off any trim and save the pieces as guides for cutting new molding.

◆ Strip painted surfaces and fill nail and screw holes with wood filler. Sand the cabinets smooth, then wipe them clean with a damp cloth.

◆ If necessary, measure and cut pieces of $\frac{1}{4}$-inch luan plywood to fit between the stiles and the wall *(right)*. With a small paint roller, coat the plywood and cabinet ends with contact cement. Press the plywood to the cabinet and secure it with $\frac{1}{2}$-inch nails.

◆ Spray the cabinet exterior and plywood with three coats of clear lacquer.

2. Securing the veneer.

◆ Hold a piece of veneer against the end of the cabinet. Run a pencil along front and bottom edges of the cabinet to mark guidelines on the back of the veneer.

◆ With a circular saw, trim the piece about $\frac{1}{16}$ inch shorter and $\frac{1}{16}$ inch wider than marked.

◆ Coat the cabinet and the back of the veneer with contact cement. Press the plywood in place, with one edge against the wall and another even with the bottom of the cabinet.

◆ Sand the protruding edge of the veneer piece flush with the end stile *(right)*, then spray clear lacquer on the sanded edge. Recoat any sanded areas of the stile.

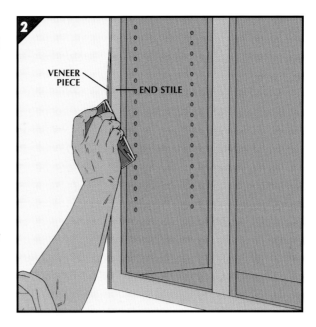

VENEER PIECE

END STILE

PEEL-AND-STICK VENEER AROUND OPENINGS

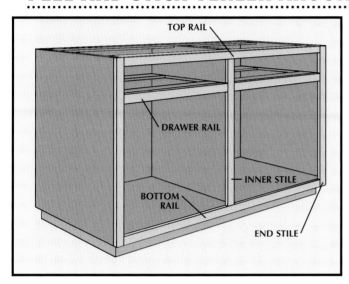

TOP RAIL

DRAWER RAIL

INNER STILE

BOTTOM RAIL

END STILE

The best sequence.

The cabinet face is composed of vertical pieces, called stiles, and horizontal ones, called rails *(left)*. Using the technique shown below, veneer each piece individually, beginning with the end stiles. Cover top and bottom rails next, followed by inner stiles. Veneer drawer rails last.

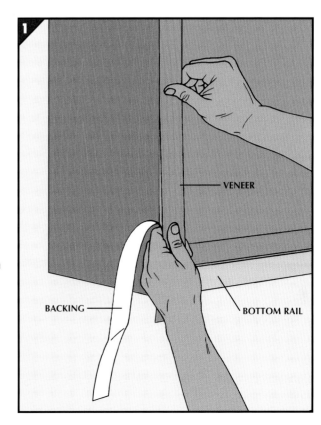

VENEER

BACKING

BOTTOM RAIL

1. Veneering end stiles.

◆ With a straightedge and utility knife, cut two strips of veneer that are $\frac{1}{2}$ inch wider and 1 inch longer than the end stiles.

◆ Peel a few inches of backing from one strip and, with the grain running vertically, lightly press it against the stile, flush with the top. Working down the stile, continue peeling off the backing and pressing the veneer against the cabinet *(right)*. Cover the other end stile in the same way.

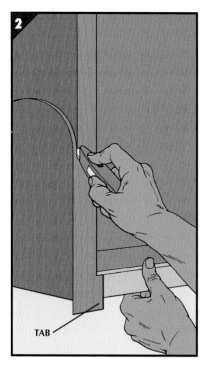

TAB

2. Trimming the veneer.

◆ Run a utility knife down the inner edge of each stile, then cut along the top of the bottom rail, leaving a small tab of veneer on the bottom rail.

◆ Next trim along the outer edge of the stile *(above)* and the bottom edge of the rail.

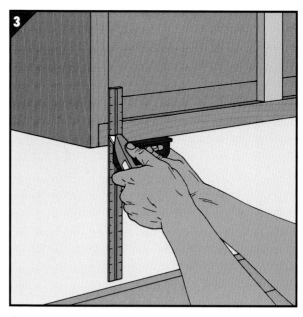

3. Covering the rails.

◆ Cut two strips of veneer $\frac{1}{2}$ inch wider than the top and bottom rails and long enough to overlap both end stiles.

◆ Press the veneer against the rails as described in Step 1, then trim the veneer along the top and bottom edges of both rails.

◆ Using a combination square as shown above, cut through the rail veneer and the tab of stile veneer at each end of the two rails. Remove the scraps thus formed, and press the rail veneer into place.

◆ Follow the same procedure to veneer first the inner stiles and then the drawer rails.

4. Finishing up.

◆ When all the peel-and-stick veneer is in place, run a hand roller along the stiles and rails to permanently bond the veneer to the cabinet face.

◆ Cut trim molding with a backsaw and a miter box to cover the joints that the cabinets form with the walls and the ceiling. Nail the molding to the cabinets with $1\frac{1}{4}$-inch finishing nails *(right)*.

◆ Sink the nail heads into the trim molding with a nail set.

◆ Conceal the nail holes—as well as joints between pieces of molding and veneer—with a wood crayon.

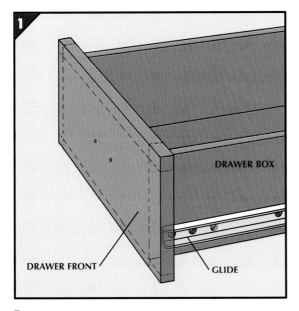

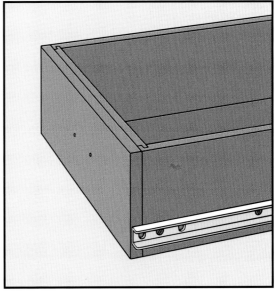

1. Putting on new drawer fronts.

◆ Remove the old drawer fronts if you can do so without damaging the drawer box. Otherwise, unscrew the drawer glides and trim each front flush with the drawer box *(dotted lines, above left)* using a fine-toothed saw. Reposition the drawer glides so that they are flush with the drawer front as shown above right, and drill two screw holes through the drawer front and the drawer box.

◆ Lay a new drawer front on the floor with the finish side down, and center the drawer box on it. Through the screw holes in the box, mark the front for pilot holes and drill them as shown on page 4. Then screw on the new front from inside the drawer.

2. Hanging new doors.

◆ Attach hinges to each door 2 to 3 inches from the top and bottom edges.

◆ With a helper holding the door in place, center it on the door opening and level it *(left)*. Then reach inside the cabinet and mark the frame for pilot holes where the hinges will attach to the cabinet frame. Drill pilot holes, and mount the door.

◆ Install the adjacent door by aligning it with the level on the one that is already in place.

◆ Mount the door and drawer handles and put felt or plastic bumpers on the inside of the doors and the drawers to protect the veneer.

If your kitchen floor is worn or damaged beyond repair, or if you just want a new look, you may want to consider using vinyl. Available in square tiles *(page 122)* or in large sheets, vinyl flooring comes in a wide variety of colors and patterns with a durable, no-wax finish. Vinyl is also easy to install; doing the project yourself will result in a significant cost savings.

One of the biggest advantages of vinyl is that it can usually be laid right over the existing floor. A variety of products are available to smooth and level the old surface in preparation for installation of a new floor. Talk to a salesperson when purchasing your new flooring, and read the manufacturer's instructions to determine what you need.

Measurements and Preparations: To calculate how much flooring you will have to buy, mea-sure the dimensions of your kitchen floor at the widest and longest points in the room and add 6 inches at each wall for overlap. If you find you will need more than one sheet, note the width of the pattern repetition on the flooring you have chosen; it is usually print-ed on the back of the sheet. For ex-ample, if your pattern repeats every 3 feet, allow 3 feet of extra width when you buy the material.

Before beginning the installa-tion, remove the shoe molding or vinyl wall base as shown on pages 20 and 22 and move appliances out of the kitchen so the new flooring can be laid underneath. Scoot these heavy items on a piece of hardboard to protect the floor.

The Finishing Touch: When the floor is in place, attach metal edg-ing at the kitchen doorways to con-ceal the edge of the vinyl sheet.

TOOLS

Utility knife
Notched spreader
Rolling pin
Metal yardstick

MATERIALS

Vinyl-flooring adhesive
Seam sealer

CUTTING THE MATERIAL TO FIT

1. Rolling out the material.
◆ Let the material adjust to room tem-perature for an hour or so; then, if you are using more than one sheet, start in one corner and unroll the larger sheet from the longest wall of the room. Leave 6 inches of overlap at each wall.
◆ When you reach a large immovable object, such as a center island, you will need to leave 6 inches of overlap as you cut around it. Reach under the roll and unroll the sheet back toward the starting wall *(right)*. Push the un-rolled section against the object and, about 6 inches above the floor, cut from the outside edge toward the cen-ter with a utility knife. When you are about 6 inches short of the vertical side of the object, cut back toward the starting wall; make this cut at least 6 inches shorter than the object's depth.

2. Fitting around a large object.

Lift the roll over the object and lower it to the floor on the other side. Holding the corner of the flap you have made in the sheet, cut at a right angle toward the outside edge of the sheet. This should give you a 6-inch overlap along all three sides of the object.

3. Reversing the roll.

◆ Unroll the sheet completely, then pull it back and reroll the sheet from the far edge as shown at left. The tightness of the inner part of the original roll compresses the pattern; unless the roll is reversed briefly, the pattern will be smaller in one part of the room than the other.

◆ Unroll the sheet again and press it into all corners, to the extent that its natural resiliency will allow.

4. Laying the second sheet.

◆ Before bringing the second sheet into the kitchen, measure the width of uncovered floor from the first sheet's edge to the opposite wall. Add 6 inches, plus the amount of overlap required to match the pattern.

◆ Unroll the second sheet completely in an area free of obstructions. Mark the above measurement on the sheet and cut. Reroll the sheet and bring it into the kitchen.

◆ Starting again from the longest wall, roll the second sheet out as far as the obstruction, then pull it over the first sheet until the patterns match *(above)*. Cut and fit the second sheet around objects as you did the first, leaving 6-inch overlaps at the walls.

5. Trimming the edges.

Pull the second sheet off the first and out of the way. At each wall and object, cut the first sheet back to about 3 inches above the floor *(left)*. Take care in making this cut—you are now close to the final trim.

BONDING THE VINYL TO THE FLOOR

1. Applying the adhesive.
Pull the first sheet halfway back upon itself. With a notched trowel, spread adhesive over the exposed floor as closely as possible to the walls and corners, but leaving bare a 6-inch strip along the line where the first sheet will meet the second.

2. Affixing the first sheet.
Lift the edge of the sheet high above the floor and slowly walk it back into place over the adhesive. Press it against the wall and into the corners as closely as its resiliency will allow.

3. Rolling out the bumps.
With a rolling pin, start from the center and roll the material toward each of its edges. Work slowly, and be sure to flatten any bulges or air bubbles in the vinyl's surface.

4. Making the final cuts.

◆ To crease the material, press a metal yardstick into the angle where walls or objects meet the floor. Then slice along the edge of the yardstick with a utility knife *(right)*. Make the cuts as straight and accurate as possible; shoe molding or wall base will cover errors up to about $\frac{1}{2}$ inch.

◆ Repeat Steps 1 through 4 for the other half of the sheet.

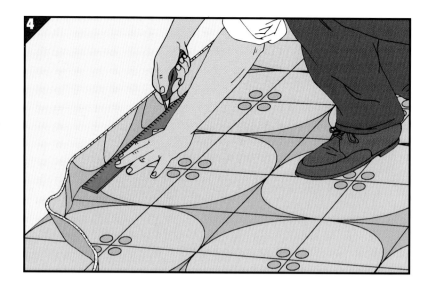

MATCHING THE PATTERN AT SEAMS

1. Cutting off the trim.

Place a metal yardstick along the overlap edge of the second vinyl sheet. With a utility knife, cut off the $\frac{1}{2}$- to 1-inch trim along this edge. On inlaid vinyl this trim is likely to be an extra-wide grout line; cut along the line so that its width matches the widths of the other grout lines in the pattern.

2. Matching the pattern.

Pull the second sheet over the first until the patterns of the two sheets match perfectly *(left)*. Note the pattern carefully to be sure the overlap continues the pattern in the same manner—a mismatched pattern will spoil the appearance of the finished job.

3. Cutting off the overlap.

◆ Place a metal yardstick along a grout line or other inconspicuous part of the pattern where the seam is less likely to show. Then, cut straight down through both sheets. Don't worry if it takes more than one pass with the knife to cut completely through the material; the important thing is that the cut be straight and clean. Remove the strips you have cut; the sheets should now abut tightly and have a perfect pattern match.

◆ Lay the second sheet as you did the first, trimming overlaps to 3 inches around objects and against walls.

◆ Spread adhesive to within 6 inches of the edge of the first sheet, and make a final trim along each wall and object.

4. Applying adhesive under the seam.

Follow the manufacturer's directions for sealing the seam between two sheets. Some vinyl flooring requires a special sealing adhesive below the sheets; with others you use regular adhesive underneath and seal the seam from the top.

◆ Pull back the butted edges on both sheets and spread adhesive over the bare floor along the entire length of the seam. Then press the sheets back in place, pushing the edges together until you get a tight fit.

◆ If seam sealer is called for by the manufacturer, proceed immediately to Step 5.

5. Sealing the seam.

Press the seam together with the thumb and fingers of one hand while applying seam sealer with the other. Wipe away any excess sealer immediately and keep off the seam for at least 24 hours.

The Versatility of Vinyl Tiles

Vinyl tiles offer virtually endless design possibilities for a kitchen floor. More often than not, tiles are laid in rows parallel to the walls of the room, but there are other options as well. You can, for example, create a diagonal checkerboard of contrasting colors, a pattern that can make a small kitchen look larger.

Learning from a Dry Run: Begin by snapping chalk lines *(page 123)* to divide the room into roughly equal quadrants, then lay tiles along the lines. For a simple parallel layout, begin the dry run at the inter-section, and set tiles along each line to the walls. The dry run for a diagonal checkerboard, explained on these pages, is somewhat more complex. In either case, if the dry run would result in cutting very small pieces of tile in order to fill in along walls and elsewhere, start over with chalk lines in slightly different locations.

Laying the Tiles: When the dry run is satisfactory, prepare the old surface as described on page 116, then begin laying the tiles. Fill in a parallel pattern one quadrant at a time, working from the center to the walls. A checkerboard pattern proceeds as shown beginning at the bottom of this page. Cut tiles to fit in spaces against walls and cabinets, taking care that the edges you cut form the outer edge of the floor, where they can be covered by baseboard.

When all the tiles are down, wipe up any excess adhesive, then press the tiles against the floor with a rolling pin or with a tile roller, which lets you do the work standing up. Keep traffic to a minimum for 48 hours to let the adhesive cure.

 **TOOLS**

 **MATERIALS**

Tape measure	Contour gauge	Vinyl tiles
Framing square	Notched trowel	Premixed adhesive
Chalk line	Scissors	Masking tape
Utility knife	Rolling pin	Paper

ESTABLISHING THE LAYOUT

1. Determining the starting point.
◆ Mark the center of the main kitchen doorway on the threshold. If there is no threshold to serve as a baseline, establish the center point on a line drawn between the corners of the doorframe.
◆ Position a framing square at the midpoint of the doorway *(right),* and draw a pencil line about 2 feet into the kitchen.

2. Marking the primary axis.

◆ With a helper, stretch a chalk line from the doorway to the opposite wall. Hold your end on the center point of the doorway, and have your helper move the other end to position the string directly over the pencil line on the floor.

◆ Holding the chalk line taut, with both ends pressed against the floor, lift the line directly upward a few inches and let go. It will snap to the floor, leaving a straight line of powdered chalk.

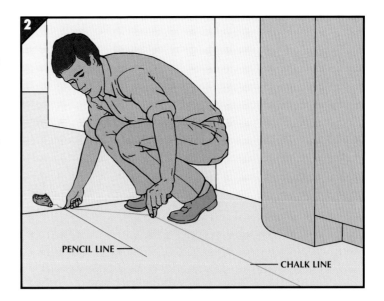

PENCIL LINE —

—— CHALK LINE

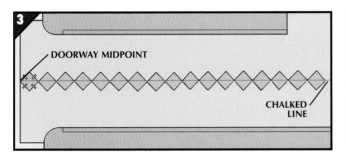

DOORWAY MIDPOINT

CHALKED LINE

3. Starting the dry run.

◆ Place a tile diagonally along the chalked line with one corner at the point marking the center of the doorway. Tape it to the floor with masking tape.

◆ Set tiles of a single color along the chalked line until you come within 1 tile width of the wall *(above)*.

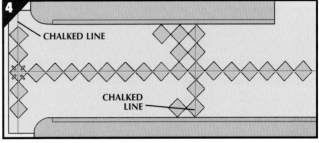

CHALKED LINE

CHALKED LINE

4. Establishing secondary axes.

◆ At about the midpoint of the dry run—and wherever the room widens into an alcove or into a T or L shape—snap a chalk line the width of the room and perpendicular to the primary axis.

◆ Lay tiles of a single color along each of these secondary axes.

STICKING DOWN THE TILES

1. Laying the first tile.

◆ Note the working time of the adhesive, and make a conservative estimate of the area you can cover with tile in that time. Pick up all the tiles from the dry run, then pour equal amounts of adhesive on both sides of the chalk line near the doorway. Spread the adhesive evenly with a notched trowel to the chalk line but not across it.

◆ Holding a tile as shown at left, set one corner on the adhesive on the baseline at the midpoint of the doorway. Align the other corner with the chalk line and let it fall onto the adhesive. This tile must be absolutely straight, since it will determine the alignment of all the rest. Adjust the tile if necessary by nudging it gently.

2. Working across the floor.

◆ Begin by laying tiles of one color, corner to corner, along the baseline. Next lay a row of tiles of contrasting colors, creating the pointed array at left. Fill in the half-tile spaces at the baseline.

◆ Continue laying rows of tiles along the sides of the point to extend it to the far end of the room, alternating colors and aligning tile edges carefully.

◆ Where the room widens, use the zigzag edge of the tiled area as a baseline from which to extend the tiles to the left or right.

CUTTING TILES TO FILL GAPS

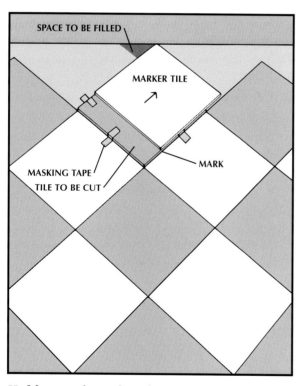

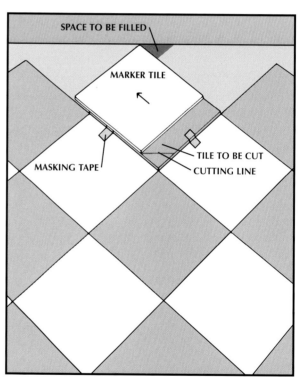

Making a triangular piece.

◆ Cut corners from tiles to fill small triangular spaces *(shaded area)* along walls. To do so, tape the tile to be cut—here a dark one—on a tile of the same color. Set a third tile on top to act as a marker.

◆ Slide the marker tile diagonally to the wall

(above, left). At the corner farthest from the wall, pencil a mark on the tile to be cut. Slide the marker tile diagonally in the other direction, and make another mark *(above, right)*.

◆ With a utility knife, cut along a straight line joining the marks, and set the triangular piece in place.

Filling a five-sided space.

◆ Tape the tile to be cut—in this case a light one—on top of a tile of the same color, then set a marker tile alongside it.

◆ Slide the marker tile diagonally to the wall, and mark where the corner farthest from the wall touches the tile to be cut. Set the marker tile on the other side of the tile to be cut and repeat.

◆ Use a utility knife to cut the tile along a straight line drawn between the two marks, and fit the five-sided piece in place.

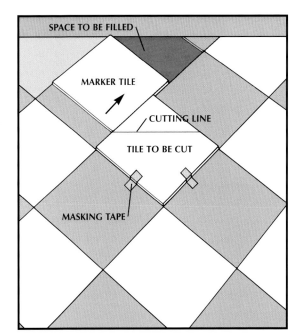

Cutting irregular shapes.

◆ To fit a tile against an irregularly shaped object, such as door molding, first cut a tile to fit the space to be filled as if the obstacle were not there.

CONTOUR GAUGE

◆ Then press a contour gauge against the irregular shape and part of the adjoining wall on either side, of it and lock the sliding fingers. Transfer the contour to the tile *(right)*.

◆ Warm the tile in a 200° oven for a few minutes, then cut it to shape with heavy-duty scissors.

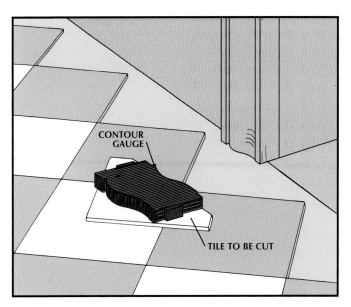

Fitting tiles under a low overhang.

◆ To fit a tile against the base of an overhanging cabinet or appliance, tape a tile-size piece of paper to a nearby tile and place a marker tile atop the paper.

◆ Slide a corner of the marker tile under the overhang and against the base. Hold a pencil against the corner as shown at right, and slide the marker tile along the base, keeping the edges parallel to the tile seams.

◆ Transfer the pencil line on the paper to a tile of the right color, and cut the tile to shape. If there is not enough room below the overhang to trowel the adhesive onto the floor, spread a thin coat on the underside of the cut tile before fitting it in place.

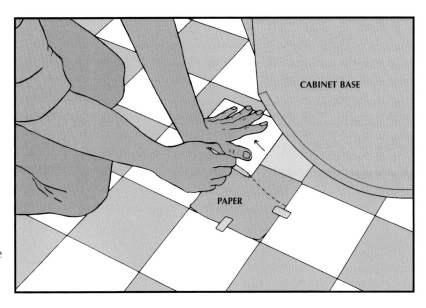

Common Bathroom Repairs

With surprisingly little time and effort, you can apply the methods described in the following pages to end drips, clogs, and other bathroom annoyances—and to replace worn-out fittings with attractive new ones. Keeping up with repairs not only makes your bathroom more comfortable, it also may prevent small problems from turning into big ones, as when an uncorrected leak damages the floor or walls.

Disassembling a bathtub faucet →

Replacing a Broken Accessory

Towel bars or a soap dish can be a handy addition to a tiled bathroom wall, but an accessory can be an eyesore if it breaks or is damaged. As shown below and at right, you can often replace the damaged item with no harm to the wall. Work carefully to avoid cracking nearby tiles, and keep them from loosening by laying strips of masking tape from one tile to the next.

A Variety of Accessories: Flush-set accessories, such as the soap dish below, are attached directly to the same backing that the tiles are mounted on. To avoid exposing the backing, replace a flush-set accessory with one of the same dimen-sions or slightly larger. Other accessories, such as the towel bar at right, are mounted to the tile surface. Replace a surface-mounted accessory with another that will attach to the same tiles; in the case of a towel bar, the new bar should be the same length as the one it replaces, so that its brackets rest on the same pair of tiles.

Some older bathrooms have recessed accessories, which are sunk into the tiled wall. You can often unscrew a recessed toilet-paper holder from its mounting bracket and install a new one, but a recessed soap dish or other sort of shelf cannot be replaced without extensive retiling.

TOOLS

Cold chisel	Electric drill with
Ball-peen hammer	carbide-tipped
Putty knife	masonry bit
Grout saw	Screwdriver
Punch	Hex wrench

SAFETY TIPS

Wear goggles as you free the accessory with hammer and chisel and whenever you drill into tile.

SETTING A SOAP DISH INTO A TILE WALL

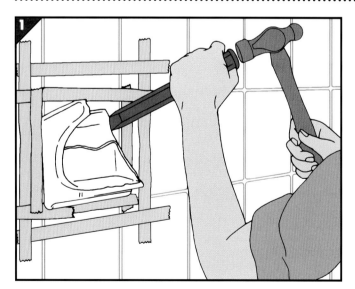

1. Removing the old soap dish.
◆ Protect the tile at the edge of the soap dish with masking tape. Hold down the nearby tiles with more tape.
◆ Remove any caulk or grout around the soap dish, then position a cold chisel at its edge. Tap with a ball-peen hammer *(above)* until the dish comes free.

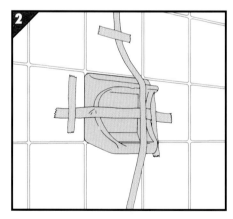

2. Positioning the new soap dish.
◆ Remove the tape and clean the exposed area with a putty knife.
◆ Apply silicone tile adhesive to the new soap dish, press it into place, and secure it with masking tape *(above)*.
◆ After 24 hours, take off the tape and grout the joints around the soap dish.

A SURFACE-MOUNTED TOWEL BAR

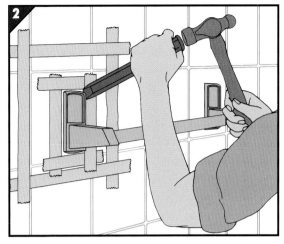

1. Preparing the surface.
◆ With a grout saw, cut out the grout around each tile to which the towel bar is attached *(above)*; this will help minimize any movement of the adjacent tiles as you work.
◆ Lay strips of masking tape around the edges of the towel bar's mounting brackets. For each bracket, add a square of masking tape over the nearby tiles.

2. Removing the old towel bar.
If you can, remove the old towel bar from its mounting brackets and unscrew the brackets. For brackets secured not with screws but with adhesive, place a cold chisel against each bracket and tap with a ball-peen hammer *(above)* to free it. Clean the exposed area and make sure any marred surface will be covered by the mounting brackets of the new towel bar you select.

3. Preparing the wall for drilling.
For screw-mounted brackets, check whether you can reuse the old screw holes; otherwise, drill new holes large enough for hollow-wall anchors.
◆ Hold a bracket in place; if it has tapered edges, position them at top and bottom. Mark the screw hole. Position the second bracket with a level and mark that hole as well. With a punch, make an indentation on each mark *(left)*.
◆ Fit an electric drill with a carbide-tipped masonry bit; keeping the drill speed as low as possible, make a hole at each indentation.

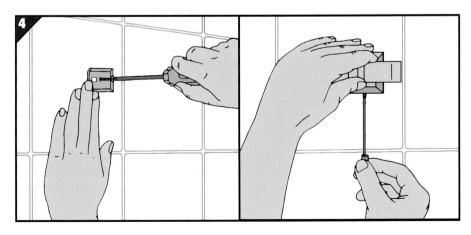

4. Installing the towel bar.
◆ For brackets without screw holes, apply tile adhesive, press the brackets into place, and allow to dry. For screw-mounted brackets, seat hollow-wall anchors in the drilled holes, then screw the brackets into place *(far left)*.
◆ Slip the towel bar onto the mounting brackets; secure a metal towel bar by tightening setscrews with a hex wrench or screwdriver *(near left)*.
◆ Regrout the tile joints that you cut out in Step 1, above.

Often a bathroom faucet with a dripping spout or leaking handles can be fixed with a small investment of time and some spare parts. Although they come in many sizes and shapes, for repair purposes most faucets are grouped into four types: stem, cartridge, disk, and ball.

Stem, or compression, faucets, depicted here and on pages 132 and 133, employ hard-rubber seat washers to provide a tight seal. When stem faucets drip, check for worn washers. You may also need to replace the stem and the seat, metal parts that come in contact with the washers. For a leaking handle, tighten the packing nut *(below)* or replace the packing washer.

Cartridge, disk, and ball faucets, all of which usually have single handles, develop drips and leaks less often. When they do, repair methods differ from one type to another, as shown on pages 134 to 137. In each case, the trick is to know how to disassemble the faucet.

Before You Begin: As with any plumbing job, locate the main shut-off valve in your house ahead of time in case of emergency. Turn off the shutoff valves below the basin and drain the faucet. If the valves will not close, turn off the main valve; drain the system by opening the faucets at the highest point in the house and working down to the lowest point. This prevents a vacuum from forming.

Plug the drain so parts cannot fall in, and protect the sink with a towel. As you work, set parts aside in the exact order you remove them to allow for easier reassembly.

TOOLS

Utility knife
Screwdriver
Adjustable wrench
Long-nose pliers
Vise
Flashlight
Seat wrench
Hex wrench

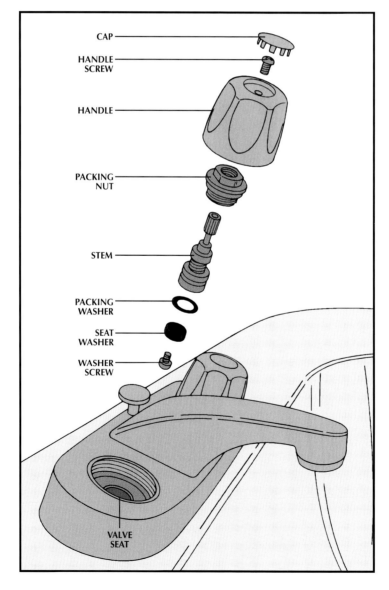

CAP
HANDLE SCREW
HANDLE
PACKING NUT
STEM
PACKING WASHER
SEAT WASHER
WASHER SCREW
VALVE SEAT

The inner anatomy of a stem faucet.

Although they vary in design, most stem faucets include the basic components shown at left. Each of the two handles is secured by a screw, often concealed under a decorative cap. The screw attaches the handle to the packing nut located at the top of the stem. Under the stem and packing washer, the seat washer closes against the valve seat to cut off the flow of water to the spout.

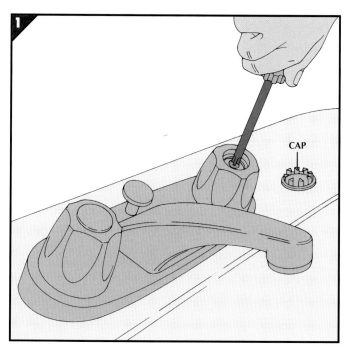

1. Removing a stem-faucet handle.

When a stem faucet drips, repair both hot and cold faucet assemblies. Do one at a time.

◆ Pry out the cap on one handle with a utility knife.

◆ Remove the screw and pull the handle straight up. If it is wedged on tight, protect the basin or base plate underneath with a towel and pry the handle off with a screwdriver. If it is very resistant, use a faucet-handle puller *(below).*

TRICKS OF THE TRADE

Freeing a Handle

A stubborn handle can be freed with a faucet-handle puller without marring the finish. Insert the center shaft into the hole on the handle, and fit the puller arms under it. Turn the puller handle clockwise to lift the faucet handle off.

CENTER SHAFT

2. Removing the packing nut.

Unscrew the packing nut with an adjustable wrench *(above).* The stem below may come out with the nut; to separate them, protect the stem with electrician's tape, clamp it in a vise, and remove the nut with the wrench.

3. Taking out the stem.

◆ Try to unscrew the stem by hand *(right).*

◆ Should that fail, set the handle on the stem and turn it in the same direction that you would to turn on the water; this will remove most stems.

◆ If the stem does not unscrew, the faucet may be a diaphragm or a cartridge type; remove the stem as described on page 132.

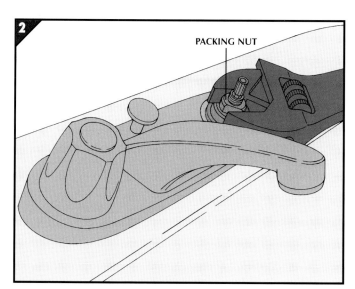

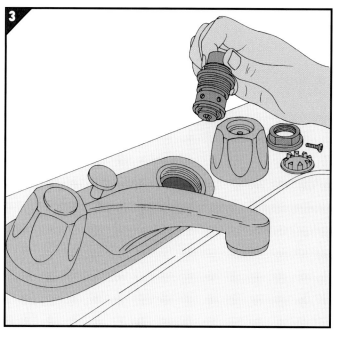

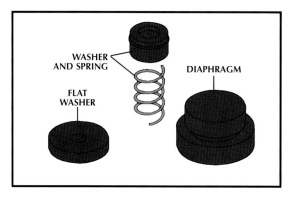

A variety of seat washers.
Different stem faucets require their own type of seat washer. Standard stem faucets use flat washers with holes for washer screws; cartridge-type stem faucets may have washers and springs. In a diaphragm stem faucet, caps called diaphragms do the work of washers, covering the bottom end of each stem. If you are not certain which washers fit your faucet, remove a valve seat *(opposite, below)* and take it to a plumbing-supply store.

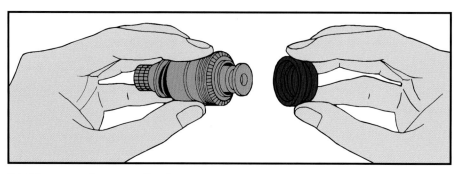

Making repairs to a diaphragm stem faucet.
Suction between the diaphragm and the valve seat may make the stem difficult to remove.

◆ Wrap the top of the stem with cloth and pull out the stem with pliers.
◆ If the old diaphragm sticks, pry it out with the tip of a screwdriver.

◆ Using a flashlight, make sure that there are no pieces of the old diaphragm remaining inside; otherwise, the new one will not seat properly.
◆ Fit the new diaphragm over the bottom of the stem *(above)*, making sure the diaphragm is snug all around.
◆ Replace the stem, the packing nut, and the handle.

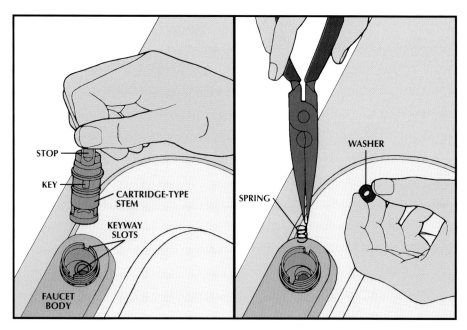

Servicing a cartridge-type stem faucet.
◆ Lift the cartridge out of the faucet *(far left)*, making sure as you do so to observe the alignment of the stop on the top of the cartridge and the keys on its side. The latter fit into two keyway slots on the faucet body.
◆ With long-nose pliers, pull the washer and spring out of the faucet body *(near left)*.
◆ Push the new spring and washer firmly into place with a finger. Insert the cartridge in the same orientation as before and attach the handle. If the spout still drips, replace the cartridge.

SERVICING A VALVE SEAT

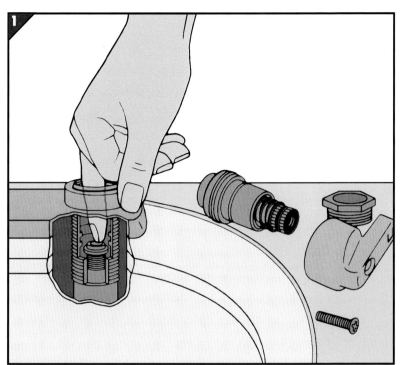

1. Inspecting the valve seat.
If the spout of a stem faucet continues to drip after you have replaced the washers, check the valve seats for signs of wear—scratches, pits, or an uneven surface. Use a flashlight to look inside the faucet body, then run a fingertip around the edge of the valve seat *(left)*. If necessary, install a new seat as shown below.

2. Installing a new seat.
◆ With a seat wrench, turn the valve seat counterclockwise and lift it out *(near right)*. Take it to a plumbing-supply store to get an exact duplicate.
◆ Lubricate the outside of the replacement with a pipe-joint compound, push it onto the wrench, and screw it into the faucet body *(far right)*.

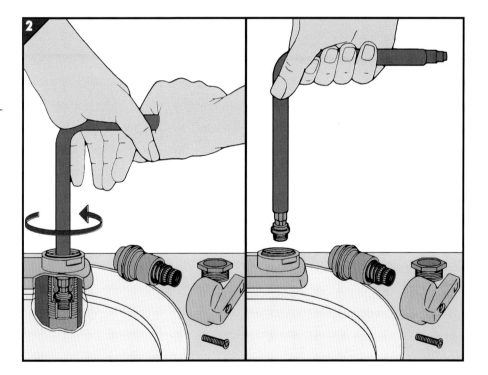

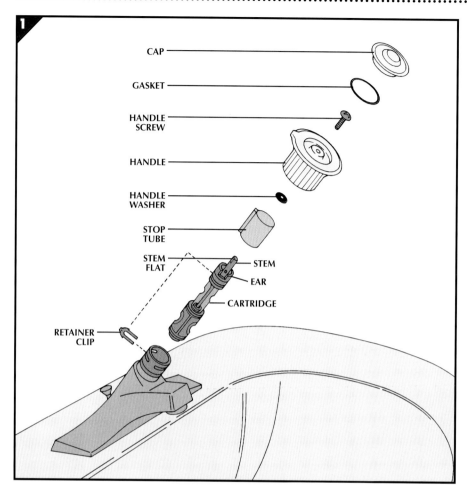

CAP

GASKET

HANDLE SCREW

HANDLE

HANDLE WASHER

STOP TUBE

STEM FLAT

STEM

EAR

CARTRIDGE

RETAINER CLIP

1. Repairing a single-lever cartridge faucet.

Fixing a cartridge faucet usually requires replacing the cartridge. When taking the faucet apart, carefully note the orientation of the cartridge ears and the stem flats, flat areas at the top of the stem *(diagram, left)*; position the replacement the same way.

◆ Remove the cap with a utility knife or a very small screwdriver.

◆ Unscrew the handle and remove it.

◆ Remove the stop tube, if there is one present.

◆ Complete the disassembly by removing the retainer clip and cartridge, as shown below.

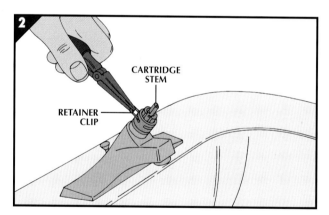

CARTRIDGE STEM

RETAINER CLIP

2. Removing the retainer clip.

◆ With long-nose pliers, pull out the retainer clip that holds the cartridge in the faucet body *(left)*.

◆ Lift out the cartridge, using pliers to grip the top of the stem if necessary.

3. Replacing the cartridge.

◆ Position the new cartridge to match the orientation of the old one. With the stem at its highest position, push the cartridge by its ears down into the faucet body.

◆ Align the cartridge ears with the faucet body slots; slide the retainer clip through the slots.

◆ Turn the stem to place the stem flats in the same position as in the old cartridge, then reassemble the faucet and turn on the water. If hot water comes out when you try to turn on the cold, and vice versa, remove the handle and stop tube and rotate the stem 180 degrees.

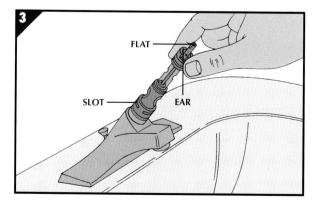

FLAT

SLOT

EAR

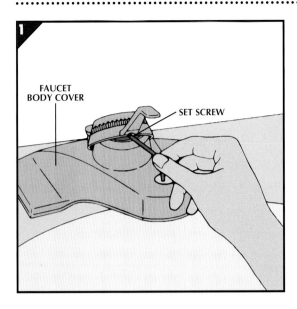

1. Getting access to a disk cartridge.

In ceramic disk faucets, leaks show up around the body of the faucet or as a puddle under the basin.

◆ Turn the faucet on full and move the handle side to side to dislodge dirt that may be lodged between the disks. If the leak persists, replace the disk cartridge.

◆ After turning off the water and draining the faucet, raise the lever as high as it can go. Unscrew the setscrew under the lever *(left)* and remove the handle.

◆ With older models, remove the pop-up lift rod *(page 138)*, remove the screws on the underside of the faucet, and take off the body cover. Newer ceramic disk faucets have a screw in the handle and a metal ring that twists off.

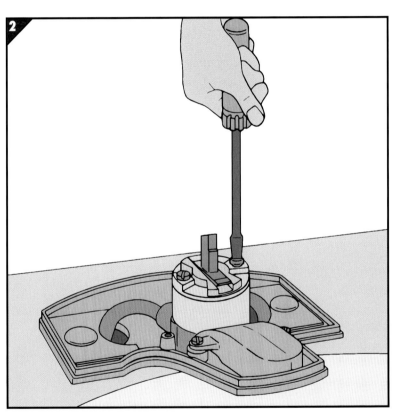

2. Removing the disk cartridge.

◆ Unscrew the bolts that hold the disk cartridge in place.

◆ Remove the cartridge and purchase an identical replacement.

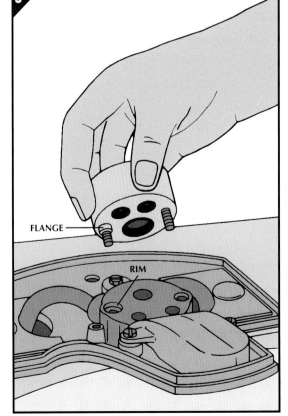

3. Installing a new cartridge.

◆ Align the three ports on the bottom of the disk cartridge with the three holes in the base of the faucet body. One of the bolt holes on the cartridge will have a flange; make sure it fits into the rim around the corresponding bolt hole in the faucet body.

◆ Replace the disk cartridge bolts, the body cover, and the handle.

SINGLE-LEVER BALL FAUCETS

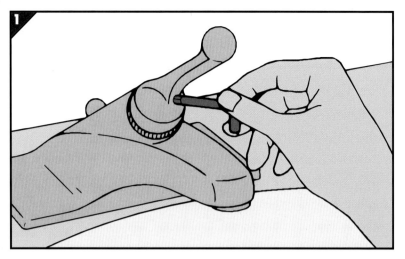

1. Loosening the setscrew.
If the spout of a ball faucet drips when the water is off, replace the two rubber valve seats and metal springs in the bottom of the faucet body.
◆ With a hex wrench, loosen the setscrew under the shank of the handle *(left)*. Do not take the screw all the way out; it is easily lost.
◆ Remove the handle.

2. Removing the cap and ball.
◆ Unscrew the cap assembly and lift out the ball by its stem; the plastic-and-rubber cam assembly will come with it.
◆ Inspect the ball; if it is rough or corroded, replace it.

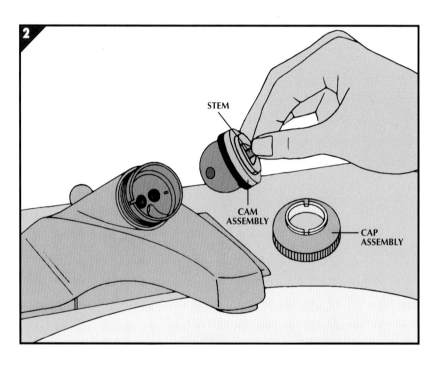

STEM

CAM ASSEMBLY

CAP ASSEMBLY

3. Installing new valve seats and springs.
With long-nose pliers, remove the valve seats and springs. Use a fingertip to push replacements firmly into place.

VALVE SEAT

SPRING

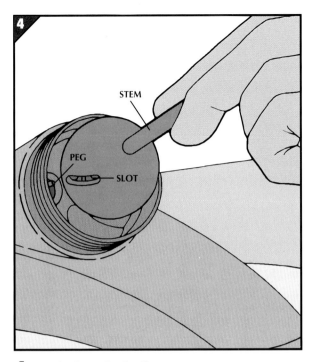

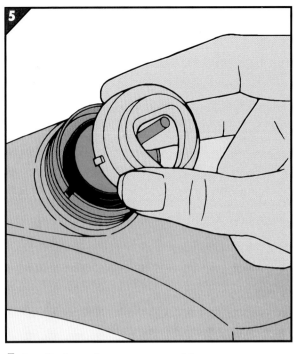

4. Replacing the ball.

A tiny metal peg projects from one side of the cavity into which the ball fits. As you replace the ball, make sure that the peg fits into an oblong slot on it.

5. Replacing the cam assembly.

◆ Replace the cam assembly so that its tab fits into the slot on the faucet body.
◆ Screw on the cap assembly.

6. Setting the adjusting ring.

◆ Turn on the water to the faucet.
◆ Move the ball's stem to the on position. If water leaks out around the stem, tighten the adjusting ring with a tool provided by the manufacturer or with the tip of a small screwdriver *(right)*.
◆ If you must tighten the ring so much that the handle is difficult to work, turn off the water, drain the faucet, and replace the entire cam assembly, including the rubber ring.
◆ Now put the cap assembly back in place. Position the handle so that the setscrew is over the flat on the stem and tighten the setscrew.

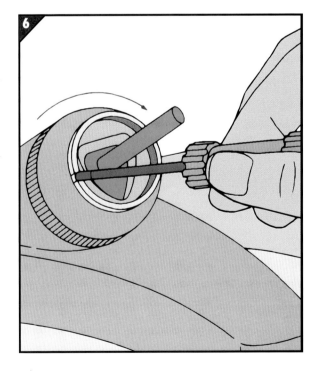

Sometimes the best and easiest repair for a worn-out bathroom faucet is to throw it out and install a new one. Replacing the washbasin faucet—or any tub and shower fittings—also helps give an old bathroom a new look with relatively little effort.

Buying the Right Fitting: If you plan to keep your washbasin, you must buy a faucet that fits the spacing of the sink's side holes. Determine the spacing by measuring between the centers of the faucet handles, or remove a faucet with a single handle to check the holes directly. Most center-set faucets *(opposite, bottom)* are designed for a washbasin in which the side holes

are 4 inches apart. You can replace a center-set faucet with a single-hole faucet *(page 141)* if its base plate covers the side holes. A wide-spread faucet *(page 142)* can accommodate side holes that are situated from 6 to 20 inches apart and must be replaced by a wide-spread set.

If your washbasin has a pop-up drain plug, you may want to replace the plug and the drain body to match the new faucet, as shown on pages 154-155. You can also follow the steps on the same pages to add a pop-up plug to a basin that does not have one; you will need to install a new drain body, T connector, and pop-up plug mechanism and purchase a faucet with a lift rod.

Tub and shower fittings are not as standardized as a sink's. Depending on the part, it is always best and sometimes essential to use replacements from the same manufacturer.

Preparation Steps: Several hours before disconnecting an old faucet or other fittings, spray all the threaded connections with penetrating lubricant. Cover the drain so that screws and small parts will not be lost. For work in a tub or shower, lay down padding or towels to avoid scarring the finish. After removing the old fittings, clean the surface beneath, removing crusty mineral deposits with a solution of equal parts of white vinegar and water.

TOOLS

Pliers
Basin wrench
Adjustable wrench
Pipe wrench
Tubing bender
Faucet-handle
  puller

Small screwdriver
Drill with a $\frac{1}{4}$-inch
  carbide bit
Hacksaw

MATERIALS

Penetrating
  lubricant
Plumber's putty
Plumbing-sealant
  tape
Washers, lock nuts,
  and other
  hardware
Braided flexible
  supply tubes

REMOVING AN OLD WASHBASIN FAUCET

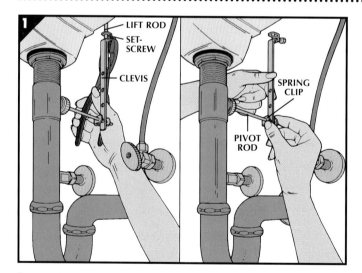

1. Freeing the pop-up plug mechanism.
Detach the pop-up plug mechanism, if any, before removing the faucet; leave the plug and pivot rod in place.
◆ With pliers, loosen the setscrew securing the pop-up lift rod to the clevis, or adapter bar, underneath the basin *(above, left)*.
◆ Above the basin, pull the lift rod up and out of the clevis.
◆ Pinch the spring clip holding the pivot rod in place *(above, right)*, and pull the clevis and spring clip free; set aside for reuse with the new faucet.

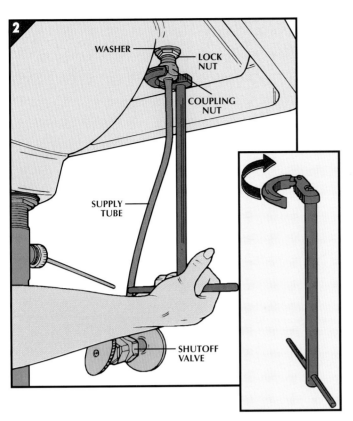

2. Disconnecting the supply tubes.

◆ Turn off the shutoff valves and drain the faucet; if you find that the valves will not turn, drain the house system as described on page 130.

◆ With a basin wrench *(inset)*, unscrew the coupling nut at the top of one of the supply tubes *(left)* and disconnect the tube.

◆ At the bottom of the supply tube, unscrew the nut attaching it to the shutoff valve.

◆ Disconnect the second supply tube in the same way.

◆ With the basin wrench, unscrew the lock nuts under the basin that secure the faucet; remove each nut and washer.

◆ Lift out the faucet, and clean the sink surface.

HOOKING UP A CENTER-SET FAUCET

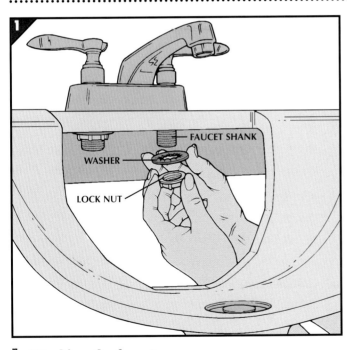

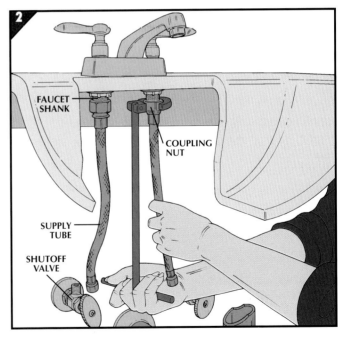

1. Attaching the faucet.

◆ Before positioning the faucet, slip a gasket and bottom plate over the faucet shanks; if these were not supplied, apply a bead of plumber's putty under the assembly.

◆ Insert the shanks into the side holes of the basin.

◆ Working underneath the washbasin, slip a washer onto one of the faucet shanks. Then thread on a lock nut and tighten by hand. Do the same with the other faucet shank.

◆ Tighten both lock nuts with a basin wrench. If you used plumber's putty, wipe off any excess with a finger.

2. Attaching flexible supply tubes.

◆ Wrap plumbing-sealant tape around the threads of the faucet shanks and shutoff valves.

◆ Insert a washer into the large coupling nut at one end of a braided flexible supply tube and hand tighten the nut to a faucet shank; attach the second supply tube the same way *(above)*.

◆ Connect each tube to its corresponding shutoff valve with the smaller coupling nut at the other end of the tube.

◆ Make a final half-turn on each nut with a wrench.

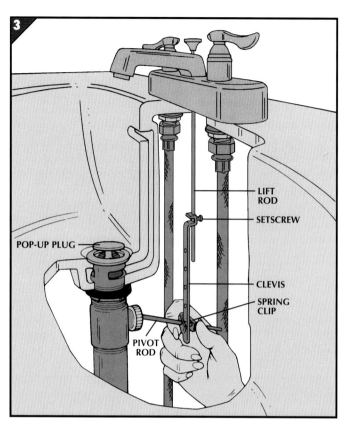

3. Installing the lift rod.

Attach the faucet's lift rod to the pop-up plug mechanism.

◆ Drop the lift rod through the hole at the back of the spout. From underneath the sink, slip the lift rod through holes in the top of the clevis.

◆ With a spring clip, secure the pivot rod to the clevis, passing the rod through one of the clevis holes. Holding the pivot rod and clevis at this connection *(left)*, pull downward to raise the pop-up plug in the drain. Adjust if necessary by moving the pivot rod to a different hole.

◆ Lock the lift rod in place by tightening the setscrew at the top of the clevis.

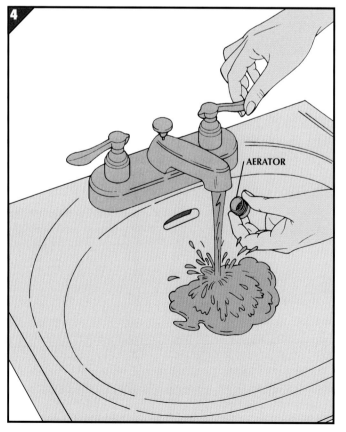

4. Flushing out the faucet.

◆ Turn on the water supply.

◆ Unscrew the aerator, an attachment in the underside of the spout that ensures an even flow of water and prevents splashing.

◆ Turn on the faucet slowly *(left)* and check under the sink for leaks. Fix leaking connections by tightening slightly with a wrench. Then turn the water on full force to flush out sediment.

◆ Turn off the faucet and replace the aerator.

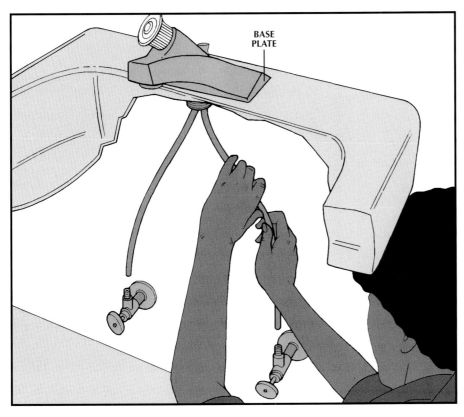

BASE
PLATE

Setting the faucet in place.

◆ Place the gasket supplied with the faucet on the base plate; if there is no gasket, substitute a bead of plumber's putty.

◆ Insert the faucet's preattached supply tubes—usually flexible copper tubing—through the center hole. Position the faucet on the sink.

◆ Under the basin, push a washer up over the tubing, followed by a lock nut. Thread the nut onto the faucet shank and tighten.

◆ With your hands, gently separate the supply tubes. Do not bend them sharply, or the faucet assembly will be useless. Put your thumbs together (left) and shape each piece of tubing to line up with its corresponding shutoff valve. Or use a tubing bender (box).

◆ If the tubing is too short, extend it with braided tubes (below, left).

◆ Complete the installation as with a center-set faucet (opposite).

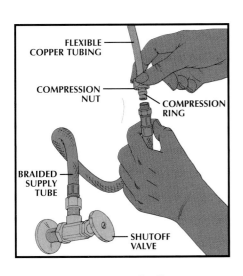

FLEXIBLE
COPPER TUBING

COMPRESSION
NUT

COMPRESSION
RING

BRAIDED
SUPPLY
TUBE

SHUTOFF
VALVE

TRICKS OF THE TRADE

To Gently Shape Tubing

A tubing bender makes it easier to shape flexible copper tubing without crimping. Slip the coiled metal over the tubing and bend to the desired shape.

Extending the supply lines.

If the flexible copper tubing does not reach to the shutoff valves, extend each piece with a braided supply tube equipped with compression fittings.

◆ Find the end of the braided tube that has a compression nut that turns in place but stays on the tube; attach that end to the shutoff valve.

◆ At the other end of the tube, detach the compression nut and compression ring and slip them onto the corresponding piece of faucet tubing. Connect the faucet tubing and the supply tube with the compression nut (above, left).

◆ Repeat the process for the second supply line.

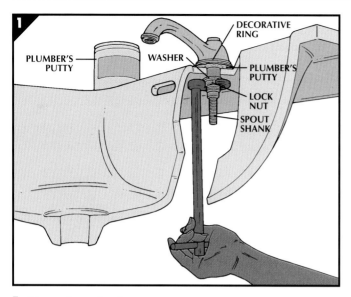

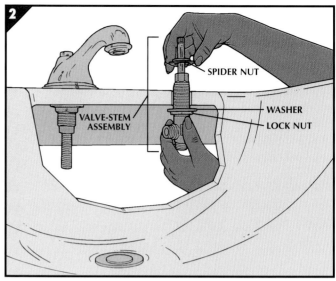

1. Mounting the faucet spout.

◆ Press a pencil-thick bead of plumber's putty around the edge of the underside of the spout.

◆ Insert the shank through the decorative ring and into the center hole of the sink. Be sure to position the spout at right angles to the back of the washbasin.

◆ Under the basin, secure the spout with a washer and lock nut; use a basin wrench to tighten the nut *(above)*.

◆ With a finger, wipe away excess plumber's putty from around the spout.

2. Installing the valve-stem assemblies.

◆ Place a washer and lock nut on one of the faucet's valve-stem assemblies. From underneath the washbasin, push the upper part of the assembly through a side hole.

◆ By hand, screw a spider nut onto the top of the assembly *(above)*.

◆ Adjust the upper and lower nuts until the stem portion of the assembly protrudes above the sink by the distance recommended by the manufacturer.

◆ Install the second valve-stem assembly in the same way.

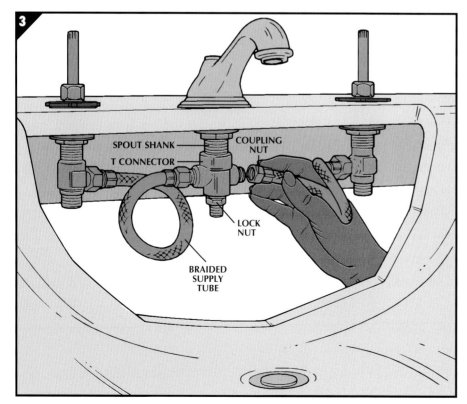

3. Connecting the spout.

◆ Place an O-ring and washer on the upper side of the faucet's T connector and slip the connector onto the spout shank; secure the connector from below with a packing nut and a lock nut.

◆ Wrap plumbing-sealant tape on the threads at each side of the T connector and around the supply connectors on each valve-stem assembly.

◆ Connect each valve-stem assembly to the T connector with a braided supply tube *(left)*. Hand tighten the larger coupling nut on the tube to the valve-stem assembly and the smaller one to the T connector. Make a final turn on each nut with an adjustable wrench.

◆ Follow the same procedures as for a center-set faucet *(page 140)* to connect the pop-up plug mechanism, attach supply tubes from the faucet shanks to the shutoff valves, check for leaks, and flush out the faucet.

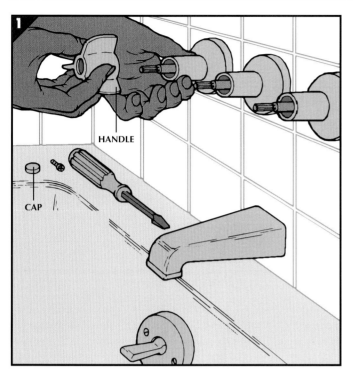

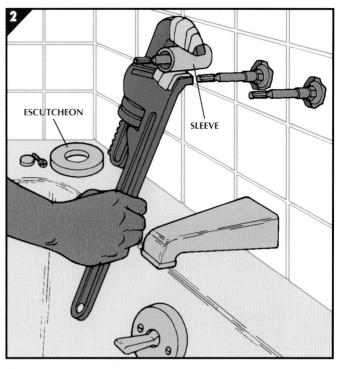

1. Removing the handles.

◆ Before starting, obtain replacement handles from the same manufacturer for best results; others can be adapted to fit *(Step 5)* but will not last as long.
◆ Turn off the water supply to the tub.
◆ Pry off the cap in the center of each faucet handle, or unscrew the cap with pliers if it has raised edges.
◆ Remove the screw holding the handle on the faucet stem, and pull off the handle *(above)*. If necessary, use a faucet-handle puller *(page 131)*.

2. Removing escutcheons and sleeves.

◆ Take off the faucet's escutcheons, or cover plates; they may be held in place by face screws or by a setscrew at the base of each escutcheon, or they may have been secured by the handles.
◆ If the sleeves are separate pieces, as here, remove them next; they may lift off, or you may need to unscrew each with a tape-wrapped pipe wrench *(above)*.

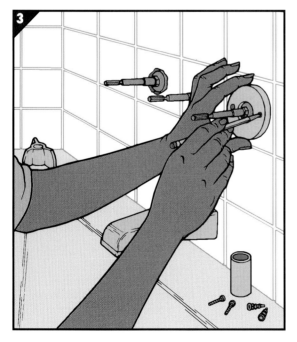

3. Installing new escutcheons.

◆ Slide each new escutcheon over a faucet stem. If the escutcheons have holes for setscrews, position the holes at the bottom.
◆ For escutcheons that are secured with face screws, center each escutcheon over a stem and line up the face-screw holes to either side of it. Mark the location of the screw holes on the wall *(left)* and make 1-inch-deep holes at the marks using a drill with a $\frac{1}{4}$-inch carbide bit. Insert the plastic screw anchors supplied with the handles into the holes, then attach the escutcheon with the face screws.

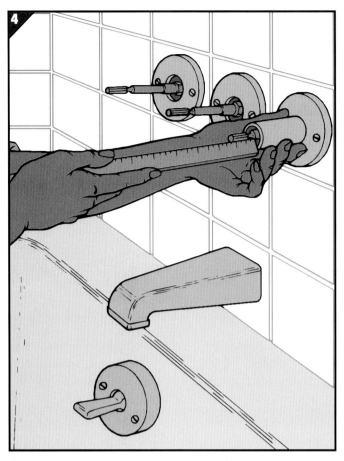

4. Inserting the sleeves.
◆ Attach separate sleeves by placing each one over a faucet stem and inserting it into the center of that escutcheon.
◆ Measure how much of the stem protrudes beyond the sleeve *(above)*; if less than $\frac{3}{4}$ inch of the stem is exposed, remove the sleeve and shorten it with a hacksaw.
◆ Attach the sleeve, usually by tightening a setscrew at the bottom edge of the escutcheon.

5. Attaching the handles.
◆ If the new handles are from the same manufacturer as the original handles, set them in place, attach with screws, and cover the screws with caps.
◆ For replacements from a different company, use handle adapters. Fit an adapter onto the ridged end of each faucet stem, then tighten the three setscrews with the hex wrench supplied with the adapter *(inset)*. Put on each handle and secure it with a screw. Snap the handle caps in place.

REPLACING OTHER BATH AND SHOWER FITTINGS

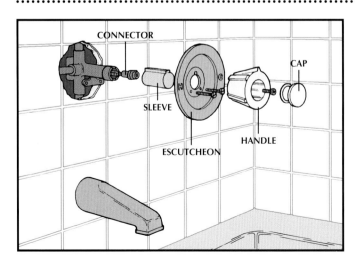

Revamping a single-handle faucet.
Always replace a single-handle tub or shower faucet with one from the same manufacturer.
◆ Pry off the faucet cap, which conceals a screw attached to the connector. Loosen the screw and pull off the handle.
◆ Unfasten the escutcheon. Remove it, the sleeve, and the connector.
◆ Install new trim by reversing the disassembly process, substituting a new sleeve, escutcheon, and handle.

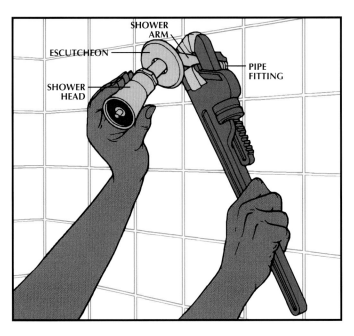

Changing a showerhead and shower arm.

◆ Pull the shower-arm escutcheon away from the wall.
◆ With a pipe wrench, carefully unscrew the shower arm from the pipe fitting inside the wall. Discard the old showerhead and shower arm.
◆ Wrap the threads on both ends of the new shower arm with plumbing-sealant tape. Screw the new head onto the arm and slide the escutcheon over the other end.
◆ Hand screw the free end of the arm into the pipe fitting. Steadying the assembly with one hand *(left),* tighten the arm with a tape-wrapped wrench until the shower head points down.
◆ Press the escutcheon against the wall.

⚠ **CAUTION** *Never allow the pipe fitting to turn or move inside the wall. This could break it and require extensive repairs.*

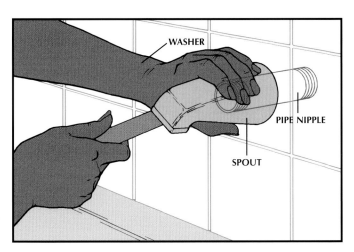

Changing a tub spout.

◆ If your spout has a setscrew at the base, loosen it and slide the spout off; replace it with any other spout using the same system.
◆ If your spout does not have a setscrew, turn the spout with a pipe wrench to remove it from the pipe nipple underneath. Take the spout to a plumbing-supply store to find a replacement with the same threading.
◆ Wrap the threads on the nipple with plumbing-sealant tape and tighten the new spout onto the nipple by hand. To finish tightening, trim a piece of wood to fit in the spout opening *(left);* use it to position the spout with its opening straight down.

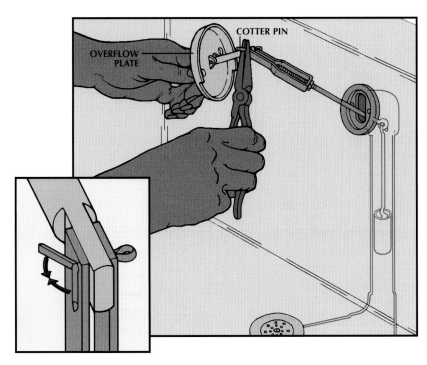

Changing an overflow plate.

◆ Remove the two screws holding the overflow plate to the tub.
◆ Pull the plate and attached mechanism out of the overflow hole far enough to reach the cotter pin *(inset)* that secures the mechanism to the back of the plate.
◆ With pliers, squeeze the ends of the cotter pin together and pull the pin out to free the plate *(left).*
◆ Attach the new plate to the old mechanism with a new cotter pin.
◆ Ease the mechanism back into the overflow hole and secure the plate with the two screws provided.

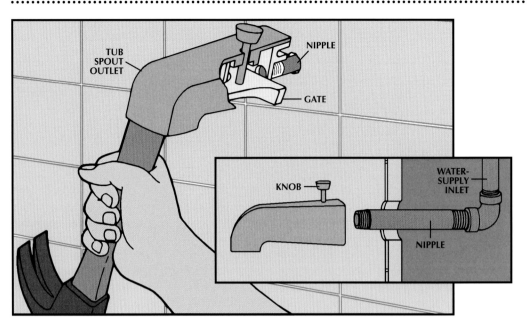

Replacing a screw-on spout diverter.

The knob of this diverter raises an internal gate that closes the pathway to the tub spout, forcing the water up to the shower head. If the mechanism malfunctions, the entire spout must be replaced.

◆ To remove the old spout, insert a piece of wood, such as a hammer handle, in the spout and turn it counterclockwise. Buy a replacement spout of the same length as the old one.

◆ If you cannot match the spout, buy an appropriately sized threaded adapter or replace the nipple *(inset)*.

◆ Apply plumbing-sealant tape to the threads and silicone sealant to the spout base.

◆ Hand tighten the spout. If you cannot complete the alignment by hand, use the makeshift wood tool or—provided the spout comes with a pad to protect the finish—use a wrench.

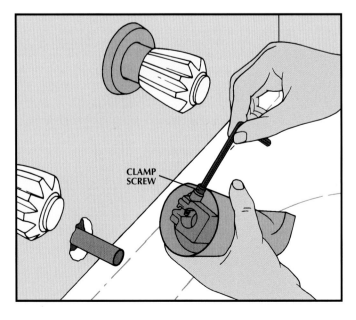

Replacing a slip-fit spout diverter.

◆ To remove this type of spout, loosen the clamp screw on the underside with a hex wrench. Grasp the spout firmly and twist it off the pipe.

◆ With the hex wrench, loosen the clamp screw on the new spout *(left)*, and twist the spout onto the pipe.

◆ Turn the spout so that the clamp screw faces up, and partially tighten the screw.

◆ Twist the spout into position and finish tightening.

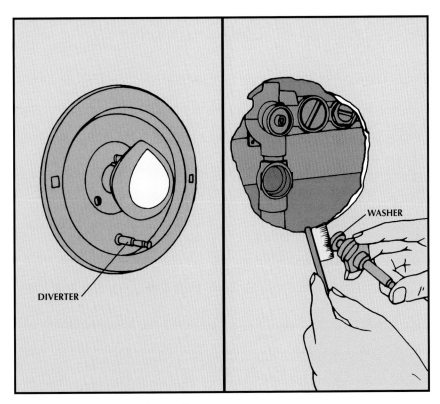

DIVERTER

WASHER

Servicing and replacing other diverter types.

For a diverter in a single-lever faucet unit *(above, left)*, remove the faucet handle and escutcheon, then unscrew the diverter.

◆ If water is not being diverted from the tub spout to the shower head properly, clean any sediment that may be adhering to the washer with white vinegar and an old toothbrush *(above, right)*.

◆ If water leaks from around the diverter or if its parts are worn, replace the entire mechanism with one of the same make.

◆ For a diverter in the center of a three-handle faucet, replace the entire cartridge if it leaks or malfunctions. Proceed just as you would for a faucet cartridge.

UNCLOGGING A SHOWER HEAD

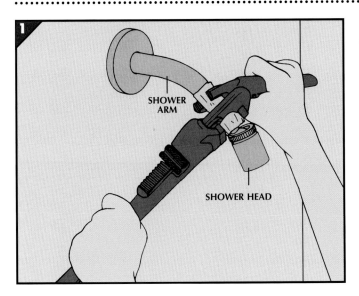

SHOWER ARM

SHOWER HEAD

1. Removing a shower head.

When the water flow from a shower head is uneven or insufficient, disassemble and clean the fitting:

◆ Wrap the shower head collar in masking tape and turn it counterclockwise with a pipe wrench. For greater leverage, grip the shower arm with one wrench and turn the collar with a second wrench *(left)*.

◆ Twist off the loosened shower head by hand.

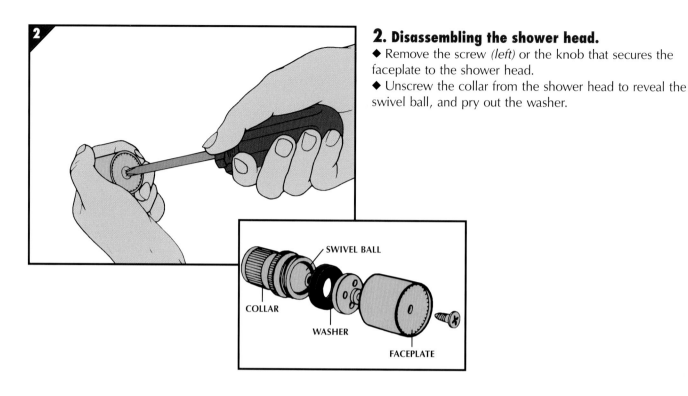

2. Disassembling the shower head.

◆ Remove the screw *(left)* or the knob that secures the faceplate to the shower head.

◆ Unscrew the collar from the shower head to reveal the swivel ball, and pry out the washer.

SWIVEL BALL

COLLAR

WASHER

FACEPLATE

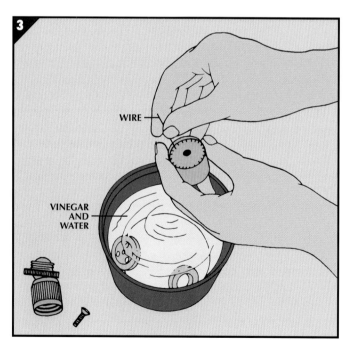

3. Cleaning the shower head.

◆ Soak the entire shower head or its disassembled parts overnight in a bowl of white vinegar and water.

◆ Scrub with steel wool or an old toothbrush, and clear the spray holes with a small wire *(left)*.

◆ Rinse thoroughly.

◆ Replace any worn parts of the shower head.

◆ Lubricate the swivel ball with silicone lubricant, and reassemble the head.

WIRE

VINEGAR AND WATER

The traditional shower head, designed simply to deliver a steady stream of water from above, is only one of many shower fittings now available. Today's alternatives include hardware with internal mechanisms that conserve water by lowering the pressure, reduce or shut off water when the temperature gets too high, or regulate the pulse of the spray to simulate a massage. Hand-held showers, attached either to the tub spout or the shower arm, allow you to maneuver the spray freely—and you can also hang the head from a bar and use it in the conventional manner.

ADJUSTING BATHTUB DRAINS

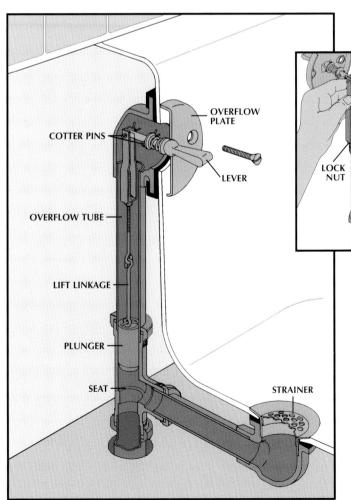

A trip-lever drain.

The key element of this type of drain is a brass plunger suspended from a lift linkage. The lever lowers the plunger onto a slight ridge below the juncture of the overflow tube and the drain, blocking outflow of water via the main tube outlet; however, any water that spills into the overflow tube can pass freely down the drain because the plunger is hollow. A leak in the drain may be due to wear on the plunger caused by repeated impact against its ridge seat. To restore a proper fit, lengthen the linkage:

◆ Unscrew the overflow plate and lift out the whole mechanism, removing any accumulated hair or debris. The upper segment of the lift linkage consists of a brass yoke from which a threaded rod is suspended; a lock nut secures the threaded rod in place.

◆ Loosen the lock nut with pliers, turn the threaded rod the desired amount—usually just a turn or two—then tighten the lock nut again (inset).

◆ Replace the cotter pins if they are corroded.

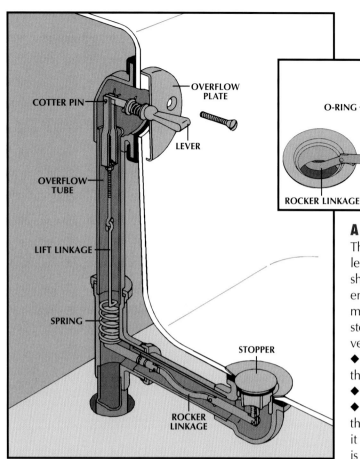

COTTER PIN

OVERFLOW
PLATE

LEVER

OVERFLOW
TUBE

LIFT LINKAGE

SPRING

STOPPER

ROCKER
LINKAGE

STOPPER

O-RING

ROCKER LINKAGE

A pop-up drain.

The lift linkage of a pop-up drain resembles that of a trip-lever drain, except that the lower end of the linkage is shaped to form a stiff spiral spring. This spring rests on the end of a separate, horizontal rocker linkage leading to the metal stopper. When the spring presses downward, the stopper rises. The stopper has a cross-shaped base that prevents small objects from passing down the drain.

◆ If the drain begins to clog, open it with the control lever, then pull out the stopper and the rocker linkage.

◆ Clean these parts of accumulated hair.

◆ Replacing the stopper can be tricky. Make sure that the bottom of the curve in the linkage faces down. Work it sideways or back and forth until the bend in the pipe is cleared.

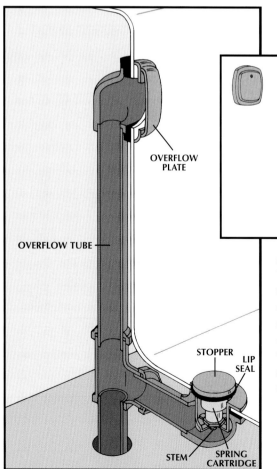

OVERFLOW
PLATE

OVERFLOW TUBE

STOPPER

LIP
SEAL

STEM

SPRING
CARTRIDGE

A toe-operated drain.

The only moving part of this type of drain is the stopper. Beneath its rubber lip seal is a spring cartridge attached to a stem. Pressing on the stopper when it is open will seal it shut; pressing again will open it.

◆ If the rubber lip seal wears out, simply un-screw the stopper and replace it with a matching one (inset).

REPLACING A THREE-HANDLE FIXTURE

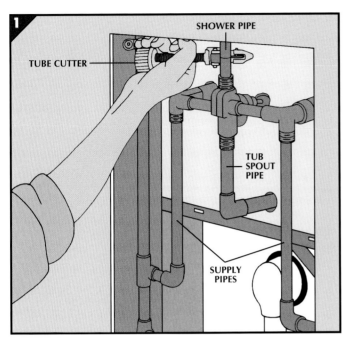

SHOWER PIPE

TUBE CUTTER

TUB SPOUT PIPE

SUPPLY PIPES

1. Cutting the pipes.

◆ Detach all handles, escutcheons, and the tub spout from the old faucet body.

◆ Look for an access panel on the other side of the wall. If there is no panel, cut through the wall, as explained below.

◆ For copper or CPVC supply pipes, cut the pipes leading into the faucet body *(left)* at points where they can easily be reconnected with fittings to the new faucet. If the supply lines are threaded steel, cut them and unthread the cut sections *(page 272)*.

◆ Take the faucet body, with its cut pipe ends still in place, to a plumbing-supply store. Buy a replacement, fittings, and spacer pipes.

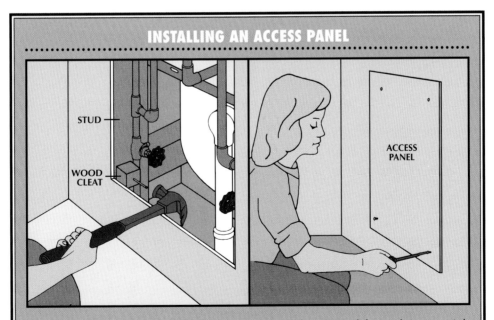

INSTALLING AN ACCESS PANEL

STUD

WOOD CLEAT

ACCESS PANEL

If a faucet body is walled in, create an access panel as part of the replacement job. To determine where to cut, measure from the floor and nearest corner to the fitting on the tub side of the wall; transfer these measurements to the other side of the wall, and punch a hole with a hammer and chisel at the indicated point. With a dry-wall saw, cut from the hole out to the studs. Draw a rectangular box, stud to stud and about 2 feet high, and cut the wall along the outline. Cut a plywood panel slightly larger than the opening. At the corners of the opening, nail wood cleats to the studs *(above, left)*. The panel attaches to the cleats with screws *(above, right)*.

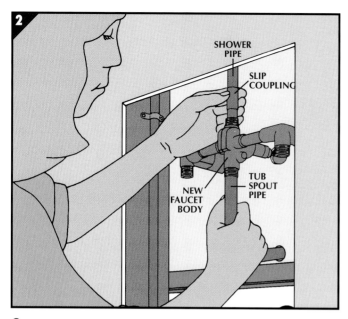

2. Connecting the shower pipe.

◆ Cut the pipes to connect the new faucet body to the shower pipe, the spout, and the supply lines. For CPVC or steel supply lines, use CPVC *(pages 272-275)* and add threaded adapters to the faucet body.

◆ Temporarily place the pipes in the faucet body, and put the assembly in position to check the pipes' lengths. Remove it and shorten them as needed.

◆ Secure the tub spout pipe and the shower pipe spacer to the faucet body, placing a slip coupling on the spacer.

◆ Set the faucet body assembly in place.

◆ Add an elbow and horizontal pipe to the tub spout pipe. Use a slip coupling to attach the shower pipe to the spacer *(above)*.

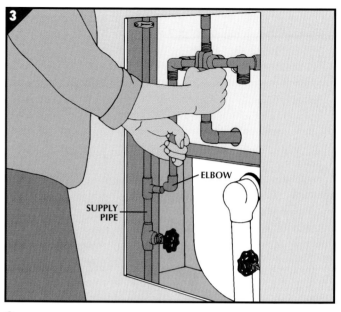

3. Connecting the supply pipes.

◆ Slip a supply pipe into one of the two openings in the faucet body.

◆ At the other end of the pipe, attach a coupling or elbow and connect it to the supply line *(above)*. Connect the other pipe in the same way.

◆ Solder or cement the pipes at both ends (see pages 269 and 270 for copper, pages 274 and 275 for CPVC or steel).

◆ Leave the access panel open for a few days in order to check for leaks.

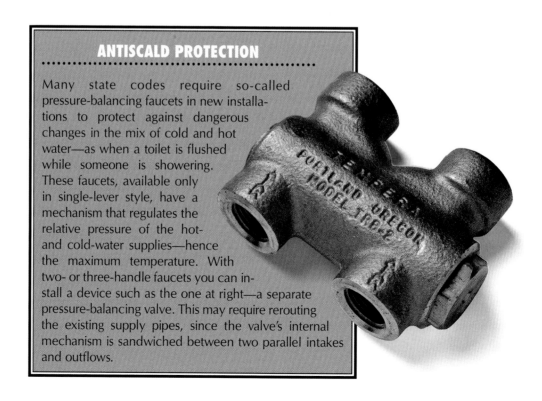

ANTISCALD PROTECTION

Many state codes require so-called pressure-balancing faucets in new installations to protect against dangerous changes in the mix of cold and hot water—as when a toilet is flushed while someone is showering. These faucets, available only in single-lever style, have a mechanism that regulates the relative pressure of the hot- and cold-water supplies—hence the maximum temperature. With two- or three-handle faucets you can install a device such as the one at right—a separate pressure-balancing valve. This may require rerouting the existing supply pipes, since the valve's internal mechanism is sandwiched between two parallel intakes and outflows.

INSTALLING A NEW SINGLE-LEVER FAUCET

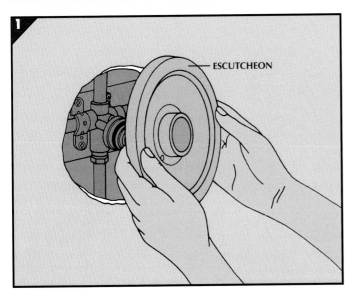

ESCUTCHEON

1. Gaining access to the faucet body.
◆ Remove the handle *(page 144)* and unscrew and lift off the escutcheon *(left)*.
◆ If you have access to the faucet from the other side of the wall, follow the procedure for removing the faucet body described on page 151 for a three-handle faucet. If you cannot gain access from the back, you may be able to re-place the faucet body from the tub side *(next step)*; do not attempt this, however, in a house with steel supply lines.

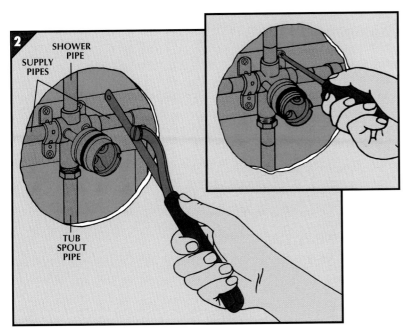

SHOWER PIPE
SUPPLY PIPES
TUB SPOUT PIPE

2. Removing the faucet from the tub side.
◆ Cut the shower pipe, tub spout pipe, and supply pipes with a minihacksaw *(left)*. It may be necessary for you to chip away tiles or wallboard for easier access.
◆ Remove the screws that secure the faucet body to the wooden crosspiece behind it *(inset)*.
◆ Lift the faucet body out of the wall.
◆ Buy a replacement faucet of the same make and model as the old one (or at least the same size), along with replacement pipe and slip cou-plings that will be used to reconnect the pipes. To calculate the total amount of new pipe need-ed, add the lengths of the four pipes in the old faucet plus at least half an inch for each length.

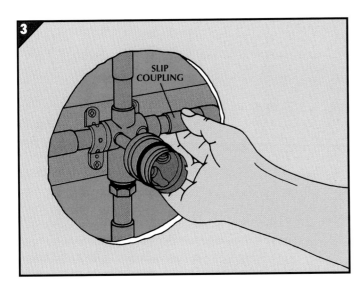

SLIP COUPLING

3. Reconnecting the pipes.
◆ Cut the new pipe into segments that will join the faucet body to the shower pipe, tub spout pipe, and supply lines; insert them in the faucet body, using threaded adapters for plastic pipe. (See pages 269 and 270 for working with cop-per pipe, page 275 for working with plastic.)
◆ Position the faucet and connect the pipes with slip cou-plings *(left)*.
◆ Secure the faucet body by screwing it to the crosspiece with pipe clamps.
◆ If you have copper pipe, remove all plastic and rubber parts from the faucet body before soldering the joints. Mount a flameproof pad between the crosspiece and the pipes for protection. (You may need to unfasten the clamps to slip the cloth through.)
◆ Screw on the escutcheon and reconnect the handle.

Over time, corrosion in the trap and drain under your bathroom washbasin can cause leaks, which are best remedied by the replacement of all or part of the drain assembly. You may also want to replace a worn pop-up plug and drain body when installing a new faucet.

For best results, spray the threaded connections in the drain assembly with a penetrating lubri-cant several hours before disconnecting the old fittings. Drain configurations vary, but most include slip-nut connections that can easily be dismantled with a wrench. If you intend to reuse a trap, be sure to put new washers under the slip nuts before putting the trap back in.

Selecting the Right Parts: If the sink is mounted in a vanity top or on a pedestal, and you are replacing all of the drain assembly, use polyvinyl chloride (PVC) fittings like those depicted here. Such pipes are durable, rustproof, and easy to work with. To replace the entire drain assembly under a wall-hung basin, chrome-plated parts are an elegant alternative. If you are replacing only some of the drain fittings, match the material of those that remain.

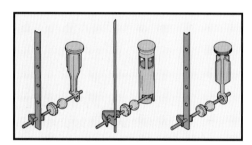

Pop-up drain plugs.

The method for removing a pop-up drain plug depends on its type. Some plugs sit atop the pivot rod and just lift out *(far left)*. Others require a quarter-turn to free them from the rod *(left, center)*. To remove the type of plug at near left, you must disengage the pivot rod from the T connector under the basin and then lift out the plug.

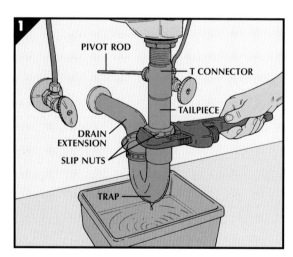

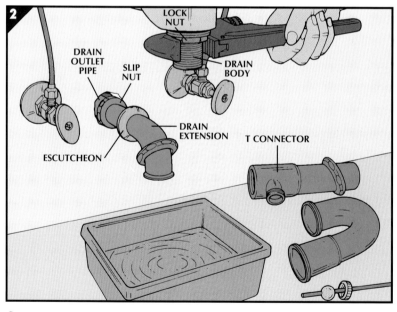

1. Removing the trap.
◆ Place a shallow container underneath the trap to catch any water remaining inside.
◆ With a pipe wrench or a monkey wrench, unscrew the slip nuts on either end of the trap, disconnecting it from the tailpiece and the drain extension *(above)*.
◆ Remove the pop-up plug as outlined above, as well as the lift rod and clevis *(page 139)*. With pliers, unscrew the retaining nut at the back of the T connector and remove the pivot rod.

2. Removing the fittings.
◆ With a pipe wrench, unscrew the T connector from the drain body, remove the lock nut and washer holding the drain body to the basin *(above)*, and push the drain body up and out through the hole in the basin.

◆ If replacing all of the drain assembly, pry the escutcheon from the wall. Unscrew the slip nut behind it, then gently remove the drain extension, being careful not to move or break pipes inside the wall. Clean the threads of the drain outlet pipe.

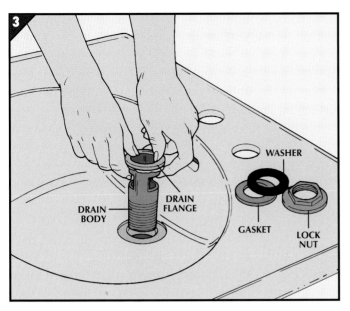

3. Sealing the new drain flange.

◆ Inside the washbasin, scrape off any old putty from around the drain opening and clean and dry the surface.

◆ Roll a short rope of plumber's putty and press it under the edge of the flange at the top of the drain body. Lower the drain body through the opening in the sink *(left)* and press down on the flange.

◆ Underneath the basin, push the gasket, washer, and lock nut onto the drain body. Hand tighten the lock nut against the bottom of the basin, then tighten one more turn with a pipe wrench. Wipe away any excess putty with a finger.

◆ If you are replacing the faucet, install the new one now, as well as the new lift rod and clevis.

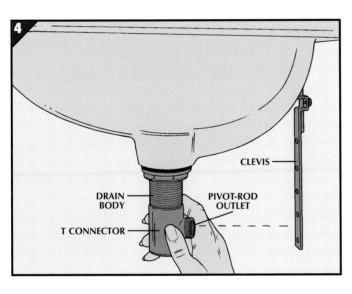

4. Aligning the T connector.

◆ Wrap plumbing-sealant tape around the threads on the lower part of the drain body.

◆ Screw the new T connector onto the drain body so that the pivot-rod outlet faces toward the clevis *(dotted line, left)*.

◆ Insert one end of the pivot rod into the T connector and attach the other end to the clevis with a spring clip, following the procedure shown on page 140.

◆ Tighten the pivot rod's retaining nut on the T connector and adjust the position of the pivot rod on the clevis as necessary.

5. Installing a new plastic trap.

◆ Wrap plumbing-sealant tape around the threads of the tailpiece and hand tighten it into the T connector. Slide a plastic slip nut and washer *(not visible)* onto the tailpiece.

◆ If replacing the entire drain assembly, loosely connect the replacement trap and the new drain extension with a plastic slip nut. Slide the escutcheon, a nut, and a washer onto the extension and insert it into the drain outlet pipe. The washer fits between the extension and the outlet pipe, but the nut slips over the pipe's outside.

◆ Align the top of the trap with the tailpiece *(right)*. Loosely connect the pipes with the nut.

◆ When the drain assembly is properly aligned, hand tighten the nuts at each connection. Turn each nut once more with a wrench. Push the escutcheon against the wall.

◆ Close the pop-up plug, fill the sink with water, then open the drain and check for leaks. Tighten any leaking joints slightly.

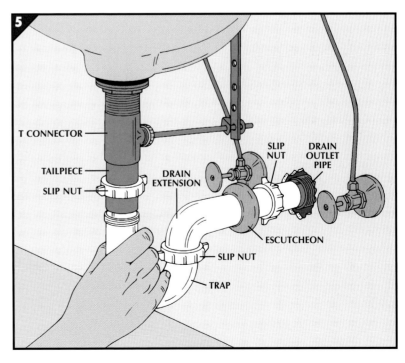

When a bathroom drain stops or slows, see if other drains are affected. If so, the problem may lie elsewhere in the house's plumbing.

A Hierarchy of Solutions: If only one drain is blocked, try a plunger *(right)*. Prepare the drain by removing the strainer, pop-up plug, and overflow plate, if present; take apart a tub's drain hardware as shown in Step 1 on page 157. Stuff any overflow opening with rags.

If the plunger fails, you can sometimes clear a tub or shower drain with water *(below)*. A third method is to use an auger—a trap-and-drain auger for a tub, sink, or shower, and a closet auger for a toilet. Avoid compressed-air devices, which often compact the blockage and may cause old pipe joints to break apart.

Chemical Drain Cleaners: Do not pour chemical cleaning agents into a blocked drain. Many contain lye, and you could be exposed to the caustic as you continue work on the stoppage. Cleaners can be helpful once a tub, sink, or shower drain is open; applied regularly, they prevent buildup of debris. Never put such cleaners in a toilet, however. They do no good and can stain the porcelain.

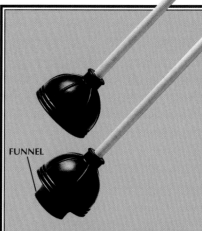

FUNNEL

A Multi-Role Plunger

An ordinary force-cup plunger is suited to many drains, but it will not fit a toilet. For the bathroom, purchase a foldout plunger instead. As shown above, its cup can take on two different shapes.

With a tub, sink, or shower drain, keep the funnel portion tucked inside *(upper photo)*. Coat the rim of the cup with petroleum jelly and center it over the drain. Make sure that standing water covers the cup completely; if it does not, add more water. Without breaking the seal between drain and cup, pump the plunger down and up several times, then jerk it away. When the drain opens, run hot water through it to flush it clean.

For a toilet, extend the plunger's funnel lip *(lower photo)*. If a clogged toilet is too full, bail out some of the contents. If the bowl is empty, add water by hand, not by flushing. Fit the plunger over the opening near the bottom of the bowl and pump vigorously, then jerk it away. If the bowl empties, pour in water to confirm that the drain is fully opened.

 TOOLS

Foldout plunger
Garden hose
Drain flusher

Trap-and-drain
  auger
Closet auger

 SAFETY TIPS

If human waste is present when you are unclogging a toilet, wear goggles and rubber gloves.

CLEARING A STOPPAGE WITH WATER

Flushing a drain with a hose.

A hose-mounted drain flusher, available at most hardware stores, will work in a shower or tub drain.

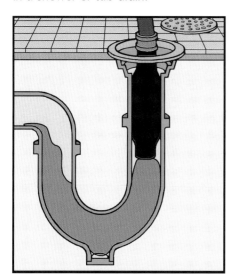

◆ Attach the drain flusher to a garden hose and push it into a shower drain; in a tub, insert it through the overflow opening past the level of the drain. Connect the other end of the hose to a faucet; for an indoor faucet, you will need a threaded adapter.

◆ Have a helper slowly turn on the hose water. The flusher will expand to fill the pipe so that the full force of water is directed at the clog.

⚠ *Do not flush a clogged drain that contains caustic clean-* **CAUTION** *ers, and never leave a hose in any drain. The cleaner could splash into your face, and the hose could draw wastewater into the supply system if the pressure should drop.*

BREAKING UP A CLOG WITH A TRAP-AND-DRAIN AUGER

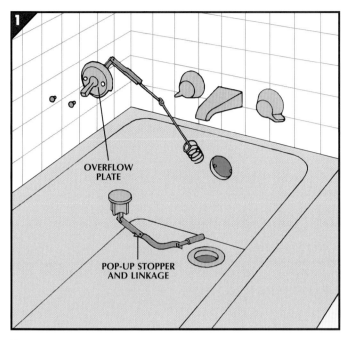

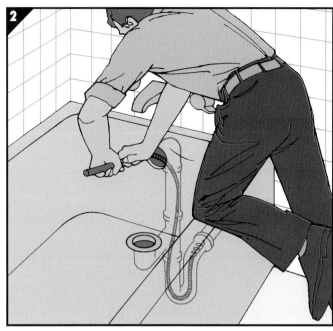

1. Gaining access to the drain.

To unclog a bathtub, unscrew the overflow plate and lift it up and out. Draw out the pop-up stopper and its linkage. Note how the parts line up so that you can put them back in the same way.

OVERFLOW PLATE

POP-UP STOPPER AND LINKAGE

2. Inserting the auger.

◆ Cranking the auger handle clockwise, feed the auger tip through the tub overflow opening.

◆ When the auger wire reaches the blockage, move the auger slowly backward and forward while cranking. Continue to crank clockwise as you withdraw the auger wire; doing so helps to prevent you from dropping the material that caused the blockage.

◆ After clearing the drain, run hot water through it for 2 to 3 minutes.

OPENING A TOILET DRAIN WITH A CLOSET AUGER

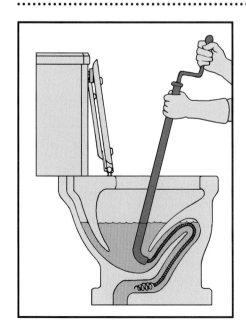

An auger meant for toilets.

The cranking handle of a closet auger attaches to a long sleeve shaped to help guide the tip of the auger into the trap. Closet augers work equally well in toilets with a front drain opening, as shown here, or with the opening at the back.

◆ Hold the sleeve near the top and position the other end against the drain opening. Crank the auger tip slowly clockwise into the trap until you hook the obstruction or break through it.

◆ Withdraw the auger while cranking the handle clockwise. If the drain remains clogged, repeat the process.

◆ When the drain seems clear, test it with a pail of water before attempting to flush the toilet.

Understanding how the mechanisms inside a toilet tank work can make their repair fairly simple. Certain parts vary, but most operate according to the same scheme. When you press the handle, a lift wire or a chain pulls a stopper off the opening to the bowl. Water rushes into the bowl. The falling water level in the tank causes a float to drop. This, in turn, opens the ball cock—the device that starts and stops the refill cycle. When the tank is nearly empty, the stopper drops into place. Rising water then lifts the float high enough to shut off the ball cock.

Diagnosing the Problem: One way to spot a mechanical breakdown is to lift the tank lid and watch a flush cycle. Also be alert to noises and leaks. The sound of water running constantly may indicate that the tank ball is not properly seated *(opposite)*. A high whine or whistle during flushing means that the ball cock needs attention *(pages 160-161)*. Visible leaks near the tank may be caused by loose bolts, worn washers, or condensation *(page 162)*.

Working Near Porcelain: Most toilets are made of vitreous china, which is easily cracked or broken. Set the lid on padding in an out-of-the-way place while working in the tank, and use gentle pressure when removing or tightening bolts. As shown on page 163, it may be safer to cut corroded seat-cover bolts than to strain to remove them with a wrench near fragile porcelain.

 **TOOLS**

Adjustable wrench	Socket wrench with deep sockets
Plastic cleansing pad or steel wool	Screwdriver
Locking-grip pliers	Hacksaw
Long-nose pliers	

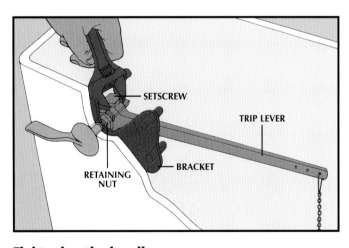

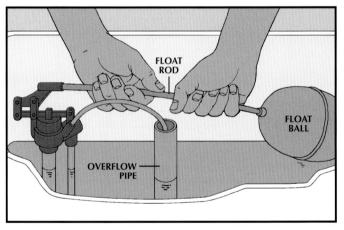

Tightening the handle.
If a toilet handle must be held down until the flush cycle is complete, the linkage between the handle and the trip lever needs to be secured.

◆ For a toilet with a bracket arrangement like the one above, tighten the retaining nut with an adjustable wrench so the bracket does not wobble but still moves freely when the handle is turned. Turn the nut counterclockwise—the opposite direction from that used to tighten most nuts. With a wrench or pliers, turn the trip-lever setscrew against the handle shaft.

◆ In models that have a one-piece handle and trip lever, tighten the nut that holds the handle on its shaft. This nut also must be tightened counterclockwise.

Adjusting the water level.
If water is cascading through the overflow pipe into the bowl, lower the water level by replacing the float ball or adjusting the float rod.

◆ Unscrew the float ball and examine it; if it is worn or there is water in it, replace it.

◆ If the ball is sound, bend the float rod $\frac{1}{2}$ inch downward with both hands *(above)*. Alternatively, unscrew the rod with pliers and bend it over a rounded surface, then put it back. The rod may break when bent; if that happens, replace it with a new one. Reattach the ball.

◆ Flush the toilet. The water should stop rising about $\frac{1}{2}$ inch below the top of the overflow pipe. If it does not, the rod must be readjusted.

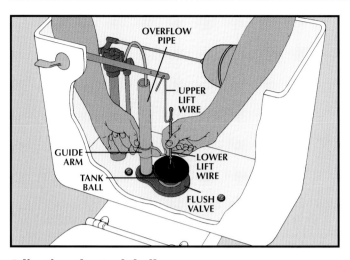

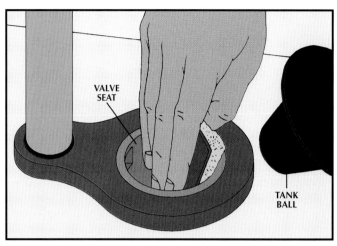

Adjusting the tank ball.

If water runs constantly into the bowl from the tank, sometimes making the toilet flush, first try reseating the tank ball.

◆ Turn off the water at the shutoff valve and remove the lid.

◆ Flush the toilet. If the tank ball does not fall straight into the flush valve opening, loosen the thumbscrew fastening the guide arm to the overflow pipe (above).

◆ Reposition the arm and the lower lift wire so the tank ball is centered over the flush valve. If necessary, straighten the lift wires.

◆ Turn the water on. If the leak persists, clean mineral deposits off the ball and valve seat (right).

Cleaning the tank ball and valve seat.

◆ Turn off the water and empty the tank.

◆ Unscrew the tank ball and wash it with warm water and detergent. If the ball is worn, replace it with a modern flapper ball hinged to prevent misalignment (below).

◆ Gently scour the seat of the flush valve with fine steel wool or a plastic cleansing pad (above).

◆ Replace the ball and turn on the water. If the valve still leaks, a special replacement flush valve seat can be placed over the old one. To replace the old valve seat completely, remove the tank as shown on page 162.

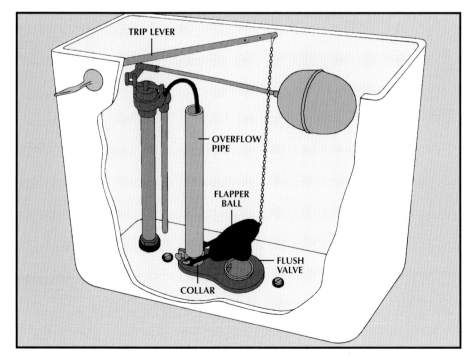

Installing a hinged flapper ball.

◆ Turn off the water, drain the tank, and remove the old guide arm, lift wires, and tank ball.

◆ Slide the collar of the flapper ball to the bottom of the overflow pipe and align the ball over the flush valve. If there is a thumbscrew on the collar, tighten it.

◆ Hook the chain from the ball through a hole in the trip lever directly above, leaving about $\frac{1}{2}$ inch of slack.

◆ Turn the water on, flush the toilet, and check whether the tank drains completely. If it does not, lessen the slack or move the chain one or two holes toward the rear of the lift arm.

REPAIRS FOR THE TANK'S FILL MECHANISM

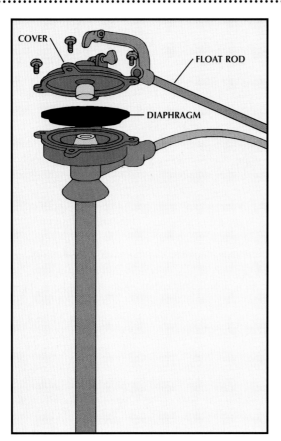

COVER

FLOAT ROD

DIAPHRAGM

Servicing a ball cock.

When a diaphragm ball cock or a float-cup ball cock develops a minor leak, repair it with parts available at plumbing-supply stores. Replace other, older types of ball cocks *(below)* rather than attempting repairs.

◆ Shut off the water and flush the toilet.

◆ Remove the top screws and lift off the cover and float rod assembly.

◆ In a diaphragm ball cock *(left),* take out and replace the diaphragm, rubber gaskets, and washers. For a float-cup ball cock like the one shown at far right, replace the rubber valve seal and washers.

◆ Attach the ball cock cover and turn the water on. If the ball cock still leaks, or appears worn-out, replace it.

A DEVICE FOR REPLENISHING THE TANK

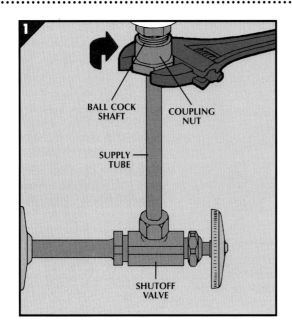

BALL COCK
SHAFT

COUPLING
NUT

SUPPLY
TUBE

SHUTOFF
VALVE

1. Disconnecting the supply tube.

◆ Turn off the water at the shutoff valve, flush the toilet, and sponge out the remaining water from the tank.

◆ With an adjustable wrench, unscrew the coupling nut on the underside of the tank that attaches the supply tube to the ball cock shaft.

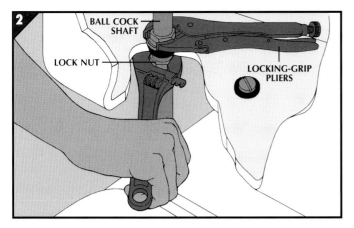

2. Removing the ball cock.

◆ Inside the tank, attach locking-grip pliers to the base of the ball cock shaft. The pliers will wedge against the side of the tank and free your hands.

◆ With an adjustable wrench, unscrew the lock nut that secures the ball cock shaft on the underside of the tank (left). Use firm but gentle pressure to avoid cracking the tank.

◆ If the nut resists, soak it with penetrating oil for 10 or 15 minutes and try again. Once the nut is removed, lift the ball cock out of the tank.

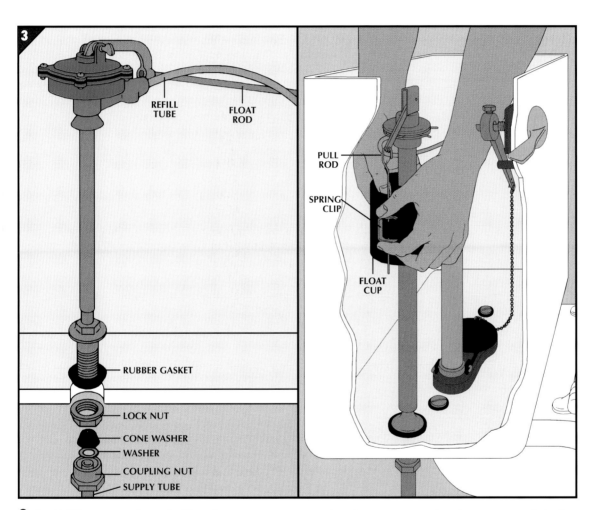

3. Installing a modern ball cock.

Diaphragm ball cocks and float-cup ball cocks are secured in place in the same way. Float-cup ball cocks require a simple adjustment as well. Float-cup ball cocks come in several heights; measure your tank depth before buying one.

◆ Put the new ball cock shank through the rubber gasket supplied with it and through the hole in the tank. Then screw a lock nut onto the ball cock shaft underneath the tank.

◆ Inside the tank, hold the base of the ball cock with locking-grip pliers. Tighten the lock nut.

◆ Insert a new washer in the coupling nut on the supply tube; some supply tubes come with built-in washers. If the tube extends through the nut and washer, place a cone washer over the tube (above, left). Screw the coupling nut to the bottom of the ball cock shaft.

◆ Attach the float rod assembly and refill tube, and turn the water back on at the shutoff valve.

For a float-cup ball cock, adjust the ball cock to change the water level in the tank. To raise the level, pinch the spring clip on the ball cock's pull rod and slide the float cup higher (above, right). To lower the water, move the cup down.

SEALING LEAKS AT BOLTS AND GASKETS

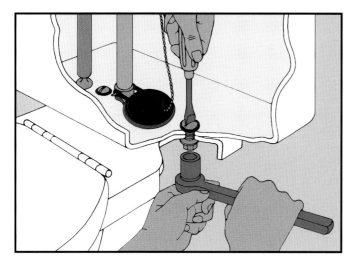

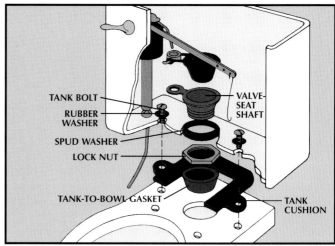

TANK BOLT
RUBBER WASHER
SPUD WASHER
LOCK NUT
TANK-TO-BOWL GASKET
VALVE-SEAT SHAFT
TANK CUSHION

Tightening the tank bolts.

Drips at the tank bolts may be caused by condensation on the tank's exterior, or by seepage from the inside. To check, pour a few drops of food coloring into the tank and hold white tissue over the bolts. If the tissue turns that color, tighten the bolts to stop the leaks.

◆ Turn off the water and drain the tank. Hold the slotted head of the bolt with a screwdriver or have a helper do it.
◆ Tighten the nut below the tank with a socket wrench and a deep socket *(above)*, or use an adjustable wrench.
◆ Turn the water back on.
◆ If the leak persists, drain the tank, remove the bolts, and replace their washers.

Replacing flush-valve washers.

If water leaks outside the toilet at the connection between tank and bowl, you must remove the tank.

◆ Turn off the water, drain the tank, disconnect the supply tube *(page 160)*, and unscrew the tank bolts.
◆ Lift the tank off the bowl and set it on its back on a padded work surface.
◆ The components that connect the tank and bowl appear above in diagrammatic form. Remove the lock nut on the valve-seat shaft protruding from the tank bottom, then pull the shaft into the tank and replace the spud washer and tank-to-bowl gasket. Reattach the lock nut.
◆ Place the tank on the tank cushion, reconnect the tank bolts, and attach the supply tube. Turn on the water.

DETERRING TOILET TANK CONDENSATION

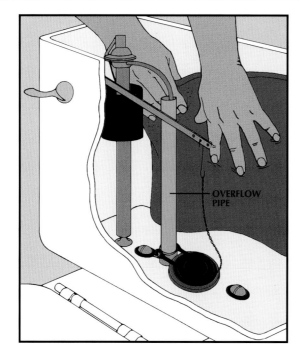

OVERFLOW PIPE

Installing insulation pads.

Condensation on the outside of a toilet tank may signal other problems, such as a constant leak from tank to bowl. If temperature or humidity is the cause, line the tank with a waterproof insulating material such as foam rubber.

◆ Turn off the water, drain the tank, and sponge it dry.
◆ Measure the inside width and depth of the tank and the height from the bottom of the tank to a point 1 inch above the overflow pipe.
◆ Cut four pieces of $\frac{1}{2}$-inch-thick foam rubber to fit the front, the back, and each side.
◆ Trim 1 inch from the width of the front and back pieces so they will abut the side pieces.
◆ Make a cutout for the toilet handle, and be sure the pads do not interfere with other moving parts.
◆ Apply a liberal coating of silicone glue or rubber cement to the inside tank surfaces; press the pads in place.
◆ Let the glue dry 24 hours before refilling the tank.

REPLACING A TOILET SEAT

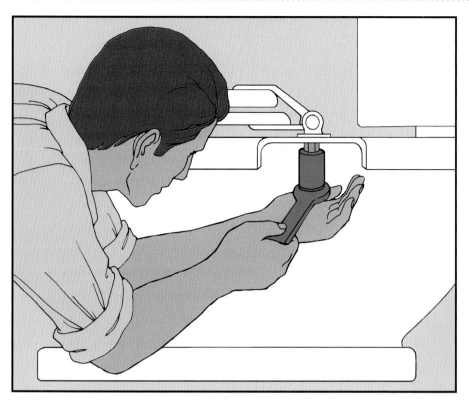

Removing the seat bolts.
To take off an old toilet seat, unscrew the nuts underneath the bowl. First try to turn the nuts with long-nose pliers. Should that fail, twist gently using a socket wrench with a deep socket. If the seat bolts are too corroded to loosen, apply the methods below.

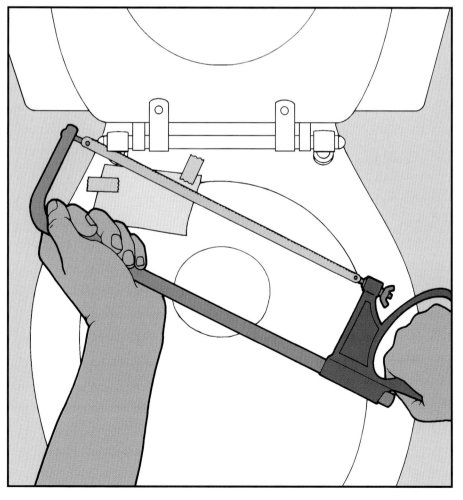

Freeing corroded bolts.
◆ Soak the bolts with penetrating oil for at least 30 minutes—overnight is better still. Then try loosening the nuts once more.
◆ If penetrating oil does not free the nuts, tape thin cardboard on top of the bowl next to the heads of the bolts to protect the china. Then, with a hacksaw, cut off the boltheads, sawing through the attached washers *(left)*.

6

Updating Your Bathroom

You can noticeably improve almost any bathroom with a variety of basic amenities. From hanging a mirror to adding an exhaust fan, the installations and modifications explained in the pages that follow not only modernize a bathroom but also make it safer, more accessible, and generally more agreeable to family members and guests alike.

Positioning a glass tub enclosure →

Hanging a Mirror

Placing a large mirror above the bathroom washbasin not only aids grooming, it seems to enlarge the room. Buy $\frac{1}{4}$-inch glass mirror and have the dealer cut it. Ask to have the edges seamed, which removes the sharp side of each edge. In determining the dimensions, plan for at least $\frac{1}{8}$ inch of clear space around the mirror to ease installation and to allow for settling of the house.

Methods for Mounting: Hanging a mirror on the wall requires special hardware, which comes in several varieties. In the system illustrated here, J clips and L clips anchor the mirror. Made of metal, J clips support the weight of the glass and provide a $\frac{1}{8}$-inch ventilation space behind the mirror to prevent corrosion. Plastic L clips keep the top of the mirror in place.

Self-adhesive felt pads stuck to the back of the mirror help to maintain the ventilation space and prevent the mirror from flexing. In areas subject to earthquakes, a bulky adhesive called mirror mastic *(box, opposite)* not only sticks the mirror to the wall but also serves instead of felt pads as a spacer.

Avoiding Corrosion: A mirror's reflective coating is easily damaged by moisture and harsh chemicals. Never mount a mirror so that it touches a backsplash; water creeping onto the backing could ruin it. Let a freshly plastered or painted wall dry for a week before installing a mirror. When cleaning the glass, avoid preparations with ammonia.

 CAUTION *If you are carrying a mirror and it starts to fall, do what the professionals do—get out of the way. Never try to catch it.*

Mirror-Handling Checklist

✔ Each square foot of $\frac{1}{4}$-inch mirror weighs more than 3 pounds. Work with a helper if your mirror is larger than 12 square feet—for example, if it is larger than 3 feet by 4 feet or 6 by 2.

✔ When you bring a mirror home, store it on edge.

✔ Salts and oils from human skin can damage mirror backing; always wear work gloves when handling the mirror.

✔ Carry the mirror on edge so it will not sag and break of its own weight. When working with a helper and navigating stairs, post the stronger person at the lower end.

TOOLS

Electronic
   stud finder
Drill
Level

MATERIALS

$\frac{1}{4}$-inch glass mirror,
   cut to size
Self-adhesive felt
   pads
J clips
L clips
$1\frac{1}{2}$-inch flat-head
   screws
$1\frac{1}{2}$-inch round-head
   screws
Mirror mastic

1. Preparing the wall.

◆ Mark the locations of the mirror's bottom corners on the wall—at least $\frac{1}{8}$ inch away from the backsplash and adjacent walls. Use a straightedge to join the marks to make a baseline for the mirror.

◆ To check for bulges in the wall, run a straight board over the area the mirror will occupy *(above)*.

◆ To determine the height of any bulge, center the board on it and, using the bulge as a pivot, push one end of the board against the wall. Have your helper measure the gap between the wall and the board at the other end and halve this distance.

◆ Flatten bulges higher than $\frac{1}{8}$ inch with a hammer.

2. Mounting the J clips.

◆ Using an electronic stud finder, locate the studs inside the mirror area nearest the ends of the baseline.

◆ Place the bottom corner of a J clip on the baseline at a stud near one end of the line. Mark the location of the clip's screw holes and drill a pilot hole $1\frac{1}{2}$ inches deep at each mark.

◆ Secure the clip with flat-head screws (above), then cover the heads with a felt pad (inset).

◆ Attach a J clip to a stud at the line's other end.

◆ For a mirror wider than 5 feet, mount a J clip on every second stud.

3. Placing the mirror in the J clips.

◆ Using a level, measure up from each J clip a distance equal to the height of the mirror plus $\frac{1}{4}$ inch.

◆ Mark and drill a pilot hole into the stud at that height.

◆ Stick two or more rows of felt pads on the back of the mirror, keeping the pads several inches in from each side.

◆ With a helper, lift the mirror. Tilt the top edge forward and lower the bottom edge into the J clips. If necessary, slide the mirror sideways into its intended position.

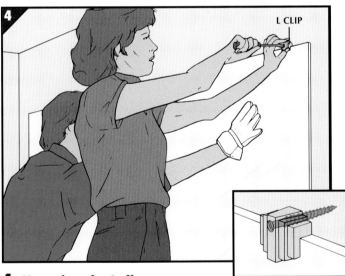

4. Mounting the L clips.

◆ Push the mirror toward the wall, listening carefully for the muted sound of felt pads making contact. A sharp sound indicates the mirror is hitting the wall; add pads on top of the first ones. Test again and add a third layer of pads if necessary.

◆ While a helper steadies the mirror, drive a round-head screw through the hole in an L clip and into each pilot hole (inset). Tighten each fastener no more than needed to prevent movement of the mirror when you push on it.

Mirror Mastic for a Permanent Bond

Mirror mastic helps secure a mirror to the wall without damage to the backing. Although particularly suited to earthquake zones because it remains resilient and will flex with tremors, mastic is messy to use and permanent. Attempting to remove a mirror glued with this adhesive usually damages both mirror and wall.

Mastic, which takes the place of felt pads on the back of the mirror, is applied after Step 2 of mirror installation. Lay the mirror facedown on a clean blanket. Using a wood scrap to avoid scratching the backing, scoop mastic onto the mirror in separate pats—each about $1\frac{1}{2}$ inches across and $\frac{3}{4}$ inch thick. Apply four pats for every square foot of mirror, keeping the adhesive at least $2\frac{1}{2}$ inches from the edges. Then mount the mirror as shown in Steps 3 and 4.

Installing a Glass Tub Enclosure

Replacing an old-fashioned shower-curtain rod with a glass tub enclosure not only helps to keep shower spray where it belongs but also adds an elegant touch to the bathroom. Most tub enclosures are designed to fit a standard 5-foot tub between two side walls and are made of glass and extruded aluminum. They come in many styles: Panels may be clear, frosted, or mirrored, and frames may be polished bright or anodized in gold or other colors.

Preparing the Tub Area: Before buying an enclosure kit, check your tub rim and side walls with a level and a framing square. If the tub is as much as $\frac{1}{4}$ inch off level, or if the walls are out of plumb by that amount, you can compensate by adjusting the enclosure's panel rollers; if the variance is much greater, an enclosure may be impractical.

For a tub with tiled walls that do not extend as high as the top of the enclosure frame, add filler tiles as needed, securing them with a waterproof bathroom adhesive.

A Sturdy Installation: Methods for securing the enclosure frame in place vary depending on whether there are studs located where the frame is to be attached. When studs are present, drill through the finished wall and attach the frame to the stud with $1\frac{1}{2}$-inch No. 8 wood screws. When studs are not present, the frame should be secured with hollow-wall anchors.

Care and Maintenance: To keep water from spraying between the panels into the bathroom when showering, keep the inner panel toward the shower head. The only upkeep required is periodic cleaning with a nonabrasive window cleaner and, when necessary, adjusting the panel rollers in their slots.

 TOOLS

Tape measure
Hacksaw with
   metal-cutting
   blade
Miter box
Metal file
Grease pencil
Utility knife
Level
Electric drill

SAFETY TIPS

If you must drill into ceramic tile with a carbide bit, wear safety goggles and use a dust mask.

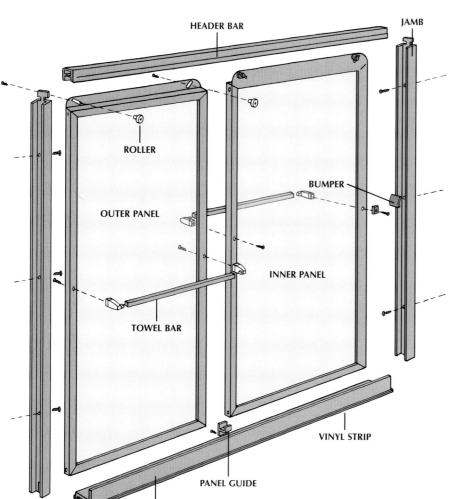

HEADER BAR

JAMB

ROLLER

BUMPER

OUTER PANEL

INNER PANEL

TOWEL BAR

PANEL GUIDE

VINYL STRIP

TUB TRACK

Anatomy of an enclosure.
The typical glass tub enclosure at left consists of a frame and sliding panels. The frame includes side jambs, a header bar, and a tub track, which is sealed against the tub rim with a flexible vinyl strip. The tempered glass panels, each with a towel bar in this example, ride inside the header bar on adjustable rollers and are held in the tub track by a panel guide. Bumpers keep the panels from hitting the jambs too hard.

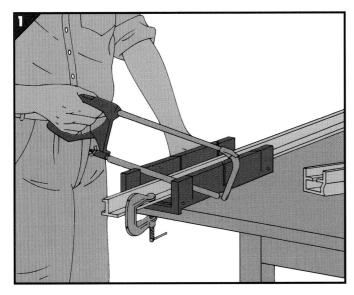

1. Cutting the pieces.

◆ Measure the tub rim between the two side walls, then subtract $\frac{1}{16}$ inch to avoid too tight a fit. Mark the tub track to this length and cut it with a hacksaw, using a miter box to ensure a square cut *(left)*.

◆ To measure for the header bar, set one of the jambs on the tub rim against a side wall and mark the wall at the top of the jamb. Mark the second wall the same way, then determine the distance between the two marks. Subtract $\frac{1}{16}$ inch and cut the header bar to that length.

◆ Smooth the cut edges of both pieces with a metal file.

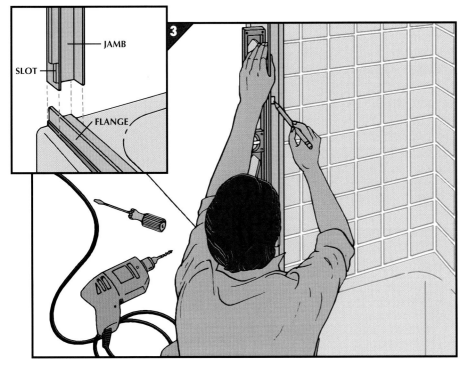

2. Fitting the tub track.

◆ Center the tub track on the tub rim, with the tall flange toward the room. Mark the position of the track on the tub rim with a grease pencil.

◆ If the enclosure kit includes vinyl sealing strips *(inset)*, press them onto the flanges on the underside of the tub track; trim off any excess with a utility knife. For kits with no vinyl strips, apply a bead of silicone caulk along the edges at the bottom of the track.

◆ Set the track on the tub rim between the marked lines. Secure it in place with masking tape until both of the jambs are installed.

3. Marking the walls.

◆ Place a jamb at one end of the tub track so that the slot in the jamb goes over the track flange *(inset)*. Adjust the jamb against the wall with a level to get it upright, then mark the wall through each screw hole. Set the jamb aside. Repeat the process for the facing wall with the other jamb.

◆ Drill holes at each mark for the fasteners: $\frac{3}{32}$-inch pilot holes for wood screws if a stud is present behind the wall, or larger holes for hollow-wall anchors. Use a carbide-tipped bit for ceramic tile.

◆ Put the bumper in place on one of the jambs, place the jamb on the track as before, and fasten the jamb to the wall. Do not install the other jamb yet.

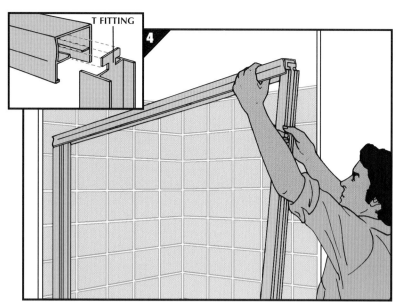

T FITTING

4. Completing the frame.

◆ Place the bumper on the unattached jamb and set the jamb aside.

◆ Slide one end of the header bar into the top of the installed jamb, inserting the bar into the jamb's T-shaped fitting.

◆ Angle the free end of the bar slightly outward and connect it to the T fitting on the unattached jamb *(inset)*.

◆ Gently lift the bottom of the jamb into place on the tub track and fasten the jamb to the wall.

◆ Remove the masking tape from the tub track now that the track is held in place by the jambs.

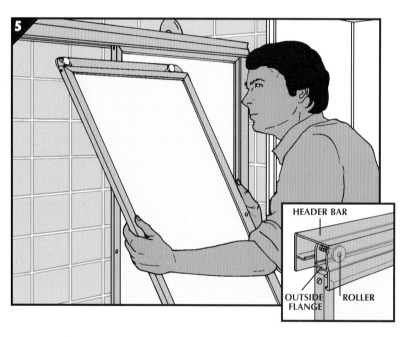

HEADER BAR

OUTSIDE FLANGE   ROLLER

5. Hanging the panels.

With the frame installation complete, put the door panels in place.

◆ Place a roller in each of the diagonal slots at the tops of the door panels; do not tighten the roller screws yet.

◆ Hold the inner panel with its rollers facing the tub. Lift the panel to set the rollers over the lip of the header bar's inside flange. Install the outer panel so that its rollers rest on the outside flange of the bar *(inset)*.

◆ Slide the panels against the jambs. If a panel does not slide freely or does not hang straight, adjust it by removing the panel from the frame and shifting the position of one or both of the rollers within the diagonal slots. Tighten each roller screw and rehang the panel.

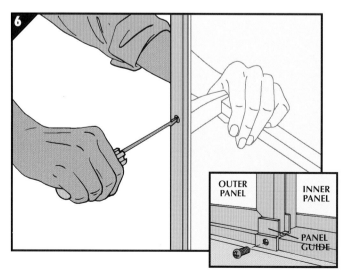

OUTER PANEL   INNER PANEL

PANEL GUIDE

6. Attaching the hardware.

◆ Secure the panel guide *(inset)* to the tub track so that it will retain the bottom edges of both panels.

◆ Attach any accessories supplied with the kit—in this case, two towel bars.

◆ Apply a thin bead of silicone caulk where the frame meets the tub and walls. Smooth the caulk if necessary with a finger dipped in liquid detergent. Let the caulk cure overnight before using the tub.

Making the Bathroom Safe and Accessible

Most bathrooms combine at least three potentially dangerous elements: electricity, water, and slick surfaces. You can improve the safety of your bathroom and the ease with which you can use it by undertaking some or all of the modest projects described here and on pages 172-175.

Measures against Falls: A water-slicked shower floor or tub can be dangerous. To reduce the likelihood of accident, add texture to either surface with grip strips *(below)*.

Also consider installing grab bars *(page 172)* as handholds on walls surrounding the bathing area. Tow-el bars are too weak to rely on. Choose grab bars made from metal tubing without sharp corners. And avoid hanging towels on them; someone could accidentally grasp the towel instead and fall.

Preventing Electric Shock: To minimize the hazards of operating electrical appliances near water, the National Electrical Code requires that new bathroom electrical circuits be equipped with a device that is called a ground-fault circuit interrupter, or GFCI. If your bathroom does not have this protection, you can add it by installing a GFCI outlet in place of the receptacle that already exists *(page 173)*.

Adaptations for Disabilities: For someone with a disability, the typical bathroom can be difficult, or even impossible, to use. Ideally, a bathroom for a family member who needs a wheelchair, a walker, or simply some assistance with standing up or sitting down is designed from the outset for their comfort and capabilities. As described on pages 174 and 175, you can also make an old bathroom somewhat more accessible with a variety of products and modifications.

APPLYING GRIP STRIPS

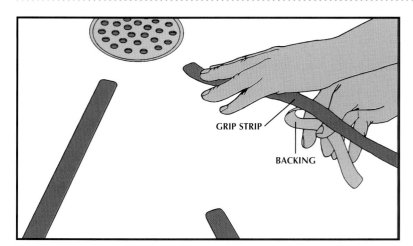

GRIP STRIP

BACKING

Laying a safe pattern of strips.
◆ Wash the shower or tub floor, clean it with rubbing alcohol, and let it dry.
◆ For a shower, plan a star pattern of strips *(below, far left)*; for a tub, arrange strips both in a chevron pointed at the drain and in parallel lines *(below, left)*.
◆ To apply each strip, peel the backing from one end and press it firmly in place, then continue peeling as you work *(left)*. If you must cut a strip, round the corners so they will not curl later.

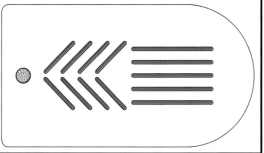

171

GRAB BARS FOR SHOWER AND TUB

1. Positioning the bar.

The grab bar shown here is designed so each flange is anchored by two screws in a stud and a toggle bolt through the wall. (To support someone weighing more than about 250 pounds, double the studs from the other side of the wall and use three screws.)

◆ Locate studs above the tile with an electronic stud finder.

◆ Drop a plumb line at the center of each stud and mark the width of the stud with masking tape at the height you intend to anchor the flanges.

◆ Place the grab bar so that two mounting holes in each flange lie on the tape. Mark all six hole locations with a pencil (above).

2. Drilling holes.

◆ At each hole location, tap a punch with a hammer to break through the slick tile glaze.

◆ Wearing safety goggles, use carbide-tipped bits to drill a $\frac{1}{2}$-inch hole through the wall for each toggle bolt. For the screws, drill a hole through the tile slightly larger than the screw diameter, then use an ordinary bit to drill a smaller hole into the wooden stud.

◆ Remove the tape from the wall.

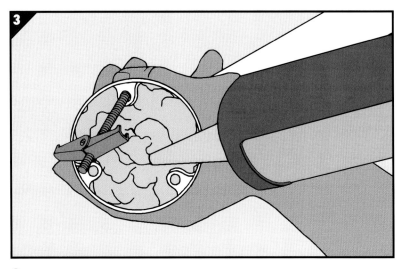

3. Mounting the bar.

◆ Insert a $\frac{3}{16}$-inch toggle bolt into its hole on a flange and fill the inside of the flange with silicone caulk (above). Prepare the other flange the same way.

◆ Position the bar on the wall, pushing the toggle bolts into place. Insert 3-inch-long screws into the remaining holes and tighten screws and toggle bolts with a screwdriver.

◆ Caulk around each flange and let dry for 24 hours.

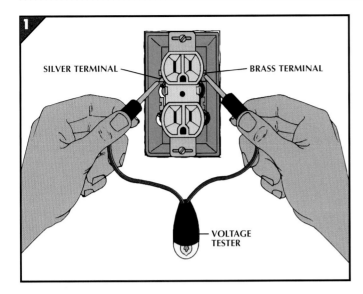

SILVER TERMINAL — BRASS TERMINAL

VOLTAGE TESTER

1. Checking for power.

◆ Turn off the electricity to the bathroom receptacle at the service panel. Then unscrew and remove the cover plate.
◆ Test for power at the receptacle with a voltage tester *(left)*. Holding the tester by its insulated wires, touch the probes to each pair of brass and silver terminals; the tester will not light if the power is off.

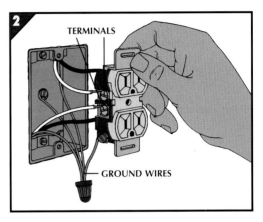

TERMINALS

GROUND WIRES

2. Removing the receptacle.

Unscrew the receptacle and pull it from the box. Look inside; consult an electrician if the wiring is aluminum, if there are no ground wires, or if the box is less than $2\frac{3}{4}$ inches deep. Otherwise, detach all wires from the receptacle terminals.

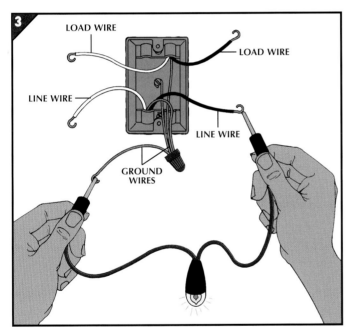

LOAD WIRE

LOAD WIRE

LINE WIRE

LINE WIRE

GROUND WIRES

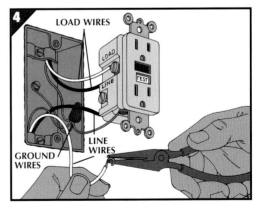

LOAD WIRES

LOAD

LINE

TEST

GROUND WIRES

LINE WIRES

3. Identifying line and load wires.

To install a GFCI receptacle, you need to know which black wire in the box brings power from the service panel.
◆ To identify this so-called line wire, stretch out all the wires so they touch neither each other nor the box. Then turn the power on.
◆ Keeping your hands away from any bare wires, touch one probe of the voltage tester to a ground wire and the other to each black wire. The one that causes the tester to glow is the line wire *(above)*; the other is called the load wire.

4. Installing the GFCI.

◆ Turn the power off. Attach the wires of the line and load cables to the corresponding terminals on the GFCI, connecting the black wires to the brass terminals. Attach the ground wire to the green terminal.

◆ Screw the GFCI into place and replace the cover plate. Turn on the power, then press the test button. If the wiring is correct, the reset button will pop out, interrupting the power going to the receptacle. Depress the button to reset the GFCI.

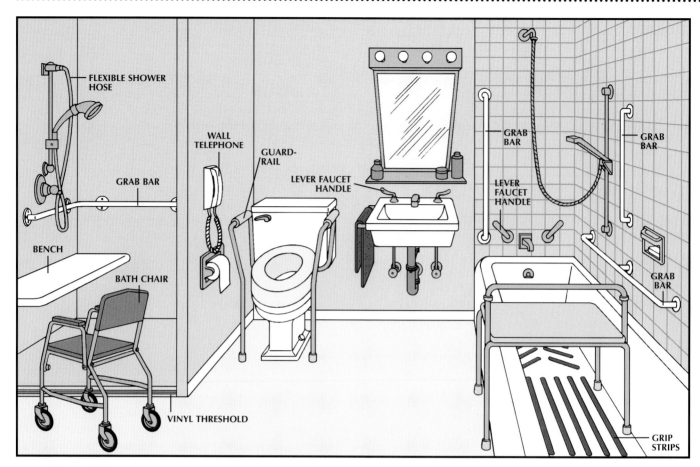

FLEXIBLE SHOWER HOSE

WALL TELEPHONE

GUARD-RAIL

LEVER FAUCET HANDLE

GRAB BAR

GRAB BAR

GRAB BAR

LEVER FAUCET HANDLE

BENCH

BATH CHAIR

GRAB BAR

VINYL THRESHOLD

GRIP STRIPS

Helpful modifications.

Few bathrooms offer all the features in the composite illustration above, but a person with a disability may find several of them beneficial.

A roll-in shower. For a family member who uses a wheelchair or bath chair, consider a shower with a low flexible-vinyl threshold; either vehicle can easily roll across, and the vinyl keeps water from flowing out. Once inside, a bather may transfer to a bench seat.

An accessible telephone. A wall phone with the dial or keypad in the handset provides a link to help.

An easier-to-use toilet. A thicker-than-usual toilet seat and adjustable guardrails may help someone who has difficulty sitting down or standing up. Alternatively, install a grab bar beside the toilet.

A nonslip floor. Floor tiles in a

bathroom are a poor choice for someone who may slip and fall. Carpet or vinyl sheet flooring are among the alternatives.

A convenient mirror. Tilt mirrors downward a bit to make them useful for a person in a wheelchair.

Lever handles. Equip faucets with long handles, rather than knobs that must be grasped.

Washbasin access. A wall-hung basin lets someone in a wheelchair roll up to the sink; insulate the hot-water pipe to prevent burns.

Grab bars and grip strips. As in any bathroom, grab bars and grip strips in tubs and showers help to prevent falls while bathing.

Seating in the bath. Place a bench or bath chair in a tub or shower; install a showerhead with a flexible hose, and mount it on a sliding bar or within easy reach.

Easing the Way for a Wheelchair

✔ A door opening 32 inches wide is usable if the bathroom opens onto a wide hallway, but an opening of 36 inches is better.

✔ Inside the bathroom, the clear floor space should be at least 60 inches square to allow a wheelchair to turn around completely.

✔ Sinks must be no more than 34 inches high, and they must not rest on a vanity.

✔ Buy an add-on toilet seat from a medical-supply store to raise the seat 4 inches—the same height as most wheelchair seats.

✔ Mount such items as the telephone at 33 to 36 inches.

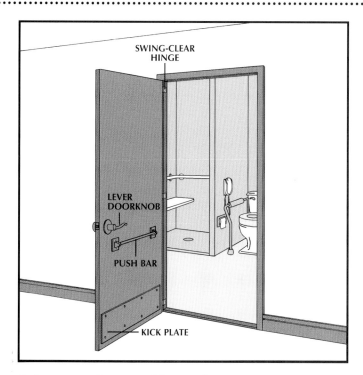

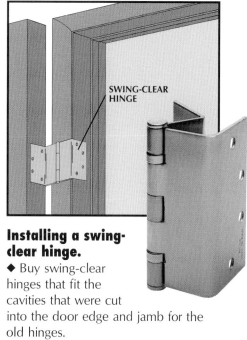

A doorway that provides easier access.

To maximize the width of a door opening, install a pocket door or a sliding door. Rehang a hinged door to open outward *(above)*; you can increase its effective width with swing-clear hinges *(right)*, which add $1\frac{1}{2}$ to 2 inches to the opening. Other useful door hardware includes a kick plate, a lever doorknob *(below)*, and a push bar to help open and close the door.

Installing a swing-clear hinge.
◆ Buy swing-clear hinges that fit the cavities that were cut into the door edge and jamb for the old hinges.
◆ Unscrew the old hinges from the door and the jamb; set the door aside.
◆ If new screw holes are required, pack lengths of dowel, coated with glue, into the existing holes. Let the glue dry overnight, then drill pilot holes for the new screws.
◆ Attach the swing-clear hinges and rehang the door.

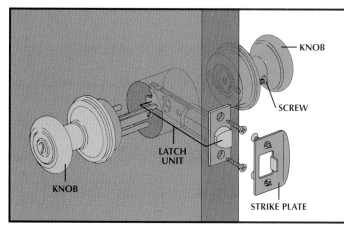

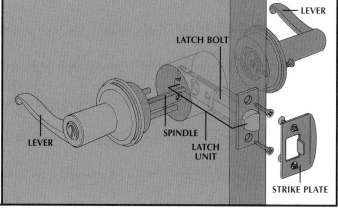

Putting in place a lever-knob assembly.
◆ Unfasten the two screws that secure the knob plate and pull it off with the knob *(above, left)*. If no screws are visible, depress the metal tab that holds one knob on its shaft. Then remove the knob and the underlying cover plate to reveal the screws.

◆ Pull off the other knob.
◆ Remove the two screws holding the latch unit in place and slide it out of the door.
◆ With a half-round rasp, enlarge the lock and latch holes as needed to accommodate the new mechanism.
◆ Set the latch unit of the lever knob in the door. Screw it to the door edge.

◆ Insert the spindle attached to one of the two lever handles so that it engages the latch unit; then install the other lever. Secure the assembly with screws *(above, right)*.
◆ Check to make sure the strike plate aligns with the latch bolt.

175

Storage space is often at a premium in a bathroom. A simple way to make more room is to install a larger medicine cabinet or a supplementary one, mounted on the wall or recessed into it. For even more space, you can discard a stand-alone washbasin and instead install a vanity with a sink in the countertop.

Considerations for a Vanity: Ready-made cabinets are available in many widths. Choose a vanity that is at least wide enough to cover the holes left in the wall by the bracket for the old washbasin but not so large that the bathroom becomes cramped *(page 216)*. For ease of installation and maintenance, choose a one-piece countertop like the one shown on page 179.

If you plan to tile, wallpaper, or paint the bathroom walls, do so before installing the vanity. This way the new cabinet will cover the edges of the finish.

Installing a Medicine Cabinet: A surface-mounted cabinet can be hung virtually anywhere *(page 180)*, but recessed cabinets require more consideration. Most are designed to fit in the space between existing studs, commonly $14\frac{1}{2}$ inches but sometimes $22\frac{1}{2}$ inches. If the cabinet location is not critical, simply fit it between the studs *(page 180)*.

A unit wider than a single stud space—or one that must be centered on a wall or above the washbasin—requires cutting out sections of one or more studs.

A Suitable Wall: The technique for cutting away studs shown on these pages applies only to nonbearing walls, which carry no weight from the structure above. Usually such walls run parallel to joists. A basement ceiling or attic floor is the best place to find exposed joists, which usually have the same orientation from floor to floor. Treat all exterior walls, and any walls about which you are uncertain, as load-bearing walls. Avoid them.

Making Holes in Walls: Whenever possible, avoid cutting into a part of a wall that might conceal pipes or wires. To check for wires, note the locations of switches, outlets, and lights on both sides of the wall and in the rooms above and below. Also observe where pipes and drains enter and leave walls and floors.

Before you cut or drill, turn off electricity to any circuit that might run through the wall. Drill only enough to penetrate the wallboard or plaster and lath, usually less than 1 inch; plan to cut studs, if necessary, as a second step. Stop at once if the drill bit hits a hard surface; it might be a pipe or electrical junction box. If you puncture a pipe, turn off the main water supply and call a plumber. Severed cables usually require an electrician's help.

 **TOOLS**

 **MATERIALS**

 SAFETY TIPS

Wrenches
Screwdriver
Cold chisel
Saber saw
Electronic stud
   finder
Utility knife
Pry bar
Level
Electric drill with
   screwdriver bit
Backsaw
Dry-wall saw

Wood shims
$2\frac{1}{4}$-inch No. 6
   dry-wall screws
Adhesive caulk
$1\frac{1}{2}$- and $2\frac{1}{2}$-inch
   finishing nails
$\frac{3}{4}$-inch brads
Scribe molding
Shoe molding
Hollow-wall
   anchors
2-by-4s
Wallboard

To protect your eyes, wear safety goggles when drilling or sawing at or above the level of your waist.

CLEARING THE WAY FOR A VANITY

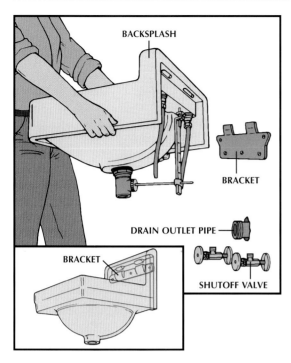

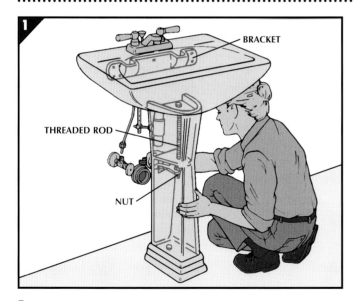

Dismounting wall-hung basins.

◆ Turn off the water at the basin shutoff valves or at the house's main valve. Disconnect the supply lines and the drainpipe assembly *(pages 139 and 154).*
◆ To remove a basin hung on a bracket behind the backsplash as shown in the drawings at left, simply lift the basin straight up.
◆ Unscrew the bracket from the wall.

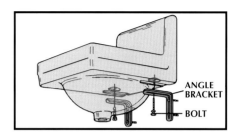

An angle bracket mounting.

To detach a basin supported from below by angle brackets, have a helper hold the basin while you loosen the mounting bolts with a wrench and remove them. Set the basin aside and unscrew the brackets from the wall.

DISASSEMBLING PEDESTAL BASINS

1. Removing a two-piece pedestal basin.

◆ Shut off the water and disconnect the water-supply lines and drainpipe assembly *(pages 139 and 154).*
◆ Look inside the pedestal for a long threaded rod connecting the basin to its base. In the absence of such a rod, simply lift the basin from its wall bracket and set it aside. Otherwise, reach inside the pedestal with a wrench and remove the nut at the lower end of the rod *(above).* Lift the basin off its pedestal and wall bracket, then remove the rod from the basin.

2. Removing the pedestal.

◆ Unscrew any fasteners you find holding the pedestal base to the floor *(above),* then lift the pedestal away.
◆ If the pedestal is secured to the floor with grout, gently rock it back and forth to break the seal. Loosen old grout from the floor with a cold chisel.
◆ For a pedestal and basin molded as a single unit, unscrew the pedestal from the floor. Then lift the entire fixture free of the basin wall bracket.
◆ Detach the basin bracket from the wall.

ANCHORING A VANITY BASE AND COUNTERTOP

1. Aligning the cabinet.

◆ Position the vanity so that shutoff valves and drainpipe are roughly centered within the frame. If the vanity has a back, mark openings for the pipes, then cut the holes with a saber saw.

◆ Push the vanity against the wall. Mark the outline of the cabinet on the wall with light pencil lines, then set the cabinet aside.

◆ With a stud finder, locate wall studs that fall within the cabinet outline. Mark the center of each stud above the outline as shown here.

2. Dealing with baseboard.

◆ For wooden baseboard, run a utility knife along the joint between the wall and the top of the baseboard section extending across the planned area for the vanity, breaking any paint seal.

◆ At one end of the baseboard section, tap a small pry bar into the joint. Place a shim behind the bar (above), then lever the molding away from the wall. Slip a shim into the gap.

◆ Continue prying and shimming to loosen the baseboard section, then pull it free and set it aside.

To remove vinyl molding, cut it at the cabinet outline with a utility knife guided by a straightedge. Peel away the piece below the pipes.

3. Securing the vanity.

◆ Reposition the vanity against the wall and level it from side to side by inserting shims under the cabinet (far left). Level the cabinet from front to back by shimming it away from the wall (left).

◆ Mark each shim at cabinet edges. Remove one shim at a time, saw it to length, and slide it back into place.

◆ For wallboard or plaster walls drive $2\frac{1}{4}$-inch No. 6 dry-wall screws through the back of the cabinet about $\frac{3}{4}$ inch from the top and into the studs that were marked earlier.

ADHESIVE
BEAD

4. Mounting the countertop.

◆ Attach as many of the faucet and drain fittings to the countertop as possible *(pages 139-142 and 155)*.

◆ Apply a bead of adhesive caulk along the top edges of the cabinet, then press the countertop into place. Wipe off excess caulk immediately.

5. Finishing up.

◆ Connect the water-supply lines and the drain *(pages 139, 141, and 155)*.

◆ If you detached a section of wooden baseboard earlier, use a backsaw to cut the baseboard at the lines marking the sides of the vanity. Discard the center section and nail the others to the wall with $2\frac{1}{2}$-inch finishing nails.

◆ Cover gaps at the sides of the vanity with scribe molding that matches the cabinet finish; attach the molding with $\frac{3}{4}$-inch brads *(above)*. Cover a gap at the floor with shoe molding secured with $1\frac{1}{2}$-inch finishing nails.

SURFACE-MOUNTED MEDICINE CABINETS

1. Hanging the cabinet.

◆ Locate studs where the cabinet will go. Have a helper hold it with at least one upper mounting hole on a stud. Mark through the upper holes and lower the cabinet. With a level, align the marks.

◆ If both marks are over studs, drive screws into the studs until the heads are $\frac{1}{8}$ inch from the wall.

◆ Otherwise, mark for the lower mounting holes as well. For marks not on a stud, drill holes for hollow-wall anchors, tap the anchors into place, and tighten. Loosen both anchor screws $\frac{1}{8}$ inch from the wall.

◆ Slip the cabinet's mounting holes over the screwheads. Drive screws through the other holes and tighten them all.

2. Adding shelves and doors.

◆ Position the shelves on the interior brackets.

◆ Attach the door hinges and the doors. Mounting systems vary, but doors commonly are first attached to the upper hinge, then adjusted for fit at the bottom hinge *(above)*.

◆ Complete the installation by affixing door catches and any hardware provided by the manufacturer.

A MEDICINE CABINET BETWEEN TWO STUDS

Cutting an opening.

◆ Use a stud finder to locate the studs on each side of the cabinet location.

◆ Draw the dimensions of the desired opening on the wall between the studs. With a level, ensure that the top and bottom lines are horizontal.

◆ Cut away the outlined section, using a dry-wall saw for wallboard. A saber saw fitted with hacksaw blades works well for plaster walls; change blades as they dull.

◆ Drive a dry-wall screw partway into each stud,

$1\frac{1}{2}$ inches above the top edge of the opening.

◆ Cut a 2-by-4 header to fit snugly between the studs, and push it up against the screws. To anchor the header, angle two screws through each end into the stud.

◆ In the same way, install a 2-by-4 sill at the bottom of the opening *(left)*.

◆ Set the cabinet into the recess. Through the pre-drilled holes on each side, drive screws partway into the studs. Level the cabinet and tighten the screws while maintaining the level.

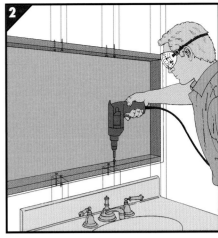

1. Cutting out studs.

◆ Mark the proposed opening on the wall, then with a stud finder locate a stud to the right and left of the outline.
◆ On the wall between these studs, mark horizontal lines $1\frac{1}{2}$ inches above and below the proposed opening.
◆ Cut away the rectangle of wall bounded by these lines and the studs.
◆ Use a backsaw to cut through studs in the cabinet space, flush with the edges of the opening *(above)*.
◆ Gently pry the stud segments away from the wall behind them. Nails that hold the wall surface to the studs may pull through, and you may have to repair some damage on the other side.

2. Framing the opening.

◆ From 2-by-4s, cut a header and a sill to fit snugly between the studs at the left and right of the opening. Screw the header and sill to the cut ends of the studs *(above)*. Fasten header and sill ends with screws that are angled into the studs at the sides of the opening.
◆ Screw vertical 2-by-4s to both end studs to provide a surface for patching wallboard.

3. Customizing the fit.

◆ If the cabinet does not fill the framed opening, cut two 2-by-4s to the height of the opening. At the sides of the planned recess, secure them to the sill and header with angled screws *(left)*.
◆ Cut and fit wallboard patches to cover the sides of the opening to the inner edges of the cabinet framing.
◆ Position the cabinet inside the framing, using shims at the bottom and sides to make it level and plumb. Drive at least two screws through each side of the cabinet, through the shims and into the framing.

Fresh Air for the Bathroom

Often stale and humid, the atmosphere in a bathroom fogs mirrors and promotes mold and mildew. Over time, the moisture can damage paint, wallpaper, and even walls.

An exhaust fan solves these problems by venting odors and humidity outdoors. The fan shown on these and the following pages also incorporates an infrared bulb to add a measure of heat on cold mornings.

Planning Steps: Before buying a fan, first determine how you will vent it. Through an unfloored attic to the roof is often the most direct route from a second-floor bathroom. With a finished floor overhead, you must run the ventilation duct between floor joists to an outside wall.

After estimating the length of duct required, use the estimator below to determine the air-handling capacity, in cubic feet per minute (CFM), of a fan that will renew the bathroom air every $7\frac{1}{2}$ minutes.

Ducting Choices: Flexible duct, best for runs of less than 16 feet, can be bent around corners or obstructions. It comes in sections that stretch to 8 feet and can be bought in kits that include a weatherproof wall or roof cap *(opposite)*, and the plastic bands needed to clamp the duct to the fan and to the cap.

Rigid duct is often a better choice for longer runs; its inner surface is smooth and offers less resistance to air flow. Rigid duct cannot be bent, so special elbow fittings are needed to detour around obstacles.

Wiring Considerations: Before planning any wiring, first check local building and electrical codes for possible restrictions. Because exhaust fans require little power, they can usually be added to an existing circuit. The most convenient power source is often a junction box mounted on an attic joist.

Switching: Since the fan and heat lamp are designed to run separately or together, you will need two switches. You can mount separate switches in side-by-side boxes, or you can use a dual switch that fits into a single box. In either case, you will need three-conductor cable to serve the two switches.

⚠️ **CAUTION** *Do not open any electrical box without shutting off power to the circuit at the fuse or circuit-breaker box and double-checking with a voltage tester.*

 **TOOLS**

Electric drill	Nail set
Keyhole saw	Voltage tester
Hammer	Pliers
Carpenter's pencil	Cable ripper
Utility knife	Wire stripper
Saber saw	Screwdriver
Tape measure	Fish tape
Putty knife	Socket wrench

 **MATERIALS**

Duct kit	Cable clamps
Dual switch	$\frac{1}{2}$-inch plastic staples
Switch box	$1\frac{1}{4}$-inch roofing nails
Wire caps	Roofing cement
Electrician's tape	
Two- and three-conductor 14-gauge cable	

 SAFETY TIPS

Wear goggles to protect your eyes from dust and flying debris while hammering or sawing. A hard hat guards against painful encounters with rafters and exposed roofing nails. Before handling insulation in an attic, put on a long-sleeved shirt, gloves, and a disposable dust mask.

Calculating fan capacity.

Use your bathroom dimensions in the estimator at left to determine the minimum air-handling capacity for an exhaust fan. If the result falls between two fan sizes, choose the larger. And for long duct runs—more than 8 feet of flexible duct or 16 feet of rigid duct—pick the next larger fan.

Length   Width   Height

_____ x _____ x _____ ÷ 7.5 = _____ (CFM)

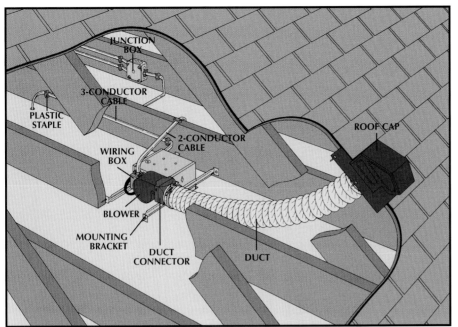

Anatomy of a fan installation.
Seen at left in an attic above a bathroom ceiling, a heater fan consists of a lamp housing fitted with a blower and a wiring box. Designed for a 250-watt heat lamp, the unit is fastened to joists with adjustable mounting brackets. A length of flexible duct, extending from the blower outlet to a hole cut through the roof, carries moisture outdoors through a roof cap. Dampers at the roof cap and inside a duct connector at the blower outlet prevent backdrafts when the fan is off. Power comes to the unit from a junction box by way of a two-conductor electrical cable. A three-conductor cable leads to a pair of switches in the bathroom below; one is for the fan, and the other is for the heat lamp.

MOUNTING AN EXHAUST FAN HOUSING

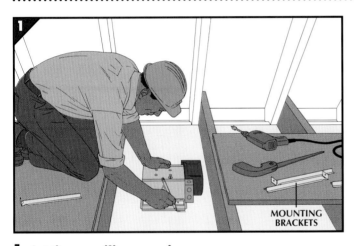

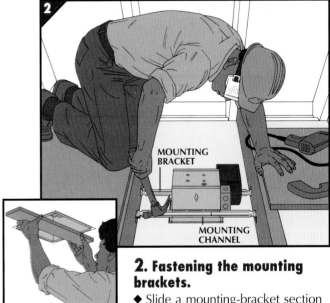

1. Cutting a ceiling opening.
◆ In the bathroom, drill a $\frac{1}{8}$-inch test hole in the center of the ceiling. If the bit hits a joist, fill the hole with spackling and drill another hole several inches away. Push a length of wire up through the test hole to mark the spot.

◆ Lay plywood across attic joists to support you and your tools and the mounting brackets for the fan. Push aside any insulation you find, then remove the marker wire. Center the lamp housing between the joists on either side of the test hole and outline the housing on the ceiling (above).

◆ Drill a $\frac{3}{4}$-inch hole at each corner of the outline, then cut along the lines with a keyhole saw, stationing a helper in the bathroom to support and catch the cutout.

2. Fastening the mounting brackets.
◆ Slide a mounting-bracket section into each end of the channel on one side of the lamp housing, then push the pieces together until they overlap. Repeat this procedure for the channel on the opposite side of the housing.

◆ While your helper in the bathroom holds a board across the ceiling opening, orient the blower outlet toward the exit point for the duct, then lower the housing through the ceiling to rest on the board (inset).

◆ Extend the mounting brackets until their nailing flanges touch the joists, and fasten both brackets with a $1\frac{1}{4}$-inch nail in each end (above).

183

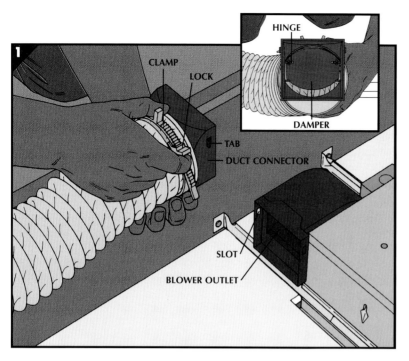

1. Attaching the flexible duct.

◆ Check that the damper inside the duct connector swings freely on its hinges, then slide a length of duct onto the circular end of the connector.

◆ Wrap a plastic clamp around the connection, then thread the clamp's serrated end through the lock. Tighten the connection by squeezing together the two projections on the clamp *(left)*.

◆ Holding the connector so that the damper hinge is at the top *(inset)*, attach the connector to the blower outlet. In this unit, tabs on the connector snap into matching slots in the outlet.

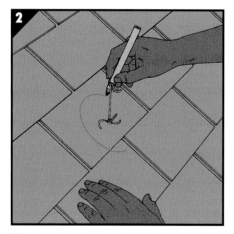

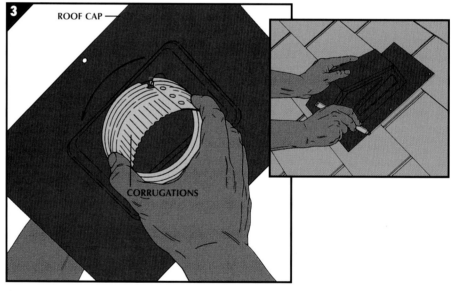

2. Making a roof opening.

◆ In the attic, hold the other duct end on the roof midway between two rafters. Mark around the duct with a carpenter's pencil, then drive a nail through the center of the circle.

◆ On the roof, find the marker nail. Draw a 5-inch-diameter circle, with it as the center *(above)*.

◆ Within the circle, pull out all roofing nails. Cut away shingles and roofing paper with a utility knife. Drill a starter hole inside the circle, then saw around the circumference.

3. Assembling the roof cap.

◆ Holding the corrugated end of the duct connector *(above)*, insert it into the underside of the roof cap. Lock the connector to the cap by turning it clockwise for some models, counterclockwise for others.

◆ Insert the connector into the roof opening, and mark the outline of the roof cap on the shingles *(inset)*.

⚠ **CAUTION** *If the slope of your roof is greater than 15 degrees, have the roof work performed by a professional.*

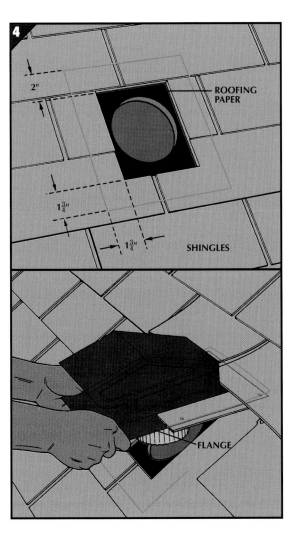

4. Installing the roof cap.

◆ Lift the roof cap out of the hole and set it aside.

◆ Within the outline marked in Step 3, measure 2 inches from the upper edge and draw a line. In the same manner, mark lines $1\frac{3}{4}$ inches in from the sides and bottom edge.

◆ Within this smaller area, cut away the shingles, but not the roofing paper *(left, top)*.

◆ Holding the cap at a 45-degree angle, slide the upper edge and sides of the flange under the shingles, and fit the duct connector into the 5-inch roof hole *(left, bottom)*.

◆ Nail the flange to the sheathing through the holes provided, lifting shingles as needed to do so. Apply roofing cement with a putty knife to seal the nailheads and shingle edges to the roof cap flange.

◆ In the attic, use a plastic clamp to connect the flexible duct to the roof cap's duct connector.

MAKING ELECTRICAL CONNECTIONS

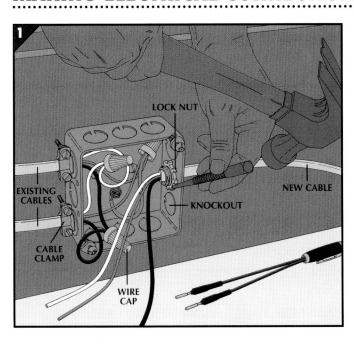

1. Tapping power.

◆ At the service panel, turn off power to the circuit you plan to extend.

◆ Remove the junction box cover, then, with a hammer and nail set, dislodge one of the removable disks called a knockout. Break it off with pliers.

◆ With a cable ripper, strip 8 inches of sheathing from a length of two-conductor cable. Use a wire stripper to remove $\frac{3}{4}$ inch of insulation from the ends of the black and white wires. Slip a cable clamp onto the cable and tighten the clamp on the cable sheathing with a screwdriver.

◆ Insert the clamp into the knockout hole and screw a lock nut onto the clamp. Tighten the nut with a hammer and nail set as shown at left.

◆ Include the new wires under the wire caps that join the old wires, connecting black to black, white to white, and bare wire to bare wire. (In some cases, larger wire caps will be needed to accommodate the added wires.)

◆ Route the cable from the junction box to the fan wiring box, securing it to joists with plastic staples *(page 183, top)*.

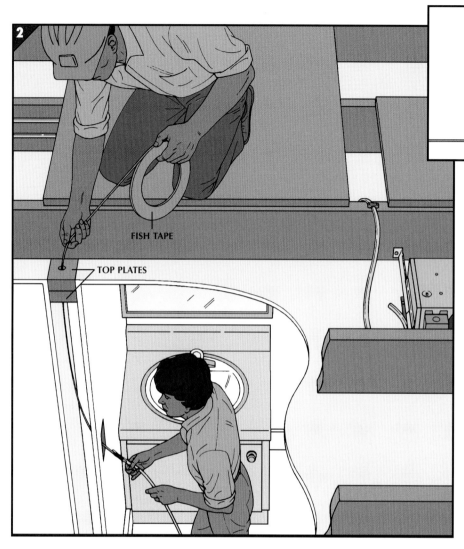

FISH TAPE

TOP PLATES

2. Fishing cable.
◆ In the bathroom, cut an opening for a new switch box in the wall near the doorway. Use the template included with the box, or the box itself, to outline the opening.
◆ In the attic, locate the top plates of the bathroom wall that has the new opening. Drill a $\frac{3}{4}$-inch hole through the plates above the opening.
◆ Push the end of a fish tape through the hole. Maneuver the tape until a helper below can pull it out through the switch opening *(left)*.
◆ Have your helper strip 8 inches of sheathing from a length of the three-conductor cable and attach the wires to the fish tape *(inset)*.
◆ With your helper feeding cable from below, pull it into the attic with the fish tape. Unhook the cable and route it to the fan wiring box.

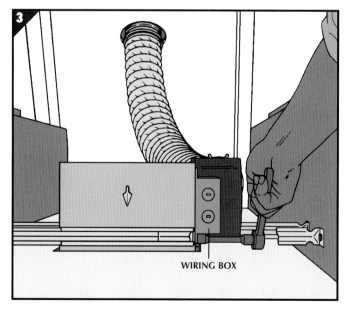

WIRING BOX

3. Preparing the wiring box.
◆ Unfasten the screw holding the wiring box to the housing. As shown at left, a socket wrench can be handy for hard-to-reach screws, most of which have hexagonal heads. Set the screw aside and remove two knockouts from the wiring box.
◆ Strip 8 inches of sheathing from the ends of both the two-conductor and three-conductor cables, then remove $\frac{3}{4}$ inch of insulation from the insulated wires in each. Attach each cable to the wiring box with a cable clamp as shown on page 185.

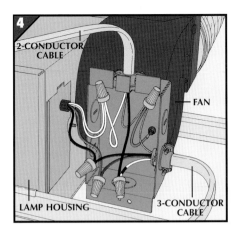

4. Wiring connections.

Using wire caps, make the following connections:

◆ Black wire of the switch cable to the black wire from the lamp housing.

◆ Red wire of the switch cable to the other colored wire from the lamp housing, blue in this case.

◆ White wire of the switch cable to the black wire of the power cable. Color the white insulation black to indicate a current-carrying wire.

◆ Bare wire of the switch cable to the bare wire of the power cable and to a jumper wire *(green)* screwed to the wiring box.

◆ White wire from the power cable to the two white wires coming from the lamp housing.

◆ Fold all connections into the box, and refasten it to the housing.

5. Adding a switch box.

◆ In the bathroom, remove a knockout from a switch box with built-in cable clamps top and bottom.

◆ With a screwdriver, loosen the clamp at the top of the box.

◆ Cut the switch cable to length, then strip off 8 inches of sheathing.

◆ Thread the cable wires into the box through the knockout, and tighten the clamp on the cable sheathing.

◆ Insert the box into the wall opening so both ears touch the wall surface.

◆ Turn the screw on each side of the box to draw the wall clamps against the inside of the dry wall *(left)*. Continue turning until the box fits tightly.

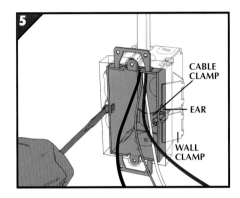

6. Wiring the switch.

◆ Using the strip gauge on the back of a two-function switch, mark the insulation of all three conductors for stripping *(left)*. The gauge shows how much insulation must be removed so that no bare wire is exposed when the conductors are inserted in the terminals.

◆ After stripping the wires, push the end of the white wire all the way into the terminal marked COMMON. Color the white insulation black.

◆ Insert the red wire into either of the two remaining terminals, and insert the black wire into the other. Screw the bare wire to the box.

◆ Fold the wires into the box and screw the switch to the box, then install the cover plate provided.

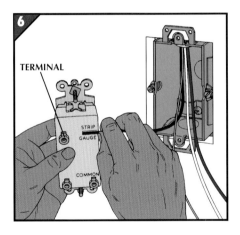

FINAL ASSEMBLY AND TESTING

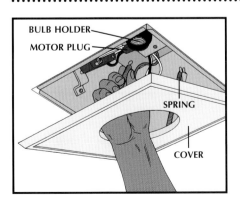

Final assembly and testing.

◆ From the bathroom, plug the fan motor into the base of the bulb holder.

◆ Hook the two cover springs to clips inside the housing.

◆ Screw an infrared heat bulb into the socket; adjust the cover to center the bulb in the opening.

◆ At the service panel, restore power to all circuits turned off for safety, then check that the switch in the bathroom operates the fan and heat lamp both separately and together.

◆ At the roof cap, confirm that the damper opens with the fan running and closes when the air flow stops.

Refinishing Floors and Walls

7

The floor and walls of a bathroom face a daily challenge from water and humidity unequaled in any other room. The following pages show how to seal the bathing area against leaks and seepage with a variety of new wall treatments—from prefabricated panels to ceramic tiles—as well as how to repair rotted areas in a bathroom floor and lay a new finish floor of tiles.

Fitting tile around a pipe →

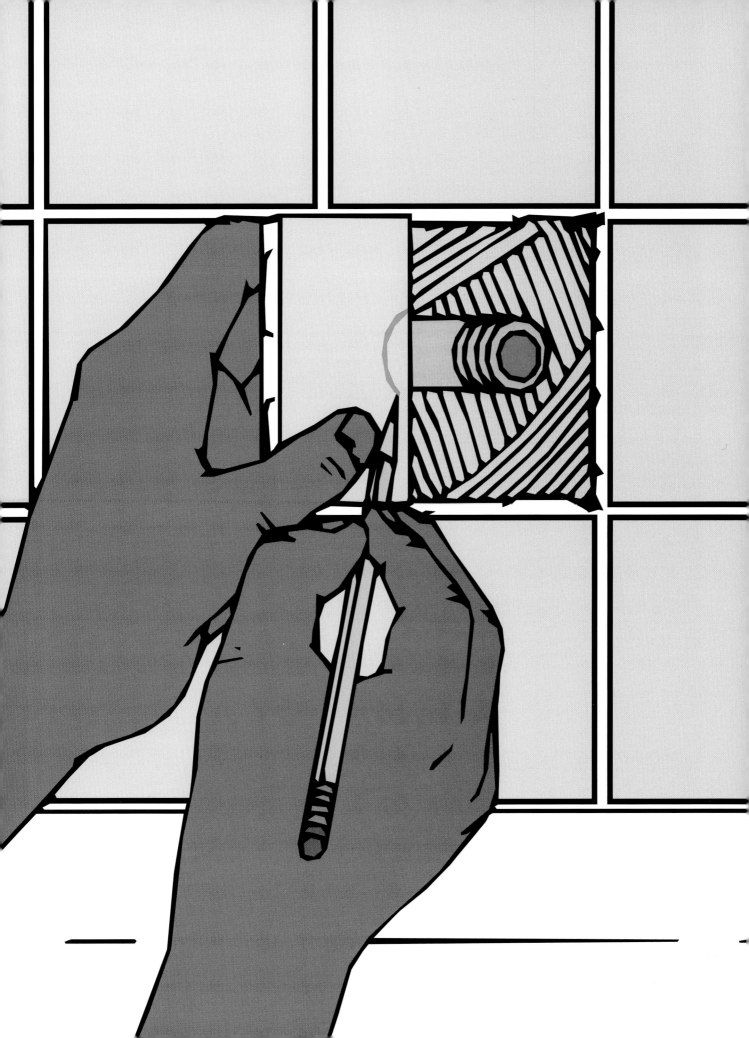

The walls surrounding a tub or shower must be durable, moisture resistant, and easy to clean. A variety of specially designed wall treatments, many in kit form, can meet these requirements handily as well as dress up an existing bathroom or complement a new one.

A Choice of Materials: Molded units of fiberglass, plastic, or acrylic are lightweight, economical, flexible, and easy to handle. Many come in three- or five-panel kits that adjust to fit standard 5-foot or smaller tubs. Extension panels sometimes are available to fit longer tubs.

The nonporous polyester and acrylic products known as solid-surface materials are heavier, more rigid, and more expensive. These walls are composed of the same material throughout, so they are very sturdy and easy to maintain.

You can install both types over nearly any clean, dry, structurally sound subsurface, including tile, plaster, wallboard, and cement.

Preparing the Area: Turn off the water supply and remove the faucet handles, tub spout, showerhead, soap dish, towel bars, and any other fittings on walls to be covered. Remove or reattach loose ceramic tiles or peeling wallpaper.

Wash the subsurface and let it dry. For wallboard, plaster, and cement walls, first seal with primer; alternatively, replace or cover these surfaces with moisture-resistant wallboard and then seal.

To avoid cracking or chipping the tub during the job, pad it with blankets or cardboard. Keep the bathroom well ventilated when working with adhesives or caulk.

TOOLS

Level	Electric drill with
Circular saw	hole saw or
Coarse file	spade bit
Orbital sander	Jigsaw
Caulking gun	Hot melt glue gun

MATERIALS

Primer	120-grit sandpaper
Panel adhesive	$\frac{1}{16}$-inch-thick
Silicone caulk	laminate shims
(color-matched	Denatured alcohol
or clear)	Hot melt glue sticks
Masking tape	Clean white rags

SNAPPING IN PREFABRICATED PANELS

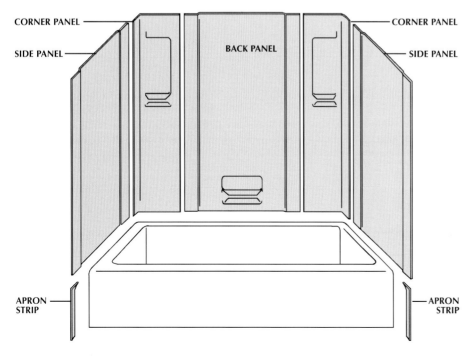

CORNER PANEL — CORNER PANEL
SIDE PANEL — BACK PANEL — SIDE PANEL
APRON STRIP — APRON STRIP

1. Preparing to install a molded tub surround.

A typical molded tub surround consists of five pieces: two corner panels, a back panel, and two side panels. Some kits, like the one at left, also include apron strips for installation on the walls in front of the tub.

◆ First, trial fit each panel. Level the top of each panel and, if the bottom edge does not meet the tub's rim evenly, draw a line across the panel marking the excess below the tub rim.

◆ With a circular saw or coarse file, trim the panel bottoms along the marked lines. Sand any rough edges.

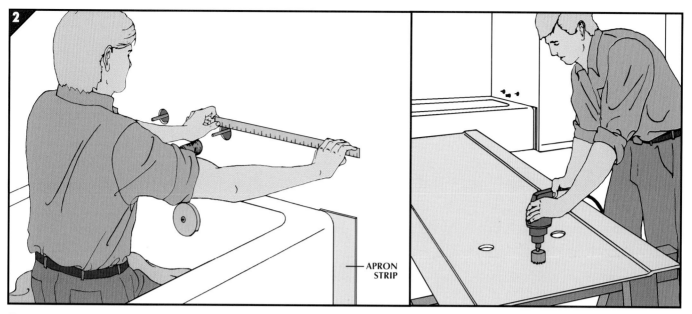

APRON
STRIP

2. Creating outlets for plumbing.
◆ If you are using apron strips, remove their backing and affix them to the wall in front of the tub.
◆ Measuring from the front edge of the tub or of the apron strip and the top of the tub *(above, left)*, make a cardboard template of the plumbing outlets. Transfer the measurements to the correct side panel.

◆ Drilling from the finished side of the panel with a hole saw or a spade bit, cut holes in the panel that are slightly larger than the pipe diameters *(above, right)*.

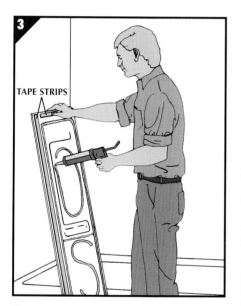

TAPE STRIPS

3. Setting corner panels.
◆ With a caulking gun, apply a $\frac{1}{4}$-inch bead of adhesive to the back of a corner panel, about 1 inch from both the panel edges and any factory-installed tape strips. Follow the pattern of straight lines around the edges and curved lines in the middle *(above)*. Put extra adhesive around shelf areas.
◆ Remove backing from the tape strips, if any, and press the corner panel into position, making sure all of it makes contact with the wall.
◆ Install the other corner panel in the same way.

4. Attaching the back and side panels.
◆ Apply adhesive to the back panel as directed in Step 3.
◆ Rest the back panel on the edge of the tub, center it between the corner panels, and press it firmly against the wall *(left)*.
◆ Apply adhesive to the side panel that attaches opposite the wall with the plumbing.
◆ Line up the panel's outside edge with the front of the tub or with the front of the apron strip, overlap the corner panel, and press it firmly onto the wall.
◆ Apply adhesive to the plumbing-wall panel and an extra ring of adhesive $\frac{1}{4}$ inch away from the edges of the cutouts. Firmly attach the panel to the wall.
◆ Caulk the top and bottom edges of the tub surround, as well as the overlapping edges of the panels.

INSTALLING SOLID-SURFACE WALLS

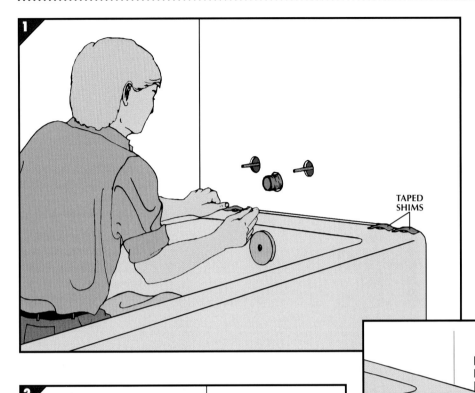

TAPED SHIMS

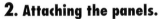

TUB RADIUS

1. Preparing for installation.

A solid-surface tub wall kit usually contains two back and two side panels, corner pieces, and matching T molding and mitered trim strips.

◆ To provide a gap for caulking, tape $\frac{1}{16}$-inch-thick laminate shims around the perimeter of the tub edge *(left)*, setting them where the ends of the panels, corners, and trim pieces will rest. Place the shims for the outside edges of the side panels $2\frac{1}{2}$ inches in from the point known as the radius, where the edge of the tub begins to curve down *(inset)*.

◆ Trial fit all panels and trim the bottom edges, if necessary, with a circular saw or jigsaw. Smooth rough edges, using an orbital sander or sandpaper.

◆ Clean the walls and the backs of the panels, corners, and trim pieces with denatured alcohol and clean white rags.

◆ Mark the center of the back wall.

2. Attaching the panels.

◆ Apply a $\frac{1}{4}$-inch bead of silicone caulk $\frac{1}{2}$ inch from the bottom edge of a back panel and a bead of adhesive 1 inch above the caulk. Apply additional adhesive as in Step 3, page 191.

◆ Resting the bottom edge on the shims, position the back panel about $\frac{3}{8}$ inch to one side of the marked centerline, and press it onto the wall.

◆ Pull the top of the panel out slightly, apply a dab of hot melt glue to the wall at each corner, then press the panel back into position and hold it in place for 10 to 15 seconds.

◆ Attach the second back panel in the same way, thus leaving a gap of about $\frac{3}{4}$ inch between the two panels.

◆ Attach the side panel opposite the plumbing wall, its outside edge $2\frac{1}{2}$ inches from the tub radius.

◆ Starting from a line drawn $2\frac{1}{2}$ inches from the tub radius on the plumbing wall, measure and cut outlet holes in the remaining side panel as in Step 2 on page 191. Apply extra adhesive $\frac{1}{4}$ inch from the edges of the cutouts and attach the panel to the wall *(left)*.

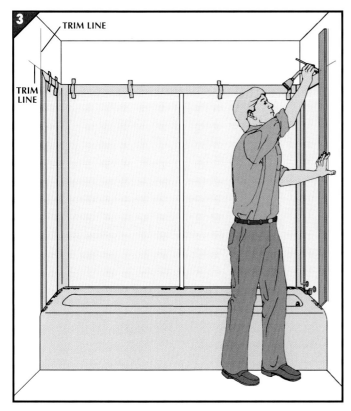

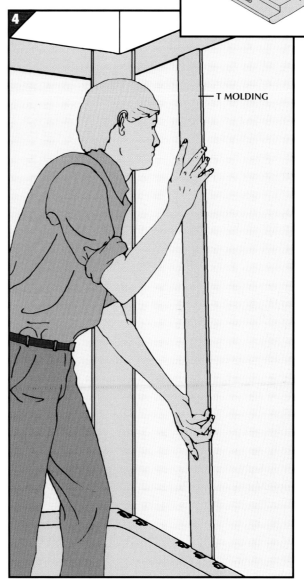

3. Fitting corners and trim strips.

◆ On the back of a corner piece, apply silicone caulk $\frac{1}{2}$ inch from the bottom and side edges and hot melt glue at the top edge; press the corner piece into place.

◆ Install the other corner panel.

◆ Measure and cut the back wall top trim to fit between the corner pieces. Attach it with a bead of caulk applied $\frac{1}{4}$ inch from each edge. Align the top edge of the trim with the top edge of the corner pieces, press the trim into position, and secure it with masking tape.

◆ To position the side trim, mark a level, horizontal line from the top of one corner piece to about 4 inches beyond the side panel edge. Place the trim piece next to the side panel, check it for plumb, and draw a vertical line along its outside edge to about 4 inches above the horizontal line.

◆ Rest the mitered end of the trim piece on the shim located between the side panel and the tub radius. Mark, then squarely cut off, the portion of the trim piece that extends above the horizontal line. Sand the cut edge.

◆ Similarly fit the side wall's top trim piece by resting its mitered end against the edge of the corner piece; mark and squarely cut off the portion extending past the plumb line.

◆ Attach the trim pieces by applying a bead of caulk $\frac{1}{4}$ inch from all edges. Secure the trim with masking tape.

◆ Repeat for the other side.

4. Finishing the job.

◆ Rest the vertical trim piece called the T molding on its shim and position it between the back panels. On the T molding, mark the length from the shim to the top trim piece and cut the molding to fit.

◆ Apply a bead of caulk about $\frac{1}{4}$ inch from the edges of the T molding, press it into place and secure it with masking tape.

◆ Mount shampoo shelves and soap dishes in the corners with caulk and small dabs of hot melt glue. Secure them with masking tape.

◆ Wait 8 to 10 hours for the adhesives to partially set. Then, remove the shims and masking tape, and caulk the gap around the tub, all of the vertical edges, and the tops of the trim and corners. Also caulk around shelves and plumbing openings.

◆ Wait 24 hours before using the tub.

The first step in replacing a bathroom floor is to examine the condition of the existing one. Damage and rot are not always visible, since the floor actually consists of three layers—the surface, or finish flooring; an underlayment of particle board or plywood; and the subfloor, which is nailed or screwed directly to the joists.

Inspecting Below the Surface: Before beginning your survey, remove the toilet *(pages 219-220)*. If the floor feels suspiciously soft or yielding in places, take up a section of finish flooring and probe for rot with a screwdriver. The damage may be confined to the underlayment or it may extend through to the subfloor.

Also check for lifted seams, buckling in the finish flooring, dampness, odors, discoloration, or other signs of water seepage around sinks, tubs, and toilets. The toilet flange presents special problems in patching the underlayment and subfloor *(pages 196-197)*.

Preparing the Surface: Once the damage is repaired—or if the three existing layers are solid to begin with—the next step depends on your choice of replacement material. Resilient vinyl—either sheet or square tiles—can be laid over the old flooring. Makers of vinyl flooring sell a variety of products to level and smooth the existing surface.

Laying a ceramic tile floor over vinyl requires a new underlayment for support *(page 195)*. Exterior-grade $\frac{5}{8}$-inch plywood or particle board is preferred because of its water resistance. You may need to trim door bottoms to add this layer—plus the tile—to the floor. Do not tile over an existing ceramic tile floor unless it is structurally sound—no cracks or water damage.

CAUTION

Asbestos

If your resilient bathroom floor was installed before 1986, the flooring and the adhesive underneath may contain asbestos. When disturbed, these materials can release microscopic asbestos fibers into the air, creating severe long-term health risks. Unless you know for certain that your floor does not contain asbestos, assume that it does and follow these precautions when making any repairs:

❗*Always wear a dual-cartridge respirator. Asbestos fibers will pass right through an ordinary dust mask.*

❗*Never sand resilient flooring or the underlying adhesive.*

❗*Try to remove the damaged flooring in one piece. If it looks likely to break or crumble, wet it before removal to reduce the chance of raising dust.*

❗*When scraping off old adhesive, always use a heat gun to keep it tacky or a spray bottle to keep it wet.*

❗*If vacuuming is necessary, rent or buy a wet/dry shop vac with a HEPA (High Efficiency Particulate Air) filtration system.*

❗*Place the damaged flooring, adhesive, and HEPA filter in a polyethylene trash bag at least 6 mils (.006 inch) thick, and seal it immediately.*

❗*Contact your local environmental protection office for guidance as to proper disposal.*

TOOLS

Electric drill with screwdriver bit
Utility or linoleum knife
Heat gun
Putty knife or stiff-bladed scraper
Chisel
Screwdriver
Circular saw
Pry bar

MATERIALS

Vinyl-tile adhesive
Latex patching compound
$\frac{5}{8}$-inch plywood or particle board
$2\frac{1}{4}$-inch dry-wall screws
Construction adhesive

PREPARING AN UNDAMAGED FLOOR FOR CERAMIC TILE

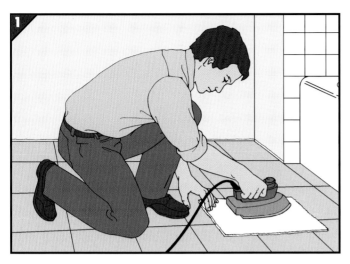

1. Leveling the finish flooring.
◆ Remove the shoe molding and base-board as described on page 178.
◆ Clean the floor thoroughly, removing all dirt and old wax.
◆ For a vinyl tile floor, rebond any loose tiles by using a hot iron, protecting the surface with an old towel *(left)*. If heat fails to activate the adhesive, lift the tile, scrape off the old adhesive, and reset the tile with new adhesive.
◆ Fill any spaces that are left with a latex patching compound available from flooring retailers.

2. Installing new underlayment.
◆ Arrange plywood or particle board sheets in a staggered pattern. The sheets should span any joints in the existing floor. To allow for expansion, leave about $\frac{1}{32}$ inch between the sheets and about $\frac{1}{8}$ inch between the outside edges and the walls.
◆ With an electric drill and a screwdriver bit, secure each sheet with drywall screws set $\frac{3}{8}$ inch in from the edges and spaced 6 inches apart over the whole surface of the sheet *(left)*.

PATCHING OLD UNDERLAYMENT

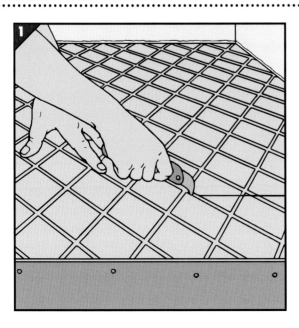

1. Removing the finish flooring.
◆ For sheet vinyl, make several parallel cuts from wall to wall with a utility or linoleum knife *(left)*.
◆ Use a heat gun to soften the adhesive along the cuts or, in the case of tiles, along the joints between them. Hold the nozzle a few inches above the floor and sweep it back and forth for about 15 seconds. Then work a putty knife blade under the flooring and gently pry it loose.
◆ Continue until the entire strip or tile comes off, then soften and scrape any remaining adhesive off the underlayment with the heat gun and putty knife.

2. Cutting out the damaged area.

◆ Poke a chisel or screwdriver through a soft spot in the underlayment to determine its thickness and set your circular saw to that depth.

◆ Cut out and remove a rectangular section of underlayment around the damaged area *(left)*.

◆ Fit an underlayment patch to the opening; make the patch the same thickness as the original. Attach the patch to the subfloor with a construction adhesive and dry-wall screws.

WORKING AROUND A TOILET FLANGE

1. Lifting out the underlayment.

◆ Stuff the toilet drain hole with rags to prevent odors and possible loss of small tools.

◆ With a circular saw, cut a rectangular section of underlayment around the damaged area *(right)*. Then cut the section in half, sawing as close as possible to the flange.

◆ Remove any screws that are attaching the toilet flange to the floor, and pull the nails out of the underlayment cutout. Ease each side of the underlayment out from under the toilet flange without putting upward pressure on the flange that would disturb the seal between the flange and the drain beneath.

2. Inserting a patch.

◆ Cut a patch of $\frac{5}{8}$-inch plywood or particle board that is the size and shape of the hole in the underlayment.

◆ Saw the patch in two so that the seam will not coincide with any subflooring joint, then notch both pieces to fit around the flange.

◆ Apply a bead of construction adhesive to the underside of both pieces of the patch, and slip them into place under the flange *(left)*. Attach them to the subfloor with dry-wall screws.

1. Cutting out the damaged area.

◆ First, increase the size of the cutout in the underlayment so it is larger than the proposed patch to the subfloor.

◆ For a plywood subfloor, cut out and remove the damaged area in the same way you removed the underlay-ment in Step 1 on the previous page.

◆ For a lumber subfloor *(above)*, re-move the nails or screws from the joists on either side of the damaged area. Saw above the centerline of the joists through the empty nail or screw holes, then lift out the boards.

2. Patching the subfloor.

◆ Cut a plywood patch to fit the cutout in the subfloor.

◆ Mark the center of the toilet drain hole on an edge of the patch that will be parallel to the joists when installed.

◆ Saw the patch in two at that point, then cut a notch in each piece to fit the flange.

◆ Run a bead of construction adhesive along the tops of the exposed joists, then slip the two pieces under the lip of the flange *(left)* and anchor them to the joists with dry-wall screws.

Installing Ceramic Floor Tiles

The challenge of laying a floor in a bathroom depends in part on the material chosen. Laying sheet flooring, for example, is more demanding than installing tiles because of the multiple cutouts required. An error can ruin an entire sheet of material but may spoil only a single tile.

Either vinyl tile or ceramic tile—shown on these and the following pages—is suitable for a bathroom floor. Both are installed in much the same way, beginning with sound subflooring and underlayment *(pages 194-195)*.

Ceramic tile, which is the more durable of the two materials, also requires the extra step of grouting to fill the seams between the rows *(pages 202-203)*.

Both jobs begin with dividing the room into four roughly equal quadrants *(below)*. Work proceeds by quadrant, with the quadrant next to the bathroom door tiled last. Tiles may be laid in rows as shown here or diagonally in an adaptation of the method for walls on page 207. In either case, you have the option of not laying partial tiles around the perimeter of the room until you have laid all the whole tiles.

Tiles and Thresholds: Most ceramic tiles have spacer lugs on their edges that assure joints of equal width. If you use tiles without lugs, buy spacers separately. Choose tiles no thicker than will come flush with the toilet flange. Always buy a few extra tiles to allow for breakage, and save fragments to practice cutting *(pages 200-201)*.

For the threshold at the bathroom door, you can use real or synthetic marble if the tiles are flush with the floor outside the bathroom. If not, shape the underside of a wood threshold to bridge the two different levels.

Adhesive and Grout: When laying ceramic tile on any surface but particle board or concrete, the strongest bonding agent is thin-set latex adhesive, a powder that is mixed with water. Use mastic with particle board, and on concrete, lay an isolation membrane—thin fiberglass backed by rubber—to prevent small cracks in the slab from shifting the tiles. Affix the membrane with mastic, and then use thin-set latex adhesive for the tile. Grout for tile joints is available with sand or without, for a smoother look.

 **TOOLS**

 **MATERIALS**

 **SAFETY TIPS**

Notched trowel	Rod saw	Ceramic floor tiles	Grout
Hammer	Grout float	Tile adhesive	Denatured alcohol
Chalk line	Caulk gun	2-by-4	Silicone caulk
Tile cutter	Small brush	Solvent	Silicone grout
Tile nippers	Small saw	Sandpaper, 80-grit	sealant

Planning a pattern.

◆ Mark the center of the rectangular area to be tiled, ignoring encroachments such as a vanity. Draw two guidelines through the center, perpendicular to each other and parallel to the walls.

◆ Position a tile with one corner at the center point, then add tiles to make a cross at the center of the area *(right)*. Use spacers between tiles without lugs.

◆ If a gap narrower than half a tile remains at the ends of either row, shift the guidelines *(right),* widening these spaces to eliminate awkward cuts on tiny pieces of tile. Reposition the tiles on the floor to check your work.

◆ Pick up all the tiles except for the one at the center of the cross. With a chalk line, establish new guidelines along adjacent edges of the tile.

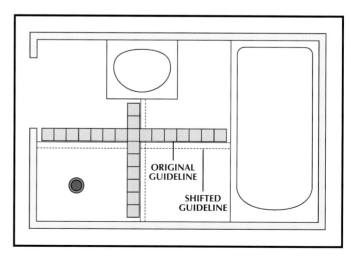

ORIGINAL GUIDELINE

SHIFTED GUIDELINE

LAYING WHOLE TILES

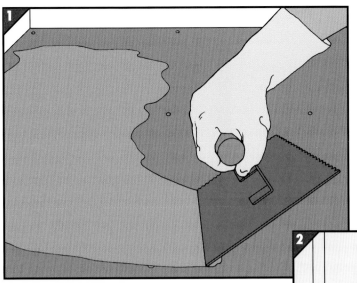

1. Preparing the surface.
◆ Spread a thin layer of adhesive on the entire floor with the unnotched side of a trowel. Work one quadrant at a time, ending at the area by the door. Avoid obscuring the guidelines.
◆ Allow this preliminary coat to dry for about 2 hours.

2. Applying adhesive.
◆ Pour about a cup of adhesive onto one quadrant. Pull the notched edge of the trowel through the adhesive at a 45-degree angle, assuring that the teeth penetrate to the floor.
◆ Use sweeping strokes to spread the adhesive evenly in the corner of the quadrant.

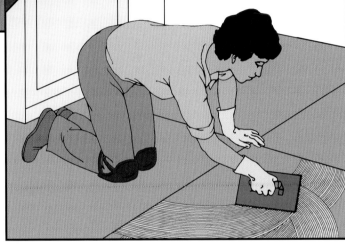

3. Setting tiles.
◆ Starting at the center of the room, set a row of tiles along the guideline, toward the wall. Work carefully; these tiles determine the alignment of all that follow. Place tiles lug to lug, pressing each into the adhesive with a slight twisting of your fingertips.
◆ Complete the quadrant in the same manner. Take care to align the first tile in each new row precisely with the tile next to it. Avoid kneeling directly on freshly laid tiles. If you can't reach across them to continue, either stop work for 24 hours while the adhesive cures or lay plywood on the tiles to protect them.

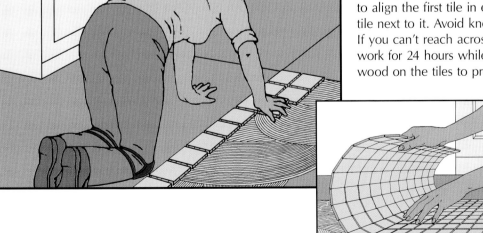

Lay mosaic tile sheets in rows, unrolling each sheet onto the surface in turn, leaving the same space between sheets as between individual tiles *(inset)*.

4. Beating in the tiles.

Cushion a straight 2-by-4 with cloth and set it on the tiles you have laid. Move the board around, gently tapping it with a hammer to force protruding tiles into the adhesive. Wipe away excess adhesive with a solvent recommended by the manufacturer.

CUTTING AND SETTING PARTIAL TILES

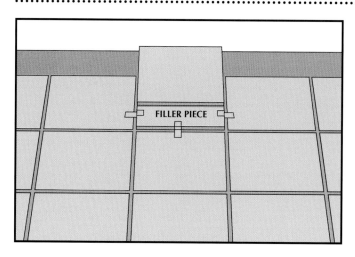

FILLER PIECE

Marking edge tiles.

◆ To make filler pieces for gaps at walls, cabinets, and bathtubs, tape a tile on top of a tile that borders the gap. This second tile will become the filler piece.

◆ Set a third tile on top of the second and slide it to the wall.

◆ One joint width from the edge of the topmost tile, mark the filler piece for cutting as shown at left *(blue line)*.

For mosaic tile, cut tiles from a sheet, trim them as needed, and set them individually.

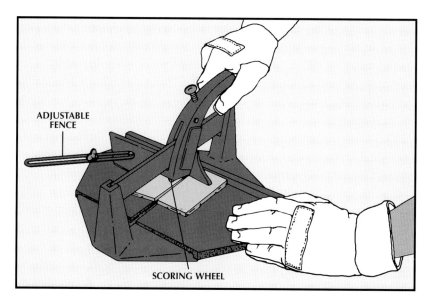

ADJUSTABLE FENCE

SCORING WHEEL

Cutting perimeter tiles.

◆ Position the cut line under the tile cutter's scoring wheel and set the adjustable fence to hold the tile in place.

◆ Score the tile with the wheel, then press down firmly with the lever to snap the tile along the line.

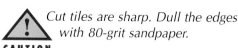 *Cut tiles are sharp. Dull the edges with 80-grit sandpaper.*

CAUTION

Making irregular cuts.

Use nippers to fit tiles to corners, doorjambs, or a toilet flange.

◆ First, make a paper pattern for the cut, then transfer the outline to the glazed side of the tile. Hold the glazed side up and break tiny pieces from the tile—less than $\frac{1}{8}$ inch at a time—to avoid splitting it.

◆ Smooth and dull the cut edges of the tile with 80-grit sandpaper.

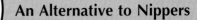

An Alternative to Nippers

Nibbling at the edge of a tile with nippers sometimes fractures tiles and nearly always leaves a ragged edge. A rod saw solves both problems.

A variety of hacksaw blade, a rod saw is a wire coated with carbide, an abrasive that cuts quickly through ceramic. The cylindrical blade allows abrupt changes in direction to make cutting a square corner as easy as shaping a wide curve.

To cut a tile, rest it on a low work surface such as a bench or a stool with the cut line near the edge. Saw vertically, repositioning the tile as needed to keep the blade close to the supporting edge. Sandpaper the cut edge.

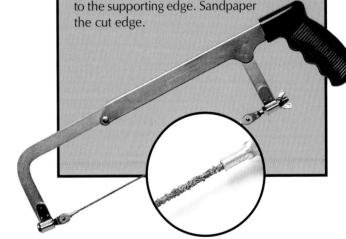

Setting partial tiles.

◆ Position each partial tile in line with its row as you did with whole tiles and press it into the adhesive.

◆ If the tile is to fit under a molding at the wall, slide the cut edge under the trim, then press the tile in place.

◆ Let tile adhesive cure for at least 24 hours before grouting the joints.

1. Grouting.

◆ Temporarily stuff perimeter joints with rolled paper towels to prevent grout from entering.

◆ Pour a cup or two of grout onto the tiles and drag it diagonally across the joints with a rubber grout float. Work in an area of 5 square feet or so, pressing grout to the bottoms of joints. Wait 15 minutes, then wipe up excess grout with a damp sponge.

◆ Grout the rest of the floor in the same manner.

◆ Keep the grout damp as it cures by mopping the floor twice daily for 3 days. Then wipe any haze of grout from the tiles with a soft cloth.

2. Caulking perimeter joints.

◆ Load a caulk gun with a tube of silicone caulk, its tip cut at a 45-degree angle, to lay a bead of caulk in each perimeter joint. Pushing the caulk ahead of the gun, as shown at right, fill the joints to the same depth as the grout between the tiles.

◆ When the silicone is tacky, dampen a rag with denatured alcohol and clean excess caulk from around the joints.

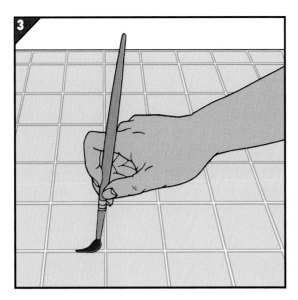

3. Sealing grout.
◆ Brush grout sealant on the joints only after the grout has fully cured. The curing period varies among sealants; check the manufacturer's instructions. Apply sealant liberally, wiping up the excess with a soft cloth.
◆ Allow the sealant to dry completely before letting the floor get wet.

ADDING A THRESHOLD

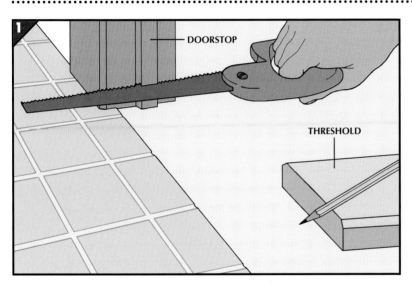

DOORSTOP

THRESHOLD

1. Cutting the doorstop.
◆ Position one end of the threshold against the doorstop to mark the doorstop for trimming.
◆ Lay a pencil flat on the threshold and drag the point across the doorstop to make a cutting line slightly higher than the threshold.
◆ Repeat this procedure for the other side of the doorway, then use a small saw to trim both doorstops *(left)*.

2. Positioning the threshold.
◆ Apply tile adhesive to the bottom of the threshold with the notched edge of a trowel.
◆ Hold the threshold as shown at right. Without allowing the adhesive to touch the floor, slide the threshold under the doorstops to the edge of the tiles and press it into place.
◆ Wipe away excess adhesive with a damp sponge.

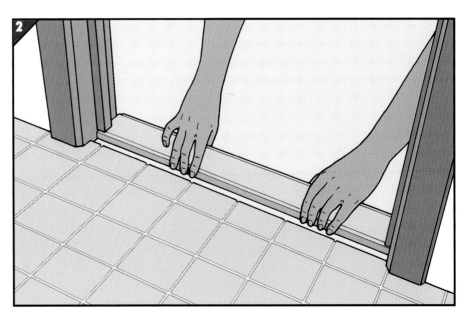

Tiling the Walls around a Tub

Few improvements add as much life and sparkle to an older bathroom as a newly tiled tub alcove, which can also provide the classic finishing touch to a renovation or new bathroom. Tile offers the practical advantage of a waterproof, durable, and easy-to-clean surface. Moreover, by replacing old, cracked tiles you may also prevent water damage to the walls and floor.

A Solid Backing: For a tiling job that will last, cement board *(page 251)* is the best choice of backing material. In an old bathroom, strip the surrounding walls to the studs *(page 222)* and nail cement board to them. During a renovation, install cement board on any wall that is intended for tiling.

Selecting Materials: For best results with tub walls, choose full-size or field tiles that are $4\frac{1}{4}$ inches square with spacer lugs on each side. Such tiles are easier to handle than larger specimens and are less likely to shift under their own weight during installation; the lugs ensure even spacing for the grout lines between tiles.

Tub surrounds are commonly tiled to a height of 72 inches above the floor—just below the shower arm, which is normally placed between 74 and 76 inches above the floor. Estimate how many field tiles you will need to cover your surround, then add extras to allow for imperfections, breakage, and cutting mistakes. Also purchase trim tiles *(opposite, top)* as edging. Trim tiles usually lack spacer lugs; establish the correct spacing between them and the field tiles with 2-inch finishing nails *(page 208)*.

When practical, buy soap dishes and other ceramic accessories from the wall-tile manufacturer. They are often the size of one or two field tiles; leave the space open as you tile, then add the accessory as shown on page 128.

Choose a Type 1 organic or mastic tile adhesive formulated for wet areas. Follow the directions on the container to select the right trowel to properly spread the adhesive. Serrated trowels—rather than the notched trowels used for floors—are common for wall tiling. To fill spaces between tiles, look for a grout with a latex additive. It is stronger, more flexible, and more water resistant than other grouts.

Final Preparations: Before beginning any work in the bathtub, pad the bottom with cardboard and old blankets to prevent shoes, tools, or falling tiles from chipping the finish. Cover the drain and overflow openings with masking tape to keep out dust, adhesive, and other materials.

 **TOOLS**

Level
Chalk line
Hammer
Serrated trowel
Tile cutter
Tile nippers
Grout float
Caulk gun

 **MATERIALS**

1-by-2 lumber	Trim tiles
Dry-wall nails	2-inch finishing
Adhesive	nails
$4\frac{1}{4}$-inch field tiles	Latex grout
with spacer lugs	Silicone caulk
Ceramic accessories	Grout sealant

 **SAFETY TIPS**

Protect your eyes with safety goggles and hands with work gloves while cutting or nipping tiles. Wear rubber gloves when mixing or applying tile adhesive and grout.

Trim tiles for a finished edge.

Although square field tiles cover most of the walls above a tub, two kinds of trim tiles are needed to complete the installation. The first are 2- by 6-inch bullnose tiles, which run along the top and ends of the tiled area. Where the end walls of a tub alcove meet the back wall, the bullnoses butt together as the field tiles do—the edge of one against the glossy face of the other. As shown in the photograph at right, the second kind of trim—called a down-corner tile—fills the square where vertical and horizontal courses of bullnose meet.

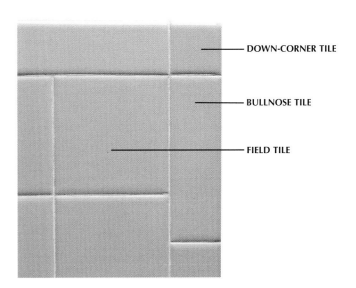

DOWN-CORNER TILE

BULLNOSE TILE

FIELD TILE

PLOTTING GUIDELINES

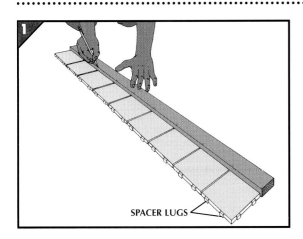

SPACER LUGS

1. Making a layout stick.

◆ Cut a piece of straight 1-by-2 lumber to a length of between 36 and 42 inches.
◆ Working on a level surface, set out a row of tiles, lug to lug, and place the 1-by-2 alongside them, one end aligned with the lugs of the first tile.
◆ Mark the width of each tile on the stick *(left)*.

For wider grout lines or when working with tiles that have no lugs, take care to space the tiles evenly, then mark the layout stick accordingly.

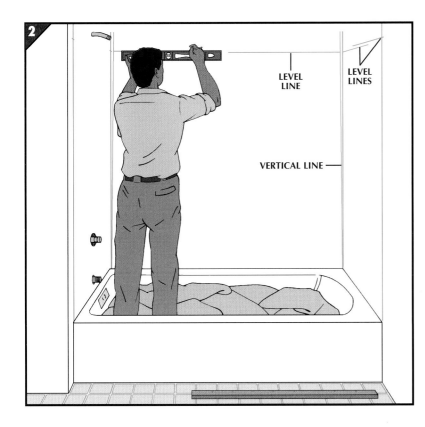

LEVEL LINE

LEVEL LINES

VERTICAL LINE

2. Checking the tub slope.

◆ Where each corner of the tub meets an end wall, draw a vertical line on the wall to the showerhead height, using a level to keep the lines plumb. Similarly draw vertical lines on the back wall from the inside tub corner. On each line, mark the planned height of the tiles, measured from the tub rim.
◆ On each tub wall, draw level lines inward from the marks on the two vertical lines. If the lines meet, the tub is level along that side.
◆ Where the lines do not meet, the higher line indicates the high side of the tub. Measure the distance between them.

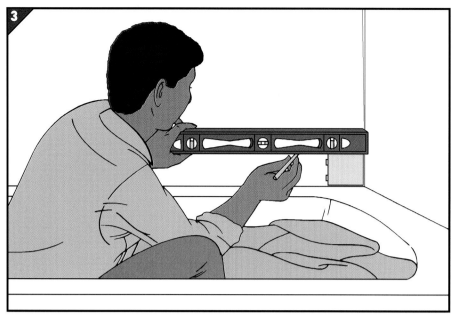

3. Marking a level starting line.

◆ If the distance between the level lines drawn on the back wall in Step 2 is less than $\frac{1}{8}$ inch, set a field tile at the high end of the bathtub's back rim. Otherwise, place the tile at the low end of the rim.

◆ In either case, place a level on top of the tile and draw a horizontal guideline across the wall *(left)*.

◆ If tub rim and guideline converge to less than a tile width, tiles must be trimmed to fit. When the distance between the tub rim and the guideline becomes slightly greater than the width of a tile, plan to fill the extra space with grout.

4. Selecting a center point.

◆ Mark the center of the guideline. Then hold the layout stick under the line so that it touches the end wall.

◆ If the center mark aligns with a joint space on the stick, the wall can be completed without cutting end tiles.

◆ If a tile would cover the center mark *(right)*, slide the stick to center a joint space on the mark. Measure the distance between the stick and the end wall.

◆ If the gap is 2 inches or more, draw a vertical guideline at the center mark. For a gap that is narrower than 2 inches, mark the wall half a tile width farther from the corner and draw the vertical line there.

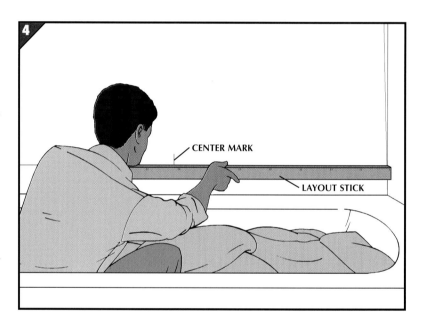

CENTER MARK

LAYOUT STICK

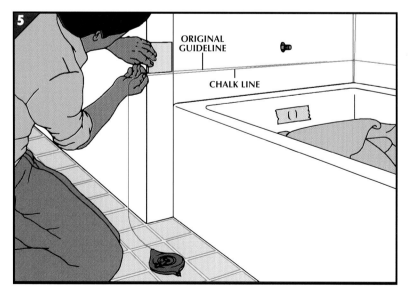

ORIGINAL GUIDELINE

CHALK LINE

5. Guidelines for end walls.

◆ Mark a horizontal guideline on each end wall as in Step 3.

◆ At an outside corner, hold a tile against the guideline where it intersects the corner. If the tile edge and corner do not coincide, tack a chalk line at the inside corner, align the tile with the outside corner, and snap a new guideline along the bottom of the tile *(left)*. Mark a vertical guideline $2\frac{1}{8}$ inches from the corner.

◆ For an end wall with no corner nearby, extend the horizontal guideline one tile width past the tub and mark for a vertical guideline.

◆ In both cases, plan for uncut field tiles at the outer edge and check with the layout stick whether this layout will create tile slivers at the inside corner. If so, either lengthen the guideline half a tile width or set half-tiles at the outer edge.

SETTING TILES IN PLACE

VERTICAL GUIDELINE

BATTEN

1. Applying adhesive.

◆ Using dry-wall nails, tack a 1-by-2 board to the back wall with the top edge at the horizontal guideline; this batten will support tiles while the adhesive sets.
◆ With the straight edge of a serrated trowel, scoop up about a cupful of adhesive and smear it on the wall near the intersection of the horizontal and vertical guidelines.
◆ Hold the trowel's serrated edge at a 45-degree angle to the wall to spread a thin, even coat of mastic over about 3 square feet of wall space *(left)*.

2. Placing the tiles.

◆ Set the first tile on the batten, side lugs against the vertical guideline. Press the tile against the adhesive with your fingertips, jiggling it slightly to help it stick.
◆ Add tiles according to the numbered sequence at left to form a pyramid. Continue the pattern upward and outward, coating the wall with adhesive as you go.
◆ Place tiles on the end walls in a half-pyramid *(inset)*, working from the outer edge toward the inside corner.
◆ Finish by removing the battens and filling in each bottom row. Allow the adhesive to cure for a few minutes before setting the tiles to keep them from sagging.

3. Accommodating the tub plumbing.

◆ If a pipe falls entirely within a tile, hold the tile below the pipe and mark its center on the edge of the tile. Cut the tile along the mark with a tile cutter *(page 200)*.

◆ Mark the width of the pipe on the cut edge of each piece *(above, left)*.
◆ Holding each piece glazed side up, use tile nippers to make a notch for the pipe *(above, right)*.
◆ For a pipe that falls at a joint, notch the edges of whole tiles to fit.

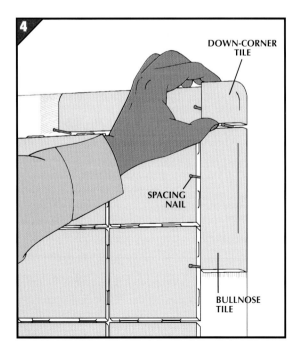

4. Adding the trim tiles.

◆ Measure the length in inches of the top row of tile on the back wall; divide by 6 to get a rough count of the number of bullnoses required. Allow $\frac{1}{8}$ inch more for each bullnose. Based on the result, plan to place the bullnoses along the top so that any partial bullnoses at the corners are about the same length.
◆ Spread enough adhesive for a few trim tiles at a time, then tap 2-inch finishing nails beside the field tiles between the spacer lugs to allow room for grout. Set the bullnoses in the adhesive.
◆ On each end wall, begin at the outside corner *(left)*. Set a bullnose above the top outermost field tile, flush with the edge and spaced away with a nail. Then set a bullnose vertically beside the field tile in the same way. Place a down-corner tile between the bullnoses. Extend the bullnose tile rows along both sides of the wall, cutting as needed at the inside corner.

FINISHING THE JOB

1. Applying grout.
◆ Let the adhesive cure for 24 hours, then remove the trim-spacing nails.
◆ Wearing rubber gloves and safety goggles, prepare a batch of grout according to the manufacturer's instructions.
◆ Trowel the mixture onto the tile surface with a rubber-faced grout float *(left)*, forcing the grout into the joints with crisscrossing diagonal strokes of the float edge. Be sure to fill the corner joints and the joint above the tub rim.
◆ Allow the grout to dry for 10 to 12 minutes. Then clean and polish the tiles as described on page 202.

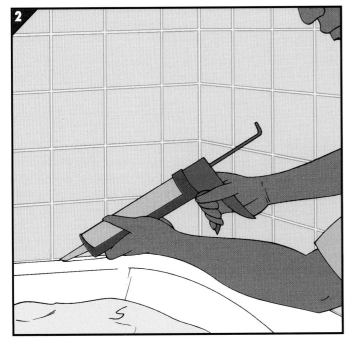

2. Caulking the tub.
◆ Wait 24 hours for the grout to cure; it will also shrink enough to form a shallow channel for a bead of caulk. Fill the bathtub with water to widen the tub-rim joint, which must be completely dry and free from dirt.
◆ Load a cartridge of silicone caulk, approved for bathtub use, into a caulking gun and cut the cartridge tip at a 45-degree angle.
◆ Place the tip at the joint and apply steady pressure on the trigger as you push the gun along the joint.
◆ To finish the bead, smooth it with a wet finger.
◆ Let the caulk cure for 24 hours before emptying the tub.

A few weeks later, apply sealant to the grout *(page 203)*.

Creating a New Bathroom

Whether you are adding a new bathroom or modernizing an old one, the details of the job will depend on a number of factors—among others, the structure of your house, the size of your budget, and your own tastes. The following pages explain the skills you are likely to need in any bathroom renovation, including planning, demolition, carpentry, laying new pipes, and installing fixtures.

Breaking up tiles to remove a bathtub →

Remodeling a bathroom or adding a new one is a complex job that requires thorough planning. You must make basic decisions about the sizes and styles of fixtures and appliances, what floor and wall coverings to install, and how to provide or modify lighting, heating, and ventilation.

Preliminary Considerations: Unless you plan simply to remove the old fixtures *(pages 218-221)* and replace them with new ones, you will need to put in additional plumbing lines. The location of existing pipes and the distance they can be extended will often dictate the layout of a remodeled bathroom and may also limit your choice of locations for a new one. Especially critical is the location of the main stack for the house, which vents out of the roof and extends down to the house drain.

The additional fixtures required for a new bathroom can reduce water flow through the supply lines if your plumbing system already has low pressure or constricted pipes. Make solutions to such problems your first order of business.

To expand a bathroom, you will need to demolish old walls and you might have to build new ones *(pages 222-227 and 250-251)*. Avoid disturbing any bearing walls; you can recognize one by following the guidelines on page 176.

A Quartet of Codes: Learn the code requirements in your area as soon as possible in the planning stage to avoid wasted time and money. Four different codes may affect work on a bathroom: plumbing;

electrical; mechanical, for heating and cooling systems; and building, for any structural changes to bearing walls, including exterior ones. Permits and specific plans are often required for each code. Your project will probably have to pass a rough-in inspection for each permit once the basic work is done, and a final inspection at the end of the job.

Pipe and Fixtures: For extending supply lines and drain lines, choose materials that are easy to work with. You do not need to match new pipe to old; adapters are available that will make the transition. For drains and vents, use polyvinyl

chloride (PVC) plastic if local codes permit; most do. PVC is lightweight, readily cut with a saw, and easily assembled with special-purpose cement. Hot- and cold-water pipes may be any of several materials; in the examples shown here and on the pages that follow, the supply pipes are rigid copper, which remains a common choice for its durability.

Select your fixtures, usually including a toilet, washbasin, and tub or shower, early in the project so that you can take their dimensions and framing requirements into account. A sampling of basic options appears on pages 214-215.

Hiding Waste Lines: Drainpipes are large—the smallest drain from a bathroom fixture has a $1\frac{1}{2}$-inch inside diameter—and concealing them can be tricky. If the new bathroom is above a crawlspace or an unfinished basement, branch drainpipes can be run between or beneath the floor joists. For a new installation above a finished part of the house, you must cut away some of the ceiling below to install the pipes, and you may also have to drill through the joists to accommodate them *(page 231)*.

Vertical drainpipes and vent pipes are usually concealed inside a structure called a wet wall that is framed with 2-by-6 studs instead of the usual 2-by-4s in order to accommodate the pipes *(pages 224-227)*. Alternatively, supply lines and drain lines can be run alongside an existing wall and concealed—within cabinets, bookcases, closets, or specially made paneling.

Tips on Positioning Fixtures

✔ In a room with an existing stack, or in which a new stack must be located in a particular area, plan the placement of the toilet first—local codes normally dictate a maximum distance between the toilet and the stack.

✔ Because a full bathtub is very heavy, the best location for the tub is along a wall or in a corner, where it can be supported by proper framing. Provide extra floor bracing as shown on page 229.

✔ Position the foot of the tub against a wall that can be opened from the other side for plumbing repairs; whirlpool tubs must be installed so that there is also access to the motor.

✔ If possible, allow space around the washbasin for towel racks, hooks, and cabinets or shelves for storage.

✔ In a windowed bathroom, try to position the basin to take advantage of natural light for shaving and applying makeup.

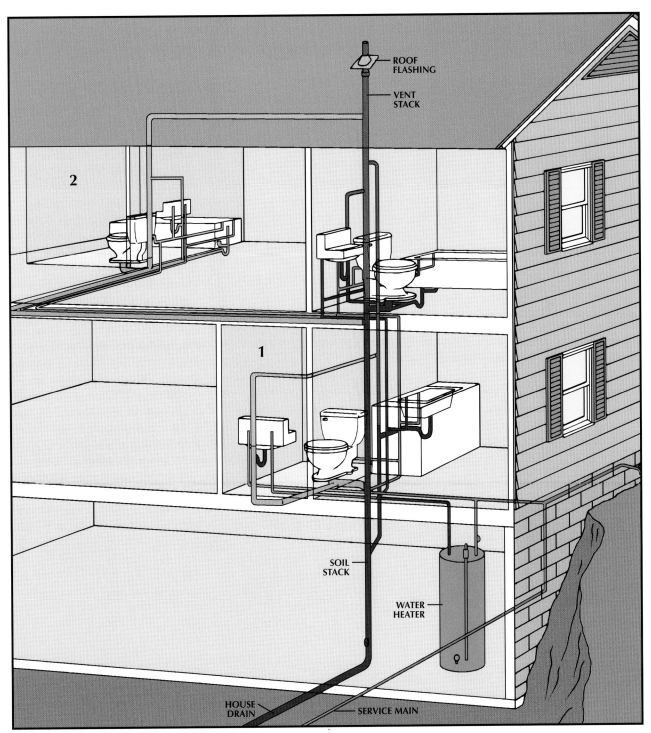

The following labels appear in the diagram:

ROOF FLASHING

VENT STACK

2

1

SOIL STACK

WATER HEATER

HOUSE DRAIN

SERVICE MAIN

Paths for new pipes.

In this simplified diagram, the plumbing for a first-floor kitchen and a second-floor bathroom, both installed when the house was built, appears in dark colors. Pipes for a powder room (1) added next to the kitchen and for a second upstairs bathroom (2) have lighter tints.

The original plumbing core consists of pipes originating in the basement. Parallel supply pipes carry cold water (blue) from the service main and hot water (red) from the water heater.

Drainpipes (gray) carry wastewater from the fixtures into the soil stack—the portion of the stack that leads down from the highest waste outlet to the house drain. Each fixture has a drain trap that prevents sewer gases from entering the house. Vent pipes (purple) linked to the vent portion of the stack exhaust waste gases through the roof.

Both the new powder room and the new second-floor bath illustrate ways new plumbing can be grafted to an existing system. The powder room con-

tains a toilet and basin. It is close enough to the original plumbing core to be tied directly to it. The new drain runs across the unfinished basement ceiling below, and new vent pipes run parallel to the stack before connecting with it on the second floor. The supply lines are extensions of nearby hot and cold vertical lines, called risers.

The full-size upstairs bathroom requires a long run of piping across a first-floor ceiling. Fixtures are vented to a pipe that crosses the attic to connect with the existing vent stack.

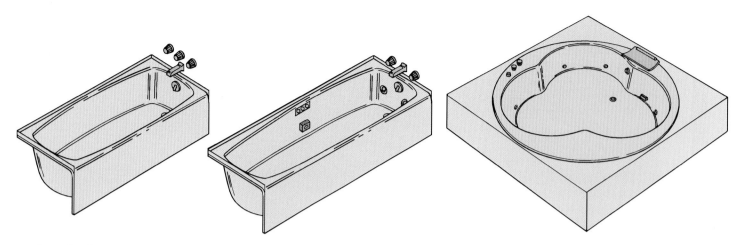

Standard tub.

This 60-inch by 30-inch tub is commonly available in fiberglass, cast iron, or steel. It may have one, two, or three skirted sides, depending on how many walls the tub will abut. You can also buy this style tub with all four sides unskirted and sink it into a floor or raised platform.

Whirlpool tub.

Equipped with a pump to circulate bathwater through nozzles in the sides, a whirlpool tub requires its own electric circuit. Modest units like this one resemble a standard bathtub and range up to 7 feet in length. A tub of this size usually fits through halls and doorways en route to the bathroom but may feel cramped to some.

Oversize whirlpool tub.

A unit wider than a standard tub offers luxurious comfort. However, it will not pass through a standard door or hall, so it is often practical only for a new bathroom near a sliding-glass door in an exterior wall. A large tub also may require extra floor reinforcement and two electrical circuits—one for the pump motor, another for a heater.

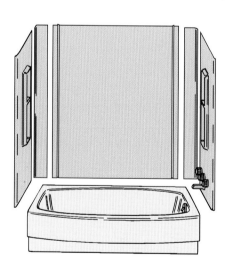

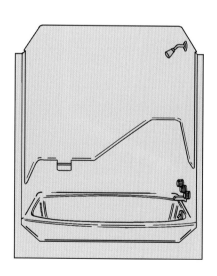

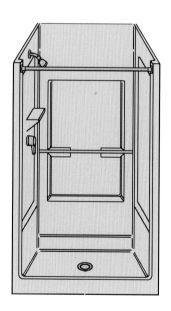

Multipiece tub surround.

Sold as a kit of separate panels, a tub surround like the one above can be carried through any doorway, then assembled as shown on pages 190-193. To prevent leaks, you must carefully maintain joints with caulk.

A seamless tub-and-wall unit.

Like a large whirlpool tub, a one-piece tub enclosure cannot fit through a standard hall or doorway, making it impractical for some renovations. This lightweight unit offers an advantage over surrounds built of separate panels: the corners remain watertight.

One-piece shower stall.

Some enclosures for showers come as a single unit like the one above; others must be assembled from panels (pages 248-249). Select a shower that you can maneuver into the new bathroom, and allow room in your layout so the shower door can swing outward.

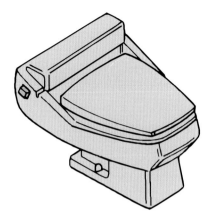

Two-piece toilet.

The traditional toilet consists of two major components, a tank and a bowl, which may be separated for certain repairs. Round bowls like the one shown here are standard, but elongated bowls are also available, at a higher price.

One-piece toilet.

A compact alternative to the two-piece version, this toilet frees wall space for shelves or cabinets. Because of their lower profile, one-piece toilets do not rely on gravity alone for flushing; instead, a special mechanism pressurizes the water that clears the bowl.

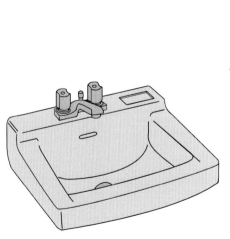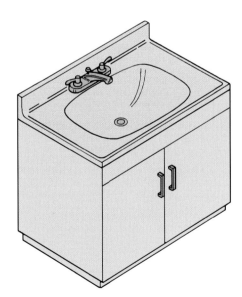

Wall-hung basin.

Requiring no cabinetry for support, a wall-hung basin occupies less space than many other kinds of sinks and so is well suited to small bathrooms. As its name suggests, this type of basin simply hangs from a mounting bracket attached securely to the wall.

Pedestal basin.

Most pedestal basins are supported by framing in the wall. The base, which is largely decorative, conceals the drain assembly while still leaving ample free space underneath.

Integral countertop basin.

Designed to be mounted onto a vanity, this type of basin is part of a small molded counter with a backsplash. The space between the basin and the backsplash may be ordered predrilled for any of the standard faucets shown on pages 139 to 142.

BASIC BATHROOM LAYOUTS

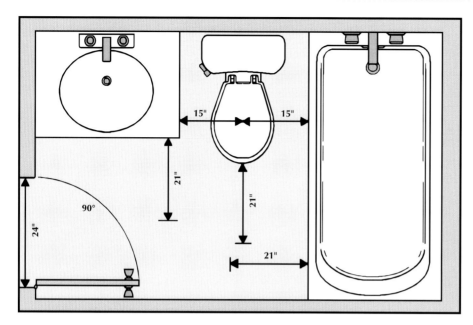

Standard clearances.

Most building codes specify minimum clearances to the front and sides of each bathroom fixture. The figures noted at left are common, but check your local code for specifics in your area. Code requirements set minimum clearances; for comfort, allow for more space if possible. Under most codes, fixtures must have a minimum of 21 inches of free space in front. Codes also commonly mandate 15 inches to each side of a toilet's centerline. A bathroom door is normally required to be at least 24 inches wide and to open through an arc of at least 90 degrees; see page 175 for the dimensions needed for wheelchair access.

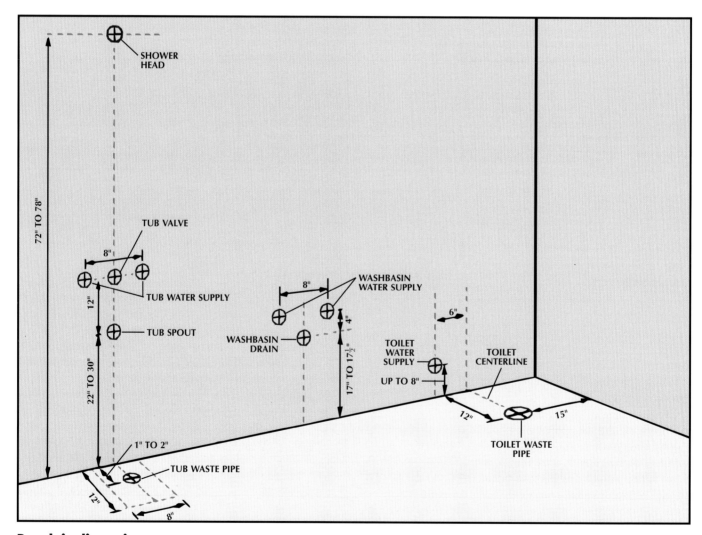

Rough-in dimensions.

After selecting fixtures and planning their placement, establish locations for pipes to enter the room. If you are using an old wall, mark the wall surface; otherwise, mark the framing members of the new wall. The measurements shown here along a single wall are typical for some common fixtures.

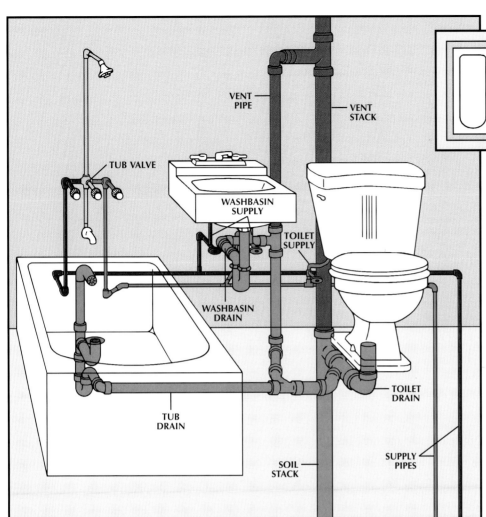

VENT
PIPE

VENT
STACK

TUB VALVE

WASHBASIN
SUPPLY

TOILET
SUPPLY

WASHBASIN
DRAIN

TUB
DRAIN

TOILET
DRAIN

SOIL
STACK

SUPPLY
PIPES

A one-wall plumbing pattern.

The simplest plan for a bathroom consolidates the plumbing along one wall, reducing the amount of cutting into the house structure and the amount of pipe installed. This arrangement may be the only choice for a small bathroom like that at left, which has rough-in dimensions identical to those in the illustration at the bottom of the preceding page.

Plumbing in two walls.

Extending supply pipes and drainpipes to two adjoining walls provides more room around the basin than a one-wall room. (Three-wall plumbing patterns are less common, since they offer few advantages.) A bathroom with plumbing in two walls generally requires more cutting of studs and joists to accommodate the pipes. To minimize such work or to bridge a door *(inset),* try to run the supply pipes underneath or between the joists directly below.

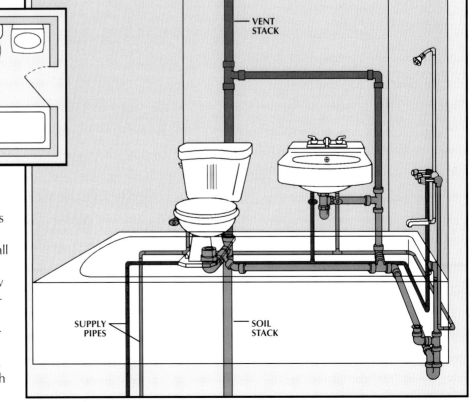

VENT
STACK

SUPPLY
PIPES

SOIL
STACK

Clearing the Way for a Major Renovation

Remodeling a bathroom usually requires that some or all of the old fixtures be removed. Enlarging a bathroom or creating space for a new one may also mean tearing down one or more walls.

Taking Out Fixtures: Always begin by cutting off water to the fixture, usually at the nearby shutoff valves in the supply lines. In the absence of such valves—or if they are stuck open—you may have to turn off the water supply to the entire house *(page 130)*. Removing most fixtures consists mainly of undoing nuts and bolts. A bathtub, however, can present a considerable challenge *(pages 220-221)*. Disposing of a plastic, fiberglass, or steel tub may be made easier with a reciprocating saw, which is available from tool-rental stores.

If you plan to reinstall your washbasin, bathtub, or toilet, handle the fixtures carefully; they are fragile and easily damaged when dropped or bumped.

Breaking Down an Interior Wall: If you plan to expand a bathroom, do not disturb a bearing wall *(page 176)*. Before starting demolition on a nonbearing wall, look for evidence of utilities—heating, air conditioning, or electricity—that may be housed within. Vents signal the presence of ducts, which can often be rerouted from the wall to the floor. Electrical switches or outlets indicate wiring that must be removed or relocated.

Supply pipes passing through a wall on the way to plumbing fixtures elsewhere may not be evident. If you find them during demolition, you will have to reroute them. Think twice about moving a plumbing wall. You can often redirect small branch drains, but large drains and stacks ordinarily must be left in place and concealed.

 **TOOLS**

Adjustable wrench
Socket wrench
Putty knife
Large groove-joint pliers
Small pliers
Screwdriver
Pry bars
Cold chisel
Dry-wall saw
Reciprocating saw
Sledgehammer
4-pound maul
Tin snips
Chalk line
Utility knife
6-inch and 12-inch dry-wall knives
Bucket
Sponge

 **MATERIALS**

Pipe caps and plugs
Rags
Picture-hanging wire
Fiberglass mesh tape
Joint compound

Capping Pipes

Cover the open ends of all pipes to keep out construction debris and, in the case of drains, to prevent sewer gas from entering the house. Plug toilet flanges with rags, and cap the other drains and the supply lines. If a pipe is threaded, screw on a cap or insert a plug of the same material. Cement a plastic cap onto unthreaded plastic pipes (the capped end must be sawed off to reopen the pipe); unthreaded copper pipes require a soldered copper cap.

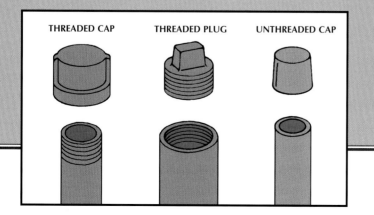

THREADED CAP   THREADED PLUG   UNTHREADED CAP

 **SAFETY TIPS**

Demolition creates dust, flying splinters of wood and metal, and other potentially dangerous debris. Wear goggles, a dust mask, and leather work gloves. Long sleeves, sturdy long pants, and boots are also in order. A cap will keep the mess out of your hair.

REMOVING WASHBASINS

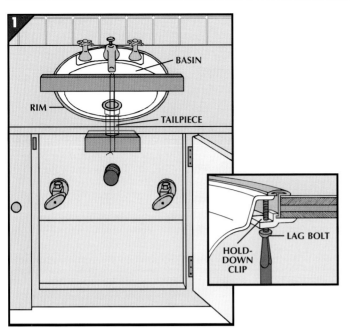

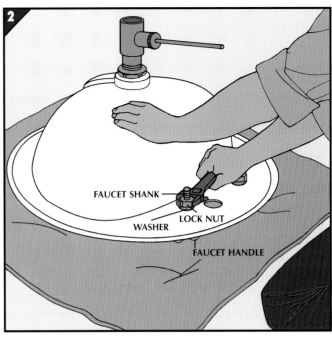

1. Freeing the fixture.

◆ Disconnect the supply lines, the pop-up linkage, and the trap *(pages 139 and 154).* Remove a wall-hung or pedestal basin as shown on page 177. Lift out a basin with a lip that rests on a vanity top. For a basin that is part of a vanity top, unscrew and remove the top.

◆ To detach a sink secured by a metal rim *(above),* lay a 2-by-4 across the basin. Bend a piece of picture-hanging wire over the 2-by-4, passing both ends through the drain hole. Twist the ends together below the tailpiece and insert a wood block between the doubled wire. Turn the block to draw it tightly against the tailpiece.

◆ Unfasten the lag bolts *(inset)* and hold-down clips and turn the block in the opposite direction to lower the basin.

2. Removing faucets.

◆ Place the basin facedown on the floor so that it is resting on the faucet handle. Pad the basin carefully if you intend to reuse it.

◆ With an adjustable wrench, unscrew the lock nuts from the faucet shanks. Lift off the washers.

◆ Turn the basin faceup and tap the faucet to break the seal of plumber's putty, if necessary, then lift out the faucet.

DISCONNECTING A TOILET

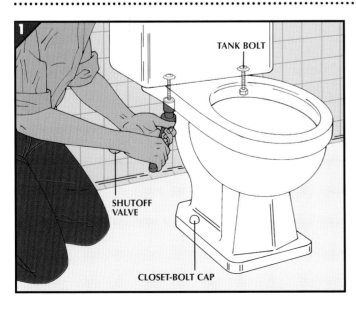

1. Disconnecting tank and bowl.

To remove a two-piece toilet, detach the tank, then unbolt and lift up the bowl. Take out a one-piece model as you would a bowl.

◆ Close the shutoff valve, flush the toilet, then bail and sponge the remaining water from the tank and bowl. Detach the supply tube as you would a sink line.

◆ For a bowl-mounted tank, unscrew the nuts under the bowl's rim with a socket wrench *(left).* Use a screwdriver, if necessary, to keep the boltheads from turning.

◆ If the tank is hung on the wall, remove the L-shaped pipe connecting it to the bowl by loosening the slip nuts at each end. Then take out the screws or bolts that hold the tank to the wall.

◆ For any type of toilet, pry the caps from the closet bolts and remove the nuts.

◆ Rock the bowl to break the seal between toilet and flange. Lift the bowl free.

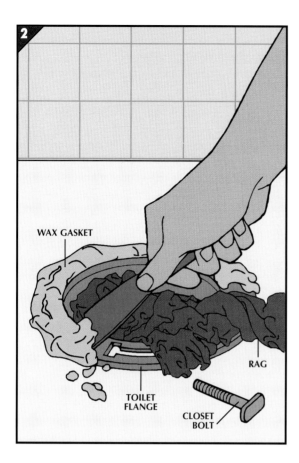

2. Scraping the toilet flange.

◆ Stuff an old rag into the toilet drain to block sewer gases.

◆ Slip the bolts out of the slots in the toilet flange and scrape away the wax gasket with a putty knife.

◆ Inspect the flange; if it is cracked, plan to replace it before seating the new toilet *(page 252)*.

TAKING OUT A TUB

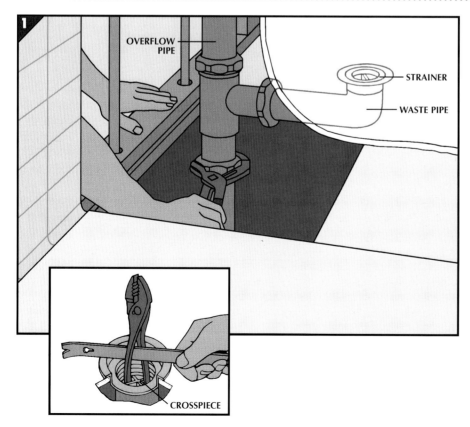

1. Disconnecting the tub.

◆ Remove the access panel in the wall behind the tub's plumbing fixtures. If there is no panel, cut a 14-inch-square hole, starting at floor level and taking care not to damage pipes in the wall.

◆ With large groove-joint pliers, loosen the slip nut connecting the waste and overflow pipes to the drain-pipe outlet *(left)*.

◆ Returning to the tub, remove the overflow plate *(page 145)* and lift linkage, and take out the strainer by removing the strainer screw. If there is no screw, raise part of the edge of the strainer with an old screwdriver, then tap the screwdriver counterclockwise.

◆ Insert the handles of small pliers into the crosspiece. Use a pry bar along with the pliers to unscrew the crosspiece *(inset)*.

Remove the spout, faucets, and shower arm, following the procedures on pages 143-145.

2. Freeing tub flanges.
◆ Remove a foot-high section of finished wall above the tub. For a tile wall, such as the one shown here, use a cold chisel and hammer to chip away the tile. For molded panels, remove the entire surround.
◆ Cut the waterproof wallboard behind the tile with a dry-wall saw; demolish cement board or plaster with a hammer and chisel.
◆ Remove screws or nails anchoring the tub flange to the studs.

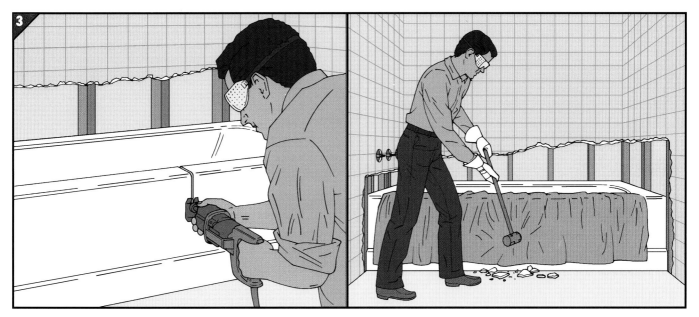

3. Removing the tub.
◆ If space allows, and you wish to save the tub, carry it out whole. Be sure to recruit enough helpers for the job. Even a lightweight fiberglass tub is hard to handle in a tight place.
◆ To demolish an unwanted tub for disposal, first examine an exposed edge to determine whether it is made of plastic, fiberglass, steel, or cast iron. Confirm your assessment by rapping the tub with your knuckles. Plastic or fiberglass tubs sound hollow. A steel tub emits a metallic ring. Cast-iron tubs respond with a dull tone.
◆ Cut up a fiberglass, a plastic, or a steel tub with a reciprocating saw *(above, left)*.

◆ Break up a cast-iron tub with a sledgehammer *(above, right)*. Wear safety goggles, long sleeves, and work gloves—and cover the tub with a drop cloth to trap flying shards.

TEARING DOWN AN OLD WALL

the holes with tin snips; wood lath can be cut with a reciprocating saw.
◆ To strip the wall, grip the edges of the holes with both hands and pull outward sharply *(left)*. Doing so will break any wall material and will even tear metal lath.
◆ Use a pry bar to lever remaining bits of wallboard from the studs to which they are nailed.
◆ Remove any electrical cables, plumbing lines, or heating ducts that run through the wall, and reroute them if necessary.

If the wall you plan to demolish was built before 1978, check the surface for lead with a kit from a hardware store **CAUTION** *and have a piece tested for asbestos by your local government or a laboratory. If either substance is present, hire a contractor trained in dealing with hazardous materials to take out the wall.*

1. Tearing away the wall surface.
◆ Turn off electricity to any cables—and water to any supply pipes—before entering the wall.
◆ With a 4-pound maul, smash numerous large holes in the wall between studs. The holes prevent the surface from peeling off in one piece—a potential cause of injury.
◆ In a plaster wall, cut metal lath from

2. Removing the second wall surface.
◆ Loosen the other surface of the wall with a maul. For wallboard, hammer next to studs; once freed, entire wallboard panels can be pushed free of the studs into the next room. For plaster, knock all the material from the wall, then pry the lath from the studs.
◆ Saw all but the end studs in half and pull them free.

3. Dislodging the end studs and soleplate.
◆ Sever both end studs with a reciprocating saw and cold chisel to create a 2-inch gap in each board.
◆ Insert a pry bar into the gap and remove one stud section. A block of wood can serve as a fulcrum to lever off the second piece *(above)*.
◆ Remove the soleplate in the same way.

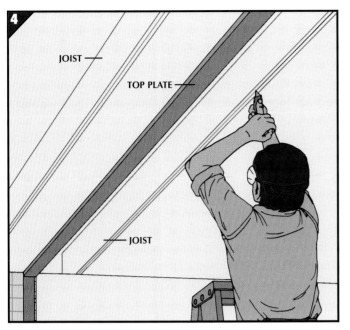

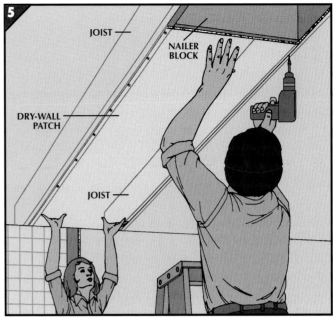

4. Removing the top plate.

◆ For joists parallel to the top plate, use a stud finder and a chalk line to mark the centers of the joists on either side of the plate. Score each line deeply with a utility knife.

◆ Use a hammer to break up the wallboard or plaster and lath between the ceiling cuts, then clean up the edges of the opening with the utility knife.

◆ Pry the top plate loose from the nailer blocks to which it is attached.

◆ For joists that cross the top plate, score the ceiling 12 inches to each side of the plate and pry both dry wall and top plate loose.

5. Patching the gaps.

◆ Cut dry wall to fit the ceiling gap. For an opening longer than 8 feet, trim sections of wallboard to end midway across either the joists or the nailer blocks.

◆ Where joists cross the gap, screw the patch to each one. Where joists parallel the gap *(above)*, drive the screws into the nailer blocks between the joists and into the edges of the joists, angling the screws slightly outward from the patch to anchor them solidly.

Fill the gap in the flooring left by the soleplate with a strip of plywood of the same thickness.

6. Finishing the ceiling patch.

◆ Apply a strip of self-adhesive, fiberglass mesh tape with a 6-inch dry-wall knife *(far left)*.

◆ Spread one coat of joint compound, holding the knife at a low angle *(left)*.

◆ Wait 24 hours to allow the compound to dry, then scrape off any ridges with the knife and apply a second coat of compound, diluting it for a smooth finish.

◆ After the second coat has dried, smooth the seam with a moist sponge. With a 12-inch dry-wall knife held at a steep angle, apply a final skim coat of compound diluted with water.

Before running new pipes, you must construct framing to support them—not only in the bathroom walls and floor, but along the course the pipes will follow through the house. Framing is also needed for most fixtures.

When attaching new framing, substitute 3½-inch drywall screws for nails of the same length where hammering could jar a nearby finished wall or floor.

Thick Walls for Pipes: Drain and vent pipes in a bathroom range from 1½ inches for a washbasin drain to 4 inches for a toilet; the small basin drain is most likely to be routed through a wall. For adequate support and concealment, an old wall of 2-by-4 studs can be made thicker with furring strips *(below)*. Or build a new wall for the plumbing, often called a wet wall *(pages 225-227)*.

Supporting Fixtures: Frame for fixtures as shown on pages 228 to 230. A washbasin set in a vanity requires no additional framing, but wall-hung and pedestal mod-els are usually supported by a crosspiece between two studs. Tubs need framing in the floor and wall, as well as crosspieces for the faucet and shower assemblies.

Running Pipes: Route the bathroom's supply pipes and drainpipes horizontally toward the vertical plumbing core of the house *(page 213)*, either through the floor joists *(page 231)* or—preferably—just below the joists. Follow local codes for joists, which are part of the basic structure of your house. Never run a long section of drainpipe through joists, since the required pitch of ¼ inch per foot cannot be accommodated.

Drill holes for pipes, in studs or joists, ⅛ inch larger than the pipe. Bore holes ½ inch larger than the pipe if you must insert it at an angle, a technique permitted by the flexibility of copper and PVC. To reduce noise, you may opt for foam pipe insulation; this requires still bigger holes. In no case, however, should holes be larger than 60 percent of the depth of a stud or joist.

ADAPTING AN OLD WALL FOR PLUMBING

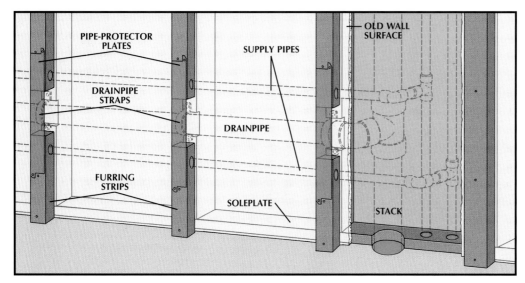

Fitting drain and supply lines.
◆ Remove the baseboard *(page 178)*.
◆ If you plan to install a stack, remove wallboard or plaster between the studs to each side. Drill a pilot hole through the soleplate and floor at the center of the stack. Expand the hole to full size with a hole saw; if necessary, drill first from above and then from below, tapping out any remaining wood with a hammer. With a spade bit, drill holes 4 to 6 inches apart for supply pipes.
◆ For studs that are not crossed by drains or vents, cut 2-by-2 furring strips the full length of the studs.
◆ Where studs will be crossed by

washbasin drainpipes or vent pipes, mark the location of the pipe run on the wall. Cut 2-by-2 furring strips to fit above and below the pipe. Remove the wall surface as needed, and notch the original studs to recess pipes that exceed 1½ inches in diameter.
◆ With an electric drill and a screwdriver bit, drive 3½-inch dry-wall screws through the furring strips into the studs.
◆ Drill supply pipe holes in the furring strips, next to the old wall surface.

After drainpipes and vent pipes are in place *(pages 232-237)*, anchor them with drainpipe straps and shield them with metal pipe-protector plates, ⅛ inch thick and long enough to extend past each supply pipe.

TOOLS

Electric drill
Hole saw,
  spade, and
  screwdriver
  bits
Electronic stud
  finder
Chalk line
Plumb bob

Utility knife
Tape measure
Carpenter's
  square
Level
Ball-peen
  hammer
Small pry bar

MATERIALS

2-by-2 furring strips
1-by-2s, 2-by-4s,
  and 2-by-6s
Larger framing
  lumber as
  needed
$3\frac{1}{2}$-inch nails

$3\frac{1}{2}$-inch dry-wall
  screws
Hollow-wall
  anchors
Cedar shims
Joist hangers

SAFETY TIPS

Constructing walls and framing with nails produces loud banging and may cause nails and wood chips to fly. Use earplugs and goggles for ear and eye protection.

A NEW WALL DESIGNED FOR PIPING

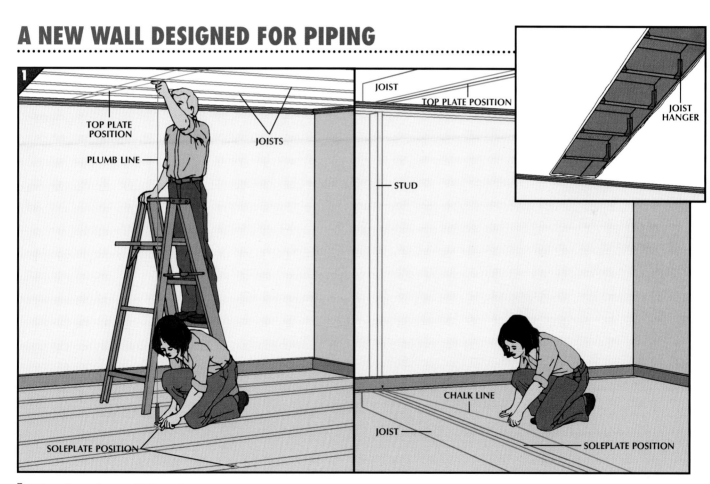

1. Planning the wall location.

◆ With an electronic stud finder, locate several ceiling joists.
◆ If the joists run perpendicular to the planned wall *(above, left),* mark for a 2-by-6 top plate on the ceiling, snapping a chalk line along each edge. With a plumb bob, transfer the marks

to the floor, then snap a chalk line along each edge of the soleplate.
◆ For joists parallel to the wall *(above, right),* find the nearest joist. Snap chalk lines for the top plate so that it extends 4 inches into the new bathroom. Transfer the top plate location to the floor with a plumb bob, and mark the edges

of the soleplate with a chalk line.

To place a wall between two joists *(inset),* open the ceiling between them and use joist hangers *(page 228)* to install nailer blocks at 24-inch intervals. (No framing is needed under the wall, if the floor is at least $1\frac{1}{8}$ inches thick.)

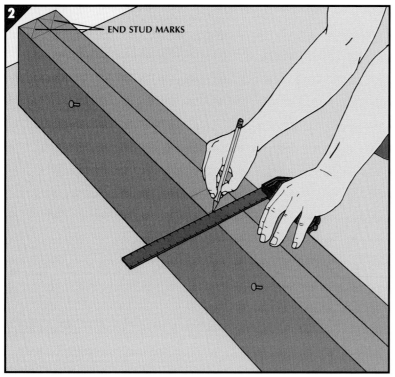

END STUD MARKS

2. Marking the top plate and soleplate.

◆ From 2-by-6 framing lumber, cut a soleplate and top plate the length of the new wall, and temporarily face-nail the boards together.

◆ Beginning at one end, mark the plates every 16 inches to indicate stud locations *(left)*. Plan for studs at both ends of the wall, making the stud space at one end narrower than 16 inches if necessary. If you plan to place the drain of a tub or shower against the wall, adjust two stud positions to center the drain between them.

CROWN

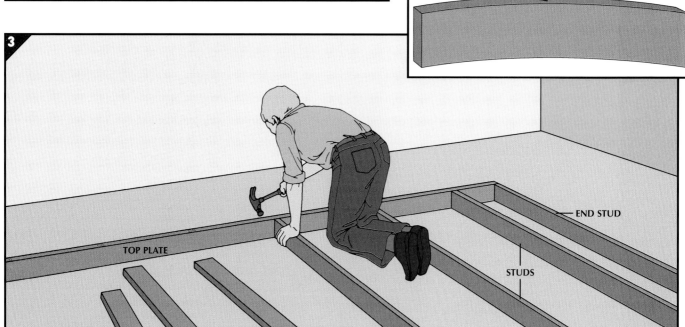

TOP PLATE

END STUD

STUDS

3. Assembling the frame.

In a tight space, you might have to nail the soleplate and the top plate to the floor and the ceiling, then toenail the studs to both of them. An easier method is to assemble the frame as

shown here and raise it into position.
◆ Every 2 feet along a soleplate line, measure the distance from the ceiling to the floor. Cut 2-by-6 studs $3\frac{1}{4}$ inches shorter than the smallest measurement. Doing so assures a frame short

enough to clear the ceiling when being raised from the floor.
◆ Fasten the studs to the top plate and soleplate with $3\frac{1}{2}$-inch nails *(above)*, making sure that any crowns face up *(inset)*.

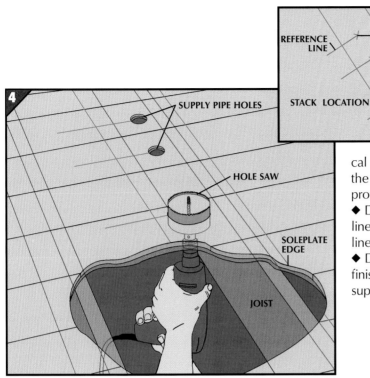

4. Cutting holes for vertical pipes.

◆ Before raising the new wall, mark the floor with the centers of holes for vertical pipes. If possible, keep holes at least $1\frac{1}{2}$ inches inside the planned wall; otherwise, you must later install pipe-protector plates.

◆ Draw reference lines from the centers across the chalked line marking one edge of the soleplate so that the chalked line divides each reference line into two equal parts *(inset)*.

◆ Drill pilot holes in the floor. Use a hole saw for the stack, finishing the hole from below if necessary *(left)*. Drill the supply pipe holes with appropriately sized spade bits.

5. Installing the wall frame.

◆ With a helper, raise the wall. If it lines up with studs inside the existing walls, attach the end studs with $3\frac{1}{2}$-inch dry-wall screws at 24-inch in-tervals *(above)*; otherwise secure the end studs with hollow-wall anchors.

◆ Push pairs of tapered cedar shims between the top plate and ceiling, one from each side. Put shims under per-pendicular joists or nailer blocks; otherwise, 16 inches apart. Drive screws through the top plate and shims, into the framing. Score protruding shims with a utility knife; snap them off.

◆ If the joists run perpendicular to the soleplate, screw it to each joist.

◆ When a floor joist runs along the wall, screw the soleplate to it at 16-inch intervals, avoiding where the pipes will go. Between joists, screw the soleplate to the floor.

◆ Locate the reference lines for the pipe holes. Measure each line and ex-tend it inward by the same amount, then drill through the soleplate *(inset)* to match the holes in the floor.

SUPPORTS FOR PIPE AND FIXTURES

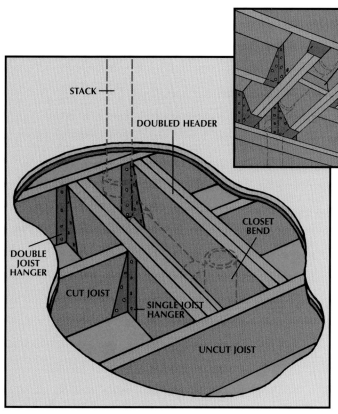

TRICKS OF THE TRADE

Hammering Nails in Close Quarters

Framing for a fixture or pipe in a restricted space, as with the closet bend at left, can be extremely difficult. One solution is to start the nail, then place the end of a 2-foot pry bar against the nailhead. To drive the nail strike farther down on the pry bar with the flat face of a framing hammer (the hardened steel of a pry bar may chip an ordinary trim hammer).

Framing for a closet bend.

◆ For a waste pipe that runs perpendicular to joists, you must cut a gap in the intervening joist. In the room below, remove a strip of ceiling, exposing the joist that blocks the planned path of the waste pipe and one joist to either side of it.

◆ Temporarily brace the middle joist with two vertical studs outside the opening, then cut out an 18-inch section of the center joist.

◆ From joist lumber, cut four boards to fit between the two uncut joists.

◆ Face-nail the boards together to make two doubled headers (above), and nail double joist hangers to both ends of each. Nail the joist hangers to the joists, then secure the headers to the cut joist with single joist hangers. Remove the temporary support studs.

◆ Support the waste pipe at the correct slope with a 1-by-2 support between the headers (inset).

The only framing necessary for a toilet waste pipe that parallels the floor joists is the 1-by-2 support.

Support for a washbasin.

◆ From a 2-by-6, cut a crosspiece to fit between the studs on either side of your washbasin.

◆ Level the crosspiece at the height specified by the basin manufacturer, and secure it with two $3\frac{1}{2}$-inch nails or screws through the studs (left).

◆ Attach the basin mounting bracket to the crosspiece after the wall is closed and finished.

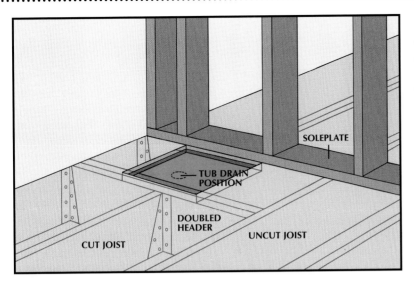

Underpinnings for a bathtub.

◆ In the floor, cut a 12-inch-square hole, one edge at the soleplate and centered side to side on the spot to be occupied by the tub drain; the tub overflow pipe and drainpipe will later connect to the drain system in this area *(page 245)*.

◆ If the opening exposes a joist and you cannot adjust the planned position of the tub, install headers as shown here. To do so, follow the procedure for a closet bend *(opposite)*.

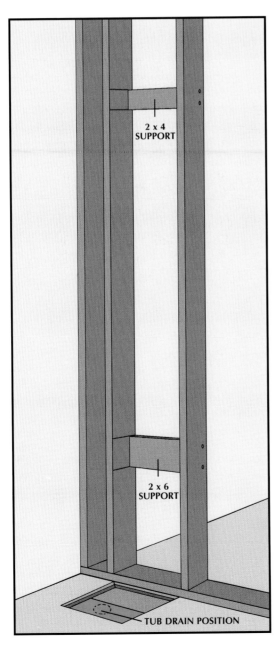

Bath and shower faucet framing.

◆ Mark the heights of the tub faucet assembly and the shower arm on the studs behind the drain end, or "head," of the tub.

◆ Cut a 2-by-6 faucet support to fit between the studs and nail it in place, recessing it into the wall according to the specification sheet provided by the faucet manufacturer.

◆ Attach a 2-by-4 support the same way for the supply pipe that will attach to the shower arm.

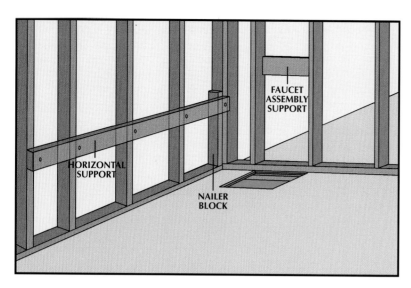

Supporting the tub.

◆ To provide the edge support needed by most bathtubs installed next to a wall, remove any wall surface to expose the studs, then cut a 2-by-4 support to extend from the planned location for the foot of the tub to the head of the tub.

◆ Level the support and nail it to studs at the height specified by the tub manufacturer. Use a vertical nailer block to attach the support at the head of the tub, as shown at left. If necessary, to anchor the other end of the support, toenail an additional stud at the end of the 2-by-4.

SAFE PASSAGE THROUGH STUDS AND JOISTS

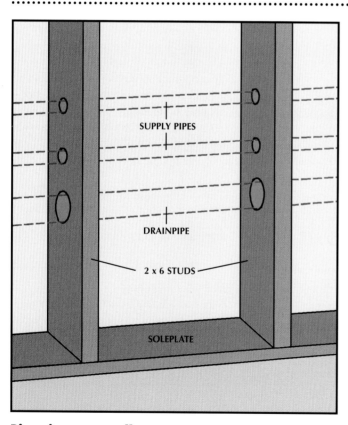

Pipes in a wet wall.

To run pipe inside a wall built for plumbing, drill holes through the studs with spade bits for the supply pipes and a hole saw for drainpipe or vent pipe. Align the holes for each pipe precisely, and try to keep them at least $1\frac{1}{2}$ inches from the edges of the studs; otherwise use pipe-protector plates (page 224). The slope of supply pipes is unimportant, but drainpipes must slant downward toward the stack, $\frac{1}{4}$ inch per foot.

TRICKS OF THE TRADE

Drilling in Close Quarters

A drill and its bit may be more than a foot long—potentially awkward for working in the $14\frac{1}{2}$-inch space between joists and studs. A right-angle drill (below) offers a solution. Available at tool-rental stores, this tool also comes as an attachment for many standard drills and easily fits between framing members.

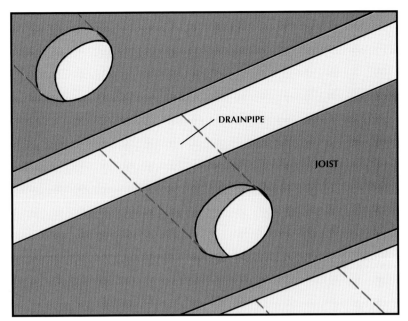

In standard joists.

Whenever possible, hang pipes under floor joists rather than cutting holes in the joists. If you must run pipes through joists, drill the holes to allow at least 2 inches between the hole and the top and bottom of the joist.

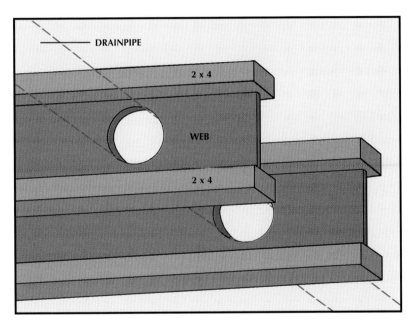

In I-beams.

Joists like those at left, consisting of a plywood web between two 2-by-4s, have become common in home construction. Do not cut the 2-by-4s, but cut pipe holes freely through the thin center piece; some I-beams come with knockout holes for the purpose.

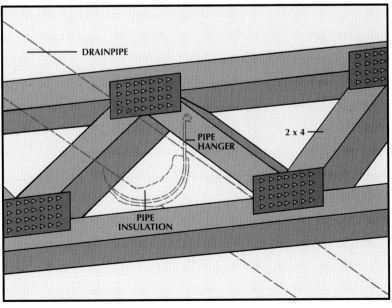

In truss joists.

Built like a bridge girder from 2-by-4s, a truss joist requires no hole drilling for pipes; when the time comes, pass them through the joists and suspend them with metal pipe hangers nailed to the cross members as shown at left. To minimize sound transferred in this particularly noisy arrangement from pipe hangers to joists, plan to fit foam pipe insulation around the pipe, as shown at left.

Drainpipes and vent pipes, collectively called the drain-waste-vent (DWV) system, are the most complicated part of a plumbing network. Work will go more smoothly if you install the DWV system before the supply lines.

Where to Start: Map your present DWV system and calculate where you will need to tie new drainpipes into the main stack. Remember that, because the pipes rely on gravity to carry the flow of wastes, they must slope downward. Plumbing codes require that a horizontal run have a pitch of $\frac{1}{4}$ inch for each foot of the run.

Check your plans against the local plumbing code before buying supplies or starting work. Most jobs that add new pipe must first be approved by building officials. Specify PVC plastic pipe: It is easily cut and joined, and along with its fittings, has smooth, continuous inner surfaces that do not obstruct waste flow. Get a plastic-pipe cutter or a backsaw and miter box to make the needed cuts, and use a utility knife or a file to remove rough burrs from cut pipe ends. To break into a cast-iron stack, rent a chain-type cutter (*page 234*).

Venting the Drains: Vents release noxious gases outside the house and equalize air pressure so that waste and water can flow freely through the drains. A vent line runs from every fixture's trap to a vent stack.

The trap-to-vent connection can be made in two ways: by stack or self-venting, in which the fixture's drainpipe drains the trap and also vents it through the roof; or by individual or branch venting, in which a separate vent line links the trap to a central stack vent.

Testing the System: You must test new drains and vents by filling the system with water. Repair any leaks that are revealed, and have a plumbing inspector check and approve the installation before you use the drains.

TOOLS

Plastic-pipe cutter, or backsaw and miter box	Dry-wall saw
	Soil-pipe cutter
	Hacksaw
	Soldering iron
Utility knife	Electric drill with extension and hole saw bits
Sandpaper or emery cloth	Plumb bob
	Saber saw
Level	Screwdriver
Hammer	Pry bar
Electronic stud finder	Garden hose
	Awl or ice pick
	50-gallon drum

MATERIALS

PVC pipe and fittings	Dry-wall screws
PVC primer	Joint compound
PVC cement	Pipe clamps
Nails	Solder and flux
1-by-2s and 2-by-4s	Slip couplings
Wood wedges	Flashing plate with rubber collar
Perforated plastic-pipe strapping	Petroleum jelly
Stack clamp	Roofing nails
	Roofing cement
	Test caps

SAFETY TIPS *Wear gloves to protect your hands while cutting cast iron, and a hard hat while working overhead, especially in an attic, where roofing nails may be exposed. When hammering or sawing, goggles help shield your eyes from flying chips.*

ROUTING DRAINS TO THE STACK

1. Joining a closet bend and a sanitary T.
Typically, the heart of a new DWV installation is an assembly of three fittings: a closet bend, receiving toilet waste; a sanitary T, with a curved inlet for smooth flow; and a closet Y, joining both and providing another waste inlet.
◆ Dry fit these components to make an assembly long enough to center the closet bend under the toilet drain hole and the sanitary T under the stack hole. Add a piece of pipe to increase the assembly's length, if necessary.
◆ Make alignment marks across each joint, to quickly assemble and orient the pieces after applying cement.
◆ Take the assembly apart, cut or file away the burrs around cut ends, and smooth them with fine sandpaper.
◆ Apply PVC primer to all assembly surfaces, inside and out, that will receive cement.

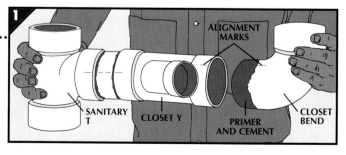

◆ Working one joint at a time, apply a thin layer of PVC cement to the inside end of the fitting and a thick layer to the outside of its matching piece.
◆ Push the parts together about 90 degrees out of line, then twist them until their alignment marks meet. Look for an unbroken bead of cement squeezing out all the way around the joint. If this bead is incomplete, quickly separate the parts, apply more cement, and rejoin. Hold the joint together for about 30 seconds.

2. Installing the closet-bend assembly.

◆ Dry fit lengths of pipe into the tops of the sanitary T and the closet bend that are long enough to reach above the floor when the closet-bend assembly is in place.

◆ Position the assembly, using a level to be sure that the sanitary T is exactly vertical.

◆ Nail a 1-by-2 across the joist space beneath the assembly to provide support. Recheck the assembly's position with a level *(right)*.

◆ Use thin wood wedges to shim the pipes tightly into the floor openings.

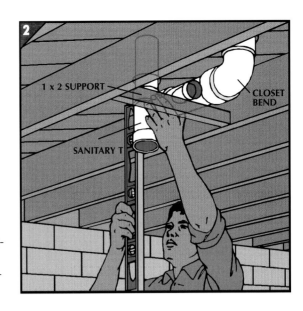

3. Running pipe to the existing stack.

◆ To extend the assembly below the joists, dry fit a short piece of pipe and an elbow to the sanitary T bottom.

◆ Nail a perforated plastic strap to a joist on one side of the planned path of the new soil branch. If the pipe will parallel the joists, attach the strap to a 2-by-4 nailed across the joist space.

◆ On the other side of the branch path, drive a nail halfway into the same joist or 2-by-4. Use a nail with a head smaller than the strap holes.

◆ Fit a length of pipe into the elbow, loop the strap under the pipe, and hook the strap onto the second nail.

◆ Try hooking the strap by different holes until the pipe slopes down from the elbow at $\frac{1}{4}$ inch per foot. To check the slope *(above)*, tape to one end of a level a strip of wood thick enough to center the bubble at the correct pitch *(inset)*. For example, a 2-foot level requires a $\frac{1}{2}$-inch strip.

◆ Couple and suspend more pipe to extend the branch, and cut the end to just reach the existing soil stack. Hang additional straps every 3 feet while maintaining the slope.

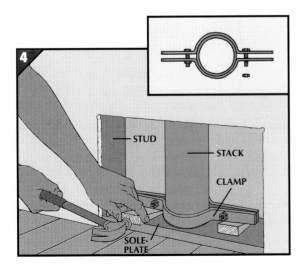

4. Bracing the stack for cutting.

To keep the top of the stack from dropping when you cut the bottom, add a brace where it enters the first floor.

◆ Find the point where the stack emerges from the basement. If it is behind a wall, locate the studs with an electronic stud finder; then, with a dry-wall saw, remove a 16- by 10-inch rectangle of wallboard between studs at floor level to reveal the stack.

◆ Position a stack clamp around the stack *(inset)*, about $\frac{1}{2}$ inch above the soleplate or the floor; tighten the clamp bolts firmly.

◆ Drive wedges between the clamp and the soleplate or floor as shown at left.

◆ Attach 2-by-4 mounting blocks to the studs, and screw the wallboard over the hole. Patch the resulting seams *(page 223)*, then repaint the wall.

TURN SCREW

5. Opening the stack.

◆ Choose a sanitary T to fit the stack and the new soil branch, and hold it against the stack at the proper height to receive the branch. Mark the positions of the top and bottom of the T on the stack.

◆ Use a chain-type cutter on a cast-iron stack *(left)*. Wrap the cutting chain around the stack and slip it into the hooks on the other side of the tool head. Position the chain $\frac{1}{4}$ inch above the top mark on the stack, tighten the turn screw to compress the spring, and move the handle of the cutter up and down until the pipe separates. Make a second cut $\frac{1}{4}$ inch below the bottom mark. Discard the cut section and stuff toilet tissue loosely into both ends of the stack.

On a copper or plastic stack, use a hacksaw to cut the pipe 4 inches above the top mark and 4 inches below the bottom mark. Save the removed section.

6. Installing a T.

◆ On a cast-iron stack, slide a pipe clamp's stainless-steel ring onto the bottom of the cut stack.

◆ Fit the neoprene sleeve of the clamp halfway onto the pipe and roll the free end of the sleeve back so the upper half folds over the lower half.

◆ Repeat the process on the top part of the stack, folding the free end of the sleeve up.

◆ Place the sanitary T in the gap of the stack and unroll the sleeves over it *(right)*. Slide the stainless-steel rings over the sleeves; tighten the screws.

◆ On a copper or PVC stack, cut the removed section into two pieces, each as long as the depth of the collars on the T, plus $3\frac{7}{8}$ inches. Solder or cement these short lengths of pipe into the end collars of the T.

◆ Two slip couplings *(far right)* will be used to connect the T to the stack. Prepare the pieces of a copper assembly by burnishing all cut ends and the

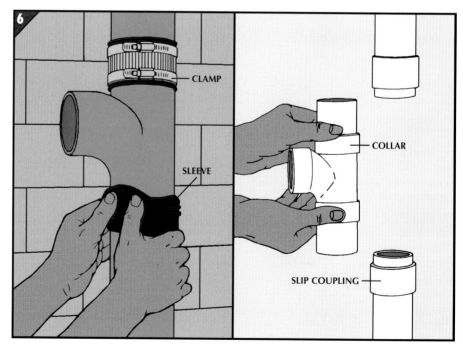

CLAMP

SLEEVE

COLLAR

SLIP COUPLING

interior of the couplings, then applying flux to these surfaces. Rub the ends of PVC pipe with abrasive cloth.

◆ Slide a slip coupling over each stack end and place the T assembly in be-

tween. Position the lower coupling over the joint, and cement or solder it in place. Repeat with the upper coupling.

◆ Cement the dry-fitted parts of the soil branch.

A DRAIN LINE FOR EACH FIXTURE

Bathtub or shower.

◆ Run pipe from the tub or shower drain to the closet-bend assembly through holes in the joists *(page 231)*, drilled at a slope of $\frac{1}{4}$ inch per foot.

◆ Install pipe in joist holes by cutting lengths that fit between the joists. Push the segments through the holes and join them with couplings.

◆ Many codes require individual vents for long drain runs. Typically a $1\frac{1}{2}$-inch pipe may be no longer than $4\frac{1}{2}$ feet from stack to fixture; a 2-inch pipe may run 5 feet. To create a separate vent, substitute a long-turn (offset) T for a coupling in the drain run *(right)*.

◆ At the closet-bend assembly, cement the pipe to the inlet in the closet Y. Do not add the trap at the other end of the run until the tub or shower is in place.

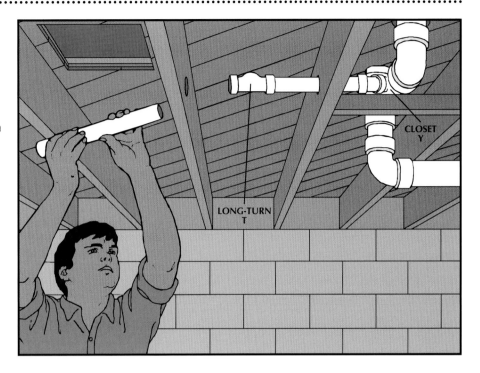

Toilet.

◆ Remove the guide pipes dry fitted earlier to both the closet bend and the sanitary T.

◆ Simulate the height of the finished floor by stacking a piece of the planned flooring atop a piece of the underlayment on each side of the closet bend. Set the rim of the toilet flange *(page 252)* on the flooring above the closet bend.

◆ Measure from the top of the flange's hub to the bottom of the closet bend's hub and cut a length of pipe to fit.

◆ While a helper braces the closet bend from below *(right)*, cement the pipe into the bend.

Washbasin.

The washbasin drain can be connected directly to the stack if no toilet on a floor above drains into the stack. (See page 237 for an alternative drainage route.)

◆ Cut a piece of pipe to join the below-floor sanitary T to a smaller one positioned at the height required by the rough-in specifications for the basin drain (page 216).

◆ Dry fit the small T to the pipe, check its height, and make alignment marks. Cement the pipe and upper T to the lower T while a helper braces it from below.

◆ Inside the wall, dry fit pipe to slope upward from the inlet of the small T. End it with an elbow facing into the room at the rough-in location for the washbasin drain (right). To the elbow, add a pipe extending 6 inches beyond the stud. Check the parts' positions, then cement them together.

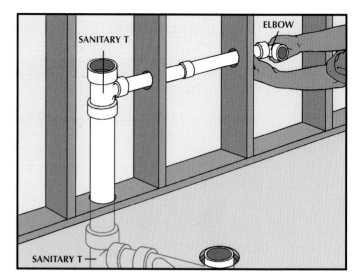

ADDING THE VENT STACKS

A stack for self-venting.

◆ Drop a plumb line from the top plate at the center of the washbasin sanitary T, and mark the position of the string on the plate (left).

◆ Mark a circle on the top plate, centered on the string position and slightly larger than the vent pipe. Cut out the circle with a drill with a hole saw bit.

◆ If the room above is floored, continue drilling through the flooring from below.

◆ Cut a length of pipe long enough to reach from the T to a point about a foot into the room above; angle the pipe into the hole, lower it to the T, and cement the joint.

Separate vent lines.

◆ To cut a vent from a tub or shower drain into the new stack, install a small sanitary T, bending upward, in the stack about 2 feet above the washbasin drain.

◆ From the long-turn T installed in the shower or tub drain line, route a vent pipe up through the soleplate and through the wall to the T fitting on the stack.

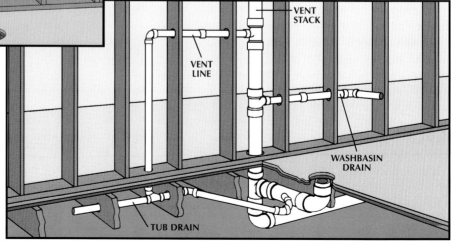

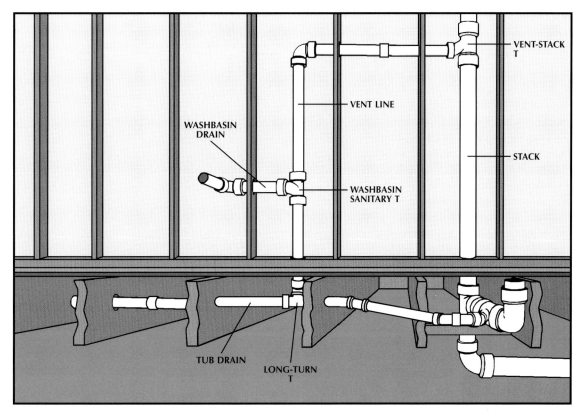

A shared vent line for two fixtures.

If your plumbing code lets you vent two traps with one line, you may be able to simplify your system *(above)*.

◆ Extend the stack upward from the top of the below-floor sanitary T to a point at least 6 inches above the overflow drain of the washbasin.

◆ Run pipe vertically from the long-turn T in the shower or tub drainpipe, through the soleplate, to the level of the washbasin drain line. Install the washbasin drain sanitary T atop it.

◆ Complete the vent with a line from this T and through the wall to one installed in the vent stack. Extend the stack through the top plate *(opposite)*.

◆ Connect the washbasin drain line to the washbasin sanitary T.

LINKING UP WITH THE MAIN STACK

A connection in the attic.

Before connecting to an existing stack, test the new system *(page 239)*, but in the attic rather than on the roof.

◆ After testing, add an elbow to the pipe extending into the upper story.

◆ Install a sanitary T in the existing stack *(page 234)*, making the top cut in the stack first. The upper section of the stack may come loose at the roof as you work; if it does, have a helper hold it in while you install the T.

◆ Cut a piece of pipe long enough to join the elbow and the T. Cement it in place.

◆ On the roof, reseal the stack with roofing cement if necessary.

A NEW VENT STACK THROUGH THE ROOF

1. Marking and cutting the hole.
◆ In the attic, drop a plumb line from the roof to the center of the stack vent. Mark the position of the string, and drive a nail into the roof through the mark. (If the stack rises directly under a rafter, alter its course with two 45-degree elbows.)
◆ Climb onto the roof and find the nail. Mark a circle around it slightly larger than the pipe. Use a utility knife to cut away shingles within the circle.
◆ Drill a starter hole inside the circle, then cut around the circumference with a saber saw.

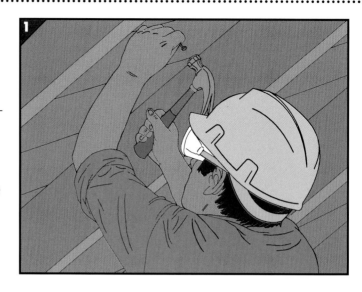

COLLAR

2. Securing the flashing.
◆ To waterproof the exit hole of the stack, install a flashing plate that has a precut hole and a rubber collar.
◆ Lubricate the inside of the collar with petroleum jelly. Slip the edge of the flashing under the shingles above the hole and align the collar over the stack hole. (If any shingle nails get in the way, remove them with a pry bar.)
◆ Lift the shingles that cover the top edge of the flashing and fasten the flashing with roofing nails.
◆ Use roofing cement to caulk exposed nailheads and shingles you may have damaged.

3. Installing the pipe.
◆ Cut a length of stack pipe to reach the distance above the roof that is specified by your code.
◆ Have a helper angle the pipe up through the collar *(right)*. Hold the flashing in place from the outside.
◆ Permanently connect this uppermost segment to the stack pipe below.

TESTING THE NEW DRAINS ALL AT ONCE

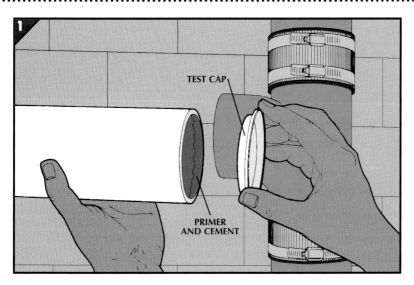

TEST CAP

PRIMER
AND CEMENT

1. Installing test caps.
When connecting a PVC soil branch to a cast-iron stack, prepare to test the system by applying cement to the inside of each open pipe. Press a test cap into place while twisting it.

For PVC or copper stacks, check your local plumbing code or with the plumbing inspector for regulations on testing the system.

2. Checking for leaks.
◆ With all drain openings blocked, pour water into the new vent on the roof to fill the drain system.
◆ If you find a leak, punch a small hole in the soil branch test cap with an awl or ice pick and drain the water into a large drum or divert it to a basement floor drain.
◆ Let the system dry overnight, then cut out the leaking joint and replace it.
◆ From the end of the run near the stack, cut off $\frac{1}{2}$ inch of pipe containing the old test cap. Cement a new test cap onto the end of the pipe.
◆ Retest the system.

◆ When the system has been inspected and approved by your local plumbing inspector, drain the water as described above.
◆ Connect the soil branch to the stack after removing its test cap. Use a sleeve and pipe clamp to join PVC to cast iron; a slip coupling and cement for PVC to PVC; and transition fittings for PVC to copper. Do not remove other test caps until you are ready to connect the fixtures.

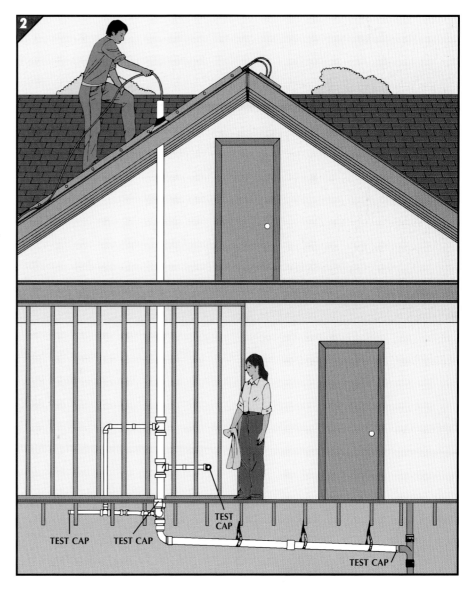

TEST CAP   TEST CAP   TEST CAP   TEST CAP

You must tap into your home's existing supply lines in order to bring water to your new bathroom. These pipes may be made of galvanized steel, plastic, or copper. Since galvanized steel is no longer in use and plastic is prohibited for supply lines by some local codes, copper is the material of choice.

To join copper pipe to steel, use a dielectric union—a five-piece transition fitting designed to prevent pipe corrosion. Copper can also be linked to plastic pipe with a two-piece adapter; a threaded copper coupling that is soldered to the copper pipe screws into a plastic collar, which has been cemented to the plastic pipe.

Pipe Sizes: Local codes dictate the diameter of a branch supply line, based on the number of fixtures that are attached to it. Most codes require $\frac{1}{2}$-inch pipe for one or two fixtures, $\frac{3}{4}$-inch for three or more.

In the system shown on pages 242 and 243, the cold-water line begins with $\frac{3}{4}$-inch tubing because it feeds three fixtures—toilet, washbasin, and tub. The hot-water line is $\frac{1}{2}$-inch; it supplies only the last two.

Installation: Choose the shortest, straightest route from existing lines to the bathroom, using angled fittings to join lengths of pipe at turns. When measuring and cutting pipe, be sure to include the distance each segment will extend into the fittings at either end. Solder all the joints in the same manner as described for the T fitting that is shown on the opposite page.

Once you reach the bathroom, bring the branch lines up through predrilled holes in the soleplate *(page 225)*, and attach 90-degree joints to extend them horizontally to the fixtures. Pages 242 and 243 show how to do this for the layout that is shown on page 216. Your sequence may vary, depending on where the branch lines enter the bathroom and where you install your fixtures.

⚠️ **CAUTION** *Use lead-free solder on copper pipes and a flameproof pad to protect nearby wooden surfaces. Use a striker to light your propane torch to reduce the risk of fire. Do not stand directly under a joint when soldering. Keep a fire extinguisher nearby, and turn off the torch before setting it down.*

 TOOLS

Tube cutter with
  built-in reamer
Flux brush
Wire fitting brush
Clean cloth

Striker
Propane torch
Hacksaw
Pipe wrenches
Plumber's abrasive
  sandcloth
Flameproof pad

 **MATERIALS**

$\frac{1}{2}$- and $\frac{3}{4}$-inch copper pipe
Fittings (T, L, wing L, coupling)
Paste flux

Lead-free solder
Penetrating oil
Dielectric unions
Pipe joint tape
Test cap

 **SAFETY TIPS**

Wear goggles, gloves, and long sleeves when soldering.

TAPPING INTO COPPER SUPPLY LINES

1. Cutting the supply line.

◆ Close and drain the system *(page 130).*
◆ Fit the jaws of a tube cutter around the section of pipe where the new line will begin. Turn the knob clockwise until the cutting disk bites into the pipe and the rollers grip the pipe *(right).*

◆ Rotate the cutter around the pipe, tightening the knob as necessary until the pipe is severed. For $\frac{3}{4}$-inch pipe, cut the pipe again $1\frac{1}{2}$ inches away from the first cut to accommodate a T fitting (for $\frac{1}{2}$-inch pipe, 1 inch away).
◆ Remove any burrs from the cut ends with the cutter's built-in reamer.

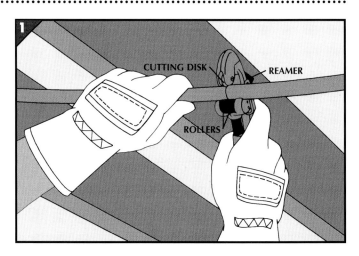

2. Installing a T fitting.

◆ Clean the inside ends of the T with a wire fitting brush. Then clean the last $\frac{3}{4}$ inch of the outside surface of the cut pipe with plumber's abrasive sandcloth until it is uniformly shiny. Do not touch this area, as oil from your hands can interfere with the bond of the solder.

◆ Brush a thin, even coat of flux on the cleaned area and fit the T over both ends of cut pipe *(right)*.

◆ Proceed immediately to Step 3, before the flux dries.

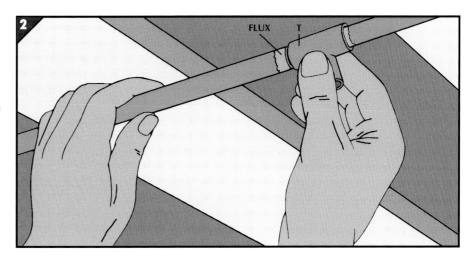

3. Soldering a T fitting.

◆ Light a propane torch with a striker and hold it with the tip of the flame touching the underside of the joint between the T and the pipe until the flux starts to bubble.

◆ Hold the tip of the solder against the top of the joint *(right)*. When the solder starts to melt, remove the torch. The solder will flow into the joint and seal the connection; examine it closely to make sure that the solder has filled the entire circumference of the joint. If there are gaps in the solder, reheat the joint and apply more.

◆ Repeat the process for the other joint. Remove excess flux and solder with a wet cloth after about 5 minutes.

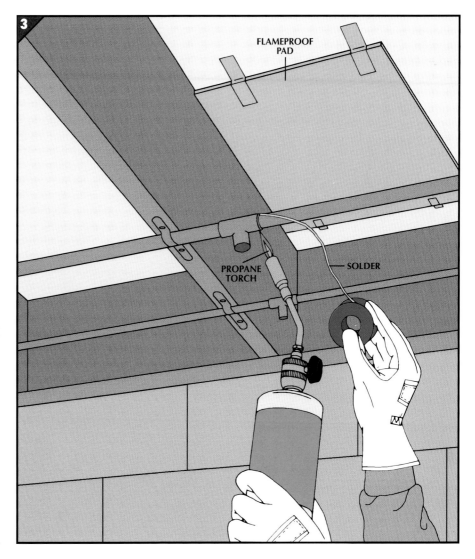

DEALING WITH GALVANIZED STEEL WATER PIPES

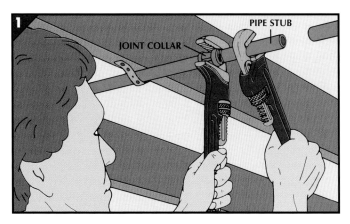

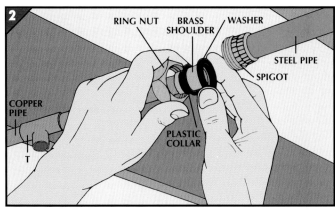

1. Cutting and removing the pipe.

◆ Close and drain the system (*page 130*).

◆ With a hacksaw, remove a 2-inch section of steel pipe between two joints.

◆ Unscrew the resulting pipe stubs from the nearest joint collars by fitting pipe wrenches to the collar and stub as shown above. Holding the collar stationary with one wrench, turn the other to remove the stub. If the joint is corroded, squirt penetrating oil on it.

◆ Next, unscrew each collar with one wrench while holding the pipe stationary with the other.

2. Attaching dielectric unions.

To join steel and copper pipe, use a dielectric union, which consists of a steel spigot and a brass shoulder separated by a rubber washer and attached with a nut and collar.

◆ Screw the spigots of two unions onto the ends of the steel pipe, and measure the gap between the spigots.

◆ Solder a copper T between two copper pipes to make an assembly 1 inch shorter than the distance.

◆ Install the copper section by assembling a union on each end as shown above and tightening the ring nuts on the spigots. Use a pipe wrench to keep the steel pipe from turning. Mark the copper pipe at each brass shoulder, then take down the copper section.

◆ Slide a ring nut and plastic collar back to the T; then clean inside a brass shoulder and outside the copper pipe. Apply flux and solder the shoulder at the mark. Repeat at the other end of the pipe.

◆ When the work is cool, wrap the spigot threads with pipe joint tape. Tighten the ring nuts on the spigots.

LINES FOR EVERY FIXTURE

1. The toilet.
◆ Run the $\frac{3}{4}$-inch cold-water line horizontally to the toilet location.

◆ Attach a $\frac{3}{4}$- by $\frac{1}{2}$- by $\frac{1}{2}$-inch reducing T at the rough-in height of the toilet inlet.

◆ Cut a 6-inch length of $\frac{1}{2}$-inch pipe to extend into the bathroom, and solder it to the T. Solder a test cap on the end.

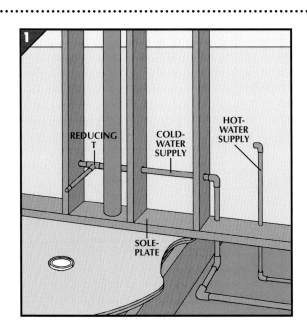

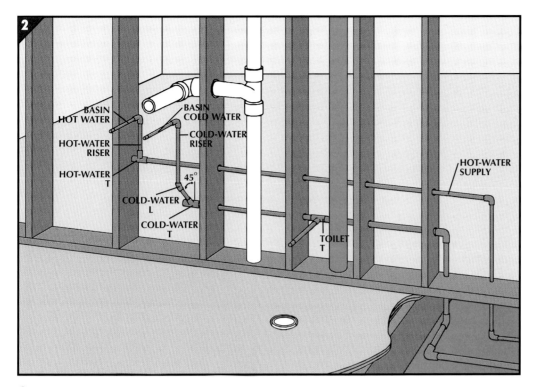

2. The washbasin.

◆ Extend a $\frac{1}{2}$-inch hot-water line below the hot-water rough-in point for the basin and install a $\frac{1}{2}$-inch T.

◆ Install a $\frac{1}{2}$-inch cold-water supply line from the toilet T under the cold-water rough-in point of the washbasin.

◆ Attach a T to the cold-water line at 45 degrees and add enough $\frac{1}{2}$-inch pipe to clear the hot-water line by 4 to 6 inches, then attach a 45-degree $\frac{1}{2}$-inch elbow—or L—so that it is pointing up.

◆ Fit the hot-water T and the cold-water L with $\frac{1}{2}$-inch vertical pipes—called risers—that extend to the height of the fixture. Attach a 90-degree L to each riser, then add a 6-inch length of pipe to each of them.

◆ Seal the ends with test caps.

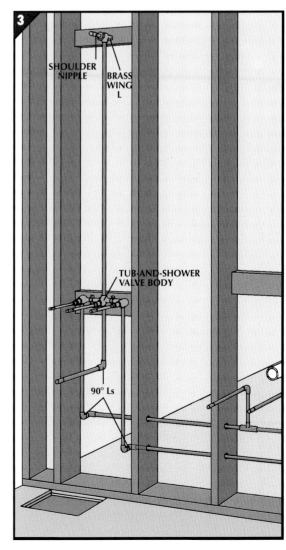

3. The tub and shower.

◆ With pipe clamps, secure a tub-and-shower valve body to the support installed earlier (page 229). Then screw the three valve stems into the valve body.

◆ Run $\frac{1}{2}$-inch hot- and cold-water supply lines horizontally through the studs and up to the valve body, using 90-degree Ls.

◆ Run a $\frac{1}{2}$-inch pipe from the shower outlet of the valve body up to the height of the shower-head. Solder a $\frac{1}{2}$-inch brass wing L to the top of the pipe and screw the sides, or wings, to the wood support. Screw a $\frac{1}{2}$-inch capped shoulder nipple into the threaded opening of the wing L.

◆ Install $\frac{1}{2}$-inch pipe from the tub-filler outlet of the valve body to the level of the tub filler. Add an L and a 6-inch-long piece of pipe and seal with a test cap.

◆ Test the entire supply system by turning on the water and checking carefully for leaks. Wait at least 24 hours before concealing the pipes or mounting fixtures.

The first fixture to install in a new or renovated bathroom is the bulkiest—the tub or shower. As noted on page 214, planning how to get the fixture from outside the house into the bathroom is essential; for example, in many homes a molded tub-and-wall unit can be brought in only through a patio door from which the sliding-glass panels have been removed. To simplify tub and shower installation, do the work before fully enclosing the bathroom.

Three Bath Options: Made of heavy cast iron or of lighter-weight fiberglass, plastic, or steel, a standard 5-foot bathtub like the one shown on these pages remains a popular choice. Instructions begin on page 246 for installing two common alternatives: a tub-and-wall unit *(pages 246-247)*, which offers finished walls and the least chance of leakage, and a shower stall of prefabricated panels *(pages 248-249)*, which is compact and easy to clean.

Framing to Match the Fixture: Tubs and shower pans alike can rest on either the subfloor or the underlayment. Select whichever is convenient; if you are installing new subfloor in the bath area, you do not need to add underlayment, but if you are preparing an old floor, you can leave the underlayment in place.

When you are installing a standard tub, strip the wall beside it to the bare studs and add a horizontal support *(page 230)*. For a tub-and-wall unit or for a shower stall, construct a separate three-wall enclosure against a bathroom wall as shown on pages 246 and 248.

Protecting the Finish: Avoid standing in the new fixture. If you must step inside, pad the bottom with cardboard and blankets.

MATERIALS

2-by-4s	Solder
$1\frac{1}{4}$-inch roofing nails	J bead
	Sealant
Tub waste and overflow kit	Corner bead
	Shower and bath fittings
Plumber's putty	
PVC drainpipe and trap	
Supply pipe	
Fiberglass insulation with vapor barrier	
Mortar mix	
Construction adhesive	
Shims	
Silicone caulk	
Flameproof pad	
Moisture-resistant wallboard	

TOOLS

Hammer	Pry bar
Screwdriver	$1\frac{1}{4}$-inch hole saw
Pliers	Trowel
Electric drill with $\frac{1}{8}$-inch bit	2-foot level
	Caulking gun

SAFETY TIPS

Wear work gloves, a face mask, and safety goggles when working with fiberglass insulation. Also wear safety goggles when you hammer nails.

EASING A BATHTUB INTO POSITION

FLANGE

RUNNER

1. Placing the tub.
◆ For a cast-iron tub—which can weigh 300 pounds or more—lay 2-by-4 runners on the floor *(left)*. Enlist three helpers to get the tub onto the runners. Two people can push the tub into place. Rest the tub rim on the horizontal support installed earlier *(page 230)*.

Handling a fiberglass, plastic, or steel bathtub requires at least one helper.
◆ For a fiberglass or plastic tub, lay a supporting bed of mortar before setting the fixture in place *(page 247)*.
◆ With all three materials, drive a $1\frac{1}{4}$-inch roofing nail into each stud, overlapping the flange with the nailhead; use a nail set to avoid hitting the tub.

2. Adding waste pipes and overflow pipes.

◆ Place a slip nut and washer on the overflow pipe and the waste pipe of a waste and overflow kit, then loosely connect both pipes to the waste T. Slide the pipes in the T to fit them to the tub's drain and overflow openings. Tighten the slip nuts.

◆ While a helper holds the assembly in place, attach the overflow plate to the lift linkage for the stopper (page 145). With the trip lever in the up position, hold the linkage against the overflow pipe at the center of the flange; adjust the length of the linkage so that the stopper is at the right height to block the waste pipe (inset).

◆ Have your helper place a large rubber washer, supplied with the waste kit, between the overflow pipe flange and the outside of the tub. While the helper holds the pipe in place on the washer, lower the lift linkage into the pipe and set the overflow plate against the inside tub wall. Connect the plate to the overflow pipe flange with screws supplied in the kit.

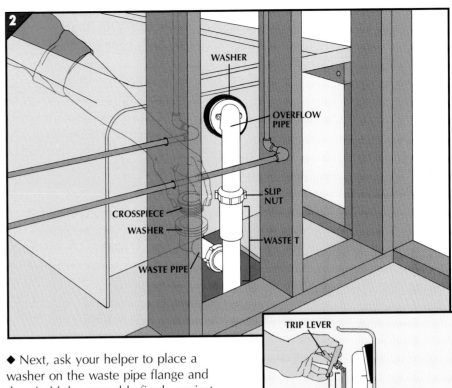

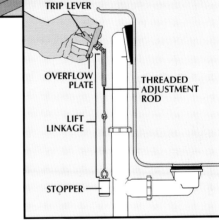

◆ Next, ask your helper to place a washer on the waste pipe flange and then hold the assembly firmly against the underside of the tub at the drain opening. Press plumber's putty under the flange of the crosspiece, and screw the crosspiece into the drainpipe by hand (above).

◆ Tighten the crosspiece by inserting pliers as shown on page 220 and turning clockwise with a pry bar.

◆ Attach the strainer to the crosspiece.

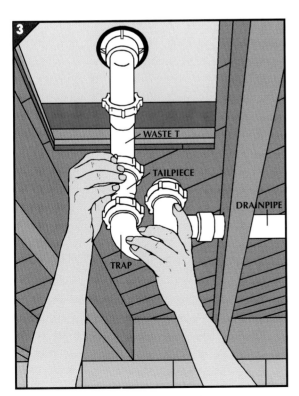

3. Connecting the trap.

◆ Working under the bathroom floor, add a tub trap to the end of the horizontal tub drainpipe (page 235), trimming the pipe so the inlet of the trap is directly beneath the tub waste T. If necessary, use an elbow and a short piece of pipe to center the trap.

◆ Measure and cut a pipe to serve as a tailpiece between the trap and the waste T.

◆ Join the waste T, the pipe, and the trap with slip nuts and washers (left); avoid cementing the trap so it can be removed if necessary for service.

1. Framing and insulating.

Before you frame for a tub-and-wall unit, check the manufacturer's instructions for special support requirements.

◆ Construct a three-wall enclosure of 2-by-4s against a bathroom wall to fit the tub-and-wall unit; locate the enclosure's plumbing wall so that you will be able to access it from behind after the unit is in place. Build the enclosure to the ceiling, doubling the studs at the end of each side wall. Provide for nailing surfaces in both the side wall and back wall where they meet. If the unit has a grab bar, add 2-by-4 backing for it.

◆ Frame for the tub's drainpipe and supply pipes *(pages 229-230),* then run the pipes *(pages 235 and 243).* After testing the supply pipes, desolder and remove the tub spout pipe stub. Wait to install it, as well as the shower arm and faucet stems, until the unit is in place.

◆ To muffle the drum of shower water on the unit's walls, staple fiberglass insulation between the studs with the vapor barrier (covered side) in *(left).* Do not insulate the stud space containing the supply lines.

2. Measuring for openings.

◆ Dry fit the tub-and-wall unit into the enclosure, and mark the back with locations for the shower, spout, and faucets. Lift the unit out and transfer the marks to the inner face by drilling a $\frac{1}{8}$-inch hole at each one; have a helper press a block of wood against the inside of the unit to keep the fiberglass from cracking as you drill.

◆ Without standing in the tub, drill $1\frac{1}{4}$-inch holes through the inner face with a hole saw, using the smaller holes as guides *(left).*

3. Setting the tub-and-wall unit.

◆ To support the bottom of the tub, spread a bed of mortar, mixed to the consistency of damp sand, about $1\frac{1}{2}$ inch deep *(right)*.

◆ If the unit includes a grab bar, apply construction adhesive to the back of the unit behind the bar before setting the unit in place.

◆ Tilt the tub-and-wall unit and push it into the enclosure *(inset)*, then lower it onto the mortar. If the unit sits too high, quickly remove it and adjust the mortar bed.

◆ Add the waste pipe, overflow pipe, and trap as for a standard tub *(page 245)*, then attach the shower arm and showerhead and faucet stems and handles *(pages 144-145)*. Working behind the unit with a flame-proof pad, solder the stub for the tub spout, then attach the spout.

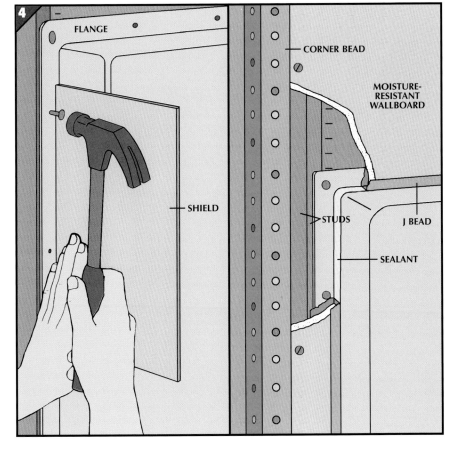

4. Nailing and finishing.

◆ Shim between studs and the flanges on the top and sides to fill any gaps.

◆ Fasten the tub-and-wall unit to the studs with $1\frac{1}{4}$-inch roofing nails driven through predrilled holes in the flanges; drill additional nail holes if necessary. While hammering, use a shield of cardboard or thin plywood to protect adjacent fiberglass surfaces *(far left)*.

◆ Finish the walls above and beside the tub-and-wall unit with wallboard that is moisture resistant. Before installing each wallboard piece, push a length of J bead onto the edge bordering the unit, mitering the metal channel to a 45-degree angle at corners.

◆ Lay a bead of sealant along the inside corner of the flange. Set the wallboard J bead in place, into the sealant, and screw the wallboard to the studs.

◆ Cover other exposed studs with moisture-resistant wallboard, finishing corners with metal corner bead *(near left)*. Hide seams with wallboard tape and joint compound *(page 223)*.

ASSEMBLING A SHOWER STALL

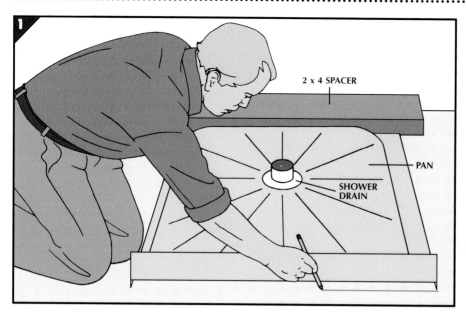

1. Marking for the shower pan.
◆ To allow for the back wall of the shower-stall enclosure, place a length of 2-by-4 against the wall in the planned shower location.
◆ Turn the shower floor, or pan, upside down and set it against the 2-by-4 spacer. With a pencil, outline the pan on the floor *(left)*.
◆ Stand a short length of pipe that is 2 inches in diameter in the drain hole. Steady the pipe as a helper lifts the pan and sets it aside, then use the pipe as a guide to draw a circle on the floor showing where the shower drain will go.

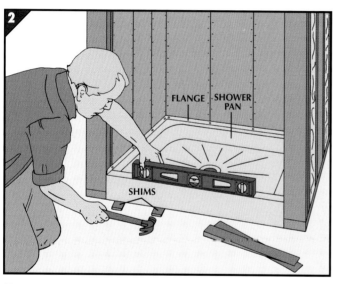

2. Installing the shower pan.
◆ Frame and insulate a three-sided shower enclosure as for a tub-and-wall unit *(page 246)*, establishing the side walls $\frac{1}{16}$ inch outside the penciled outline of the pan.
◆ Add supports for a showerhead and faucets *(page 229)*. Draw a large X through the planned center of the drain, then cut a 5-inch-square hole around that point, leaving the ends of the X as reference. Run supply pipes and drainpipes *(pages 235 and 243)*, leaving the shower arm and faucet stems until after the panels are in place. For a shower, the trap may be located either under the pan drain or at the end of a drainpipe leading to a wall beside the enclosure.
◆ Some shower pans—but not all—are meant to be supported on a mortar bed. Check the manufacturer's instructions and lay the mortar *(page 247)* if it is called for.
◆ Set the shower pan securely on the floor inside the enclosure, and level it with shims if necessary *(above)*.
◆ Fasten the shower pan flanges to the enclosure studs with roofing nails.

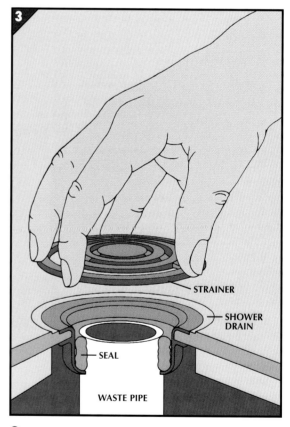

3. Connecting the drain.
Shower pans may be connected to a drainpipe by any of several systems. In the example shown here, a rubber, doughnut-shaped seal from the shower kit fits tightly between the pan's drain hardware and the drainpipe. After pressing the seal in place, screw on the strainer *(above)*.

4. Cutting holes for plumbing.

◆ Dry fit the side panel that will house the plumbing connections, seating it on the pan flange below. Mark the panel from behind with the positions of the faucet and shower arm connections as with a tub-and-wall unit *(page 246)* if access permits. Otherwise, measure the location of each pipe from the end stud and transfer those measurements to the panel.

◆ With a $1\frac{1}{4}$-inch hole saw, cut openings in the panel for the shower arm and faucet stems *(left)*.

5. Assembling the shower stall.

Since sealant dries quickly, try for a speedy installation. Avoid smearing sealant on shower stall panels; it can be hard to remove.

◆ Run a bead of sealant in the back flange of the shower pan. Set the back panel in the flange, temporarily holding the panel in place with a roofing nail just above its top flange.

◆ Apply sealant to the channel on the right edge of the panel *(left)* and to the right flange of the pan; add sealant to the right side panel's edge.

◆ Put the side panel on the pan flange and interlock the edges of the back and side panels *(inset)*. Lightly anchor the side panel with a nail above the flange.

◆ Install the left panel the same way.

◆ Check that the panels meet snugly and remain square and plumb to the pan; if necessary, shim under the flanges. Then secure all three with nails just outside the flanges, using a punch or nail set to avoid scarring the finish.

◆ Finish the walls above and beside the panels as with a tub-and-wall unit *(page 247)*. Add the shower arm and showerhead, faucet stems and handles, and a shower curtain and rod.

Completing the Room

Depending on the extent of your bathroom project, you may need to add new walls—a step best performed after installing the bathtub and any other large items. An ordinary partition wall resembles the wet wall that is described on pages 225-226, but with one difference. The studs and soleplates and top plates of a partition wall are 2-by-4s rather than 2-by-6s, because no plumbing must be concealed inside the wall.

Installing a door in such a wall is a simple matter of nailing a factory-made, prehung door to the sides and top of a rough doorframe built as part of the partition. Buy the door assembly ahead of time, and use its measurements as starting points for the built-in doorway.

A Sequence of Final Steps: Before hanging the door, you probably need to arrange for a rough-in inspection for each permit. In most areas, these inspections take place after the walls are framed but not closed and the ducts, wiring, and pipes are in place but not connected to any fixtures.

Once these inspections have been completed, close the walls with moisture-resistant wallboard or, where it is needed, cement board *(box, opposite)*. Then paint the ceiling, finish the walls, and put in the finished floor. See Chapter 7 for floor- and wall-surfacing techniques. Hook up the lighting and the appliances, and then complete the job by adding a door, a sink, and—as depicted on pages 252-253—a toilet.

Hanging a Door: A prehung door assembly *(below)* consists of two halves that are pushed into the rough doorframe from opposite sides of the wall. The door itself comes hinged to the inside of one of the sections, with the casing and doorstop already attached to the top and side jambs.

Many doors come with predrilled doorknob holes and bolt channels. To install a doorknob-bolt assembly—using a lever knob *(page 175)* for greater accessibility—drill a hole into the jamb for the bolt; chisel mortises on the door and jamb for the bolt and strike plates.

 **MATERIALS**

2-by-4 studs
Nails
Wood shims

Spacing blocks
Prehung door
Doorknob assembly

 **SAFETY TIPS**

When hammering, wear safety goggles to protect your eyes from flying debris or loose nails.

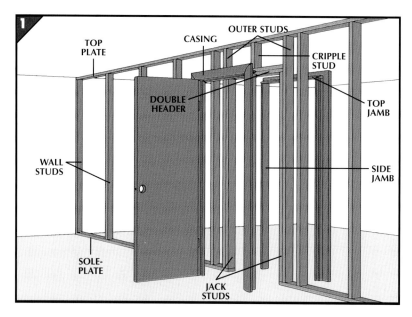

1. Building the wall and doorframe.

Construct a partition wall of 2-by-4s using the methods on pages 225-226, but avoid nailing the soleplate near the area that must later be cut for the doorway.

◆ At the planned door location, install two outer studs, spacing them $3\frac{1}{2}$ inches farther apart than the width of the prehung door's top jamb.

◆ Cut two jack studs $1\frac{1}{4}$ inches shorter than the top of the top jamb. Nail them to the outer studs flush with the bottoms of the studs.

◆ Place two headers, one atop the other, across the tops of the jack studs and nail them in place.

◆ Attach a cripple stud between the double header and the top plate.

◆ Cut away the soleplate between the jack studs where the doorway will be.

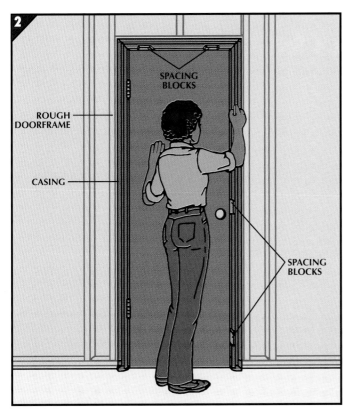

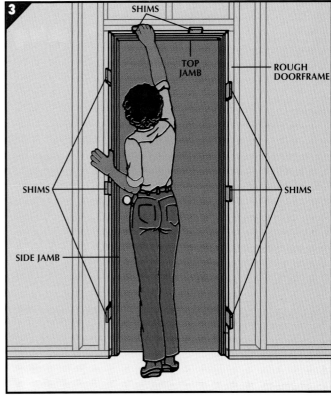

2. Installing the prehung door.

After closing the wall and applying a finished surface, install the prehung door.

◆ Remove the shipping braces holding the door assembly together. Prehung doors are often nailed closed for shipping; free the door before installing the assembly.

◆ Plan to attach the section containing the door first; if the second section will be installed from inside the bathroom, place it there before beginning.

◆ Slide the first section into the opening in the wall.

◆ Insert three $\frac{1}{8}$-inch spacing blocks between the strike side of the door and the side jamb, and two blocks between the top of the door and the top jamb (above).

◆ Nail the casing to the rough doorframe.

◆ Remove the blocks, open the door, and walk through.

3. Completing the job.

◆ From the other side of the wall, insert two $\frac{1}{4}$-inch tapered shims between the top jamb and the rough frame, and three between each side jamb and the frame (above).

◆ Break off the excess portion of each shim. With the door open, secure the shims in place by driving nails into the jambs, through the shims, and into the frame.

◆ Slide the other half of the door assembly into position so that it fits snugly into the first section; the two attach with a hidden tongue-and-groove joint.

◆ Nail the casing to the wall.

◆ Nail the jambs to the frame at 1-foot intervals.

Special Forms of Wallboard for a Bathroom

Ordinary wallboard becomes soft and spongy in a damp setting, so its use should be avoided for bathroom walls. Instead, close the walls with moisture-resistant wallboard, or with cement board for areas you intend to tile.

Moisture-resistant wallboard, called "greenboard" for its green, water-resistant face paper, has a core saturated with asphalt to resist absorption and softening. Cut and install greenboard as you would any wallboard, but do not employ it on ceilings, where it has a tendency to sag; ceilings are the only bathroom surface for which ordinary wallboard is often used.

Cement board, commonly available under the trade name Durock, consists of an aggregated Portland cement held together by fiberglass mesh. To cut it, score through the surface skin of cement and the mesh below with a utility knife, making several passes and substituting new blades as necessary. Then snap the board along the cut, and plane the edge with a rasp. Alternatively, cut cement board with a circular saw and a carbide-tipped blade; wear safety goggles and a dust mask. Make any necessary holes by scoring the desired shape onto the cement board, then smashing out the marked area with a hammer. Cement board should be secured in place with $1\frac{1}{2}$-inch hot-dip galvanized roofing nails or with special screws called wafer-head fasteners. Space the nails or screws no more than 8 inches apart.

Hooking Up a Toilet

Begin toilet hookup by installing a shutoff valve and a plastic toilet flange *(below)* if you moved a toilet drain or added one during a bathroom renovation. Before cementing the flange in place, remove the rag that was stuffed into the drain earlier, then replace the rag until you are ready to set the toilet. If you are in-stalling a new toilet on an old drain, you usually can use the existing flange and valve; start with Step 3 on the facing page.

In either case, the new toilet's dimensions must match the wall-to-drain distance in your bathroom. Furthermore, water-conserving toilets, which have been mandated by federal law since 1994, require the use of a $\frac{3}{8}$-inch supply tube be-tween the shutoff valve and the toi-let tank.

To conceal the bolts anchoring the toilet to the floor, there are plas-tic caps available that snap in place and there are porcelain caps that are secured with putty.

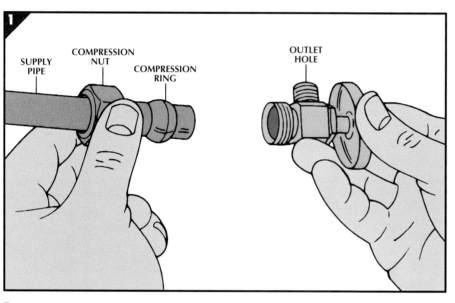

MATERIALS

Shutoff valve
Toilet flange
PVC cement
Toilet flange screws
Wax gasket
Plumber's putty
Closet bolts and
  caps
Toilet supply tube

1. Attaching a shutoff valve.
◆ Cut the supply pipe 2 inches from the wall, then slide an escutcheon over the stub and press it against the wall.
◆ Slip the compression nut and com-pression ring that came with the valve over the pipe.
◆ Position the valve on the pipe with the outlet hole pointing up. Tighten the nut one turn past finger tight.

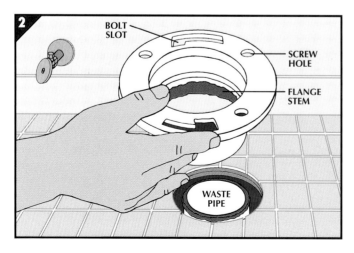

2. Seating the flange.
◆ Apply PVC cement to the inside of the flange stem and the outside of the waste pipe. Push the flange onto the pipe so that a line drawn between the bolt slots is perpendicular to the wall, as shown at left, then im-mediately rotate the flange a quarter-turn, positioning the slots an equal distance from the wall.
◆ Drill through the screw holes into the subfloor (on a tile floor, use a masonry bit). Secure the flange with toilet flange screws.

⚠ *Work quickly when you are setting a* **CAUTION** *toilet flange; PVC cement dries permanently within 30 seconds.*

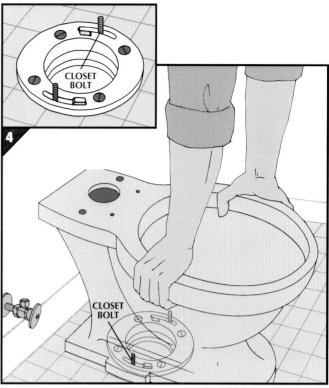

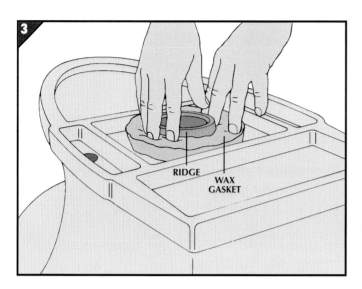

3. Attaching the wax gasket.

◆ Turn the toilet bowl upside down and set it on padding.
◆ Slip a wax gasket over the ridge around the waste hole. With your fingers, press the gasket firmly against the bowl bottom *(above)*.

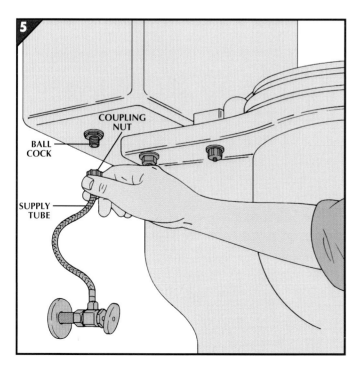

4. Setting the bowl.

◆ Insert a closet bolt head downward into each bolt slot *(inset)*, positioning them equidistant from the wall.
◆ Lower the bowl onto the bolts *(above)*. Press down firmly on the bowl, rocking it slightly. Do not raise it from the floor; doing so will break the seal between toilet and drain.
◆ Level the bowl from side to side and front to back. If necessary, shim with copper or brass washers without lifting the bowl up.
◆ If using plastic bolt caps, slip a cap base onto each bolt, followed by a metal washer and a nut. Tighten the nuts finger tight, then a quarter-turn more with a wrench. Trim the bolts with a hacksaw as needed and snap the bolt caps in place.
◆ For porcelain caps, secure each bolt with a washer and nut, then attach the caps with putty.

5. Connecting the water supply.

◆ Attach the toilet tank as shown on page 162, and bolt on the seat and cover.
◆ Wrap plumbing-sealant tape onto the threads on the shutoff valve and on the base of the ball cock, which protrudes under the tank.
◆ Screw the compression nut on one end of a toilet supply tube to the outlet hole on the shutoff valve; fasten the coupling nut on the other end to the ball cock *(left)*.
◆ Open the valve, flush the toilet, and check for leaks. If necessary, tighten the nuts a fraction of a turn at a time until the leaks stop.

Home Plumbing Basics

Whether you are repairing a leaking pipe or adding a new washbasin, the task is simplified if you know how your home's plumbing is laid out and how to work with common pipe materials. These plumbing fundamentals, set forth in the pages that follow, will also help you to diagnose problems—and may enable you to fix the difficulty without an expensive visit from a professional.

Applying primer to a plastic supply pipe →

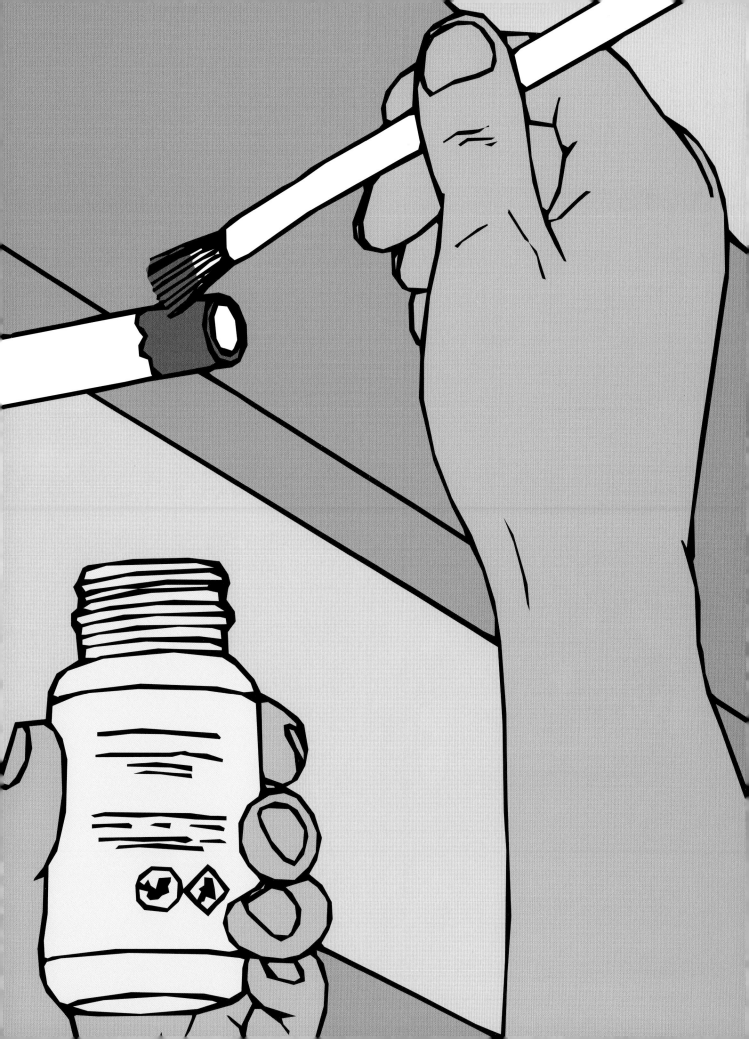

Many of the tools necessary for plumbing repairs and improvements are multipurpose instruments, such as screwdrivers, pliers, hammers, and adjustable wrenches. With the addition of the few specialized tools shown here, you can be ready not only to meet most plumbing emergencies but also to install and replace pipes and fixtures.

Included in this tool kit are implements for loosening and tightening plumbing hardware, cutting and soldering pipe, and clearing clogged sink and toilet drains. There is no satisfactory substitute for any of these tools, which are designed for the hardware unique to plumbing or for work in awkward spaces, such as under the sink.

Seat wrench.
The repair of faucet leaks caused by worn valve seats *(page133)* requires a seat wrench. With a square tip on one tapered end and an octagonal tip on the other, the wrench fits the two most common types of seats in a wide range of sizes.

Spud wrench.
The wide-spreading, toothless jaws on this wrench firmly grasp large nuts found on toilets and sinks. The jaws, which lock in place once opened to the desired width, are shaped to fit into tight spaces.

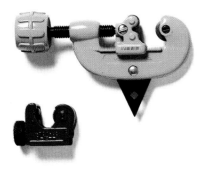

Tube and pipe cutters.
Depending on the type of cutting wheel installed, these devices cut either plastic or copper pipes. The built-in triangular reamer on the larger cutter scrapes away burrs around the cut edge, leaving it smooth. A minicutter is handy when working in tight spaces.

Pipe wrench.
The serrated teeth and spring-loaded upper jaw of this durable tool tightly grip pipes while you hold or turn them. The spring allows you to release the wrench's grip and reposition the tool without readjusting the jaws.

Basin wrench.
This self-adjusting tool's long handle is used primarily to reach otherwise inaccessible nuts that fasten faucets to washbasins and kitchen sinks.

Plunger.
A fold-out plunger has a flexible extension called a funnel. Extended as shown here, the funnel helps to unclog toilet drains. Folding it inside the cup converts the plunger for clearing tub, sink, and shower drains.

Faucet-handle puller.
To remove stubborn faucet handles, enlist the aid of this device. The jaws of the puller fit under the handle and pull it free as the threaded center shaft is tightened against the faucet stem.

Propane torch and flameproof pad.
To solder copper pipe or tubing—or to disassemble soldered joints—use a propane torch. With a flame spreader attached, the torch also thaws frozen pipes (page 265). For any of these applications, protect nearby house framing with a flameproof pad.

Augers.
The trap-and-drain auger, shown here coiled with its handle, is used for clearing sink and tub drains; the handle slides along the snake as it progresses into the drain. For toilets, use a closet auger, which is shaped to direct the flexible shaft into the toilet trap and has a handle at the top.

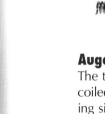

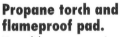

Although fixtures and pipe materials vary, all plumbing systems share two basic components: a supply system to deliver water that is safe to drink and a drain-waste-vent (DWV) system to remove wastewater quickly and reliably.

System Basics: Water enters the house through a single pipe. This conduit passes through a water meter and then branches into hot- and cold-water supply lines, both of which carry water that is under pressure.

The DWV system includes drainpipes, which work by gravity, and vent pipes, which do not carry water; instead they allow gases to escape through the roof. Vents also equalize air pressure in the drains in order to prevent partial vacuums that could retard drainage. Underneath sinks, showers, and bathtubs—but inside toilets—water-filled bends that are known as traps prevent gases in the drains from entering the house.

Local Codes: Plumbing is controlled by local regulations that have the force of law. Observing these codes, besides being necessary, helps ensure the success of plumbing projects. For example, a roof vent is usually a single pipe, 3 to 4 inches in diameter. In the colder parts of Canada and the United States, snow and ice could block such a vent; codes there specify wider vent pipes.

Checking Water Use: Water meters show how many cubic feet of water are being consumed. Knowing how to read a water meter allows you to check how much water goes to a specific purpose such as lawn watering. Simply read the meter before and after the task, then take the difference. Convert readings from cubic feet to gallons with the calculator below.

Though some meters show a single easy-to-read figure as an odometer does, others have multiple harder-to-interpret dials *(bottom)*.

Cubic feet of water		
_____ x 7.5 =	_____	**gallons**

Converting to gallons.
To translate water-meter readings in cubic feet to gallons, multiply the difference between two readings by 7.5.

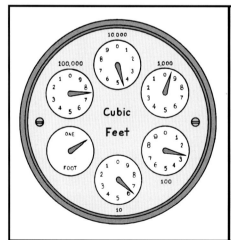
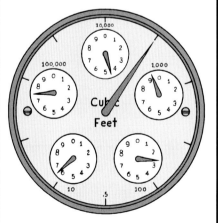

74,926). Note that on a six-dial meter *(far left)*, the smaller digit lies clockwise from the hand on some dials, counterclockwise on others.

The dial labeled 1 on a six-dial meter—and the pointer that sweeps the edge of a five-dial model—measure fractions of a cubic foot, a feature helpful in detecting leaks. To confirm a leak, turn off all fixtures, then check whether this indicator on the meter continues to advance, however slowly.

Reading a water meter.
On water meters with multiple dials, each is labeled with the number of cubic feet required to rotate the pointer a full turn. Thus each mark on the dial labeled 100,000 corresponds to 10,000 cubic feet of water. To take a reading, note the smaller of the two digits nearest the pointer, beginning with the 100,000 dial and ending with the dial labeled 10. The five digits from the dials provide the current reading (here,

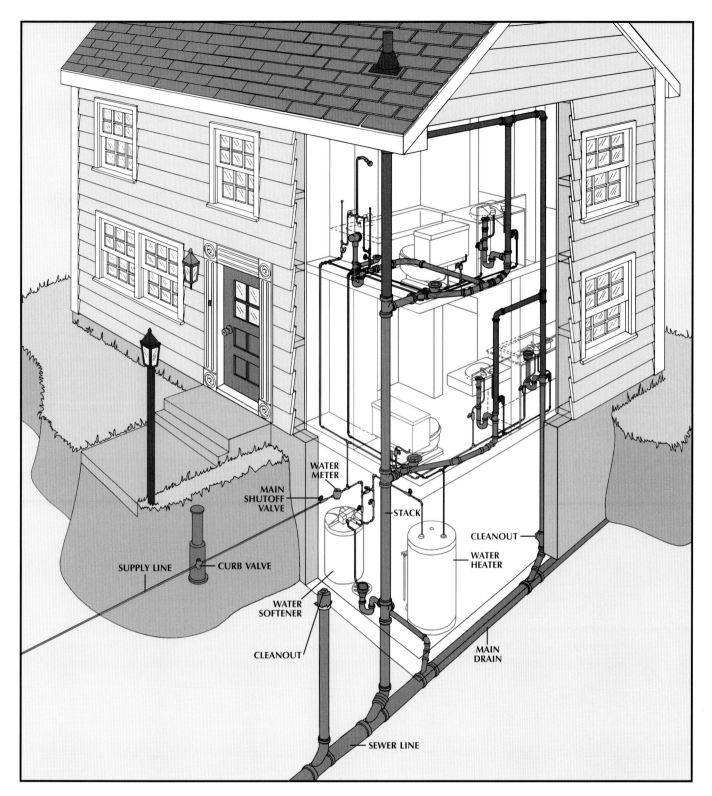

WATER METER

MAIN SHUTOFF VALVE

STACK

CLEANOUT

WATER HEATER

SUPPLY LINE

CURB VALVE

WATER SOFTENER

CLEANOUT

MAIN DRAIN

SEWER LINE

Anatomy of a plumbing system.

Typically, water reaches a house through a supply line controlled by two valves—an underground curb valve owned by the utility and the main shutoff valve in the basement. Past this valve is the water meter, beyond which the supply line divides. One branch supplies cold water to fixtures *(blue);*

the other supplies the water heater, often by way of a water softener *(pages 290-294).* Hot-water pipes *(red)* lead from the heater to the fixtures.

Drainpipes *(gray)* carry wastewater away from the plumbing fixtures to vertical stacks. These conduits lead to the house's main drain, which con-

nects to a sewer line. Cleanouts in both the stacks and the main drain provide access for unclogging the drain system.

Vent pipes *(purple)* channel gases from the drains through the upper portion of each stack and then outdoors through the roof.

Pipes and fittings, the prime constituents of a household plumbing system, not only can be assembled in any number of configurations but also exhibit considerable variety in their own right. For example, several different materials may be used for the supply pipes in residential systems, and still other materials are acceptable for the drain-waste-vent (DWV) portion of the network. (To determine what kind you have, simply examine the pipes in your basement, garage, or behind an access panel, and match them to the photographs on these pages.) As for fittings, they are designed for many roles—splicing straight lengths of pipe (called a run), allowing direction changes and branching, linking pipes of differing diameters, and so on. Some common sorts of fittings for the supply lines are shown opposite; DWV counterparts appear on page 262.

Keys to Buying Materials: Cost, durability, and ease of installation are among the important factors in choosing the materials for a repair job or an addition to your plumbing system. But before you make a purchase, check the code of your local jurisdiction. Some codes prohibit a particular material in one part of a plumbing system but not in another, and the local code may dictate the method used to join components. Among allowed materials, you can mix and match: Special transition fittings will create secure connections between dissimilar pipes; and if the pipes are made of different metals, an appropriate fitting will prevent an electrochemical reaction that could erode a joint.

All piping is sized by inside diameter. When replacing pipe, determine its inner diameter *(pages 262-263)* and buy new pipe of the same size.

SUPPLY PIPES AND FITTINGS

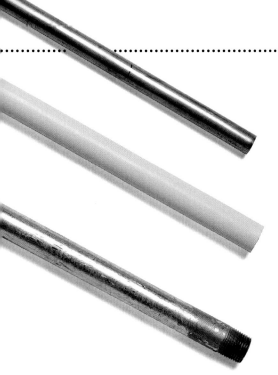

Rigid copper.
This metal, joined with durable solder, resists corrosion and has smooth surfaces for good water flow. A thin-walled version called Type M is the least expensive and will serve well for most repairs.

Chlorinated polyvinyl chloride (CPVC).
A rigid plastic formulated with chlorine so that it can withstand high temperatures, CPVC is a popular supply-pipe material for its low cost, resistance to corrosion, and ease of assembly: Fittings are secured by solvent cement. For residential use, most codes specify a so-called Schedule 40 pressure rating, stamped on the pipe.

Galvanized steel.
Used for supply as well as drain-waste-vent lines, this material is found only in older homes. Although it is the strongest of supply-pipe materials, galvanized steel is prone to corrosion over time. Runs of threaded pipe are joined by threaded fittings; the entire length between fittings must be removed and replaced to complete a repair.

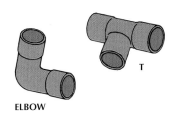

ELBOW

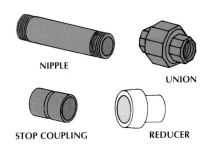

NIPPLE

UNION

STOP COUPLING

REDUCER

COPPER-TO-CPVC ADAPTER

THREADED ADAPTER

Bends and branches.

The direction of a supply pipe is changed by a fitting called an elbow, available in 45- and 90-degree turns. A T fitting joins a 90-degree branch run to a straight run of pipe.

Straight-line fittings.

Many sorts of fittings are used to join pipes in a straight run. A straight piece of pipe called a nipple extends a run or fitting a short distance—from 1 to 12 inches. A union holds two pipes within an assembly joined by a threaded nut, allowing disassembly without cutting. Couplings, unlike unions, are unthreaded and permanent. A stop coupling like the one shown here has interior shoulders for a secure fit in new installations; a slip coupling, which has no shoulders, slides over existing pipe and is used for repairs. A reducer, also known as a bushing, attaches pipes of different diameters by reducing the opening at one end.

Transition fittings.

As the name implies, these fittings allow a run of pipe to change from one material to another. Copper-to-CPVC adapters join the two most common kinds of supply pipe, both unthreaded. Threaded adapters join threaded pipe to unthreaded—and also are used to connect pipes to a variety of other plumbing components, such as a spigot or tub spout. Connecting steel pipe to copper requires another special-purpose fitting: a dielectric union, which prevents an electrolytic reaction between the two metals.

DRAINPIPES AND FITTINGS

Cast iron.

This is the strongest material available for DWV piping, and its heavy weight helps contain noise generated by active drains. Cast-iron pipe comes in two types, identified by the methods used to join them: hubless *(left)*, which uses easily installed fittings; and hub and spigot, joined by a cumbersome procedure utilizing molten lead and oakum.

Copper.

Although mostly chosen for supply lines, copper pipe also comes in larger drain-waste-vent forms. Because copper DWV pipe is comparatively costly, however, it is seldom chosen for new installations.

ABS.

This plastic pipe, acronymically named for acrylonitrile butadiene styrene, is less expensive and more durable than PVC, but many codes prohibit its use because of low resistance to chemicals and a low ignition point. Where ABS is allowed in homes, a Schedule 40 pressure rating is recommended.

Polyvinyl chloride (PVC).

A rigid plastic pipe material like CPVC but less able to withstand heat, PVC is lightweight, easy to install, corrosion resistant, and inexpensive. In addition to its DWV uses, it can serve for cold-water supply lines. Codes usually specify a Schedule 40 rating for homeowners.

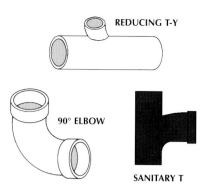

REDUCING T-Y

90° ELBOW

SANITARY T

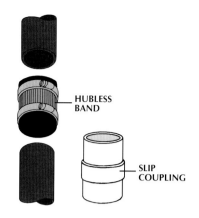

HUBLESS BAND

SLIP COUPLING

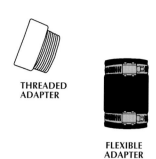

THREADED ADAPTER

FLEXIBLE ADAPTER

Bends and branches.

A 90-degree elbow fitting (also known as a quarter-bend) makes a right-angle turn in DWV piping. Among the fittings that join two runs of drainpipe are a reducing T-Y, which connects a branch pipe to a larger diameter drainpipe, and a sanitary T, a fitting that joins a fixture drain to a vertical stack.

Straight-line fittings.

A hubless band—used to join hubless drainpipe—consists of a tightly fitting neoprene sleeve that is held in place over a joint by a stainless steel collar and clamps. A slip coupling, like its supply-system counterpart, slides over pipes to connect them in a repair.

Transition fittings.

A threaded adapter, as in the supply system, joins threaded pipe to unthreaded and also connects pipe to various special drain-system components, such as cleanout plugs and traps. A flexible adapter made of a rubberlike, specially treated PVC connects unthreaded drainpipes of any material; the fitting is slipped over the pipe ends and its built-in clamps tightened.

MEASURING PIPES

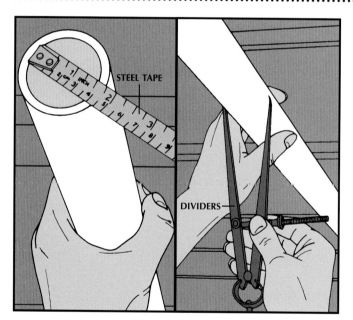

STEEL TAPE

DIVIDERS

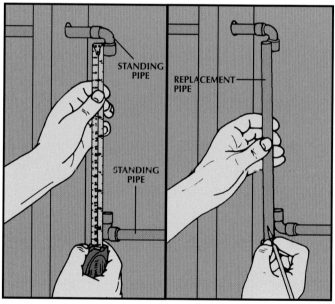

STANDING PIPE

REPLACEMENT PIPE

STANDING PIPE

Finding the inside diameter.

Pipes and fittings are sized according to their inside diameter, called nominal size.
◆ To determine this figure for pipe that is already cut, simply hold a ruler or steel tape across an end of the pipe and measure from one inner wall to the other (above, left).
◆ If the pipe is part of an uncut run, you must proceed indirectly. First, fit dividers (above, right), calipers, or a C clamp against the pipe, then measure the space between the instrument's arms to get the outside diameter; repeat several times, and average the readings. Finally, convert the average outside diameter to inside diameter by referring to the chart opposite.

Measuring the replacement pipe.

◆ After cutting out or unthreading damaged pipe, buy the appropriate type of replacement pipe, making sure the piece is several inches longer than the gap. (See pages 269 to 277 to determine the correct pipe material and adapters for the plumbing being repaired.)
◆ Attach the new fittings on the ends of the standing pipes.
◆ Hold a steel tape to the farthest point the new pipe can extend into each of the two fittings (above, left). Alternatively, hold the replacement pipe up to the gap and mark the exact length—including the depth of the fittings—with a pencil (above, right).

CALCULATING PIPE DIMENSIONS

Reading the chart.
Always choose replacement pipe with the same inside diameter (ID) as the old pipe. To determine a pipe's inside diameter without cutting it, measure its outside diameter (OD) and use the conversion chart below. The chart also specifies the socket depth of fittings used with the various pipe sizes and types. For example, the socket depth of fittings for $\frac{3}{4}$-inch plastic pipe is $\frac{5}{8}$ inch. When you cut a length of replacement pipe, be sure to account for the fittings at both ends—twice $\frac{5}{8}$ inch, or a total of $1\frac{1}{4}$ inches.

COPPER

	Outside Diameter (OD)	Inside Diameter (ID)	Depth of Fitting Socket
Supply	$\frac{3}{8}$ in.	$\frac{1}{4}$ in.	$\frac{5}{16}$ in.
	$\frac{1}{2}$ in.	$\frac{3}{8}$ in.	$\frac{3}{8}$ in.
	$\frac{5}{8}$ in.	$\frac{1}{2}$ in.	$\frac{1}{2}$ in.
	$\frac{7}{8}$ in.	$\frac{3}{4}$ in.	$\frac{3}{4}$ in.
	$1\frac{1}{8}$ in.	1 in.	$\frac{15}{16}$ in.
Drains	$1\frac{3}{8}$ in.	$1\frac{1}{4}$ in.	$\frac{1}{2}$ in.
	$1\frac{5}{8}$ in.	$1\frac{1}{2}$ in.	$\frac{9}{16}$ in.
	$2\frac{1}{8}$ in.	2 in.	$\frac{5}{8}$ in.
	$3\frac{1}{8}$ in.	3 in.	$\frac{3}{4}$ in.
	$4\frac{1}{8}$ in.	4 in.	1 in.

GALVANIZED STEEL

	Outside Diameter (OD)	Inside Diameter (ID)	Depth of Fitting Socket
Supply	$\frac{3}{8}$ in.	$\frac{1}{8}$ in.	$\frac{1}{4}$ in.
	$\frac{1}{2}$ in.	$\frac{1}{4}$ in.	$\frac{3}{8}$ in.
	$\frac{5}{8}$ in.	$\frac{3}{8}$ in.	$\frac{3}{8}$ in.
	$\frac{3}{4}$ in.	$\frac{1}{2}$ in.	$\frac{1}{2}$ in.
	1 in.	$\frac{3}{4}$ in.	$\frac{9}{16}$ in.
	$1\frac{1}{4}$ in.	1 in.	$\frac{11}{16}$ in.
Drains	$1\frac{1}{2}$ in.	$1\frac{1}{4}$ in.	$\frac{11}{16}$ in.
	$1\frac{3}{4}$ in.	$1\frac{1}{2}$ in.	$\frac{11}{16}$ in.
	$2\frac{1}{4}$ in.	2 in.	$\frac{3}{4}$ in.

CAST IRON

	Outside Diameter (OD)	Inside Diameter (ID)	Depth of Fitting (If Not Hubless)
Drains	$2\frac{1}{4}$ in.	2 in.	$2\frac{1}{2}$ in.
	$3\frac{1}{4}$ in.	3 in.	$2\frac{3}{4}$ in.
	$4\frac{1}{4}$ in.	4 in.	3 in.
	$5\frac{1}{4}$ in.	5 in.	3 in.
	$6\frac{1}{4}$ in.	6 in.	3 in.

PLASTIC

	Outside Diameter (OD)	Inside Diameter (ID)	Depth of Fitting Socket
Supply	$\frac{7}{8}$ in.	$\frac{1}{2}$ in.	$\frac{1}{2}$ in.
	$1\frac{1}{8}$ in.	$\frac{3}{4}$ in.	$\frac{5}{8}$ in.
	$1\frac{3}{8}$ in.	1 in.	$\frac{3}{4}$ in.
Drains	$1\frac{5}{8}$ in.	$1\frac{1}{4}$ in.	$\frac{11}{16}$ in.
	$1\frac{7}{8}$ in.	$1\frac{1}{2}$ in.	$\frac{11}{16}$ in.
	$2\frac{3}{8}$ in.	2 in.	$\frac{3}{4}$ in.
	$3\frac{3}{8}$ in.	3 in.	$1\frac{1}{2}$ in.
	$4\frac{3}{8}$ in.	4 in.	$1\frac{3}{4}$ in.

First Aid for Frozen Pipes

A house that is properly constructed and heated is safe from plumbing freeze-ups even in the midst of a severe cold snap—unless the heating system breaks down. If that should happen, the best way to keep pipes from freezing and bursting is to drain the entire plumbing system *(page 268)*. Also drain the plumbing in a house that will be left empty for the winter *(page 266)*.

Although a house may be well built, if its pipes run through a basement, crawlspace, laundry room, or garage that is unprotected, they may be vulnerable to cold. To avoid resulting problems, consult the checklist at right.

Coping with Leaks: If a pipe freezes despite your precautions, the first symptom may be a faucet that refuses to yield water. But all too often, the freeze-up is announced by a flood from a break. Ruptures are especially likely near joints or bends in the plumbing. When a leak occurs, turn off the water supply and apply a temporary patch *(page 267)*.

Getting Ready to Thaw Pipes: As you prepare to warm a frozen section of pipe, close the main shutoff valve most of the way. The movement of water through the pipe aids thawing and helps protect against

later refreezing. Keep the affected faucet open to let water vapor and melted ice run out. Since leaks may go undetected until the pipe thaws, guard against water damage by spreading plastic drop cloths, and have extra pots and pails ready. Then warm the pipe by one of the methods at right and on page 266.

Electrical heaters of one kind or another are generally safest for thawing both metal and plastic pipe. Since electricity and water together pose a shock hazard, plug the appliance into a GFCI-protected outlet, which cuts power to the appliance if it detects conditions that could lead to injury.

TOOLS

Electric heating
   tape
Propane torch with
   flame spreader
Hair dryer
Heat gun
Heating pad
Heat lamp
Work lamp

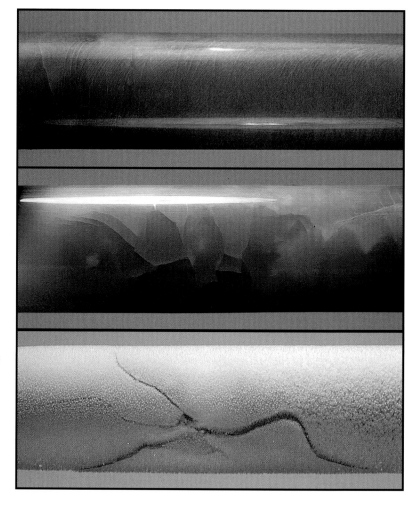

Three steps to a ruptured pipe.

Unlike most substances, water expands when it freezes—a fact that can easily burst a pipe. Three stages in the freezing and rupture of a pipe are shown in the transparent tubing at right. Frost forms first on the inner surfaces of the pipe *(top photograph),* then ice crystals begin to take shape *(middle).* With freezing complete, the pipe cracks *(bottom).* By melting freeze-ups quickly, you may be able to avoid the final stage—and preserve your supply pipes from further harm.

How to Keep Pipes from Freezing

✔ Protect exposed pipes ahead of time with insulation made to retard freezing, or warm them with thermostatic heating tape *(right)*.

✔ When no commercial insulation is at hand and pipes must be protected immediately, wrap several layers of newspaper loosely around the pipes and tie the paper on with string.

✔ If you have no time to install insulation, open faucets so a trickle of water moves through the pipes.

✔ Keep a door ajar between a heated room and an unheated room with pipes so that the unprotected area will receive heat.

✔ If power is available, plug in an electric heater or heat lamp, or hang a 100-watt bulb near vulnerable pipes. Keep the heat source a safe distance from walls, floors, ceilings, and nearby combustibles.

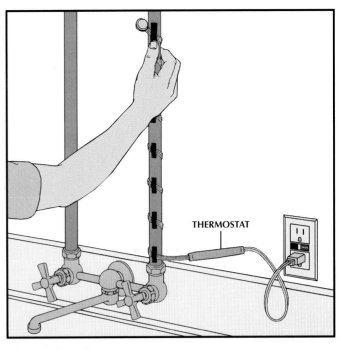

THERMOSTAT

Electric heating tape.

To thaw a frozen pipe, wrap the tape in a spiral around the pipe, allowing about two turns per foot. Secure the spiral with PVC-type electrical tape *(above),* which will stay in place during temperature changes.

Most electric heating cables come with built-in thermostats and can be left plugged in permanently: When the temperature drops toward freezing, the thermostat activates the cable and warms the pipe. Cover the pipe and heating cable with nonflammable fiberglass pipe insulation as a second layer of protection against freezing.

FLAME SPREADER

FLAMEPROOF SHEET

A propane torch.

Equipped with a flame-spreader attachment, available at most hardware stores, a propane torch can thaw metal pipes rapidly and effectively during a power outage, if used with care. Place flameproof sheeting between the pipe and nearby framing. Apply heat near an open faucet first, then work gradually along the pipe *(arrow).*

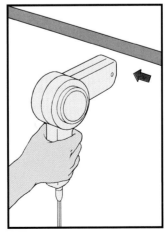

A hair dryer.

If you have power, use a hair dryer instead of a propane torch; the dryer will work more slowly, but you will avoid dealing with an open flame in close quarters. An electric heat gun can also be used to thaw pipes. As with a torch, make sure pipes never become too hot to touch.

⚠ **CAUTION** *Use a torch only on metal pipes, not plastic ones. Never let the pipe get too hot to touch; boiling water and steam inside a pipe can cause a dangerous explosion.*

A heating pad.
Wrapped and tied around a frozen pipe near an open faucet, an ordinary heating pad can be left in place to thaw ice slowly but effectively.

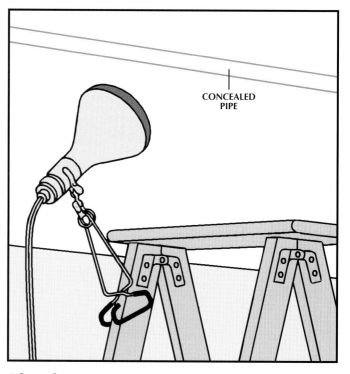

CONCEALED
PIPE

A heat lamp.
If a suspected ice blockage is behind a wall or above the ceiling, set an electric heat lamp nearby. Keep it at least 6 inches from the wall to avoid scorching paint or wallpaper. For greater flexibility in handling, you can screw the bulb into the socket of a portable work lamp (above).

WINTERIZING AN EMPTY HOUSE

When you leave a house empty and unheated for the winter, take steps to weatherproof the plumbing. First turn off water to the house. Cut power to the water heater. For a hot-water heating system, turn off power to the boiler and drain it. Next, open the radiator valves, and remove an air vent from a radiator on the top floor.

Then empty the rest of the plumbing, including the water heater and any water-treatment devices, as described on page 16. For a well system, drain the storage tank and dry off the pump, unless it is submerged in the well.

Flush and bail out each toilet. Then pour at least a gallon of plumber's antifreeze—not the toxic automotive variety—into the tank and flush the toilet again. Doing so frostproofs both the trap and the flushing channels.

For other fixtures, pour antifreeze down the drain very slowly so that it displaces water in the trap rather than mixing with it.

Often the first sign of a leaking pipe is a spreading stain on a wall or ceiling or a puddle on the floor. Before trying to trace the leak, shut off the water supply to prevent further damage and to reduce pressure on the damaged section so you can repair the hole.

Minimizing Water Damage: Where leaking pipes are concealed above the ceiling and a water stain is visible, place a waterproof drop cloth on the floor and position a basin under the wet area. Poke a hole through the ceiling or remove a section of it to let any remaining water drain out—and stand out of the way! To deal with water leaking from a ceiling light fixture, shut off the electricity, then drain the fixture by removing its cover.

If you find a leak too late to avert a flood, construct a makeshift dam from rolled-up rugs to prevent water from spreading to other rooms. For a bad flood, you may need to rent a pump with a submersible motor. If the situation is desperate, call the local fire department.

Patching the Leak: Purchase a pipe-repair sleeve *(below)* to make a secure temporary patch. To make permanent repairs, replace the leaking section of pipe *(pages 268-277)*.

For a drainpipe, leaks are likeliest at the joints; sometimes a lead joint can be resealed as shown below at right. Otherwise, as with a supply pipe, replace the leaking pipes and joints.

TOOLS

Screwdriver Hammer
Wrench Cold chisel

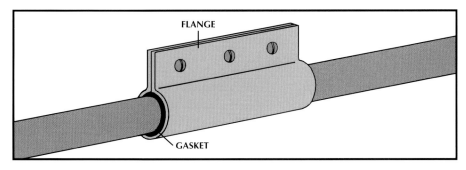

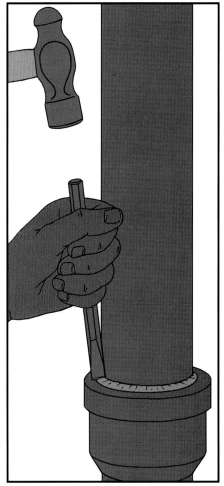

Installing a pipe-repair sleeve.

Measure the outside diameter of the leaking pipe *(page 260)*, then at a hardware or plumbing-supply store buy a temporary pipe-repair sleeve to fit. The pipe-repair sleeve seals a leak by means of a rubber gasket. Spread apart the flanges of the sleeve and then slip the sleeve around the damaged section, making sure you turn the flanges away from the hole. Finally, tighten the sleeve with a screwdriver or a wrench.

Fixing a lead-caulked drain joint.

If water seeps from a lead-caulked drain joint, tamp down the lead inside the hub of the pipe with a hammer and cold chisel *(right)*. Since the lead is soft enough to be reshaped over a weak spot, this procedure often reseals the joint.

Repairing and Replacing Pipe

A plumbing system's pipes, no matter what kind, are unlikely to remain problem-free forever. Sooner or later—perhaps because of corrosion, a leak at an aging joint, or the bursting of a frozen pipe—some mending will probably be necessary.

Measure for the replacement pipe as explained on page 262, and begin any supply-line repair by draining the system *(box, right)*. The methods for making repairs depend on the material of the pipes involved. You can use pipe and fittings that match your current piping, or introduce a different material—replacing a run of copper with CPVC, for example. Some of the most common ways of mending broken pipe are described opposite and on the following pages.

Copper Piping: Copper is connected to copper by heating the metal with a propane torch and drawing molten solder into a pipe-and-fitting joint—a process called "sweating." The solder for supply pipes must be lead-free; other solders are acceptable for copper drains. Because the flame can be a hazard to your home's structure and its wiring, cover the area be-hind the piping with a flameproof pad. Keep a fire extinguisher nearby, and turn off the torch before setting it down. For complex repairs, do as much of the assembly as possible at your workbench.

Connect copper to plastic with transition fittings; several types are available.

Plastic Piping: Assemble rigid plastic pipe only when the air temperature is above 40°F. Different types of plastic require their own primers and cements: Never use PVC primer on a CPVC repair, for instance. The basic methods used to join PVC and CPVC are the same, however *(page 275)*.

A third type of plastic, ABS, requires no primer. To repair ABS pipe with PVC replacement pipe, install a rubber adapter or consecutive male and female adapters in conjunction with primer on the PVC side and a light green transition cement on both sides.

⚠️ **CAUTION** *Solvent cements are toxic and flammable. When you apply them, you must make sure the work area is well ventilated.*

SHUTTING DOWN THE SUPPLY SYSTEM

Before making repairs to the supply system, shut off the house water supply. First, close the main shutoff valve. Then, working from the top level down, open all hot- and cold-water faucets—including all tub, shower, and outdoor faucets—and flush all toilets. Open the drain faucets on the main supply line, the water heater, and any water treatment equipment you may have. To refill the system after the repair has been completed, close all the faucets, then open the main shutoff valve. Trapped air will cause faucets to sputter momentarily when you first turn them on again.

SAFETY TIPS

Goggles and gloves provide important protection when you are soldering copper pipe.

TOOLS

Tube cutter	Flux brush	Fine-tooth
Hacksaw	Groove-joint	hacksaw or
Plumber's	pliers	minihacksaw
abrasive	Striker	Pipe wrenches
sandcloth	Propane torch	Ratchet pipe
Metal file	Flameproof pad	cutter
Round file	Small, sharp knife	Nut driver or
Wire fitting brush	Adjustable wrench	socket wrench

MATERIALS

Replacement pipe and fittings	Applicator brushes
Clean cloth	Plumbing-sealant tape
Paste flux	Grounding clamps
Solder	Grounding wire
Miter box	2 x 4 lumber
Adapters	Stack clamps
PVC or CPVC primer	Chalk
PVC, CPVC, or ABS cement	Newspaper or paper towels

REPLACING COPPER WITH COPPER

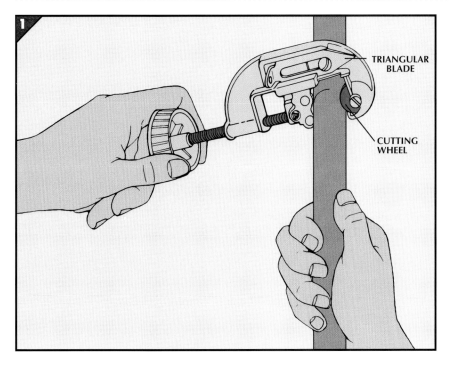

TRIANGULAR BLADE

CUTTING WHEEL

1. Using a cutter.

Although a hacksaw may be needed for a hard-to-reach section of broken copper pipe, use a tube cutter if possible.

◆ Slide the cutter onto the pipe and turn the knob until the tube cutter's cutting wheel bites into the copper. Do not tighten the knob all the way.

◆ Turn the cutter once around, retighten the knob, and continue turning and tightening. Once the piping is severed, loosen the knob, slide the cutter down the pipe, and cut through the other side of the broken section.

◆ With the cutter's triangular blade, ream out the burr inside the standing pipe. Remove the ridge on the outside with a file. (For a hacksaw cut, remove the inner burr with a round file.)

◆ Use the tube cutter to cut and ream replacement pipe.

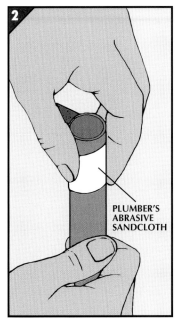

PLUMBER'S ABRASIVE SANDCLOTH

2. Preparing the cut ends.

With a piece of plumber's abrasive sandcloth—not a file or steel wool—clean the cut pipe ends to a distance slightly greater than the depth of fittings that you will use to connect them. Rub until the surface is bright.

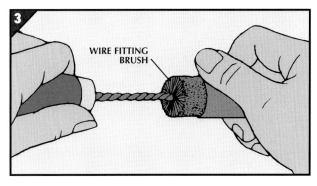

WIRE FITTING BRUSH

3. Cleaning the fittings.

Scour the inner surfaces of the sockets of each fitting with a wire fitting brush. Once the surfaces of the fittings and pipes have been cleaned, do not touch them: Even a fingerprint will weaken the joint.

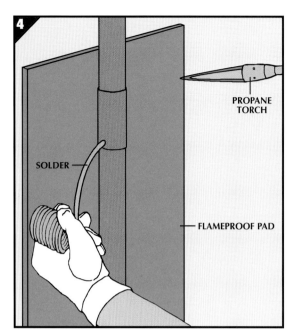

4. Assembling and heating a joint.

◆ Brush a light coat of flux over the cleaned surfaces, place the fitting between the standing pipe and the replacement section, and twist it a quarter-turn.
◆ For a slip coupling on a vertical pipe, shown here, gently crimp the coupling with groove-joint pliers just enough to hold it in place.
◆ Place a flameproof pad in back of the joint.
◆ Light the torch with a striker. Holding the tip of the flame perpendicular to the metal and about a half-inch away, play it over the fitting and nearby pipe.
◆ Touch a piece of solder to the fitting *(left)* until it melts on contact. Do not heat further or the flux will burn off and the solder will not flow properly.

5. Soldering the joint.

◆ Touch the solder tip to the pipe where it enters one end of the fitting. Keep the solder at that point while the capillary action of the flux draws molten solder into the fitting to seal the connection.
◆ Remove the solder from the joint when a bead of metal completely seals the rim.
◆ Wipe away excess with a clean cloth, leaving a shiny surface.
◆ Apply solder to the other end of the fitting in the same way, then sweat the other joint.

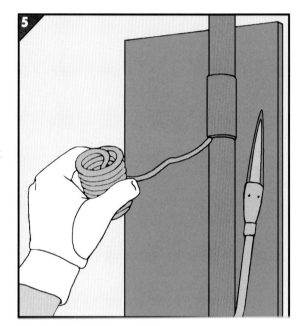

TRICKS OF THE TRADE

Dos and Don'ts of Sweated Joints

Good sweated joints *(below, left)* are achieved by careful handling of flux and solder. Spread the coat of flux thinly and evenly. Excessive residue can cause corrosion; too little flux will create gaps in the bond between solder and copper. Do not overheat the fitting or direct the flame into the socket: If the flux burns—indicated by a brownish black coloring—the bond will be imperfect. Never direct the flame at the solder, and be sure to remove the solder as soon as capillary action sucks it around the full circumference of the joint. If solder drips, it has been overheated or overapplied, and the capillary action will fail. Thick, irregular globs of solder at the edges of sweated joints are a sign of a bad job *(below, right)*.

MATING PLASTIC TO COPPER

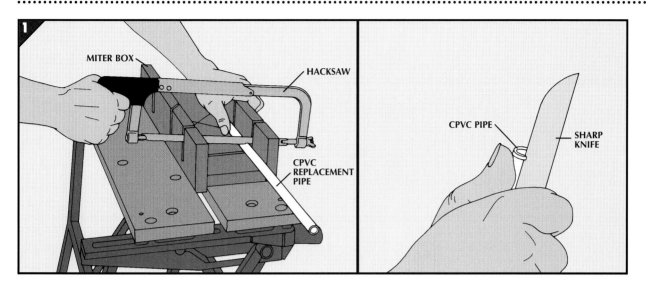

1. Cutting the pipes.

◆ Cut out the broken section of copper pipe with a tube cutter or hacksaw and ream the ends of the standing pipes *(page 269)*.
◆ Cut the CPVC replacement pipe with a tube cutter or hacksaw. If you use a hacksaw, place the pipe in a miter box and brace it with your thumb as you make the cut *(above, left)*.
◆ Ream the ends of the replacement pipe.
◆ With a small, sharp knife *(above, right)*, trim the ends' inside edge to aid water flow and the outside edge to improve the welding action of the solvent.

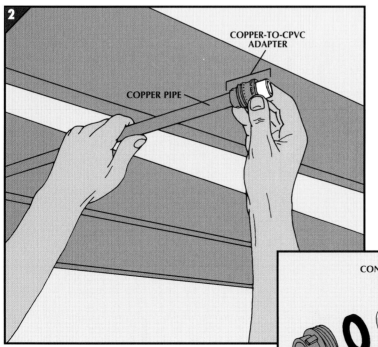

2. Adding the adapters.

◆ Unfasten two copper-to-CPVC adapters *(inset)*.
◆ Solder the copper ends of the fittings to the cut ends of the copper pipe *(page 18)*.
◆ After the soldered joints have cooled, position the threaded CPVC portion of each fitting against the copper portion with a rubber washer placed between them.
◆ Slide the connecting ring over the CPVC portion of each fitting and hand-tighten it *(left)*.
◆ With an adjustable wrench, tighten the fittings just beyond hand tight.

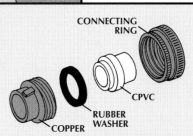

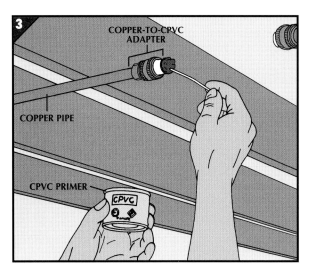

3. Priming and cementing the joints.

Work as quickly as possible with solvent cement. It sets in less than 30 seconds.

◆ With an applicator or clean cloth, apply a coat of primer to the inside of the sockets of the adapters *(left)* and to the outside pipe surfaces that will be fitted into the adapters.

◆ With a second applicator, spread a coat of CPVC cement over the primed surfaces at the ends of the CPVC pipe.

◆ Spread a light coat of cement inside the adapter sockets.

4. Fitting the replacement pipe.

◆ Working rapidly, push one end of the CPVC pipe into an adapter.

◆ Pull the free ends toward you until enough space opens for the CPVC pipe to slip into the second adapter *(right)*.

◆ Give the CPVC pipe a quarter-turn to evenly distribute the cement inside the sockets.

◆ Hold it firmly for about 10 seconds.

◆ Wipe away any excess cement with a clean, dry cloth. Do not run water in the pipe until the cement has cured (about 2 hours at temperatures above 60°F).

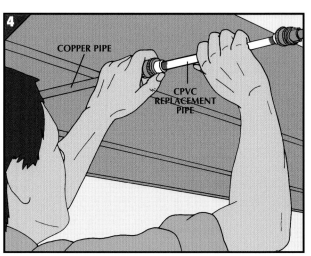

REPAIRING STEEL PIPE WITH PLASTIC

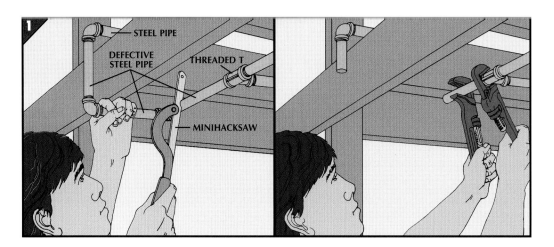

1. Removing the steel pipe.

Once in place, a threaded pipe cannot be unscrewed as one piece. In the situation here, CPVC replaces three runs of damaged pipe.

◆ Near the outer ends of the damaged section, cut the pipe with a fine-tooth hacksaw or minihacksaw *(above, left)*. Remove the intervening piping.

◆ Unthread the remaining stubs of pipe from their fittings. Hold a fitting stationary with one wrench and turn the pipe with another wrench. The jaws must face the direction in which the force is applied *(above, right)*.

If a union is near a damaged section, cutting is unnecessary. Hold the pipe steady with one wrench, unscrew the union with a second, then unscrew the other end of pipe from its fitting.

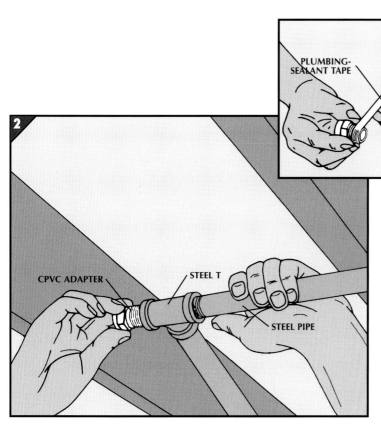

2. Adding CPVC adapters.

◆ Wrap plumbing-sealant tape around the threads of two CPVC adapters *(inset)* and screw them into the steel fittings by hand *(left)*.

◆ With an adjustable wrench, tighten the adapters just beyond hand tight.

3. Measuring and test-fitting replacement pipe.

◆ Push CPVC pipe into an adapter socket as far as it will go. Mark the desired length, allowing for the socket depth of the fitting that will go at the other end.

◆ Cut that section of pipe to length with a hacksaw in a miter box *(page 271)*.

◆ Push the fitting—in this case, an elbow—on the other end. Measure and cut the next length of CPVC pipe, push it into the next fitting, and continue dry-fitting the replacement piping in this way.

◆ At each connection, draw a line across the fitting and adjacent pipe *(right)* as a guide for reassembly and cementing.

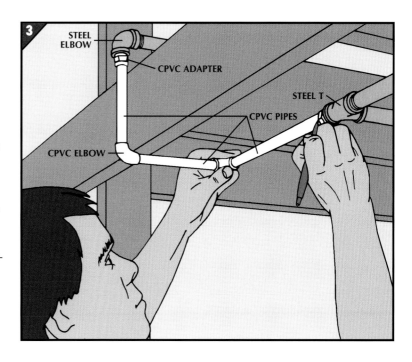

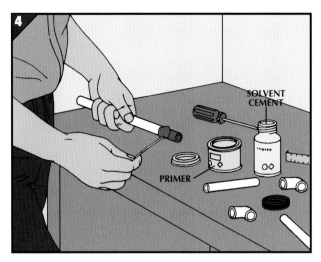

4. Cementing the CPVC pipe.

◆ Disassemble the dry-fitted pipe sections.

◆ At a well-ventilated workbench, ream and trim all pipe ends *(page 271)*.

◆ Apply primer and solvent cement *(page 272)* to a pipe and fitting that will form an outer section of the assembly *(left)*.

◆ Push the pipe into the fitting, give it a quarter-turn, and align the marks. Hold the pieces together for about 10 seconds.

◆ Continue cementing pipe and fittings together until all but the last pipe is in place. Leave this pipe detached.

5. Beginning the installation.

◆ Check to make sure that the CPVC adapters are dry. If they are not, dry them with a clean cloth.

◆ Apply primer to the sockets of both CPVC adapters.

◆ Spread solvent cement in the socket of the adapter that will receive the pipe at the completed end of the CPVC assembly. Apply primer and then a coat of cement to the end of that pipe.

◆ Push the pipe into the adapter socket as far as it will go. Give the pipe a quarter-turn to spread the cement.

◆ Line up the marks on the pipe and adapter and hold the pieces together for about 10 seconds *(right)*.

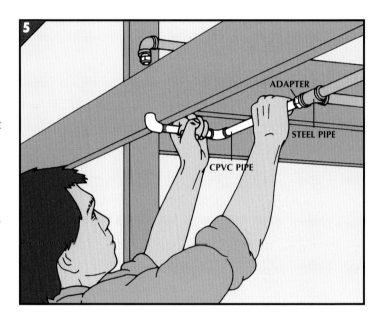

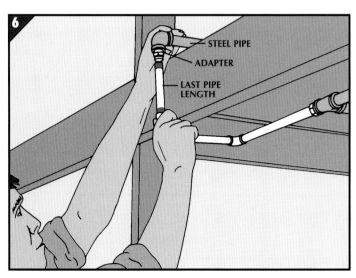

6. Adding the last pipe.

◆ Apply primer and cement to the second adapter, the last fitting on the CPVC assembly, and both ends of the unattached pipe.

◆ Push one end of the pipe into the assembly fitting. Gently maneuvering the assembly *(left)*, push the other end into the adapter socket as far as it will go.

◆ Give the pipe a quarter-turn to spread the cement, and hold the pieces together for about 10 seconds. Do not run water in the pipe until the cement has cured (about 2 hours at temperatures above 60°F).

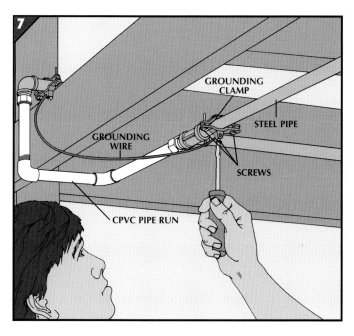

7. Installing a grounding jumper.

If the replaced section of steel pipe was part of your home's electrical grounding system, you must install a grounding jumper to maintain continuity.

◆ At one end of the cut steel pipes, fit both pieces of a grounding clamp *(photograph)* around the circumference of the pipe. Fasten the two pieces together with screws on either end of the clamp.

◆ Measure and cut a length of grounding wire to extend between the clamp and the other cut steel pipe.

◆ Insert the wire into the small opening on top of the clamp and secure it with the corresponding screw.

◆ Install a clamp on the other steel pipe and secure the end of the wire in its opening *(left)*.

FIXING PLASTIC PIPE

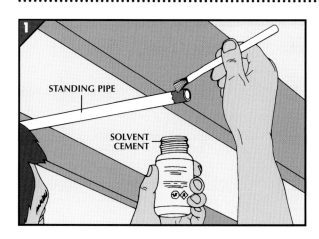

1. Preparing the joint.

◆ Cut out the damaged pipe with a hacksaw or tube cutter.

◆ Hold the replacement pipe against the gap and mark it, then cut it with a tube cutter or hacksaw and miter box.

◆ Ream and trim the pipe ends *(page 271)*.

◆ Prime the ends of the standing pipes and one socket on each of two couplings.

◆ Apply a liberal coat of solvent cement to the coupling sockets and on the ends of the standing pipes *(left)* to a distance matching the socket depth.

◆ Push the couplings onto the pipes, give them a quarter-turn to spread the cement, and hold the pieces together about 10 seconds.

2. Inserting the replacement pipe.

◆ Prime the exposed coupling sockets and ends of the replacement pipe, then apply cement.

◆ Working quickly, push one end of the replacement pipe into a coupling, then gently bend the pipes until the opposite end fits into the other coupling *(right)*.

◆ Give the pipe a quarter-turn to spread the cement, and hold the pieces together for about 10 seconds.

◆ Wipe off any excess cement around the pipe or fittings with a clean, dry cloth. Do not run water in the pipe until the cement has cured (about 2 hours at temperatures above 60°F).

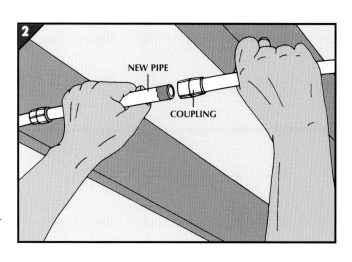

MENDING CAST-IRON DRAINPIPE

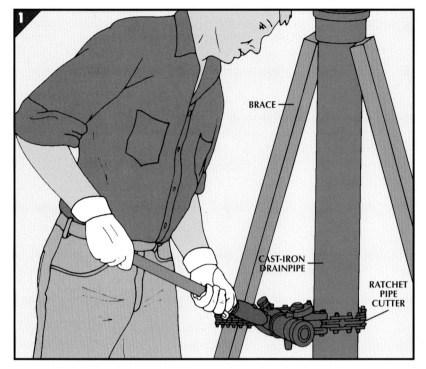

BRACE

CAST-IRON
DRAINPIPE

RATCHET
PIPE
CUTTER

1. Removing the broken pipe.

The easiest way to cut cast-iron pipe is with a ratchet pipe cutter, available at rental stores. Before cutting vertical drainpipe, support it with stack clamps, or brace 2-by-4s against a joint above the section to be removed *(left)*, hammering the braces into position for a secure fit. Make sure that no one runs water in the house during the repair.

◆ With chalk, mark off the area to be cut out.

◆ Wrap the chain around the pipe and hook it onto the body of the tool.

◆ Tighten the knob, turn the dial to CUT, and work the handle up and down until the cutting disks bite through the pipe.

◆ If badly corroded pipe crumbles under a pipe cutter, rent an electric saber saw and metal-cutting blade.

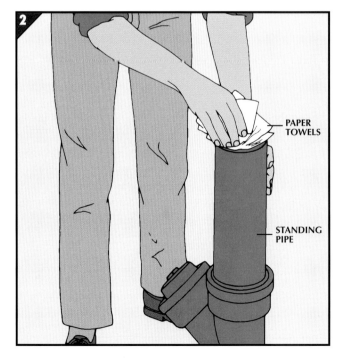

PAPER
TOWELS

STANDING
PIPE

2. Cutting the replacement pipe.

◆ Immediately after removing the damaged section, stuff newspaper or paper towels into the standing pipes *(left)* to block dangerous sewer gas.

◆ Measure the gap in the pipe and transfer that measurement, less $\frac{1}{4}$ inch, to a cast-iron, PVC, or ABS replacement pipe.

◆ Lay cast-iron pipe across two level 2-by-4s, spaced to support the pipe ends, and cut it to size with a ratchet cutter or saber saw.

◆ Cut PVC or ABS with a hacksaw and miter box.

◆ With a sharp knife, ream and trim the ends of the plastic pipe *(page 271)*.

3. Inserting the replacement section.

Hubless bands *(page 262)* join cast-iron drainpipe to replacement pipe.

◆ Slide a clamp onto each standing pipe and tighten the clamps to hold them temporarily in place.

◆ Slip the neoprene sleeves of the fittings onto each pipe until the pipe ends bottom out inside the sleeves *(near right).*

◆ Fold the lip of each sleeve back over the pipe.

◆ Work the replacement pipe into the gap between the sleeves *(far right)* until it is properly seated.

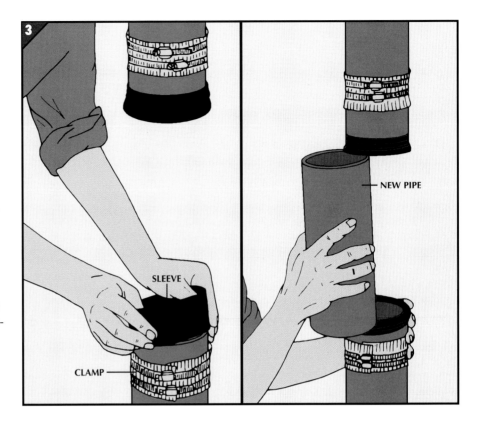

SLEEVE

CLAMP

NEW PIPE

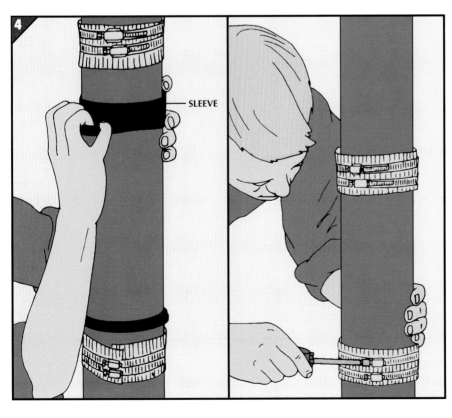

SLEEVE

4. Completing the repair.

◆ Pull the folded lips of the sleeves over the replacement pipe *(far left).*

◆ Loosen the clamps and slide them toward the replacement section until they are centered over the joints. Tighten them again with a nut driver *(near left)* or socket wrench.

◆ Run water through the drainpipe in order to test the repair; if a joint leaks, take it apart and reassemble the hubless band.

Unclogging Drains

When a sink empties slowly or not at all, the cause is usually debris blocking the drainpipe or trap just below. If other drains show the same symptoms, the problem is in the main drain or its branches *(below)*.

A Choice of Methods: To unclog a drain, try the simplest remedy first, then proceed stepwise with the progressively more demanding procedures shown on pages 279 and 280. A force-cup plunger offers the easiest way to loosen an obstruction and flush it away. A more powerful alternative is a stream of water delivered by a drain flusher *(page 280)*.

Should the obstruction resist these measures, try a trap-and-drain auger, or snake. This flexible steel coil is twisted into the pipes like a corkscrew to dislodge debris.

Some blockages may require that you open a sink trap or a cleanout in the main drain. Before doing so, turn off water to the entire house *(page 268)* and flush all toilets. Since wastewater may be trapped above a cleanout, be ready for a dirty torrent as you remove the plug that seals the cleanout opening. If you have no success with the snake, call a plumber, who can bring an electric-powered auger that is capable of dealing with the most stubborn obstruction.

Chemical Solutions: Drain cleaners may work effectively against a slow-flowing drain, and routine use every few weeks helps to prevent future clogs. But resist the temptation to pour these agents through standing water into a drain that is completely clogged. Extended contact with the lye or acid in drain cleaners can damage pipes and fixtures. Also, if you must later open a trap or a cleanout, drain cleaner in the pipes may splash on exposed skin or furnishings.

> ⚠️ **CAUTION** Do not use a plunger, auger, or chemical cleaner in a sink equipped with a garbage disposer. Instead, disconnect the disposer's outlet pipe and clear obstructions as shown on page 280, Step 4.

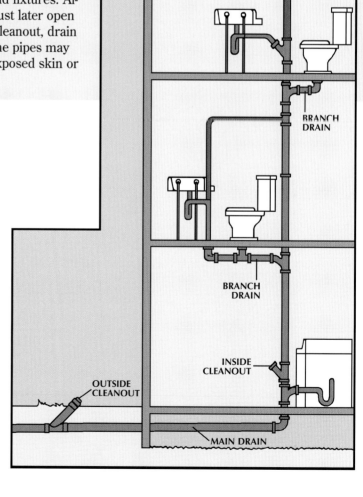

ROOF VENT

STACK

BRANCH DRAIN

BRANCH DRAIN

INSIDE CLEANOUT

OUTSIDE CLEANOUT

MAIN DRAIN

Finding the clog.

To clear a blocked pipe, pinpoint the obstruction by observation and deduction, then work from the drain—or cleanout, if available—immediately above.

For example, if the second-floor sink in the diagram at right is stopped but the toilet is clear, the clog is in the sink trap or the branch drain between the two fixtures. When all second-floor fixtures drain properly but all top-floor fixtures are stopped up, the clog is in the stack between floors. If all the drains back up, the problem is in the main drain. Most houses have only one cleanout plug for the main drain. It is near the foot of the stack in old houses; newer systems have an exterior cleanout within 5 feet of the foundation.

TOOLS

Force-cup plunger
Trap-and-drain
  auger
Adjustable pipe
  wrench
Bucket
Bottle brush

MATERIALS

Mop, rags, and
  sponges
Plastic bag
Petroleum jelly
Electrical tape
Plumbing-sealant
  tape
Penetrating oil

SAFETY TIPS

Wear rubber gloves and safety goggles when using drain cleaners or working through a cleanout in a stack or main drain.

OPENING A SINK DRAIN

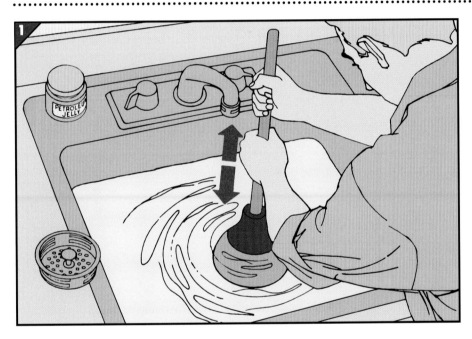

1. Starting with a plunger.
◆ Remove the sink strainer. In a double sink, bail out one side—the side with the garbage disposer, if there is one—and plug the drain with a rag in a plastic bag. In a washbasin, remove the pop-up drain plug; most lift out or can be turned and then lifted. Make sure there is enough water in the sink to cover the base of the plunger cup.
◆ Spread petroleum jelly on the cup's rim. Lower the plunger at an angle and compress the cup to push out air. Then seat it over the drain. Without breaking the seal, pump the plunger up and down 10 times, then quickly pull it away. If the drain stays clogged after several attempts, try an auger *(below)*.

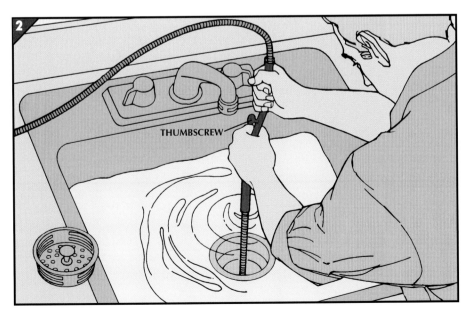

2. Using an auger.
◆ Push the tip of the auger into the drain until you feel it meet the obstruction, then slide the handle within a few inches of the drain opening and tighten the thumbscrew.
◆ Crank the handle clockwise with both hands while advancing the auger into the drain. Continue cranking and pushing the auger, repositioning the handle as necessary, until the auger breaks through the obstruction or will not go any farther.
◆ Withdraw the auger by cranking it slowly and pulling gently.

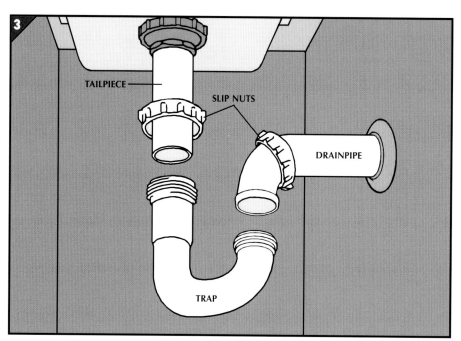

3. Removing the trap.

◆ Bail out the sink and place a bucket under the trap. Wrap the jaws of a pipe wrench with electrical tape, then loosen the slip nuts holding the trap to the tailpiece and drainpipe. Lower the trap slowly, allowing water to run into the bucket.

◆ If you find an obstruction in the trap, remove it, then clean the trap and the drainpipe with a bottle brush and detergent solution. Wrap the threads at both ends of the trap with plumbing-sealant tape, then replace the trap and tighten the slip nuts.

◆ If the trap was not blocked, clear the branch drain *(below).*

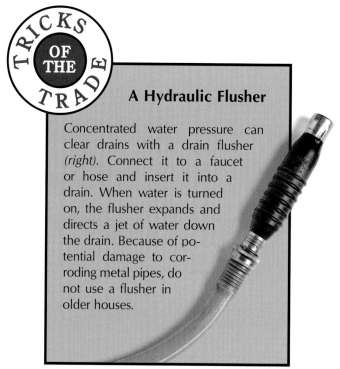

TRICKS OF THE TRADE

A Hydraulic Flusher

Concentrated water pressure can clear drains with a drain flusher *(right).* Connect it to a faucet or hose and insert it into a drain. When water is turned on, the flusher expands and directs a jet of water down the drain. Because of potential damage to corroding metal pipes, do not use a flusher in older houses.

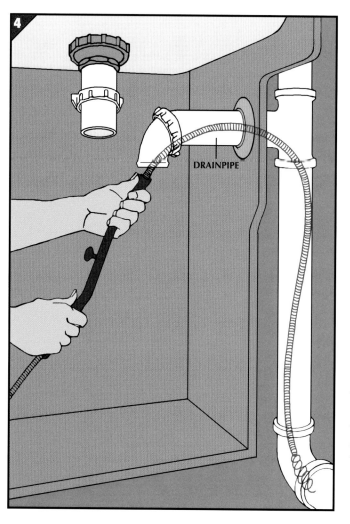

4. Cleaning beyond the trap.

With the trap removed, crank the auger into the drainpipe. The blockage may be in the vertical pipe behind the fixture or in a horizontal pipe—a branch drain—that connects with the main drain-vent stack serving the entire house. If the auger goes in freely through the branch drain until it hits the main stack, the blockage is probably in the main drainage system. In that case, identify the most likely location of the blockage *(page 278),* open the drain just above it, and use the auger to clear the pipe.

CLEARING THE MAIN DRAIN

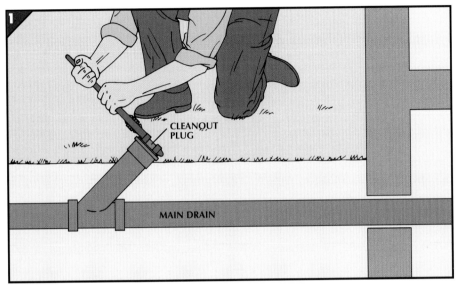

1. Opening the main cleanout.
Look for an outdoor cleanout at ground level within 5 feet of the foundation. The cleanout plug may be screwed into a Y fitting *(left)* or into the top of a vertical pipe that descends to a deeply buried main drain. Unscrew the cleanout plug with a pipe wrench. If the plug does not turn, apply penetrating oil around the perimeter, then try again. Depending on the extent of corrosion, the oil may take several days to free the plug. To gain more leverage, slip a section of pipe over the wrench handle to increase its effective length.

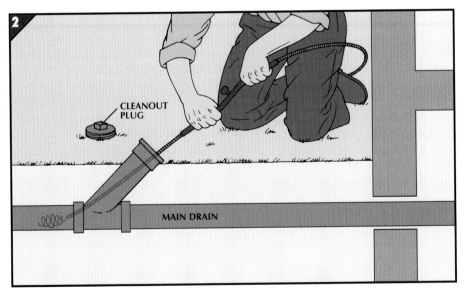

2. Working through the cleanout.
Standing water in the cleanout or drainpipe indicates that an obstruction lies between the cleanout and the sewer. Work an auger toward the sewer to clear the blockage *(left)*. If this does not work, recap the cleanout and notify a plumber.

An absence of standing water reveals that the obstruction is in the main drain under the house, or in the lower stack. Grease the threads of the cleanout plug and recap the pipe. Find the lowest drain opening or cleanout in the house and clear the blockage with an auger.

Increasing the Flow of Water

When the kitchen sink takes too long to fill, or the force of a shower is inadequate, the cause may be nothing more than a clogged faucet aerator or shower head. If water flow is weak at several fixtures, however, the problem lies in the supply system.

Low Pressure at the Source:
First make sure that the main shutoff valve is fully open *(page 259)*, then check the water pressure *(below)*. Most municipal systems provide water at a pressure of at least 50 pounds per square inch. For a lower reading, ask your neighbors whether their pressure is satisfactory. If so, there may be a leak in the pipe between the city main and your house. When the municipal system itself has low pressure, a pump and pressure tank hooked to the main supply line may be the best solution *(page 285)*.

In a home served by a well, the source of the problem may be a low setting on the pump's pressure switch. You can increase pressure by adjusting the switch *(page 285)*.

Blockages in the Plumbing:
Where water pressure to the house is adequate, compare the main shutoff valve with the diagrams on the next page. If it is a globe valve, a type that restricts water flow, replace it *(page 284)*.

With the flow-rate chart at right, you can determine what areas of the house may have pipes or valves that have become clogged over time with mineral deposits. Clean or replace clogged valves *(page 284)*. As a last resort, consider installing new pipes *(pages 268-277)*.

TOOLS

Pressure gauge
Graduated bucket
Stopwatch
Pipe wrench
Small open-ended
  wrenches

Adjustable wrench
Wire brush
Propane torch
Flameproof pad
Pliers (two pairs)

MATERIALS

Penetrating oil
Plumbing-sealant
  tape
Solder

Flux
CPVC primer and
  cement

SAFETY TIPS

When soldering copper pipe joints or heating and loosening old ones, wear gloves and safety goggles.

DIAGNOSING THE PROBLEM

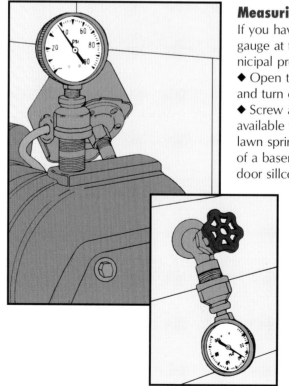

Measuring water pressure.
If you have a well, simply read the gauge at the pump *(left)*. Check municipal pressure as follows:
◆ Open the main shutoff valve fully and turn off all faucets and appliances.
◆ Screw a pressure gauge, which is available from hardware stores and lawn sprinkler suppliers, to the faucet of a basement laundry tub or an outdoor sillcock *(inset)*.
◆ Turn on the faucet or sillcock all the way and read the gauge. Take readings at different times of the day, since municipal pressure varies according to volume of use.

MINIMUM FLOW RATES	
Fixture	**Gallons per minute**
Laundry tub	5
Kitchen sink	4.5
Bathroom basin	2
Bathtub	5
Shower	5
Sillcock	5

Taking a flow-rate test.

This chart lists flow rates at various points in a residential plumbing system. To check the flow rate at a fixture, remove any aerator or other flow-restricting device such as a low-flow shower head. Turn the faucet full on and measure the time needed to fill a graduated bucket or other container. Divide gallons by minutes and record the result. Concentrate your efforts to improve flow at points where rates fall short of the figures in the chart.

VALVES AND HOW TO CLEAN THEM

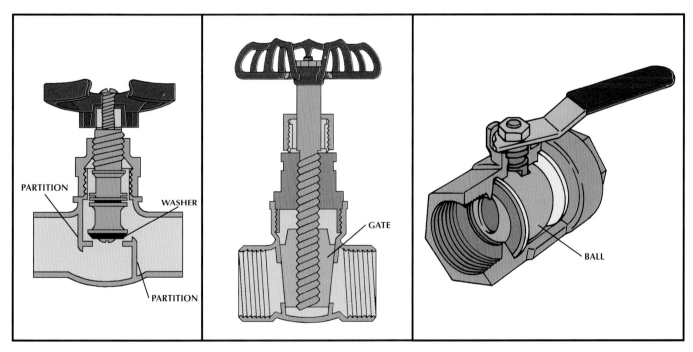

PARTITION
WASHER
PARTITION
GATE
BALL

Three common valves.

Globe valves *(above, left)* can be identified by a bulge at the base. They contain a rubber disk that presses against a seat in order to block the flow of water. Although useful as shutoffs to fixtures and branch lines, they contain partitions that impede the flow of water, making globe valves unsuit-

able as main shutoffs. A gate valve *(above, center)* has a gate that raises or lowers as the handle is turned. This unrestrictive design often serves as a main shutoff. Ball valves *(above, right)* fully open or close with a quarter-turn of the handle, which is an advantage if a line must be closed quickly. Like gate valves, ball valves provide an unrestrict-

ed flow and are therefore appropriate for main shutoff valves.

When installing a main shutoff, obtain a valve equipped with a waste, a small drain that can be opened to empty the supply line for plumbing repairs.

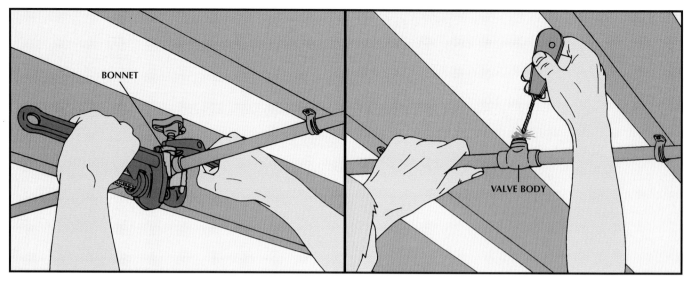

Servicing a clogged valve.

Ball valves *(page 283)* are unlikely to need cleaning; the ball scrapes off deposits as it turns. Clean a globe or gate valve as shown here:

◆ Close the main shutoff valve and drain the supply system *(page 268)*.

◆ Grip the valve body with a pipe wrench to relieve strain on pipes and loosen the bonnet with an adjustable wrench *(above, left)*. Remove the bonnet and valve stem.

◆ Scour the valve interior with a wire brush designed for cleaning copper fittings *(above, right)*. Bend the shaft of the brush to reach deep inside the valve body.

◆ Reassemble the valve, then shut off the faucets that were opened to drain the system and turn on the water.

REPLACING A VALVE TO IMPROVE FLOW

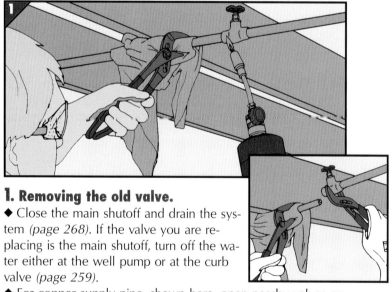

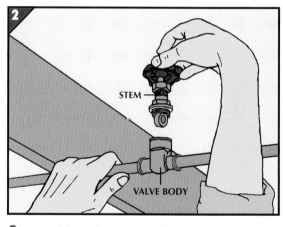

1. Removing the old valve.

◆ Close the main shutoff and drain the system *(page 268)*. If the valve you are replacing is the main shutoff, turn off the water either at the well pump or at the curb valve *(page 259)*.

◆ For copper supply pipe, shown here, open nearby valves on the line to protect their internal components from heat, and grip the adjacent pipe with a rag. Heat one of the soldered joints with a propane torch *(above)*, then pull the pipe out of the valve body, taking care not to bend the pipe. If necessary, turn off the torch and use pliers to pull apart the heated joint before it cools *(inset)*. Repeat for the other joint.

In the case of CPVC pipe, cut the pipe on each side of the valve *(page 275)*. For threaded steel pipe, cut the pipe on one side of the valve; use wrenches to unthread the two cut sections to expose the nearest pipe unions *(page 272)*.

2. Attaching the new valve.

Copper pipe: Solder the valve in place *(pages 269-270)*. Open the valve or remove the stem before soldering to protect the washer *(above)*. When the work cools, insert the stem and turn on the water.

Steel pipe: Adapt the procedure on pages 272 to 274: Attach adapters to the unions and valve inlets and extend CPVC from the inlets to the unions. After the CPVC cement cures, open the valve and turn on the water.

CPVC pipe: Add threaded adapters to the valve inlets. Cement a short spacer to one adapter; slide a coupling over the spacer. Cement the other adapter to the cut supply line, then join the spacer to the supply line with the coupling. Wait for the cement to cure, open the valve, and turn on the water.

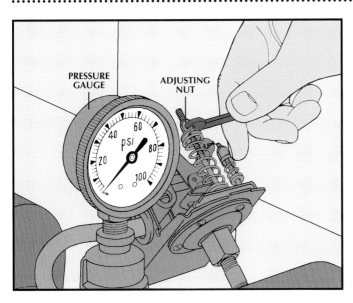

Resetting a pressure switch.

Inadequate flow from a well may result from a low pressure setting. If the pump and pressure tank are rated for a pressure higher than the pressure gauge indicates, try raising the pressure switch setting 5 pounds per square inch. Maximum ratings are usually printed on the components; if they are not, get the figures from the distributor or manufacturer.

◆ Turn off power to the pump.

◆ Remove the cover from the pressure switch, which is located near the pressure gauge *(page 282)*.

◆ With an open-ended wrench, turn the nut atop the taller of the adjustment springs two full turns clockwise *(left)*.

◆ Replace the cover and restore power.

◆ Observe the pump through one operating cycle to see that the pressure does not exceed the desired level.

A HELPING HAND FOR THE WATER COMPANY

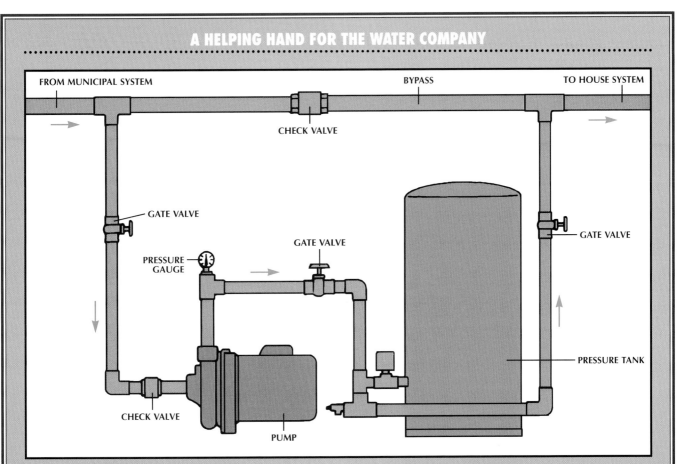

Spliced into the supply line, a pump-and-pressure-tank arrangement like the one shown here solves the problem of chronically low pressure in a municipal water system. The pump delivers water from the supply line to a T that connects to the tank inlet. The tank stores the water under pressure. When you turn on a faucet or other fixture, water rushes from the tank through the inlet T and into the house system. The resulting drop in tank pressure trips a switch that activates the pump, which operates until pressure is restored. Gate valves in the system can be closed to bypass the pump and tank for maintenance or repair. Check valves, which allow water to flow in only one direction, guard against water flowing backward into the municipal system.

Pipes can vibrate loudly—and annoyingly—if anchored too loosely to the house framing. More often, however, shrieking or banging sounds coming from your plumbing are a result of water-pressure problems.

Silencing Screeches: In houses close to a water tower or pumping station, abnormally high water pressure is common. It causes bubbling in the pipes, which produces squeals or groans and, over time, can erode valve seats, break apart joints, and make faucets leak.

To confirm that the pressure is too high, measure it close to where the supply line enters the house *(page 282)*. A reading higher than 60 pounds per square inch calls for a pressure-reducing valve near the main shutoff *(below)*.

Cures for Banging Pipes: A phenomenon called water hammer is responsible for the percussive sounds that are often heard when a valve closes abruptly. This sudden halt to the flow of water causes a momentary pressure pulse that produces a loud bang when the rush of water collides forcibly with the closed valve.

Excessive water pressure can cause water hammer, but if pressure is normal, you can correct the problem with a shock absorber or an air chamber installed close to the fixture in question *(opposite)*. Shock absorbers cost more but require no maintenance; air chambers must occasionally be drained.

 TOOLS

Pipe wrench
Propane torch
Flameproof pad

 **MATERIALS**

Solder
Flux
CPVC primer and cement
Threaded adapters

Supply pipe, fittings
Drain cock
Shutoff valve
Plumbing-sealant tape

 **SAFETY TIP**

Wear gloves and safety goggles when soldering copper pipe joints.

A DEVICE FOR LOWERING WATER PRESSURE

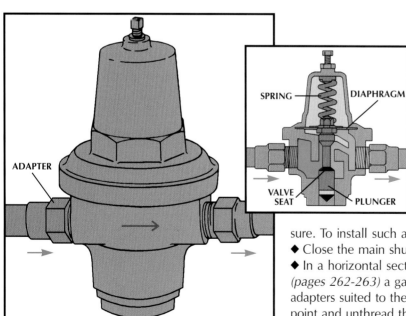

A pressure-reducing valve.
Added to the main supply line *(left)*, this device automatically lowers to a preset level the pressure of water entering the house.
Water on the house side of the valve *(inset, light blue)* presses against a spring-loaded diaphragm to regulate pressure. When the pressure exceeds the value set with an adjustment screw atop the device, the diaphragm bulges upward to lift a plunger toward the valve seat, partially closing the valve and reducing pressure. To install such a valve:
◆ Close the main shutoff and drain the system *(page 268)*.
◆ In a horizontal section of the main supply line, measure and cut *(pages 262-263)* a gap large enough to accommodate the valve and adapters suited to the type of pipe; for a steel pipe, cut at the desired point and unthread the cut sections *(page 272)*.
◆ Secure the valve in place as described on page 284, positioning it so that the arrow on the body points in the direction of water flow.
◆ Turn on the water.

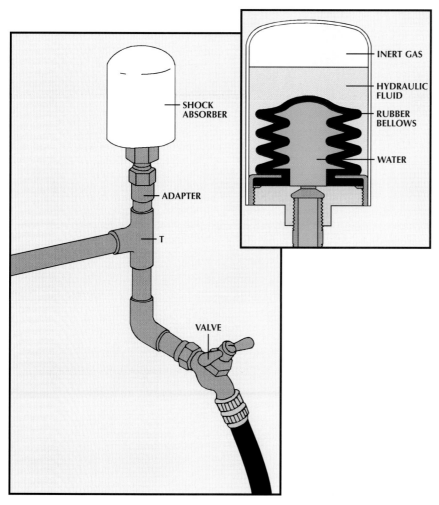

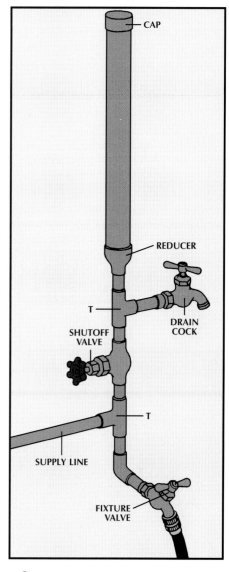

A shock absorber.

Placed near a valve that causes water hammer *(above)*, a shock absorber prevents this annoyance with a bubble of gas that cushions the pressure pulse caused by closing a valve *(inset)*. The bubble is isolated from the water in the pipe carrying the pulse by a rubber bellows surrounded by hydraulic fluid. To install a shock absorber:

◆ Close the main shutoff valve and drain the system *(page 268)*.

◆ Fit a T to a horizontal section of the pipe supplying the valve.

◆ In the top of the T, place a short pipe and threaded adapter that accommodates the shock absorber. Use plumbing-sealant tape to make the threads watertight, then screw on the shock absorber and tighten it with a pipe wrench.

◆ Connect the fixture to the bottom of the T.

◆ Turn on the water.

Making an air chamber.

In this alternative to a shock absorber, a column of air cushions pressure pulses that cause water hammer. To assemble an air chamber:

◆ Close the main shutoff and drain the system *(page 268)*.

◆ Install a T as for a shock absorber.

◆ To the upper opening of the T, add a valve and a faucet to serve as a drain as shown above.

◆ Top off this assembly with an air chamber consisting of a pipe having at least twice the diameter of the supply pipe, capped at one end. (For best results, make the air chamber about 2 feet long.) Connect the air chamber to the supply line with a reducer.

◆ Turn on the water.

Over time, the chamber may partially fill with water, reducing its effectiveness. Empty it by closing the shutoff and opening the drain cock.

A typical household consumes up to 150 gallons of water a day. That amount can be cut a third or more by conserving water *(checklist, right)* and by modifying plumbing fixtures to reduce the amount of water they discharge.

Indoor Fixtures: Installing a water-saving aerator makes a kitchen faucet more efficient. In a shower head, a flow restricter *(below)* reduces the stream from 5 gallons a minute to as little as 2 gallons a minute while delivering an adequate spray. Lowering the volume of water in an old-style large toilet tank can cut the amount of each flush in half *(opposite, top)*.

Water and fuel are saved by insulating exposed hot-water pipes so that the water does not lose heat as fast as it would in uninsulated pipes. Kitchen hot-water dispensers and refrigerated drinking water also eliminate losses that occur while waiting for the water to become hot or cold.

Regular Maintenance: An obviously dripping faucet or running toilet is easy to locate, but water often seeps through worn fixtures without obvious signals. Check faucets, spigots, and toilets for leaks throughout the house at least twice a year, and repair them with the techniques shown in Chapter 5.

Outdoor Conservation: Make the most of water applied to lawns and gardens, especially in hot, dry weather. A sprinkler timer prevents wasteful overwatering. Some timers must be set for each watering; others, like the one shown at the bottom of the opposite page, are programmable for longer periods.

Spreading a layer of mulch on garden beds and cutting grass high reduces evaporation, as does watering in the evening.

Water Recycling: A gray-water reclamation system like the one illustrated on pages 124 to 125 filters water drained from sinks, tubs, showers, and washing machines. The water can be used to irrigate gardens and lawns or, in some states, to flush toilets.

TOOLS

Wire brush
Pipe wrench

MATERIALS

Plumbing-sealant
tape

Water dam
Food coloring

Water-Saving Tips

Kitchen

✔ Soak dirty dishes and pans instead of rinsing them with running water.

✔ Turn on the dishwasher only when it is full; select a water-saving cycle.

✔ Minimize use of the garbage disposer; compost vegetable waste instead.

Bathroom

✔ Take a short shower instead of a bath, since filling a tub requires more water; turn water off while soaping and shampooing, on again for rinsing.

✔ Run water intermittently while washing your hands and face, brushing your teeth, or shaving.

✔ Flush the toilet only for human waste.

✔ Adjust the flush mechanism to a lower water level.

Laundry

✔ Wash full loads whenever it is possible.

✔ Lower fill level for small loads.

✔ Presoak heavily soiled clothes.

Lawn and garden

✔ Select plant varieties that need little water.

✔ Consider watering with a soaker hose instead of a sprinkler, and turn it on in the evening to minimize evaporation.

✔ Cover swimming pools to save 50 gallons of water on a sunny day.

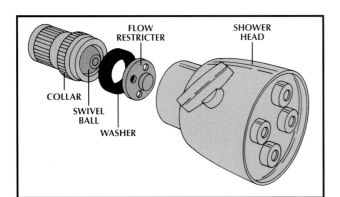

A shower-head flow restricter.

◆ Remove the shower head from the shower arm *(page 147)*.
◆ Unscrew the collar from the shower-head assembly and insert a flow restricter as illustrated at left. Reassemble the shower head.
◆ Clean the shower-arm threads with a wire brush, wrap them with plumbing-sealant tape, then reinstall the shower head.

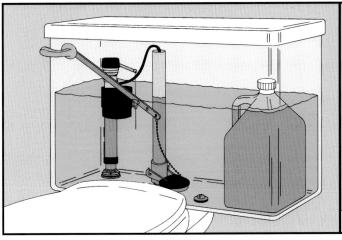

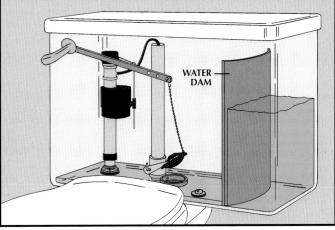

Reducing toilet-tank volume.

Place a water-filled plastic bottle in the tank *(above, left)*, or install a self-sealing water dam, a plastic sheet that retains some of the tank water during a flush *(above, right)*. Do not allow either addition to interfere with the flushing mechanism.

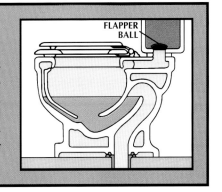

TRICKS OF THE TRADE

Detecting Toilet Leaks

Often invisible and inaudible, a tank-ball or flapper-ball leak can be a big water waster. To check your toilet for such a leak, pour food coloring into the tank and wait 20 minutes. If water in the bowl becomes tinted, replace the old tank ball or flapper ball.

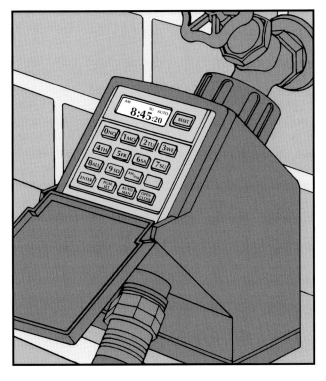

A lawn-watering timer.

The battery-powered device shown at left contains an electrically operated valve controlled by a timer that can be programmed for a weekly cycle of lawn watering. Install such a device as follows:

◆ Wrap the threads of the sillcock and the timer with plumbing-sealant tape.

◆ Screw the timer to the sillcock and the sprinkler hose to the timer.

◆ Program the timer with the instructions provided, then open the sillcock.

Improving Water Quality

Whether it comes from a municipal water company or a private well, your household water may contain impurities. Fortunately, a wide range of water-treatment equipment is available to homeowners, and each device may be used with others to cure almost any combination of conditions.

Testing the Water: The first column of the chart on the opposite page describes the signs of possible water-supply problems. If any of these indicators are present, your water should be tested. You may be able to conduct the investigation yourself with a home test kit *(opposite, bottom)*. Some conditions, however, require professional analysis. Your local board of health can provide a list of water-testing laboratories.

If you suspect that there is lead in your water, have a commercial laboratory run a test. A problem with lead is likeliest in older homes, which may have copper plumbing joined by lead-containing solder or—especially in large cities—may be linked to the water main by lead entry piping.

Since there is no sure way for a homeowner to detect the presence of bacteria, a laboratory test should be made for any new well. An existing well should be tested every 6 months if contamination is known to occur in the area. Your local board of health will do a bacterial analysis at no charge. The extension service of the county or state department of agriculture also may offer free tests.

Hard Water: Calcium and magnesium are responsible for the widespread condition known as hard water; these minerals reduce the efficacy of soap, corrode appliances, and can even block pipes. Treat the problem by installing a water softener—a device that can also remove other impurities. A few regular maintenance procedures will keep a softener running smoothly *(pages 292-294)*.

A Range of Filters: Many styles of filters are available to treat water, and they can be used either alone or in conjunction with a water softener. Install the filter in the line ahead of a water softener to screen out sediment *(page 295)*. Replenish neutralizing, oxidizing, and carbon filters according to the manufacturer's instructions—as often as every 3 days or as infrequently as every 3 years, depending on the type of filter.

Other Water-Treatment Units: A reverse-osmosis purifier forces water through a thin membrane to remove unwanted materials. Some reverse-osmosis units are designed to serve the entire house system. More commonly, these devices have a smaller capacity, and are attached under a sink to provide drinking and cooking water from a single tap. The membrane must be replaced periodically.

Chemical feeders inject a small amount of chemical solution into the water to counteract pollutants. Supply the feeder with chemicals on a regular basis.

TOOLS

Broom
Wet/dry vacuum
Adjustable wrench
Oven baster
Screwdriver
Socket wrench
Pliers

Strap wrench
Pipe cutter
Propane torch
Flameproof pad

MATERIALS

Supply pipe and fittings
Gate valves
Plumbing-sealant tape
Solder
Flux

SAFETY TIPS

Gloves and safety goggles provide protection when soldering pipe.

Common Water Problems and Their Remedies

Problem	Cause	Solution
Low sudsing power of water. Soap deposits on fixtures and clothes. White scale in pipes and water heaters.	Hard water (contains calcium and magnesium)	A water softener.
Rusty deposits in sinks, tubs, and washing machines and on washed fabrics. Water left standing turns reddish.	Iron compounds	If the problem is minor, a water softener. Otherwise, an oxidizing filter.
Green or blue stains in fixtures served by copper pipes. Red stains below faucets in fixtures served by steel pipes.	Corrosion of pipes by acidic water	If the problem is minor, a neutralizing filter. Otherwise, a chemical feeder with an alkaline solution.
Water has a "rotten egg" smell, blackish tinge, tarnishes silver.	Hydrogen sulfide	If the problem is minor, an oxidizing filter. Otherwise, a chemical feeder with a chlorine solution, followed by a sand filter.
Water has a yellow or brownish tinge or an unpleasant taste or odor.	Tannins, algae, humic acid, or other organic substances	If the problem is minor, a carbon filter. Otherwise, a chemical feeder with a chlorine or alum solution, followed by a sand filter or, for potable water only, a reverse-osmosis unit.
Water has an alkaline or soda taste.	Sodium salts	A water softener or oxidizing filter.
Water has a chlorine odor.	Excessive chlorine	A carbon filter or reverse-osmosis unit.
Water has a cloudy or dirty appearance; seats, valves, and moving parts in appliances wear out quickly.	Suspended particles of silt, mud, or sand	A sediment or sand filter.
Intestinal disorders and disease result from drinking the water.	Coliform bacteria from improperly disposed sewage nearby	Correct improper sewage disposal and add a chemical feeder with a chlorine solution, followed by a carbon filter.
Poisoning or disease results from drinking the water.	Lead, herbicides, pesticides, chlorine	A carbon filter.
	Nitrates, chlorides, sulfates, lead, chlorine	A reverse-osmosis unit.

DO-IT-YOURSELF TESTS

With various home test kits, you can easily test water for hardness, pH (the degree of acidity or alkalinity), the presence of minerals or organic substances, and several other conditions. In some tests, paper strips are dipped in water and change color when certain elements are present. Other tests use chemicals dropped into a water sample; again, a change of color indicates impurities.

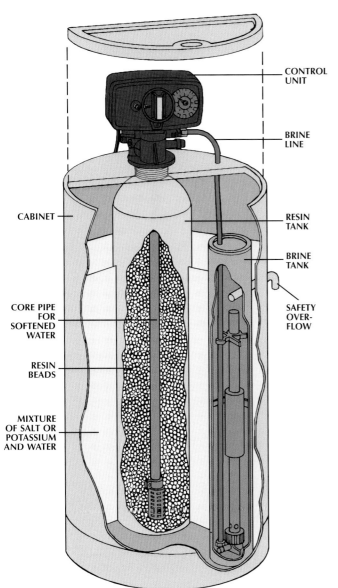

CONTROL UNIT

BRINE LINE

CABINET

RESIN TANK

BRINE TANK

CORE PIPE FOR SOFTENED WATER

SAFETY OVER-FLOW

RESIN BEADS

MIXTURE OF SALT OR POTASSIUM AND WATER

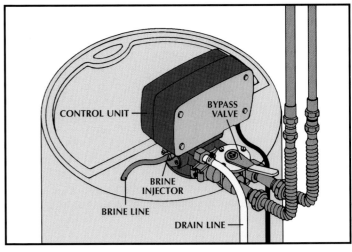

CONTROL UNIT

BYPASS VALVE

BRINE INJECTOR

BRINE LINE

DRAIN LINE

Anatomy of a water softener.

A water softener passes hard water over resin beads in a central tank; the resin contains salt or potassium, which is exchanged for the calcium and magnesium impurities in the water during its transit. Periodically, the beads must be chemically revived and the impurities removed. This is accomplished by a process called backwashing: Brine, formed by mixing water with a supply of salt or potassium outside the resin tank, is washed over the beads, recharging them and also carrying away the accumulated calcium and magnesium. An electrically powered control unit regulates the backwash cycle with either a timer or a meter that keeps track of water use. A bypass valve, used during maintenance tasks, allows water to flow to the household without passing through the softener.

Inspecting the salt or potassium.

Check on the salt or potassium supply once a week.
◆ Remove the lid of the cabinet and look inside.
◆ If a hard crust has formed on the salt or potassium supply, break it into pieces with a broom handle *(right)*.

Accumulated dirt in the cabinet means the salt or potassium contains impurities. Correct the situation as follows:
◆ Wait until the supply is low. Unplug the softener, lift the lid, and empty the cabinet with a wet/dry vacuum.
◆ Clean the cabinet with an abrasive bathroom cleanser. Rinse thoroughly.
◆ Vacuum out the remaining water. To prevent corrosion, rinse out the vacuum before putting it away.
◆ Replace the salt or potassium with a pure product.

CRUST

SALT OR POTASSIUM

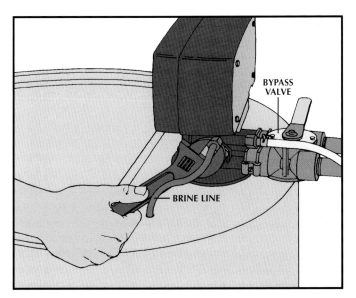

BYPASS VALVE

BRINE LINE

Clearing the brine line.
Every 6 months, check the brine line for blockages.
◆ Unplug the softener, turn the bypass valve to divert the water supply, and set the control-unit dial to the backwash position to relieve pressure on the brine line. On a unit without an integral bypass valve, close the inlet valve and open the nearest water faucet.
◆ Loosen the compression nut connecting the brine line to the control unit and pull the line free *(left)*.
◆ If there is an obstruction in the line or the inlet, use an oven baster to flush it out with warm water.
◆ Reattach the brine line.

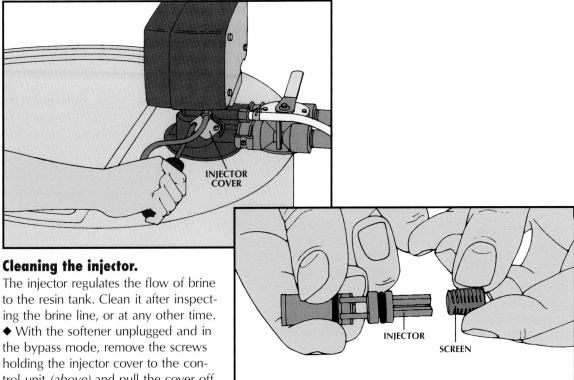

INJECTOR COVER

INJECTOR   **SCREEN**

Cleaning the injector.
The injector regulates the flow of brine to the resin tank. Clean it after inspecting the brine line, or at any other time.
◆ With the softener unplugged and in the bypass mode, remove the screws holding the injector cover to the control unit *(above)* and pull the cover off.
◆ Turn the injector counterclockwise by hand or with a socket wrench and then pull it from its housing.
◆ Remove the small filter screen from the injector *(above, right)*.
◆ Clean a clogged screen in warm, soapy water; replace a broken one. Remove any obstruction in the injector by blowing gently. Do not use a sharp object to remove a blockage.

◆ Replace the screen, screw the injector back into its housing, replace the injector cover, and tighten the screws.
◆ Turn the bypass valve to restore the water supply, reset the control-unit dial for normal operation, and plug in the softener. On a unit without an integral bypass valve, close the open water faucet and open the inlet valve.

REPLACING THE SOFTENER CONTROL UNIT

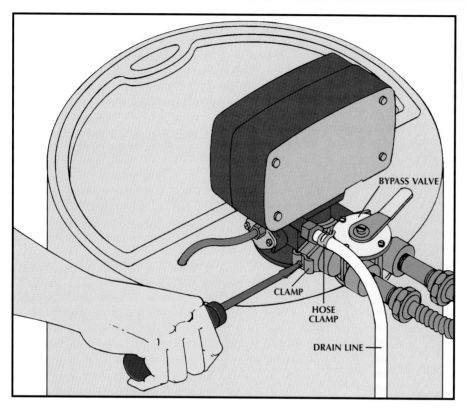

BYPASS VALVE

CLAMP

HOSE CLAMP

DRAIN LINE

1. Disconnecting the control unit.
◆ Unplug the softener, put it in bypass mode, and set the control-unit dial in the backwash position to relieve pressure on the brine line. On a unit without an integral bypass valve, close the inlet valve and open the nearest water faucet.
◆ Remove the brine line *(page 293)*.
◆ Loosen the screws on the clamps that hold the bypass valve to the control unit *(left)*, then pull the valve from the unit. On a unit without an integral bypass valve, unscrew the fittings joining the inlet and outlet pipes to the control unit and pull out the pipes.
◆ With a pair of pliers, compress the prongs of the hose clamp on the drain line, and pull the line free.
◆ Push the pipes back to provide space to remove the control unit.

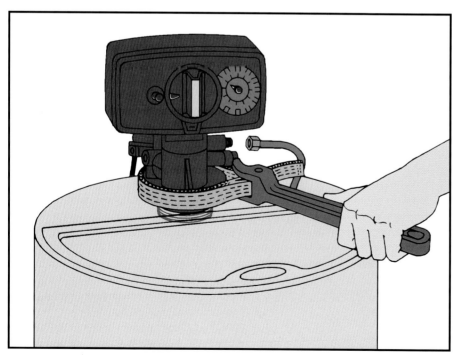

2. Replacing the control unit.
◆ Tighten a strap wrench around the neck of the control unit and turn in a counterclockwise direction until the control unit is free.
◆ Set a new control unit on top of the cabinet and turn it clockwise by hand, then tighten it with the strap wrench.
◆ Replace the bypass valve or the inlet and outlet pipes, and reconnect the brine line and the drain line.
◆ Turn the bypass valve to restore the water supply, reset the control-unit dial for normal operation, and plug in the softener. On a unit without an integral bypass valve, close the open water faucet and open the inlet valve.

ADDING A WATER FILTER TO THE MAIN LINE

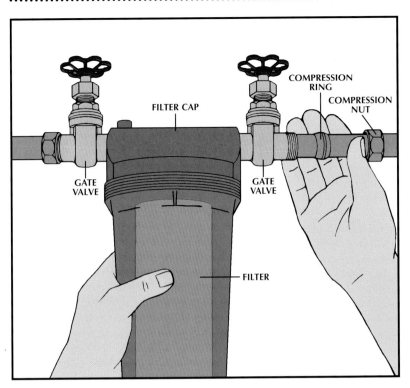

A horizontal line installation.

◆ Turn off the water at the main shutoff valve and drain the supply pipe *(page 268)*.

◆ Using plumbing-sealant tape, thread a gate valve *(page 283)* with exterior threads onto each side of the filter cap and tighten them until each valve is in an upright position.

◆ Measure and cut out a section of the supply pipe long enough to accommodate the filter and valves *(page 262)*.

◆ Slide a compression nut and compression ring over each cut pipe end, fit the valves over the pipe ends, and tighten the nut and ring onto each valve.

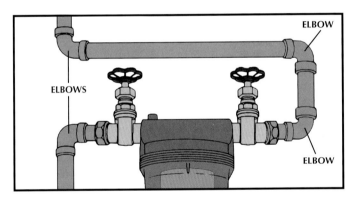

A vertical line installation.

◆ Turn off the water at the main shut-off valve and drain the supply pipe *(page 268)*.

◆ Cut out a 4-inch section of the pipe and attach elbows to each cut end.

◆ Create a loop, installing the filter in the lower leg of the loop with gate valves, as shown at left.

◆ Attach the loop to the elbows on the supply pipe.

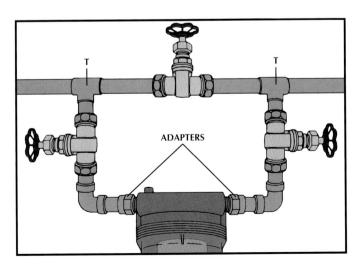

Creating a bypass loop.

◆ Turn off the water at the main shutoff valve and drain the supply pipe *(page 268)*.

◆ Create a bypass loop, using compression fittings, gate valves, and elbows.

◆ Attach the filter to the loop with two threaded adapters wrapped with plumbing-sealant tape.

◆ Cut out a section of the supply line long enough to accommodate the bypass loop *(page 262)*, insert a T fitting at each end of the pipe, and install a gate valve between the two T fittings.

◆ Attach the loop to the T fittings on the supply pipe.

INDEX

PICTURE CREDITS

10, Photograph, Renée Comet; 19: Photograph, Renée Comet; 31: Photograph, Renée Comet; 83: Photograph, Porter-Cable Power Tools; 96: Photograph, Renée Comet; 125: Photograph, Fred Sons; 131: Photograph, Renée Comet; 141: Photograph, Renée Comet; 149: Photograph, Moen Corporation; 152: Photograph, Renée Comet; 156: Photograph, Renée Comet; 175: Photograph, Renée Comet, prop courtesy Stanley Hardware; 201: Photograph, Renée Comet; 205: Photograph, Renée Comet; 228: Photograph, Renée Comet; 230: Photograph courtesy Porter-Cable Power Tools; 256: Photograph, Renée Comet; 257: Photograph, Renée Comet; 260: Photograph, Renée Comet; 261: Photograph, Renée Comet; 264: Photograph, Ken Kay; 270: Photograph, Renée Comet; 275: Photograph, Renée Comet; 264: Photograph, Ken Kay; 280: Photograph, Renée Comet; 291: Photograph, La Motte Company.

Illustrators: James Anderson, Jane P. Anderson, Jack Arthur, Terry Atkinson, George Bell, Frederic F. Bigio, Laszlo Bodrogi, Adolph E. Brotman, Roger Essley, Nicholas Fasciano, Charles Forsythe, Gerry Gallagher, Donald Gates, William J. Hennessy, Elsie J. Hennig, Walter Hilmers, Jr., Fred Holz, John James, John Jones, Al Kettler, Dick Lee, Gerard Mariscalchi, John Martinez, John Massey, Peter McGinn, Joan McGurren, Robert Paquet, Eduino J. Pereira, Jacques Proulx, Daniel Rodriguez, Michael Secrist, Ray Skibinski, Tyrone Taylorand Patrick Wilson/Totally Incorporated, Vantage Art, Inc., Anthony Woolridge, Whitman Studio, Inc.

ACKNOWLEDGMENTS

The editors also wish to thank the following individuals and institutions: Ted Adams, Fluid Systems, Santa Barbara, Calif.; Christopher Baldwin, Middleburg, Va; Allan Biggers, Charlotte Pipe and Foundry, Charlotte, N.C.; John Brown, Kohler Company, Kohler, Wis.; ohn Bryan, Fairfax Tile Co., Fairfax, Va.; Petro Exis, Gaithersburg, Md.; Tom Buckley, Washington Suburban Sanitary Commission, Laurel, Md.; John Chapski, Porter-Cable Corp., Jackson, Tenn.; William Collins, Reston, Va.; Terry Cooper, Cabinetpak Kitchens, Silver Spring, Md.; Carla Conte, Rain Bird®, San Diego; Theresa L. Dagenhart, Long's Corporation, Fairfax, Va., J. Paul De Boek, Kitchen Face Lifts, Sterling, Va.; Ed De La Vergne, Cabinet Facers of Virginia, Reston, Va.; Cheryl L. Douglas, Long's Corporation, Fairfax, Va.; Feeny Manufacturing Company, Muncie, Ind.; Carol Gore, Middleburg Millwork, Middleburg, Va.; Alice Herrold, Wood-Mode, Inc., Kreamer, Pa.; Debbie Hartnett, Josam Company, Michigan City, Ind.; Steve Hassett, Falls Church, Va.; Sue Jones, Genova Products, Davison, Mich.; Hope Herring, Rockville, Md.; Scott Keener, Cabinet Facers of Virginia, Reston, Va.; Melvin and Ken Keller, Bethesda Plumbing and Heating, Rockville, Md.; Andrew G. Kireta Jr., Copper Development Association, Crown Point, Ind.; Larry Knapp, Formica Corporation, Cincinnati; LaMotte Company, Chestertown, Md.; Robert L. Kreutzer, Tatro Plumbing Co., Inc., Garden City, Kans.; Jim Kuhnhenn, Silver Spring, Md.; Mary Levine, Tile Promotion Board, Jupiter, Fla.; Eddie Lichliter, Kitchen Face Lifts, Accokeek, Md.; Max Limpert, Star Water Systems, Kendallville, Ind.; Ron Lips, Metropolitan Bath and Tile, Wheaton, Md.; Sandra W. Lunte, KraftMaid Cabinetry, Inc., Cleveland; Bob Marcotte, Stanley Hardware, New Britain, Conn.; Mark Market, The Home Depot, Alexandria, Va.; Robin Martin, Town & Country Baths, Washington, D.C.; Sue McHugh, Silver Spring, Md.; Randy Millar, Highland Homes, Inc., Trafford, Pa.; Wally Nabors, Star Water Systems, Kendallville, Ind.; Deborah Nelson, Rev-a-Shelf, Inc., Jeffersontown, Ky.; John Owens, Owens Electric, Inc., Springfield, Va.; Chuck Pfeiffer, Trible's, Inc., Springfield, Va.; Allen E. Pfenninger, Moen, Inc., North Olmsted, Ohio; Don Pierson, Long's Corporation, Fairfax, Va.; Mac Price, Freelance Appliance Service, Inc., Fort Washington, Md.; Progress Lighting, Philadelphia; Quality Doors, Duncanville, Tex.; Nancy Rapp, Bristolpipe, Bristol, Ind.; Ridgid Tool, Elyria, Ohio; Louise Reynolds, Silver Spring, Md.; Robert St. Clair Jr., St. Clair Appliance Distributors, Inc., Alexandria, Va.; Ralph Sorrentino, Kitchen Face Lifts, Blasdell, N.Y.; Wayne Sorrentino, Kitchen Face Lifts, Sterling, Va.; Denny Speas, NIBCO, Inc., Elkhart, Ind.; John Sullivan, Falls Church, Va.; Michael Sydorko, Crescent Plumbing, Alexandria, Va.; Theresa Szalkowski, International Approval Services, Cleveland; Bill Taylor, Formica Corporation, Cincinnati; James Teasley, Falls Church Supply, Falls Church, Va.; Joe Teets, Fairfax, Va.; George W. Thornton, Thornton Plumbing and Maintenance, Alexandria, Va.; Richard Tripp, Long's Corporation, Fairfax, Va.; John Troxell Jr., Wood Mode Fine Custom Cabinetry, Kreamer, Pa.; J. Paul Trueblood, Falls Church, Va.; Marvin Walker, Falls Church Supply, Falls Church, Va.; Michael S. Warlick, The Home Depot, Alexandria, Va.; Water Ace Pump Company, Ashland, Ohio.